Effective onscreen editing: New tools for an old profession

"No p‸[a]ssion in *the wor~~l~~ld is equal~~l~~* to the p‸[a]ssion *to al~~l~~ter someone* else's dr‸[a]ft." *—H.G. Well~~l~~s*

The "a" on your typewriter seems to be stuck!

[GH1] The "o" on your keyboard isn't working, and the "l" is stuck!

by Geoff Hart

February 2008

Library and Archives Canada Cataloguing in Publication
Hart, Geoffrey J. S., 1962–
Effective onscreen editing: new tools for an old profession / Geoffrey J.S. Hart.
Includes bibliographical references and index.
Also available in electronic format.
ISBN 978-0-9783227-1-7
1. Editing--Data processing. 2. Text processing (Computer science) 3. Microsoft Word (Computer file) I. Title.
PN162.H37 2008 808'.027028553684 C2008-901067-1

Diaskeuasis Publishing
112 Chestnut Ave.
Pointe-Claire, Quebec
H9R 3B1 Canada
www.geoff-hart.com

Diaskeuasis Publishing

Dedication

To Shoshanna Green, wife and fellow word geek, for partnership in all things editorial and in the more important things that make life worth living and books worth writing.

Acknowledgments

"Think not those faithful who praise all thy words and actions; but those who kindly reprove thy faults."—Socrates, philosopher (469?–399 B.C.)

"For what I have published, I can only hope to be pardoned; but for what I have burned, I deserve to be praised."—Alexander Pope

A book of this scope would have been impossible without the assistance of many individuals. First and foremost, my thanks to the many authors who worked with me so patiently while I learned the tools of my (onscreen) trade. Second, my thanks to the many kind and sometimes lost souls who belong to two e-mail discussion groups: Copyediting-L (www.copyediting-L.info) and Techwr-L (www.techwr-L.com). Much of what I've presented in this book comes from my own explorations of the nooks and crannies of various software while seeking answers to the questions that arise while doing battle with Word and other programs. But I've also learned much from many experts who selflessly give hours of their time helping amateurs—including me, an increasingly long time ago. Third, my thanks to Woody Leonard for helping me begin my long and often strange journey in Microsoft Word well-armed and confident that Word's many idiosyncrasies had solutions, even if they weren't obvious. Subscribe to Woody's free newsletters via his site (http://office-watch.com/), and buy his books; they're great resources for coping with all things Microsoft, and you'll be thanking Woody and his team for their tireless efforts to make Microsoft software usable by mere mortals.

The core of this book is derived from my column on onscreen editing for *Intercom* magazine (www.stc.org/intercom/), published by the Society for Technical Communication. Maurice Martin, Cate Nielan, and Ed Rutkowski provided a valuable second set of eyes and reality check on what I'd written. The chapters in this book that overlap with my published columns have all been substantially revised and expanded, but the originals provided a sound basis on which to build thanks to their editorial efforts. Jane Lyle and Hilary Powers provided a crucial reality check on the substance of an early draft of this book, and many suggestions for improvement; Shoshanna Green performed the copyediting. Since I continued to tinker right up to the last minute, any errors are my fault, not theirs.

Last but not least, a vote of thanks to the Microsoft Word development team. Microsoft Word has many quirks, bugs, and outright disastrous features, but on the whole, not significantly more than most other software I've used over the years. Moreover, since you folks aren't the ones who decide what problems to fix and when to fix them, it's time we stopped blaming you for these problems. (A note to your managers, however: Isn't it time you folks stopped adding useless new features and breaking existing features that used to work just fine? Instead, please spend some time making Word more stable and fixing existing features. It's insufferable that well-known bugs such as those that infest autonumbering and Word's tendency to forget the editor's name have been around since the mid-1990s.) Griping aside—and it's a very long aside some days—I've come to consider Word an indispensable tool over the years, and one that lets me quickly and efficiently earn a very good living doing what I love. For that, my congratulations and my thanks.

A word on copyright

If you're reading this book on your computer and you didn't pay for it, please read on. I promise I'll be brief and not overly moralistic.

If a friend gave you this e-book and deleted their copy, that's fine—people give away printed books all the time, and everyone should have the right to do the same thing with e-books. If you received a potentially pirated copy, please remember that this book is a copyrighted commercial product and that I make my living selling it. (Two hungry kids, and all that—are we feeling guilty yet?) I chose a price sufficiently low that price shouldn't be a barrier to obtaining a copy. If you're working as an editor (who else would read this book?), you'll repay your investment in about 10 minutes of work by applying the tips. Plus, the cost of the book is tax-deductible—make that 5 minutes of work.

If you're a teacher at a recognized educational institution, or a trainer giving courses, "fair use" does not give you the right to provide free copies of this book to your students. Please contact me to discuss bulk purchasing. I give very favorable bulk discounts to teachers, and particularly to students; I used to be an indentured educational slave, and will never look a ramen noodle in the eye again. If you're living somewhere where wages are far below what's necessary to afford the book's North American cost, contact me to see if we can negotiate a fair price. I'm willing to be reasonable.

End of plea, beginning of lecture!

Table of contents

(continued)

(continued)

(continued)

1. Overview and introduction

Chapter 1. My goal and approach in this book

"What merit there is in my thinking is derived from two peculiarities: (1) My inability to be familiar with anything. I simply can't take things for granted. (2) My endless patience. I assume that the only way to find an answer is to hang on long enough and keep groping."—Eric Hoffer

In this book, my goal will be to teach you how to apply the skills you've learned as an on-paper editor in an onscreen editing environment. I'm going to assume that I don't need to teach you to edit; this book is *not* a course in editing or grammar. I'm also going to assume that you already understand the basics of using the Windows or Macintosh operating system installed on your computer, so I won't explain these basics unless they're helpful things you might have missed. But if you're not already proficient in using your computer, I recommend that you invest some time becoming proficient before you read this book.

The book is, as the title says, an overview of using computer software to edit. Of course, there's little reason to make the effort of learning onscreen editing if there's no benefit to be obtained from learning how to edit using a word processor. In Chapter 2, I'll explain how you can benefit from transferring your editing skills into this new medium. Although *I* no longer do much editing on paper, this does not mean that *you* have to edit exclusively on the screen; for some editors, there's a good case to be made for adopting only some of the approaches that I'll describe. Indeed, most of the techniques that I'll teach you in this book can be used to improve the effectiveness of your on-paper editing—the trick is to use the computer for things that computers do best.

In general, my approach will be to discuss the key principles involved in editing, then explain how the computer can help you apply those principles more effectively. Although I've attempted to make these techniques applicable to any word processor, learning how to apply them is easier with concrete examples. For this reason, I've chosen Microsoft Word to demonstrate the principles of onscreen editing. At the time I wrote this book, Word was the word processor most often used by editors—overwhelmingly so—and provided some of the most powerful tools for onscreen editing; unlike other programs, such as Word-

Perfect, it's also available on the Macintosh. Because many editors, myself included, work on Macintosh computers, I've also explained some of the key differences between the Macintosh and Windows where they are relevant. Because roughly one-third of Windows users continued to use Word 97 and 2000 as of late 2006, I've focused on those versions and their Macintosh equivalents, Word 98 and Word X. Most of the principles remain the same in more recent versions, though some menu locations and various idiosyncrasies of the software have changed. I've summarized the more important changes in Appendix III.

The concepts I'll demonstrate using Word should be easy to implement in other software if you're prepared to do a little research to find out how that software works. WordPerfect remains a popular choice, particularly among lawyers and in many government offices, but unfortunately, I haven't used it in recent memory. Since I'm *not* an expert in WordPerfect, you'll have to study the software to learn how to apply the techniques in this book most effectively. Where relevant, I've mentioned other software technologies that are useful in onscreen editing, such as Web browsers with which you can research issues of fact or style.

Because editing is heavily contextual and depends strongly on the human factor, I'll describe some of the key human aspects of the author–editor relationship in Chapter 3, along with some of their more important consequences. I'll use that information as the basis for developing an effective process for managing the editing process and relationships with authors, starting with a discussion of initial negotiations with the author, including setting your rates, and continuing through to the final follow-up that is either useful or necessary once you've completed a job. By all means, adapt this process to meet your specific needs, but be sure

Out with the old? The adamant refusal of so many people to upgrade to the newest versions of Word has irritated Microsoft sufficiently that their latest advertising campaign depicts users of older versions of Microsoft Office as dinosaurs blundering ineffectively around the office. Microsoft would do well to ponder why these people feel no need to upgrade, and to remember that dinosaurs ruled the Earth for millions of years before being replaced by smaller, more nimble competitors. OpenOffice, anyone?

you understand why each part of the process is recommended before you consider omitting it.

The meat of this book can be found in the four sections that follow this introductory material:

- **Mastering the tools:** A description of the software tools you'll use to apply your existing editing skills to onscreen editing.
- **Identifying and overcoming barriers:** Technology is and will remain imperfect for some time, and there are many problems you must learn to solve even once you master your tool skills.
- **Coping with the human factor:** Editors and authors are both human, and must work together to edit and revise a manuscript. This section explains how myriad human quirks interfere with this process, and offers suggestions on how to eliminate or at least lower the barriers to success.
- **A four-step approach to implementing onscreen editing in the workplace:** To conclude the book, I'll describe how you can apply the tidy theory presented in this book to the messy real-world editing environment.

Before we begin, I'd like to make a distinction between the two main types of editing that you'll be asked to perform:

- **Substantive editing** focuses on the organization, logic, and clarity of the content. It also verifies the internal consistency of a document (e.g., the Executive Summary must match the Conclusions) and external consistency with the broader consensus in a field of endeavor. In short, substantive editing focuses on the "big picture" items.
- **Copyediting** focuses on lower-level issues of grammar, punctuation, and consistency of formatting and word use, as well as conformity with a publisher's style guide. Thus, it focuses more on the "micro" level of sentences and the phrases that make up sentences.

Not all editors accept these exact definitions, and indeed, there's considerable overlap between the two types of editing. Moreover, most editors are called upon to perform both functions; for example, I routinely do a substantive edit during my first pass through a manu-

Words, words, words: Want a quick primer on some of the more common terms relating to onscreen editing? Check the Glossary!

script, performing necessary copyediting along the way, then do at least one additional final pass to catch any copyediting errors I missed while focusing on larger issues. (This approach is nearly ubiquitous among editors, with the usual personal variations just to confuse things.) Rather than leaning too heavily on these two definitions, I prefer to emphasize that we must perform different kinds or levels of editing at different times. In this book, I'll use these two types of editing as broad categories to clarify the context for certain tasks, but don't get too hung up on the definitions. (I've summarized these and other potentially unfamiliar terms in the glossary.)

Useful redundancies? Here and there, you'll come across text that you're sure you've seen elsewhere in the book. You're not imagining things. Rather than forcing you to "flip pages" to find these details—something that is much easier to do with a paper book than the PDF version, but annoying even then—I've repeated the basics of what you need to know right where you need to know them. Where more details are necessary, I'll provide an appropriate cross-reference.

Chapter 2. Advantages of onscreen editing

"In products of the human mind, simplicity marks the end of a process of refining, while complexity marks a primitive stage. Michelangelo's definition of art as the purgation of superfluities suggests that the creative effort consists largely in the elimination of that which complicates and confuses a pattern."—Eric Hoffer

Given that on-paper editing has worked perfectly well for several centuries, why should we waste our time "fixing what works" by moving editing onto the computer? Largely because on-paper editing doesn't work all that well; like the dog that sings opera, the noteworthy point is that it sings at all. Computers can greatly facilitate most traditional editorial tasks. Moreover, given that most manuscripts are now being created on the computer, printing them out just so they can be edited is both inefficient and ecologically wasteful. But it's the efficiency argument that proves most persuasive to authors, editors, and managers who must work under tight deadlines. This group increasingly includes everyone who earns their living working with words.

So if the main reason to adopt onscreen editing is efficiency, what efficiency advantages does it offer us?

Minimize errors when incorporating edits

When an author, editor, or secretary must retype handwritten edits, some are inevitably missed. One rough and unscientific count based on personal experience suggests that even skilled secretaries miss or misinterpret up to 5% of the handwritten corrections, and authors who are not professional writers—the majority of most editors' clientele—are even less accurate. In addition, the transcription process routinely introduces new errors into manuscripts when the typist misreads an editor's poor handwriting (one of my particular sins) or mistypes a correction.

Onscreen editing eliminates these problems because the edits are already present in the file, and so long as we carefully review our work before sending it to the author, those edits should contain no typos or other errors. The automation provided by a word processor's revision tools can also help ensure that the person who incorporates the corrections into the final file won't miss any edits. Of course, it's still possible to err by incorrectly dealing with a given edit; for example, I've seen authors skip a correction (by accidentally clicking the "Find" button to find the next edit), accept edits that should be rejected (by clicking the "Accept" button), or reject edits that should be accepted (by clicking the "Reject" button). Because variants of this problem also occur in on-paper edits, this suggests that whether you edit on the screen or on paper, it's still necessary to perform quality control on the results.

Reduce revision time

With on-paper editing, the best-case scenario is that the typist responsible for entering the corrections into the word processor file carefully reviews their own work to catch any corrections that they missed during the first pass and any errors they introduced in making those corrections. Unfortunately, this step is often skipped by busy workers, and when it's not skipped, it can double the time required to incorporate all the corrections. Even if this extra step were not necessary, retyping handwritten corrections into the original word processor document increases turnaround times. In effect, the edits must be "written" twice (once on paper and a second time in the word processor) and checked at least one extra time.

With onscreen editing, all corrections are made directly in the file, and this eliminates the time required to transfer those edits from paper to computer. Because this also eliminates transcription errors, there is no need to fix this category of error in a subsequent stage of the review. There is also a small but important benefit in terms of clarity: because edits are typed rather than handwritten, they are easier to read and understand, and are thus less likely to be misinterpreted.

Edit faster and more consistently

On-paper editing relies on slow and inefficient handwritten comments. Even for those few annoying editors who always get their edits right the first time, with no need for revision, it can be frustrating and time-consuming to repeatedly write the same type of comment by hand, perhaps dozens of times in even a short manuscript. Moreover, even the best editors have difficulty finding every instance of a given word or problem in a paper copy of a manuscript; if it becomes apparent several hundred pages into an edit that, for example, a specific word has been used incorrectly, the editor must re-read the entire manuscript to seek out all instances of that word—a tedious, slow, and error-prone process.

Onscreen editing solves these problems in a variety of ways. For example, most editors eventually learn to type edits faster with a keyboard than they could possibly write them with pen or pencil, and most can type the edits faster than the authors who would otherwise have to retype the edits. (Dedicated "typing pools" staffed by experienced typists that make such corrections for authors are generally a thing of the past.) This is particularly true when the edits involve extensive rewriting, which may require considerable juggling of words and phrases before attaining a satisfactory result; on a computer, an entire chunk of problematic text can be copied and pasted in a few keystrokes, then revised quickly by inserting new words, deleting old ones, and dragging around the rest until we're satisfied with the result. The results are also easier for authors to read, understand, and review, since there's no sticky correction fluid or pools of glistening red ink covering the errors made *en route* to finding a solution.

Modern word processors also let us automate repetitive, tedious work. For example, it's now possible to insert a standard comment such as "this reference is missing from your bibliography" with a few keystrokes rather than manually typing the same comment potentially dozens of times per manuscript. (My personal record is close to twenty repetitions of a single comment in a short manuscript.) Similarly, it's far faster to replace all instances of one term (e.g., an incorrectly used technical term) with another in a single step, using a global search and replace operation, than it is to hunt down each occurrence of the term and make the change manually. If only some occurrences of the term are likely to be incorrect, you can't perform a global search and replace, but you can still use the search tool to quickly and easily find all occurrences of the problematic wording.

But some things remain the same

None of these advantages minimizes the editor's role in the editing process: providing human insight into writing problems and applying human experience to solve those problems. Onscreen editing is one of the surprisingly few areas in which the promise of the computer revolution (freeing humans to perform creative work) has actually been fulfilled. Once we understand how to edit on the screen, we can combine the advantages made possible by computerization (potentially flawless execution of simple, repetitive tasks) with the unparalleled strengths of the human mind (performing complex semantic analyses and determining how to solve problems). Learning to edit on the screen has the potential to make us better editors, to free us from the drudgery of many traditional editorial tasks, and to allow us to concentrate on the best way to improve the author's ability to communicate.

None of these benefits *force* us to work exclusively on the screen. For example, it's possible to use the search tools in the word processor file to find each occurrence of a word, then manually fix the problems on a printed copy if that works better for you. The key is to use the computer for what it does well: *supporting* our work. Each of us will find different ways to do that, using the tools and techniques described in this book.

Chapter 3. Writing and editing are *human* endeavors

"For me, good editing is a … testimony that one's words are worthy enough to require close attention."—James McConkey, *Nurture for the damn ego*

"Tact is the ability to describe others as they see themselves."—Abraham Lincoln

"Writing, in a way, is listening to the others' language and reading with the others' eyes."—Trinh T. Minh-Ha, *Woman, native, other*

If you believe that editing involves nothing more profound than correcting typographical errors and changing words or phrases to suit your personal taste or the dictates of someone's style guide, your editorial career will be short and inglorious. In reality, editing is about helping our author colleagues communicate clearly with their audience in a manner that makes both the author and their employer look good and that satisfies the audience that they've understood the author. We achieve this happy result when the audience understands the intended message with as little mental effort as possible; important messages may be challenging indeed, but their *presentation* must never be. To achieve this goal, we must also communicate effectively with authors, because writing is a *human* endeavor, and most authors are both proud of what they've accomplished and deeply insecure about the quality of their writing. When we take on the role of editor, our work can easily be seen as critical of the author, since the essence of our role is to find errors and thereby demonstrate the author's fallibility. Sometimes we must alter their writing quite dramatically to achieve the goal of communication with readers. How can such an activity *not* damage the author's self-confidence, bruise their pride, and anger them?

The answer lies in turning editing from an adversarial activity, in which we become the author's nemesis and unflagging critic, into a partnership in which the author clearly sees us as their ally in the struggle to communicate. An editor and author working together can achieve synergies that neither could achieve alone. We editors may be unable to write an original work, but are well equipped to detect flaws or gaps in the writing that authors cannot detect because they lack the necessary critical distance; the authors, of course, are experts in the concepts that they want to communicate. As editors, we have training that most writers lack in how to detect and correct flawed writing, and the desire to put those skills to work in the service of our authors. The author–editor relationship is clearly a human relationship, and editing is equally clearly a human interaction. To become a truly effective editor, we must thus engage in a mutually respectful dialogue with the author.

In this book, I've defined *onscreen* editing as editing without a pen by using a word processor or similar tool. It doesn't matter whether the edited text will eventually be printed or will remain forever on the computer screen. Successful onscreen editing requires more than merely altering text in a word processor; that would be no more than rewriting or revising the manuscript. Rather, the approach must preserve and enhance the author–editor dialogue by using technology as a way to facilitate this communication, not as an end in itself. In using this technology, we must constantly strive to go beyond simply facilitating our editorial tasks; we must also make it easier and more effective for authors to revise their manuscript in response to our suggestions.

Modern word processing technology provides impressive results, but does not inherently encourage or discourage a dialogue between author and editor. In particular, current word processors provide little or no support for simultaneous revision of a manuscript by several people. This turns the dialogue into an exchange of messages, often separated by considerable time—the equivalent of collaborating on a job using handwritten letters rather than a telephone or putting our heads together over a ream of paper spread across a desk in the author's office. Although this approach *permits* the give and take that is part of any such dialogue, it does not *promote* this dialogue and cannot replace a true discussion; in a discussion, the author and editor can immediately respond to each other's concerns and reach an acceptable compromise. That's an unfortunate lack, because such discussions reinforce the feeling of a true partnership and help authors and editors to see each other as allies rather than adversaries. For this reason, I encourage you to develop an approach in which you encourage authors to identify any changes they disagree with and discuss them with you. In this manner, you have a chance to explain your concerns (i.e., why you originally proposed a change), emphasize that other readers are likely to encounter the same problem, and propose one or more solutions; in turn, the author has a chance to explain what they were trying to say, and to adapt your suggestions as required to accomplish their goal.

This is all very well in theory, but authors and editors are both human, and prone to all the flaws that afflict human communication. We all have annoyances, prejudices, fears, and a measure of unfamiliarity or discomfort with the unique editorial process that develops in each author–editor relationship. Ignoring these problems ensures that we'll fail as editors. An author may never learn to like us, or we may dislike an author's stylistic and other choices, and this friction will inevitably raise the level of tension. This tension makes communication more difficult, but should never be allowed to prevent communication. We must remember that our role is first and foremost to help authors communicate with their audience; we do so by helping authors make effective choices, but in the end, the author has the final say. (Only in a few workplaces such as magazines do we have the authority to overrule authors, and even then, we must use this power judiciously.) Our editing must thus show sensitivity to the author's feelings, must tactfully point out and explain problems, and must suggest solutions that let the author feel their voice is appreciated and preserved. This approach helps authors to recognize the value of editing, and encourages them to work with us in a friendly or at least professional way.

A standard process

The overall process of editing on the screen is much the same as the process of editing on paper, but with a few quirks related to the computer medium. In this section, I've presented a simple overview of a process used by many editors that has worked well for me for some 20 years, and that should work equally well for you with a little modification to suit your personal tastes and unique circumstances. Most of the steps in this process should be familiar to any experienced editor, but if you've been skipping a step, I highly recommend giving it at least one try. Each of these steps solves an important problem, and avoiding any step may someday cause you considerable grief. The goal of the process is to ensure that you understand what is required of you, that the author shares that understanding, and that you'll be paid fairly for the work you do.

Determining your pay rate

If you're working for the same employer as your authors, you probably won't be charging them for your time. Thus, most of this section on setting fair rates of pay won't be relevant to you. However, editors in some workplaces are treated as a cost center and editing expenses are charged back to the author's budget. Since the accounting methods used to determine this chargeback vary widely among workplaces, I can only suggest that you talk to the appropriate manager at your workplace to learn the details of how they handle chargebacks. You may not be able to change this system, but you may gain some insights into pricing that will inform your relationship with that manager.

Editing should be a profession that brings us considerable joy and intellectual satisfaction, but it must also earn us a living and should never be the sole source of joy and satisfaction in anyone's life. Each of our lives offers a strictly limited number of hours, and that number decreases steadily, hour by hour. The rate we charge for our work must thus compensate us adequately for spending an hour of our time on someone else's priorities rather than doing something else that we'd rather be doing: spending time with a loved one, reading a good book, or traveling to distant lands. As Henry David Thoreau observed, "The cost of a thing is the amount of what I will call life which is required to be exchanged for it, immediately or in the long run."

On this basis, I set a standard rate for my time that is unaffected by the nature of the work an author asks me to do: whether they want me to check the page numbers in a layout or rack my brain rewriting a document from scratch, an hour of my time will cost them the same amount. Other editors set different rates for proofreading, copyediting, and substantive editing. Except where this is mandated by an employer's pricing policy, and they have no bargaining power to negotiate a change, I don't understand their rationale. An hour spent on any of these activities is an hour we can no longer spend on our own priorities, and we should be compensated for that lost hour.

There are obvious exceptions. The most important arises when we really need the work, and are competing with other editors willing to work for less money. In that situation, we must choose a rate we can justify to the client because if we fail, they'll take their work elsewhere, particularly if they don't understand the value of our work and will award a contract solely on the basis of price. The only good solution to this predicament involves developing an understanding of the going rates in our part of the world or in our field (i.e., what clients are willing to pay) and a matching understanding of the competition we face (i.e., what rates we'll be competing against). Organizations such as the Society for Technical Communication (www.stc.org) and local groups of editors such as the Editorial Freelancers Association in the U.S. (www.the-efa.org) and the Editors' Association of Canada (www.editors.ca) are good places to learn this information.

If you're willing and able to do *pro bono* work, then by all means feel free to award certain clients a much lower rate than you'd ordin-arily accept. For example, lately I've been working with an expanding network of authors in China, and given that Chinese budgets are so far below those in North America, I've chosen to accept less money for my work in exchange for the pleasure of establishing an ongoing relationship with these authors. Similarly, it may be possible to offer lower rates for work that we particularly enjoy and could never obtain if we charged our standard rate; literary editing is a good example, because this work generally pays far less than technical editing but offers other compensations, such as the satisfaction of helping authors tell a memorable story.

How do you set a rate? The number of questions I've received on this issue suggest that the calculation is sufficiently inobvious that it requires some discussion. The most common approach involves the following steps (I've provided some basic numbers solely as examples to make the math easy):

1. Decide on the gross amount that you want or need to earn per year. In this total, include the cost of your taxes, medical and other insurance, vacation pay, and a pension fund. (These expenses can amount to an additional 30 to 50% of your base salary.)
   Example: $48 000
2. Decide how many weeks you want to work per year.
   Example: 48 weeks
3. Divide your salary by this number of weeks to estimate the income you must generate every week.
   Example: $48 000/48 weeks = $1000/week
4. Decide how many hours you want to work per week.

Example: 20 hours (unrealistic, but let's have fun with this!)

5. Divide your weekly wage by this number of hours to estimate the hourly income you must earn.

   Example: $1000/20 hours = $50/hour

The result of these calculations becomes the basic, non-negotiable hourly rate you require to earn the desired income. It's possible to work for less money for some clients if you can charge other clients more (or work more hours) to make up the difference.

The calculation is clearly simple in principle, but far more complex in reality. For example, the numbers I've chosen in this example were intentionally simplistic to make the calculations easy. In particular, the notion of 20 hours of work per week assumes that you can realistically generate this much paid work, and ignores the many hours of paperwork and other activities (such as marketing your services) that don't directly earn you any money. Moreover, the resulting rate may be well above what local clients are willing or able to pay. The important thing about this calculation process is not that the numbers are precise, but rather that it gives you an objective starting point for estimating your rate. You'll still have to subject that rate to a reality check to determine whether it's feasible.

Now let's apply a similar process to the task of bidding on a job. If we're very fortunate, our client trusts us enough to simply pay an hourly rate on the assumption that we won't abuse this privilege. I'm fortunate that I can work with many of my clients on this basis, but a growing number of clients have begun to ask for fixed-price bids both so that they can budget for my services and so that they can cap the amount they'll eventually have to pay. To provide a fixed estimate that will earn the desired amount, we must learn to estimate how long a job will take and thus, how much to charge for the work. To do this successfully, we must be able to estimate both our productivity and the amount of work we'll be required to do. Once you know (for example) how many words you can edit per hour, and the number of words in the job, it's easy to calculate a cost for the job.

For example, let's assume that we can charge the $50/hour we just calculated, can edit 1000 words per hour (including all time spent in authorial hand-holding and in record-keeping), and have been offered a 10 000-word job. The calculation becomes the following:

- 10 000 words divided by 1000 words/hour = 10 hours
- 10 hours @ $50/hour = $500
- To this amount, add any additional expenses you'll incur: travel, postage, telephone calls, library research… whatever!

The most difficult part of this calculation is determining our productivity. Although many rules of thumb exist to help estimate productivity, these rules are too general to be useful because they cover a wide range of editors and a wide range of projects. As a result, some of these numbers are actively misleading because they reflect neither our personal productivity nor how that productivity changes for different types of work. The only way to usefully estimate our productivity is to track that productivity for long enough that we obtain a good feel for our own ability to handle a range of jobs. For example, I've been tracking my productivities (total number of words in a document, total number of hours required to edit the document, and thus, my rate in words per hour) for more than 5 years, for a wide variety of clients and types of work. As a result, I have a strong idea of the full range of productivities that I've been able to achieve for work ranging from near-total rewrites to quick and easy copyedits. This lets me bid on a range of projects, sight unseen, with reasonable probability of earning my desired hourly rate. There is *no* substitute for this kind of self-knowledge.

If you're just getting started, and have no productivity data on which to estimate editing times, avoid the rules of thumb related to pages per hour that you'll often hear bandied about. Instead, ask to see a copy of what you will be editing before you commit to a price. (This is wise even if you do have decades of productivity statistics. Authors retain a remarkable ability to surprise us!) Skim through the manuscript sufficiently thoroughly that you can identify both the good and the bad parts, then edit a few pages of the bad parts to estimate how long this work will take you. From this, you can calculate your productivity on the worst parts of the manuscript and predict with some confidence that the rest of the manuscript should be easier. Applying the worst-case estimates increases the likelihood that you'll still earn your desired rate of pay should the rest of the manuscript prove unexpectedly difficult. Unless you're intimately familiar with a particular client's style, and can thus predict the difficulty of the work you'll be doing, it's always best to expect the worst and charge accordingly.

Simple tracking: I track my own productivity about as simply as you can imagine—using a simple table in Microsoft Excel. When I start and stop work, I jot down the times and use that information to calculate how long I've spent on a manuscript. If you need something a bit more formal, there are many programs available to automate the process. Have a look at my list of utility programs in the references section, under the category of "time tracking" programs.

Although we can offer our clients a discount for work that ends up being considerably easier than expected, I don't generally recommend this. If the client wants to pay us a fair rate for the job, they should agree right from the start to pay based on how long the work actually takes. If they want a fixed price, and are thus trying to place the entire risk of a cost overrun upon us, then they shouldn't expect a discount. In the long run, even with careful estimating, we'll inevitably encounter some manuscripts that take longer than expected to edit, and earning a slight bonus when a job is easier than expected compensates us for the inevitable, unexpectedly difficult jobs. One useful compromise I've adopted for first-time clients is a hybrid approach: I offer to work on an hourly basis, but with a maximum price established based on my worst-case productivities. If I can beat that worst-case price, I pass along the savings to the client and thereby encourage them to work with me on an hourly basis in the future.

Initial negotiations

When we first begin to work with an author, the process should start with a clear definition of what the author expects of us. In particular, we must clearly define the nature of the edit. We should never rely on nominally standard terms such as "copyediting", since it's only a slight exaggeration to state that every client has a different definition of what such editing involves; naïve authors often specify something as uninformative as "a light edit", whereas seasoned pros may use an idiosyncratic definition qualified by dozens of specifications and clauses. In my experience, a clear and detailed description of what we will do is far more effective than any more general definition can ever be. Consider, for example, the details of and differences between the following two descriptions:

- **Substantive or structural editing:** This activity involves heavy editing of a manuscript to ensure that both the content and the structure are logical, clear, and effective. In addition to rewriting where necessary to improve the clarity of the text, this form of editing ensures that the organization and flow of the text effectively communicate the intended message, and that the text and graphics work effectively together. This editing also ensures that the manuscript contains no internal contradictions and is consistent with the body of knowledge in a field; attaining this knowledge is not essential for working in a given field, but it does add considerable value to our work. Although this editing may require heavy revision, no entirely new material will be written; any omissions will be identified for the author to resolve.
- **Copyediting:** Copyediting involves editing for grammar, usage, spelling, punctuation, and other mechanical aspects of style. It also involves checking the *internal* consistency of these aspects and of facts *within* the manuscript, but does not include confirmation of facts, quotations, or references.

Whether or not you agree with these specific definitions, the important point is the level of detail they provide. Each definition clearly defines exactly what you will do for the author, rather than leaving it to their imagination.

Initial negotiations with an author should include a discussion of other details, such as the style guide the author expects us to use and what kinds of things (e.g., formatting) we should feel free to correct without querying the author. In addition, because we'll be working on a computer, we must specify what word processor will be used and what file formats are acceptable. The ideal situation is one in which we use the same word processor as the author, thereby removing the worst of the potential format incompatibilities. Graphics formats are a particular source of problems, since graphics embedded in a word processor occasionally display incorrectly. Both these issues provide a good example of the kind of negotiation we should engage in with authors: Can we edit graphics directly in the software used to create them, or does the author want to make corrections based on our feedback? Could we review graphics in Adobe's PDF (Acrobat) format? Acrobat eliminates most display problems, but PDF files are difficult to edit; they let us add annotations and comments, but prevent substantive editing. In such cases, it's more effective to ask the author to copy the text from figures into a word processor document that we can then edit.

Initial negotiations should also address a key brass-tacks issue: how you'll communicate with and exchange your work with the author. I'll discuss this in some detail towards the end of this chapter.

Contracts are *not* optional

There are occasional situations in which we can safely work without a contract. These typically involve a long-term client who pays promptly and with no fuss, and whose financial stability (which we should investigate periodically) is excellent. For example, I've been working with a former employer for several years, and have full confidence that I understand their needs and that they'll pay me on time and in full. Those rare times when there's been a misunderstanding, we've worked together to resolve the problem with minor fuss and bother and no hard feelings on either side. As a result, I have never required this client to sign a binding contract. What I have done instead is clearly specify in writing or e-mail any unusual details that don't fall under our existing understanding of the nature of my work.

This is about the only situation in which we should even consider working without a contract, and the archives of the Copyediting-L (www.copyediting-L.info) and Techwr-L (www.techwr-L.com) discussion groups are full of tales of woe that could have been eliminated by means of a simple contract.

At a minimum, a contract represents a straightforward description of the entire nature of the work we will do and ensures that we make at least some effort to discuss the proposed work. The contract thus summarizes and formalizes the results of the preliminary negotiations that lead up to the start of a job, and specifically states the basis for payment. If human communication were always clear and precise, and free of subjective considerations and assumptions, such a statement might never be necessary. But given the fallibility of such communication, a written statement of intent is essential to minimize the risk of misunderstandings. The goal of creating a contract is to eliminate misunderstandings so you can work productively together, not to club a recalcitrant author into submission through deft blows with a lawyer. The fact that swarms of lawyers earn a lucrative living resolving contract disputes should be a clue that we cannot entirely eliminate this risk, but that doesn't mean we shouldn't try.

Indeed, when worse comes to worst, a contract becomes our only tool for ensuring that a difficult client treats us with respect and pays us for the work we've done. It also ensures that if the scope of the work changes, we can insist on compensation for that new work, and can specify our understanding of the expanded scope in an amendment to the contract. Most clients are neither evil nor incompetent, but some are, and these are the ones against whom we desperately need a contract for protection. Many clients are overworked, overtired, and unfamiliar with the nature of our work. Again, a contract educates them and thereby protects us against their misunderstandings and ensures that we can meet their needs—something we can't do unless we first understand those needs.

Never begin work on a project, no matter how lucrative or how tight the deadline, until you have at least a firm statement of intent signed in writing. E-mail messages may constitute this proof, but I suspect that because e-mail messages are relatively easy to forge, the jurisprudence in this area will continue to evolve for some time. A printed and signed contract is still your best bet for any large or expensive job; e-mail may be acceptable for smaller jobs. Even if you have not hired a lawyer to review the contract (an excellent idea for large, expensive, or potentially risky or contentious work), a written and signed statement counts as a legally binding contract in most jurisdictions. Unfortunately, legal English is not the same English spoken by editors, and what seems to us to be clear wording may conflict with the legal definitions of certain terms or may violate certain local regulations designed to protect both parties. In a perfect world, we wouldn't need such protections. But then again, were it a perfect world, we editors would have to find honest work.

In an emergency (e.g., you've worked without a contract and the author refuses to pay you), you have one final protection: copyright law. Under modern copyright law, any rewriting of text that you have done for an author is copyrighted in your name until you receive payment for that work and transfer the copyright for your work to the author. (Of course, the original, unedited text that surrounds your edits is copyrighted in the author's name.) If an author refuses to pay you, you have a legal right to insist that they not use your writing. In some cases, sending a copy of the edited manuscript to the author's publisher with a note that you have not been paid and that use of any of your edits represents a violation of your copyright will encourage an author to pay; publishers are quite rightly scared of the costs of a lawsuit resulting from their publication of your work without your permission. If the author is publishing the work by themselves, as is often the case with corporate clients, a good lawyer can still obtain a court judgment that forces the client to withdraw any copies of your work from circulation, often at great expense to the publisher, and may even be able to obtain punitive damages from a sympathetic court. The downside of such a strategy is that it can earn you an undesirable reputation among potential clients, it can be expensive to pursue such legal action, and the outcome is not guaranteed. But if all else fails, don't neglect this strategy.

Initial edits

Having agreed upon the nature of the job, we can move on to our initial edit or edits. In on-paper editing, most editors insist on performing at least two passes through a document: once to correct all the major problems, and a second time to correct anything we missed the first time, as well as any errors we introduced through our editing. In more demanding jobs, we may need three or more passes through the text to ensure that we're satisfied with the quality of the work. This doesn't change when we move to onscreen editing, so plan to allow time for at least those two passes. Where possible, allow some time to elapse before you revisit a document. For example, I try to arrange my schedule so that I can do my final edit at least one day after the initial edit, since experience has shown that this elapsed time gives me the necessary critical distance to approach the manuscript with fresh eyes and lets me spot errors I would otherwise have missed. In addition, the delay gives me time to ponder what I've read and develop a fuller understanding of the manuscript that helps me focus more intensely on communicating the right meaning.

When we've completed the initial edit, we return the manuscript to the author and cross our fingers. We may never see the document again, and once it's in the eager hands of the author, we have no control over what will happen to our edits. If we're lucky, we'll get a chance for a second or even third edit (see *The final edit*, later in this chapter) to correct any errors the author introduced in response to our edits, but that's a luxury freelancers must often forego.

One key point to keep in mind at this stage: Authors will not agree with all of our edits. Sometimes this is because they simply don't understand the problem. Other times, it's because we guessed wrong and made a change that altered the meaning or that made no sense to the author. In both cases, it's important to emphasize that we're willing to work with the author to explain why a seemingly unnecessary change was necessary, or why we misunderstood the original wording badly enough to introduce an error through our edits. If *we* misunderstood something, it's clear that other readers will make the same mistake, and that's why the problem needs to be fixed, not ignored. Make sure that authors know they should never disregard a revision without clearly understanding why we made that change, and that they should feel free to discuss and resolve the problem.

Saved work and backups

Computers and the software that infests them remain unreliable tools. Both the operating system and the word processors we use as our primary tools crash unacceptably often, and the only solution is to save our work frequently. (For details on how to configure software to automatically save our work and create backup files, see *General behavior of your word processor* in Chapter 4. If your software doesn't provide comparable features, teach yourself to manually save the document every 5 to 10 minutes, or whenever you've completed a particularly difficult part of the edit.) The rule of thumb is that you should save a document sufficiently frequently that if your system crashes, you won't mind redoing all the work performed since the last time you saved a document.

Most important of all, whenever you finish your editing for the day, make a safe, reliable backup. This seems self-evident, but many friends and colleagues have lost large amounts of work (and potentially lost a client due to missed deadlines) because they failed to make adequate backups of their work. What with viruses and other malware, robberies, floods, inattention due to fatigue, and other unfortunate occurrences, you'll eventually lose a computer file, and sometimes even the whole computer. The only way to protect yourself against such disasters is to make ongoing backups of the files that you're editing.

Appendix I provides a comprehensive overview of what you need to know to develop a successful backup strategy.

Particularly in the middle of the editing cycle, where you may exchange a file with authors several times before finalizing the manuscript, you should retain copies of at least the following files:

- **The original manuscript submitted by the author:** If your word processor or operating system let you "lock" a file so that it can't be modified, this is a helpful way to protect the file, but the important thing is not to work in that original file.
- **The first version you will work on:** I find it simplest and most convenient to save a new copy of the original file as soon as I open it for the first time, and add "-e" (for "edited") to the file name as a reminder. For example, if the original is named *Geoff.doc*, the edited version becomes *Geoff-e.doc*.
- **Backups after each major work session:** For example, for long and complicated edits where it may become necessary to return to a previous version and start over from that point, it's helpful to create "checkpoint" versions. Using the same names as in the previous example, I might use *Geoff-e-November 11.doc* as the version completed at the end of that day, or *Geoff-e-November 11-10 AM.doc* after doing a major bit of fixing up, early in the morning before the coffee has taken effect and thus, before I'm sure that I'm thinking clearly.
- **The original copy of the revised manuscript received from the author, plus the first version you're editing:** These might become *Geoff-r.doc* and *Geoff-r2.doc*, respectively. Alternatively, I may replace the "-r" (for "revised) with the date of the version.

Ad hoc backups: Until you've developed a full-fledged backup strategy, here's a useful tip for protecting your valuable files: create an e-mail account with Google or any other online service that offers a large amount of storage space. (Most now offer at least 1 Gig of storage.) You can now e-mail yourself a copy of each file whenever you feel the need to create a backup, whether that's after a couple hours of work or at the end of the day.

The final edit

In an ideal situation, we'll have a chance to see an edited manuscript after an author has incorporated our edits. This is our last chance to catch anything we missed the first time—and it's often distressing how many things we miss, particularly when we're in a hurry—but more importantly, it's our chance to fix any problems the author has introduced while reviewing our edits. If it's possible to do so, try to include a full final edit in the contract, and include the cost of this edit in the estimated cost.

When we're confident that the author will communicate with us to resolve any unclear comments or to negotiate alternatives to our suggested changes, we can simply assume that the author accepted all our edits or has inserted comments to explain why not. In that case, we can read through the final version of the manuscript looking for any errors that escaped us the first time. However, if we suspect that the author will disregard some of our changes without understanding why we proposed them or responding to us to describe the problem, it may be fruitful to compare the final version of the manuscript with the original edited version to ensure that all our comments were addressed. This comparison is particularly important for manuscripts with implications for human health and safety or with legal implications. If you followed my advice in the previous section, you'll always have a copy of your edited version of the manuscript to use in this comparison. If you expect

Checking on the author: As a general rule, it's safer if the editor implements the corrections, since it's our job to be obsessive about doing everything right and we obsess better than most authors. This approach has an additional advantage: it lets us identify those cases when an author thinks they've responded appropriately to a comment, but they really, really haven't. If the author wants to do all the implementing, it's worthwhile comparing the document we sent them with the final document that they returned so we can catch any errors and determine whether they've rejected any edits that shouldn't have been rejected without some discussion. Most modern software offers a "compare documents" feature that provides a quick reality check.

that this final edit will be necessary, be sure to include it in your plans and budget for that part of the job.

Follow-up

Once we've returned a manuscript to an author and submitted our invoice, the hard part is over. But that doesn't mean we're done yet. Editing is a human endeavor, and keeping in touch with the author is a way to maintain a friendly working relationship. The goal of this follow-up is to help the author understand that they're more than just an invoice to us and that we're still willing to work with them to resolve any of the myriad small details that somehow never seem to be resolved the first time through. We should expect to be compensated for significant, ongoing work after we submit our invoice, but it's a kindness to the author and a wise investment in an ongoing relationship to answer a few follow-up questions, free of charge, while the author puts the finishing touches on their manuscript. In my experience, that kind of willingness to treat an author as something more than a supply of ready cash repays itself ten-fold in customer loyalty and free word-of-mouth advertising.

Archiving

It's wise to retain copies of edited files for some time after submitting an invoice for the work, since it becomes necessary to return to an old manuscript surprisingly often. At least once per year, I've had to supply an author with an old copy of a file when they lost their only copy to a virus or a computer crash. In addition, we may want to see how we handled a specific editing problem or style issue for a past client, read an old manuscript that explains a difficult concept we must understand before we can tackle a new job, or simply review our own work to see the kinds of edits we do sufficiently often to justify creating macros or other shortcuts. (See Chapter 11 for details on automation.) When I first decided to work as a freelancer, my archives of old manuscripts also provided a valuable source of contact information for past clients, a useful source of references, and (with the author's permission, of course) a portfolio of my work.

Archival copies should also include all correspondence with an author during the course of our work, as well as copies of any correspondence, contracts, invoices, and other relevant information. This is useful for legal reasons, but it also preserves knowledge that may prove useful in future dealings with a client. Such records may alert us to payment difficulties, idiosyncrasies of how clients prefer to work with us, and other useful tidbits.

Of course, there's an important exception to any rule, and when it comes to archiving, that exception can have important consequences. In some cases, a client may request that we either destroy all copies of the work we've done for them, or protect that work in such a way that only we will ever be able to see it. For example, I once completed work for a client whose manuscript involved highly confidential material related to law enforcement and certain pending court cases. As a result, the client requested that I exclude his manuscript from my archives and delete all copies once the work was complete. (I did so, but did not erase the final copies for several months after completing the work, just in case; as it happens, the client did indeed require a second copy of the manuscript files later.) If you work with confidential or classified material, it may be necessary to use passwords to protect the edited files or perhaps even purchase special-purpose encryption software such as PGP (www.pgp.com) that can protect the information from prying eyes. If the consequences of these files falling into the wrong hands are serious, we must take correspondingly serious measures to protect ourselves and our clients.

Communication and file-exchange issues

Even if most of our work is eventually done on the computer, there are certain practical matters that can't be fully computerized. The biggest one involves how to communicate with our authors, and in this section, I'll discuss the main options and how to handle the main issues effectively. The next-biggest problem involves how to transfer original and edited manuscripts between author and editor. If we'll be editing manuscripts on the screen, it doesn't seem to make much sense to exchange them with our authors on paper, but there are good reasons why this might sometimes be necessary. In this section, I'll also discuss several of the considerations you'll need to account for to successfully exchange files with authors.

Communication

As I've mentioned previously, the author–editor relationship should be a dialogue, not a one-way transfer of information. The purpose of dialogue is to develop a means of working effectively together—ideally in a friendly manner, but at a minimum, in a professional manner. There are several key goals that define the types of communication that must take place over the course of this dialogue:

Getting to know each other

During this first phase, we begin the dialogue that initiates a relationship with the author. In addition to all the formalities (introductions and other pleasantries) that accompany any first-time conversation with someone we've never met, this initial dialogue provides our opportunity to reassure the author that they're in good hands and to build their confidence in us. It's also our chance to get a feel for whether we should be equally confident in the author. An author who seems disorganized or evasive sends a strong message that we should take extra care to define schedules, confirm understandings about the work, and protect ourselves (by, for example, signing a contract before beginning the work).

Reaching a mutual understanding

The next step in the dialogue is to identify the nature of the work that will be required and explain to the author what this involves. *Never* assume that you and the author understand each other based solely on an initial discussion. *Always* summarize this discussion so the author has a chance to confirm that you've understood their needs correctly, and offer them a chance to provide their own summary that confirms whether they've understood our needs.

Who's responsible? It's particularly important to ensure that authors understand their responsibility in the editorial process. Although we always make a good-faith effort to introduce no errors, the author is the real expert, not us, and must confirm that our work is correct. (We do our best to ensure correctness, but it's rare that we have the same level of expertise as the author.) When there's any doubt, they must learn to ask us for clarification rather than simply accepting a questionable edit and thereby introducing a preventable error into the manuscript.

Resolving differences of opinion

It's rare for us to agree with an author about everything, whether that agreement concerns their needs or the details of specific edits. There's a famous saying that "the client is always right—even when they're wrong", and it's important to keep that in mind. We are experts in our profession, but most of the authors we work with are experts in *their* profession, and if we're unable to persuade them that we're right by means of logic, appeals to authority (e.g., a respected style guide), and examples, it's necessary to take a long step back and recognize that it's the author's manuscript, not ours. In the end, the author has final authority, and all we can do if we disagree strongly enough with their choices is to insist politely but firmly that our names not be associated with the resulting manuscript.

Solving problems

Most of the time, editing a manuscript is quite straightforward, but every now and then, problems arise. These may result from an error on our part, an unusually critical reviewer of the author's work, or a problem with a word processor file. The hardest thing for most editors to learn may be to take responsibility for our own errors and strive to make things right for the author. When that's necessary, we should do that without trying too hard to absolve ourselves of blame. But when we did do everything right, and the author still blames us for a problem, we need to learn how to make things better without defending ourselves so strongly that we alienate the client. Often, the best approach is to steer the conversation to a discussion of how we can make things better rather than focusing on who to blame. (Of course, some clients *should be* fired when they become more trouble than they're worth. But that should always be a last resort, when all else has failed.) Some authors simply need to vent steam and get over their stress, and providing a quiet and sympathetic sounding board is sometimes all that's necessary to get past the problem.

Arranging payment

When we first negotiate the terms of the contract, one of those terms should always be the payment date and the penalties for late payments (typically, interest charges or other fees). To avoid a situation in which we're forced to invoke those penalties, we should remind clients of the payment deadlines on our invoice, and send a polite reminder if we haven't been paid well before the deadline. If the deadline passes, we're well within our legal rights to insist on payment of any penalty fees, and I've done this with government departments that had no excuse other than incompetence for late payment. For other clients, it may be wiser to accept a slightly late payment without insisting on our rights; the penalty fee may not be large, and is unlikely to be large enough to make it worth the risk of alienating the client and losing their future business. Try to get what is owed to you and to avoid letting clients take advantage of you, but think carefully about how hard you can insist without endangering your relationship.

"Relationship management"

Because some clients may only take advantage of our services infrequently (e.g., when we only edit a client's annual report), it's important to keep in touch so they know we still exist. At a minimum, send out "season's greetings" and New Year's wishes in December, and never use specific greetings such as "Merry Christmas" unless you know the client's religion. If you know of any other important holidays your client may observe, such as the Chinese new year or Indian Diwali festival, send out appropriate greetings for that holiday too—ideally in the client's native language if you can learn the correct protocol. (I've researched and stored copies of Chinese, Finnish, French, Japanese, Italian, and Spanish greetings, and I'm working on expanding my repertoire.)

How often should you communicate with authors? Any of the difficulties I mentioned earlier in this section may indicate a need for immediate communication. But don't stop with the bare minimum. Always confirm that you've received any material that they send you, and contact them within a day or two if they haven't confirmed that they received something you sent them. With e-mail, there are no guarantees that your message made it past misconfigured spam filters, antivirus software, and network-based e-mail filters. Without being annoying about it, keep clients advised of your progress towards a deadline (provide appropriate status updates), and warn them of any potential delays as far in advance as possible so you won't have to surprise them with a missed deadline; it's always better to negotiate an extension well in advance than to simply return work late, with no explanation.

Think ahead, too, and alert your most important clients to any impending absences or busy periods. For example, whenever I know that I'll be leaving on vacation, I warn all my key clients at least a month in advance—but I tell them that I'm leaving a week earlier than my actual date of departure. That way, if any work arrives at the last minute—and it always does—I have an extra week to handle it. Please note that I'm not advocating that you lie to clients; in an ideal world, I won't work right up to my point of departure because I really will need a few days to pack, get the pets taken care of, clean house, pay bills, stock the fridge for my return, and so on. Similarly, if I receive enough advance warning to know that I'll be buried with work at a particular time, I'll warn my clients that I'm unlikely to be available at that time. This allows them to adjust their schedules to send me work before or after that busy period with the minimum possible disruption. It may also have the salutary effect of reminding clients that you exist and that they should send you more work.

How to communicate with authors is a bit of a judgment call. Each individual has their own preferences; busy people often prefer e-mail because they can answer at their leisure, nervous people often prefer a phone call because they can interact with you in real-time until you've soothed their nerves, and legalistically inclined people may prefer a fax or registered letter so they have a printed record of your conversation. No one method is inherently superior, so it's more a question of paying attention to the other person's needs and learning what kind of communication they prefer. When in doubt, ask them! It constantly amazes me how many people prefer to assume that they know what a client wants and avoid asking; many end up with an unpleasant surprise when it turns out that they guessed wrong.

One final issue related to communication concerns the fact that a modern editor's clients are often scattered around the world; I currently have clients and colleagues on every continent except Antarctica and in most time zones. For me, e-mail works best because my correspondents can receive their e-mail and respond at their convenience; there's never any risk of accidentally waking them with a phone call (or of being awoken myself, as has happened once or twice) in the middle of the night. However, a phone call has sometimes been necessary, and in that case, it helps to know when it's appropriate to call. Many current atlases will allow you to calculate time zones, either directly (from times marked on the map) or indirectly (each 15° of longitude is roughly equivalent to a time difference of 1 hour later if your client is east of you, and 1 hour earlier if they live to the west). The easiest way, though, is to use a resource, such as the World Time Server (www.worldtimeserver.com), that lets you enter your current date and time and learn the corresponding date and time anywhere in the world.

Security and confidentiality

At the start of this section, I noted that there are reasons why we might not exchange files with our authors by e-mail, even if we'll be working entirely on the screen to edit and revise a manuscript. The biggest reason is security, which can become quite important when the material we're editing is confidential and must be protected. Unfortunately, although e-mail is highly convenient, it provides little or no security in its basic form. There are several other issues we need to be aware of so we can protect ourselves.

If security is important, take appropriate precautions to protect yourself against viruses and other nasty programs (collectively referred to as "malware") that can damage the software components of your computer, harvest e-mail addresses, record your keystrokes, and sometimes even steal documents. These precautions are doubly important for editors because the worst-case scenario is that we might inadvertently transmit this malware to a client after it has damaged our own computer. At a minimum, every computer user connected to the Internet now needs at least the following basic protections:

Antivirus software

Symantec's Norton Antivirus (www.symantec.com), available for both Mac and Windows, has been a steady, reliable choice for many years, but its performance has degraded in recent versions, and an increasing number of users have begun to complain of various problems caused by the software. Fortunately, there are many alternatives. For Windows computers, AVG (www.grisoft.com) and F-Prot (www.f-prot.com) are two alternatives with good reputations; for the Macintosh, check out Intego's Virus Barrier (www.intego.com) or ClamXav (www.markallan.co.uk/clamXav).

Antispyware software

Spybot Search and Destroy (www.safer-networking.org/en) and Ad-Aware 2007 Free edition (www.lavasoft.de) are two well-respected free programs for Windows, but they have consistently rated poorly compared with paid solutions such as Web-Root Spysweeper (www.webroot.com). As I write this, there are no comparable free utilities for the Macintosh, because no spyware has been reported for the Macintosh. However, Intego (www.intego.com) offers antispyware functionality in its Internet Security Barrier software.

A software firewall to keep out intruders

Zonelabs (www.zonelabs.com) offers the excellent free Zonealarm software for Windows users, but lately, the Comodo (http://www.comodo.com/) firewall software has received better ratings. Intego (www.intego.com) offers NetBarrier for Macintosh users. Both Windows XP and Macintosh OS X offer built-in firewalls, but the software is generally not as sophisticated as commercial software, and you should consider both programs only as a short-term solution.

If you have a high-speed connection, it's also worthwhile installing a hardware firewall for extra protection. Most commonly, this will be

Passwords everywhere: If you install a router or another hardware firewall, learn how to change the administrator password that comes with it. Many products come with a default password installed at the factory, and if you don't change this password, anyone who purchased the same hardware can use that password to gain access to your computer. Any password can be cracked with enough effort, but there's no sense making the task easy for a spy. To choose a strong password, use at least eight keyboard characters, preferably a mixture of letters and numbers and possibly even one or more of the characters found above the number keys on your keyboard. The password should not contain common words found in a dictionary, or use any publicly available information about you, such as your birth date. Of course, the password must also be something you'll remember. If, like most of us, you have trouble remembering the dozens of passwords that modern life may require, record your password somewhere safe: far from your computer, where a thief cannot easily find it.

included in a device called a "router" that you connect between your computer and its physical connection to the Internet (such as a cable modem). Macintosh users have traditionally been safe from the vast majority of security problems, but this may change at any time with little warning. Unfortunately, we're currently in the middle of an "arms race" between the developers of ways to break into computers and those who try to defend us against such intrusions. Brian Livingston's excellent *Windows Secrets* newsletter (http://brianlivingston.com) offers a wealth of useful information on Windows security, including a regularly updated "security baseline" that reports the state of the art in protecting your computer—and your client's information.

Apart from conscious attempts to cause us harm, the most common problem we encounter involves misdirected e-mail. For example, I have two regular correspondents with very similar e-mail addresses, and because my e-mail software helpfully tries to automatically complete addresses as I type, I've occasionally sent a friendly letter to the wrong friend. There's no foolproof way to prevent such natural human errors, but we can take steps to reduce the frequency of such problems. The most obvious and most effective is to simply pause and carefully check the e-mail address we've just typed before sending the message; if the address is at all cryptic, as many are, it's worthwhile to look up the client in our address book rather than simply assuming that we've guessed right. If our e-mail software tries to save time by completing addresses as we type, we should consider creating distinctive aliases (shortcut names that take the place of a full address) for easily confused addresses. Another trick I've used with considerable success is to keep a copy of an author's original message (containing the file they want me to edit) in my e-mail software's In Box. That way, I can simply select that message and reply to it, eliminating the need to type an address at all.

Another problem relates to the ongoing backups of data that are performed by the computer staff of our Internet service provider (ISP) and that of our client. These backups are generally a good thing, because they're our main protection against the occasional disasters that strike computers before messages are delivered. But if we're transmitting a confidential document that absolutely must not be read by anyone other than us and our client, those backups are a very bad thing indeed: the staff at the ISP should not have a chance to read the manuscript if they happen to be bored, unethical, or outright corrupt. Although it's also possible for someone to intercept e-mail and files as they travel over the Internet between our ISP and that of our client, that's a low risk because we're simply not an attractive target unless we're engaged in military research, investment banking, or other high-security fields. But if we are working in those areas, our clients will almost certainly provide an appropriately secure solution.

If the client does not provide or propose a solution, it may be worthwhile learning how to encrypt our documents—that is, to use utility software such as PGP (www.pgp.com) to encode the document in such a way that only someone with the correct password can possibly decrypt the document and read its contents. If that level of industrial-strength security strikes you as unnecessary, you can often achieve an adequate level of protection with nothing more complicated than a judiciously chosen password. Most word processors provide some form of password protection (in Word, for example, open the Tools menu and select Protect Document), but it's generally weak protection, and many free or inexpensive utilities exist for cracking these passwords. A nice compromise between that weak protection and a full-blown security system is to use a file compression utility such as StuffIt for Windows and the Macintosh (www.stuffit.com) that allows you to protect the compressed files with a password; one particularly nice feature of this software is that the developer provides free decompression utilities that you can ask your client to install.

Secure transmission of passwords

Of course, if the goal of using a password is to protect an e-mailed file from snoops while the e-mail is in transit, it makes no sense to include the password in the same e-mail message—yet surprising numbers of people, including many Web sites I've used, follow exactly that approach. This makes about as much sense as leaving your car keys in the door lock. If security is important, you may not even want to send the password by e-mail in a subsequent message. Instead, telephone your client and communicate the password orally.

E-mail alternatives

In addition to security problems, there are several additional limitations you may encounter with e-mail:

- **File size:** Most service providers limit the size of e-mail attachments to around 5 megabytes, though there are increasingly many exceptions. For larger files, we may be able to compress the file using software such as StuffIt (www.stuffit.com).
- **Attachment formats:** Because some viruses are transmitted in Word's .doc files and in compressed "archive" formats (particularly the .zip format used by Windows and Macintosh computers), many antivirus programs and corporate e-mail servers routinely block these files. To get past these guardians, we may need to rename files to use innocent extensions such as .txt (shorthand for the "text" file format). However, we then need to teach clients to rename the file with the correct extension (such as .zip) so that their software will be able to open it.
- **Confirmation of receipt:** Although we can sometimes request an automatic confirmation that our message arrived (such as when we and the author are using the same software), more often we need to rely on the author to confirm that they received the file.

If you can't resolve these kinds of problems or the security issues I discussed in the previous section, you may need to investigate alternatives to e-mail. The first and most obvious option is to use a courier service to hand-deliver a CD (protected by a hard plastic case and a padded envelope) containing the edited file. If you work near your client, you can also hand-deliver the CD. Diskettes (floppy disks) are generally a poor choice because they are fragile, and it's easy to inadvertently overwrite the files they contain—something that can't happen with a CD. There are also persistent anecdotal reports (some more credible than others) that diskettes are vulnerable to the electromagnetic fields generated by older or poorly maintained models of the X-ray scanners and other security devices used to protect against terrorists—and particularly vulnerable to the metal-detector wands we all endure at the airport. Last but not least, some newer computers (particularly laptops) have eliminated diskette drives.

You can also use FTP (file-transfer protocol) software to transfer files directly to a client. FTP is inherently more secure than e-mail, particularly if you use a variant called "secure FTP", because the full file never comes to rest on anyone else's computer during transit. (Bits and pieces of the file travel different routes through the Internet, so only a professional spy would be able to intercept and reassemble these packets.) You can find a range of free and inexpensive FTP programs from reputable download sites such as TuCows (www.tucows.com) and most computer magazine sites. If your client has established a secure FTP server, they can provide the necessary information on how to connect to that site and transfer the file. If you only need to occasionally take advantage of this technology, a range of free FTP sites is available. These allow you to upload a file to a private, secure server hosted on the company's Web site, from which your client can download it to their own computer. For example, here are some alternatives that I've either used or seen recommended by credible sources:

- You can purchase paid software such as Apple's Mac.com service for Macintosh and Windows users (www.mac.com), which provides both Web-based e-mail and space for file transfers. It also provides a useful free backup program, boringly named "Backup", that you can use for offsite backups of your important files.
- Dropload (www.dropload.com) allows you to upload files as large as 100 megabytes and specify the e-mail address(es) of the person or people who can download it. The files are deleted from the server after 7 days. The program is offered free, but donations are requested.
- Mediafire (www.mediafire.com) claims unlimited disk storage space plus up to 100 megabytes per file. Files remain until you delete them.
- MegaUpload (http://megaupload.com) provides up to 250 megabytes of free upload space per file (up to 2000 megabytes plus password protection with a paid premium subscription).
- SendThisFile (http://sendthisfile.com) offers a free service with no stated maximum file size, but with minimal security and only 3 days to download the file, or a paid service with full security and various "business account" options.
- Yahoo offers 30 megabytes of free storage via their Briefcase service (http://briefcase.yahoo.com).
- YouSendIt (www.yousendit.com) offers free uploads of up to 1000 megabytes via a secure channel, accessible only by those to whom you give the file's Web address. There are also paid "business solutions" that were not defined when I was writing this book.

Storage durations: If you use any of these services to transfer files, carefully investigate how long the service keeps the files on their server. If they don't automatically delete the files for you within a short period of time, leave yourself a note to ensure you won't forget to delete the file once the client has received it. You do have to place a measure of trust in the integrity of the people who operate these services, but given that their business depends on demonstrating their integrity, such services are a safe bet for most purposes.

II. Mastering the tools

"One of the universal rules of happiness is: always be wary of any helpful item that weighs less than its operating manual."—*Terry Pratchett, Jingo*

Although personal computers have been around in one form or another for nearly 25 years, they're still primitive things compared with what they will eventually become. Moreover, most computer software is still designed by programmers who are unfamiliar with the modern science of user-centered design. As a result, the software we use for on-screen editing initially appears uncomfortable and awkward to most editors, and many never try to overcome that bad first impression; instead, they feel too intimidated to use the software, or simply learn to tolerate its many annoyances. My informal observations of a great many computer users over the years suggests that the fear of screwing something up or of demonstrating one's incompetence is the single greatest barrier to overcoming these problems and learning to use a computer efficiently. It helps to remember, as I've often noted to the occasional petrified victim of the computer, that even if they're smarter than we are, we can still turn them off whenever they annoy us.

Once you get past the initial intimidation factor, you quickly begin discovering how to make the computer your tool rather than your nemesis. Time invested in learning how software works will repay itself a hundredfold in subsequent time savings. Moreover, most software can be simply but extensively customized until you find a combination of settings that works well for you. In this section, I'll teach you how to personalize your editing environment so that it becomes a comfortable place to work, with the additional benefit that doing so will improve your editing speed and accuracy. I'll also teach you to pay close attention to how you work so you can recognize editorial tasks that are particularly suitable for automation: these are tasks that take up lots of time, whether because we do them so often or because they're so cumbersome that they devour our time whenever we must do them.

Most computer users master a core set of perhaps two dozen tasks, and never bother learning anything more about their software. That's a shame, since modern software offers an incredible depth and breadth of features that could make our lives enormously easier. If you don't have the time to purchase and memorize a detailed book on your software, I've found an alternative that works well for most people: Every day, spend a mere five minutes exploring a single menu choice you've never used before and figuring out what it does. (If the menu choice introduces another dozen options, concentrate on each one in turn, one feature per day.) Spend a moment thinking about whether that feature of the software could help you work faster or better, and by the time a year of exploration has gone by, you'll have explored most of the software's nooks and crannies. Or, if you don't want to spend the time, read this section of the book; I've already done most of that work for you.

Chapter 4. Personalizing how your software works

"The reasonable man adapts himself to the world; the unreasonable one persists to adapt the world to himself. Therefore all progress depends on the unreasonable man."—George Bernard Shaw (1856–1950)

Among the most productive places to start your explorations of how software works are the "control panels" that each operating system uses to control how we interact with our computers. These settings affect the performance of the operating system as a whole, but each program also has something to say about the computer's behavior. In the context of editing, it's our word processor's Options (Windows) or Preferences (Macintosh) menu choice that governs how the software interacts with us and with the operating system. This menu choice most often appears under the Tools menu (as is the case in many versions of Microsoft Word), but may instead appear under the File or Edit menus. In the most recent version of the Macintosh operating system (OS X), the Preferences menu choice has been moved under the menu that bears the name of the software (e.g., Word, InDesign).

In this chapter, I'll discuss our personalization options both at the level of the operating system (*Overall behavior of your computer*) and at the level of our word processors (*General behavior of your word processor*). In the first section, I'll provide general details for both Windows and the Macintosh; in the second, I'll describe the general features that should be available in most programs. Last but not least, I'll extend this discussion to focus on how Microsoft Word has implemented the general list of word processor features (*General behavior of Microsoft Word*). If you're using another word processor, such as WordPerfect, the descriptions in the first parts of this chapter will give you an idea of what features to look for in that software, and the last part of the chapter will illustrate the kind of changes you can try to make in your own word processor.

Overall behavior of your computer

Control panels are small programs we can use to define the characteristics of a wide range of our interactions with our computers, including most aspects of how we interact with the computer through its hardware and operating system and how that interaction produces what we see on the screen. The three most important groups of settings for editors are those for the keyboard, those for the mouse or other pointing device (hereafter, "mouse" for all such devices), and those for the screen display. All three groups of settings can be accessed via control panels in the Windows and Macintosh operating systems, with one exception; in Macintosh OS X, these are now called "preference panels". Preference panels are functionally identical to control panels, but have a slightly different interface. For the sake of simplicity, I'll refer to all tools for reining in the computer as "control panels" henceforth.

Keyboard and mouse settings

The three main keyboard settings that affect our interactions with the computer are how long it takes for the computer to recognize that we're holding down a key, how fast the computer then repeats the specified action for that key (e.g., types a letter of the alphabet or scrolls the screen), and the roles of each key on the keyboard. Both Windows and the Macintosh operating system use one or more control panels to define how these functions work.

Here are the settings you should experiment with:

Keyboard control panel

The "delay before repeating" and "repeat rate" are obviously useful in slowing down the keyboard response (increasing the delay before the computer recognizes a keystroke and reducing the number of times that input occurs before you release the key). These options should be set low enough that we don't insert a string of repeated characters each time we touch the keyboard. Unfortunately, this also slows down keystrokes that would benefit from an immediate response and fast repetition, such as moving the cursor through a document using the arrow keys. For these kinds of actions, we want to *accelerate* the keyboard response. Finding the correct balance between delaying and acceler-

Why not Linux? Although I recognize the growing popularity of the Linux operating system and the OpenOffice software suite, it simply wasn't possible for me to cover this software too. The features described in this chapter should have obvious equivalents in Linux and OpenOffice, and I encourage you to look for them.

For control freaks: To find your computer's control panels:

- **Windows:** The specific location varies slightly among versions. From Windows 2000 onwards, open the Start menu, select Settings, then select Control Panel.
- **Macintosh OS 9 and earlier:** Open the Apple menu and select Control Panels.
- **Macintosh OS X:** Open the System Preferences utility found in the Dock, or open the Apple menu and select System Preferences.

ating the keyboard requires some experimentation. To strike the optimal balance, spend some time paying attention to whether you're most annoyed by occasional repeated characters or by a long delay before scrolling begins, and adjust the keyboard response rate accordingly.

Mouse control panel

Once we've learned to use a mouse or other pointing device, most of us quickly discover that the default settings make the mouse move faster or slower than we like, and that we have to click the main button faster or slower than we prefer to double-click (for example, to launch a program or select a word). To strike the right balance, spend some time adjusting the "tracking speed" until the cursor moves fast enough to get you to the desired location quickly but not so fast that you're constantly overshooting the target. Similarly, experiment with the "double-click speed" until it's sufficiently slow you can select icons with a single click but not so slow you inadvertently select words or launch programs because your computer thinks you double-clicked.

Depending on which operating system and version you're using, the language settings may appear in the Language, International, or Keyboard control panel. (If you can't find it, search the online help for the phrase "keyboard layout".) Look for the country and language combination for the language you use most often. In Canada, for example, you have a choice between Canadian English and Canadian French. Pressing certain keys on the keyboard will produce different results with these two settings; since French uses many accented vowels and English does not, the French keyboard layout is optimized to let typists enter accented vowels in a single keystroke, whereas the English keyboard layout often requires two keystrokes. Here are typical locations for these settings:

Try the keyboard instead: If you've spent any significant length of time playing with your computer, you've noticed you can use either the mouse or the keyboard to select things and move around the screen. Keyboard shortcuts are more efficient for many purposes, particularly during editing, and learning these shortcuts will make most editorial tasks more efficient. For details on efficient ways to move around a document and select text from the keyboard with the keyboard faster than is possible by mouse alone, see Chapter 5.

- **Windows:** In Windows 2000 and later, open the Keyboard control panel, select the Input Locales tab, then select the desired keyboard layout under the heading "Input language".
- **Macintosh:** In OS 9, open the Keyboard control panel. In OS X, open the International preferences panel, select the "Input Menu" tab, and scroll down until you find the desired setting. Select that setting so that a checkmark appears beside it.

Most computers ship with the keyboard configured to support the language used in the region where the computer was sold (e.g., U.S. English in the United States), but if you installed the operating system yourself, you had the opportunity to specify your preferred language early in the installation process. In that case, you may need to find the installation disk for your operating system if you want to add another keyboard layout.

If you frequently need to type characters from other languages, open the language control panel and select a keyboard layout that lets you accomplish this task easily. For example, the "U.S. International" setting in Windows lets you enter most accented characters by pressing the Control key plus a key that represents a specific accent, followed by a character such as a vowel, to produce an accented version of that character; for example, pressing Control + ' (the single quotation mark), then releasing both keys and typing the letter *e*, produces *é*. The corresponding keystrokes on the Macintosh are implemented by pressing the Option key plus a key that represents the accent, releasing both keys, then typing the letter that should receive the accent; for example, Option + *e* followed by the letter *e* produces *é* for any keyboard layout.

If you routinely work in two or more languages, the ability to change keyboard layouts on the fly, without having to visit the language settings each time, can be very useful. The same control panel that lets you select the keyboard layout you'll be using also lets you define additional keyboard layouts and the keyboard shortcut that lets you switch between them:

- **Windows:** The default shortcut is left Alt key + Shift.
- **Macintosh:** The default shortcut is Command + Spacebar.

If you're only working in a single language, you'll more often find this keyboard shortcut annoying and disorienting, because it's easy to inadvertently switch keyboard layouts and suddenly start typing gibberish. If you're concerned that this will happen to you and you won't remember my explanation, disable this shortcut now, before it can cause any problems. All you need to do is deselect this option in the language control panel, or choose a different keyboard shortcut that you won't accidentally trigger.

Display settings

Three aspects of your video settings can prevent computer use from turning into a visual nightmare: the screen resolution, anti-aliasing, and the refresh rate. Each can be changed via the Monitor control panel (older versions of the Macintosh operating system) or the Displays control panel (modern versions of Windows and Macintosh OS X).

Screen resolution determines how many dots (*pixels*) will be displayed on the screen. At higher resolutions (more pixels), screen images will be sharper and potentially less fatiguing to view, but text and icons will be smaller than they would be at a lower resolution. The Display control panel lets you choose from a range of larger default icon and text sizes to compensate for this shrinkage, and you should spend a few moments playing with these alternative sizes to find one that won't leave you squinting at your monitor. Most computer users now use a resolution of at least 800×600 because it represents a good compromise between sharpness and size, but many other resolutions are available. Experiment with resolutions until you find one that lets you show the desired amount of text on the screen, thereby reducing the amount of scrolling you must do and providing a better view of page layouts, without making the text so small that you squint and develop eyestrain.

If you use a traditional CRT (the TV-like displays that most of us have used until recently), you can select a wide range of resolutions with little difficulty; CRTs create pixels using a beam of electrons, and can increase or decrease the number of pixels simply by modulating the size and spacing of that electron beam. However, the physical resolution of an LCD monitor is fixed when the display is manufactured, and even though you can choose other resolutions, doing so often leads to fuzzier images: if you're asking the monitor to display more pixels than it actually possesses, it has to fake those extra pixels. This is where *antialiasing* comes in. The video software on your computer uses this trick to simulate the existence of more pixels on the screen than the display actually possesses. As a result, you'll be able to see finer details than the monitor's physical structure should really allow. Microsoft's ClearType and Apple's Quartz software provide antialiasing on both LCDs and CRTs. Not everyone likes the effect of this trick, since it may create a certain amount of blurriness with older video cards and monitors, but if it works for you, it can greatly improve your ability to read text without squinting. And if it doesn't work, simply turn off this feature.

Last but not least, pay careful attention to the *screen refresh rate* for your computer. On LCD monitors, the image is created once and remains unchanged until the video software changes it, so refresh rates aren't an important factor. However, the image on a CRT display is painted by a beam of electrons sweeping across the screen, and by the time the beam reaches the end of the screen, the first pixels have begun to fade. This leads to flickering as the fading pixels are suddenly "refreshed" and replaced by bright, newly painted pixels. For many computer users, a refresh rate of 60 Hz (sixty times per second) is sufficient, but if you're at all sensitive to flicker, that refresh rate will drive you crazy. Screen flickering is sometimes more obvious in your peripheral vision, so try looking beside the screen to see if you notice any flicker. If you do, increase the refresh rate to 75 Hz or greater to eliminate it. Even if you don't consciously notice the flicker at a low refresh rate, higher refresh rates tend to be less visually fatiguing. Most modern video cards let you adjust the refresh rate to at least 75 Hz for most screen resolutions, but older cards may be unable to do so at the highest resolutions or if you're displaying the maximum possible number of colors onscreen simultaneously. Select the highest refresh rate that your video card can produce for the desired screen resolution, and if that rate isn't sufficiently high to eliminate flicker, you'll either have to decrease the screen resolution, decrease the number of colors displayed on the screen, or upgrade your video card.

"Hardware" settings

Computer hardware gets its name because it's inherently hard on your body—your own personal editing equipment. Although there are no compelling studies that show an increased risk of health problems for otherwise healthy, physically active computer users, overuse injuries (also called "repetitive stress injuries") are a potential problem if you're going to spend hours whacking away at your keyboard without interruption. Appendix II (*Protecting yourself from injury while using the computer*) provides a detailed explanation of how to set up a safer, more comfortable work environment that will minimize the risk of such injuries.

General behavior of your word processor

Most software, fresh out of the box, fits our preferences about as well as a new pair of shoes that haven't yet been broken in accommodate the unique shapes of our feet. The blisters caused by new software may be metaphorical, but they're no less painful than the real ones. Working comfortably on the computer screen will only become possible if you learn how to "break in" the software—that is, learn how to customize it so it works the way you want it to work.

The good news is that most modern word processors provide a bewildering array of options for configuring their behavior. That's also the bad news, since discovering which options work best for you can take quite some time. Fortunately, I've played with most of these settings at one time or another, and in this section, I'll discuss the groups of settings that are most likely to make your editing life easier. Because there are too many options for me to describe without turning this book into a user manual for your word processor, I've focused on the ones most likely to provide a good payback. But don't limit yourself to my suggestions: spending some time exploring the specific options that your software provides occasionally reveals an obscure setting that is highly relevant to your specific work or your unique needs.

General settings

In this section, I'll focus on the general groups of configuration options provided by most modern word processors. (A later section will illustrate how these options work in various versions of Microsoft Word.) In any word processor, you'll find several groups of broadly useful settings that you should explore until you understand which ones help you edit more effectively and which ones will get in your way until you disable them. These settings fall into several main categories:

General settings

These control things such as the measurement units the software uses to describe the page, how it handles repagination, and how it updates links to things that may change, such as automatically updating page numbers. The settings may also include the locations of key types of files (such as backups).

View settings

These control how the word processor displays certain useful things: images, special codes used to perform calculations (e.g., to insert the page number) or create links (e.g., to insert cross-references), nonprinting characters that the software uses to indicate the presence of special formatting (such as tab stops and paragraph markers), the listing of paragraph and character styles, the scroll bars and rulers that appear at the edges of windows, and how the text wraps within the window.

Typing settings

These define whether newly typed characters replace (overwrite) or are inserted within existing text, whether the software lets you automatically select entire words, whether you can drag text around the screen with the mouse instead of using cut and paste, and various special key definitions such as whether the Insert key switches between overwriting text and inserting text.

Print settings

If your file includes coding for information that must be calculated on the fly (such as page numbers or the current date), these set-

> **What's a style anyway?** Not comfortable with paragraph and character styles? Never even heard of them before? See the section *A primer on templates* later in this chapter to learn the most important details.

tings control whether the coding or the actual information will appear when the file is printed. They also control what special features (such as comments and tracked edits) will appear in the printout.

Save settings

These define whether the software creates a backup copy of your work, whether it uses certain special tricks (good or bad) to save your work, how to recover damaged files, and whether and where it saves information that helps you recover from a crash.

Spelling and grammar settings

These define whether the software will check spelling and grammar while you type, or only on request, and may perform other useful tricks such as determining which dictionaries to use during spellchecks.

"Track changes" or "revision tracking" settings

These control how your edits are recorded, how they will appear on the screen, and how the software handles edits of a single document by multiple reviewers.

User information settings

These settings are how you identify yourself to the software so it can keep track of who you are; for example, this lets the software add your name to all revisions and lets you to edit your own revisions without tracking these modifications as additional changes. These settings also let you conceal this information if you need to perform anonymous ("blind") reviews.

Compatibility settings

A miscellaneous group of settings that allow you to deal with changes in how the software works between the current version and previous versions. These settings may also help resolve issues related to font mismatches between operating systems and between European and Asian versions of the software.

Autocorrect and autoformat

These settings control whether and how the word processor will fix things such as typos as you work, and whether it will let you automatically replace short keywords with longer phrases to save wear and tear on your fingers. These settings may also cause the software to automatically format text as you type, and knowing this can help solve some bemusing typing problems.

Display settings

Most software also provides a range of screen display options to help you customize how the screen appears. (See *Display settings* earlier in this chapter for a discussion of the main factors that affect the display for all programs on your computer.) These include:

View modes

Most software offers at least a page layout view that simulates what a printed page will look like, plus a "normal" view that emphasizes the content rather than the layout. Some programs offer additional views, such as an outline mode that displays only the headings and thus reveals the document's overall structure more clearly than if you had to scroll through it. There may also be a full-screen view that provides a display with minimal clutter so you can concentrate more easily on the words.

Rulers and guides

These visual references help with the positioning of text.

Zoom (magnification)

These tools let you increase or decrease (magnify or reduce) the size of the type and graphics to make them easier to read or fit more or less information on the screen simultaneously.

Text wrap

"Wrapping" prevents lines of text from running past the right edge of the screen, thereby forcing you to scroll the window horizontally to see the ends of each line. This won't work in a page layout view, where text must necessarily run off the screen if the page being displayed is too large to fit on the screen; in that case, you must zoom in or out until the whole page fits on the screen.

Styles

Most software offers various ways to manage which paragraph and character styles are displayed. See *A primer on styles and templates* later in this chapter for more information on the use of styles.

Font name and size

This information is useful for determining whether authors have changed the font used for a chunk of text and, in so doing, have overridden a style definition.

Working with windows

Editors tend to open several programs simultaneously, and often several windows or documents in each program. As a result, it pays to learn how to arrange and move between multiple windows and how to switch between programs on your computer. The most useful things to know are:

- How you can keep two or more windows open simultaneously, and any limitations on the maximum number of available windows.
- How to resize and rearrange these windows both manually and automatically to fit your changing needs (e.g., to focus on a single document or to compare several documents).
- How to switch quickly between programs and between open windows within a single program.
- How to split a window or open a new window into a single document so you can see two parts of that document simultaneously.

Most software provides a range of other useful configuration options. For example, you can usually customize:

- The contents of menus and toolbars.
- Which toolbars are displayed and which are hidden.
- The keyboard assignments used to send the software specific commands or activate certain features.

In the next several sections of this chapter, I'll provide specific examples of how all these types of settings have been implemented in Microsoft Word. If you're using other software, spend a few moments looking through its online help or printed manual using the setting names that I've used in this chapter, plus a few likely synonyms, to see whether and how your software implements comparable settings. Most modern software can do all or most of what Word can do with a little coercion; the challenge lies in learning how.

General behavior of Microsoft Word

To modify Word's various configuration options, open the Options (Windows) or Preferences (Macintosh) dialog box, then patiently work through each category of setting until you've modified those settings in a way that seems logical, then plan to return to that dialog box as often as necessary until you've adjusted the settings to your satisfaction. To access these options in Word:

- **Windows:** Open the Tools menu and select Options.
- **Macintosh before OS X:** Open the Tools menu and select Preferences.

- **Macintosh OS X:** Open the Word menu and select Preferences.

It's important to understand that these settings only affect how Word behaves on *your* computer. If you're working with authors who haven't customized their version of Word the same way you have, they won't see the document the same way you see it. Keep this in mind when you're communicating with your authors and referring to the way documents should appear on the screen; you may need to explain things differently, or show them how to customize their own version of Word so they can see the same thing that you're seeing.

In the following sections, the names of the settings (e.g., General) refer to the tabs in Word's Options or Preferences dialog box. The names of these tabs and the wording of the specific options I'll be describing may vary among the different versions of Word, but they should be close enough that you can figure out which setting is which.

General settings

Word's General settings govern three main features that you should consider adjusting:

Measurement units

This setting lets you specify the units that will appear on the software's horizontal ruler (and in Print or Layout viewing mode, a vertical ruler too). This setting also defines the units that will be used when you specify indents, tab positions, and other formatting information in various dialog boxes. This setting is most important if your editing responsibilities also include formatting the document (for example, to conform with the submission guidelines for a publisher).

Background repagination

With this function enabled, Word will constantly recalculate the length of the document and your position within the document. This is important if you must edit a manuscript to reduce its length so that it fits within an allotted space. Note that in most versions of Word, this page count is only accurate if you're working in Print or Layout view.

> **Where did the options go?** In some versions of Word, you can't access the Options or Preferences dialog box if no document is open on the screen. If Word won't let you open this dialog box, simply create a new blank document and try again.

Update automatic links at open

If a document contains links to graphics files, spreadsheets, and other objects that exist outside the document, selecting this option ensures that you'll see the most recent versions of those objects that are available when you open the document. This is important if you'll be editing manuscripts that contain external components such as graphics that may be undergoing revision by someone else while you edit. If you're also responsible for editing these components or comparing them with the text to ensure that the descriptions match, select this option.

View settings

The View settings govern how Word displays the contents of a file, and there are several groups of settings on the View tab. Here, I've focused on those that are particularly important to editors.

Show settings

The Show group of settings governs certain aspects of the non-text display that may be important to you:

ScreenTips: If you select this setting, and hold the cursor over text inserted or deleted using revision tracking, Word displays the name of the editor, the date and time of the edit, and the nature of the edit (e.g., "inserted" to identify new text added by the editor). In addition, if you select text before inserting a comment (using the Comment feature under the Insert menu), Word will highlight that text in yellow, as if you'd run a highlighter marker over the selected text. Moving the cursor over the highlighted text will pop up a yellow balloon that contains the editor information plus the full text of the comment. If ScreenTips is deselected, you'll still see the comment markers (e.g., mine look like [GH1]), but to see the actual comment, you must double-click on the comment marker to open the Comments pane at the bottom of the screen.

Image placeholders: If you're working on a slower computer, and a graphics-heavy document is scrolling slowly enough to reduce your productivity, select this option to replace the graphics with empty boxes (placeholders) and speed up the screen display.

Field codes: Word uses field codes to calculate various things, such as the current page number, and to offer various special features, from cross-references to index entries. If you need to edit these codes, as is most commonly the case when you must edit a manuscript's index, select this checkbox so you can see and edit the fields.

Bookmarks: If you're responsible for inserting cross-references or checking their validity, or if you want to see how these special features have been inserted so that you can make the formatting consistent, select this checkbox. Bookmarks will resemble {field code} on the screen. (Note the curly brackets.)

Nonprinting character settings

The Nonprinting Characters group of settings determine which of several visual cues Word should display to help you understand what you see on the screen. Consider the following settings:

Tabs: If you'll be editing a manuscript to fix spacing problems before it is sent for layout in desktop publishing software, it's helpful to display tab markers (—>) so you can delete any that have been entered by mistake; most often, authors incorrectly use tab characters to indent the beginning of a paragraph instead of defining that initial indentation in the paragraph's style definition.

Paragraph markers: In some documents, particularly those in which the author has not indented the first line of each new paragraph and has provided no space between paragraphs, it can be difficult to determine where one paragraph ends and the next one begins. When that's the case, it's helpful to display paragraph markers (¶) that reveal these breakpoints.

Window settings

The Window Settings group of options defines what interface tools Word will display. Consider selecting the following options:

Style area width: If you're responsible for ensuring that paragraph and character styles have been applied consistently and in conformity with a publisher's style guide, it helps to display the styles used for each paragraph in the margin. To do so, enter a sufficiently large number in this field that most of each style name will fit in this area; the style area itself will appear to the left of the paragraphs of text. To eliminate this display, set the style area width to zero.

Horizontal and vertical scroll bars: These settings define whether you will see a scroll bar at the bottom and right sides (respectively) of the document window. If space is limited on your screen and you want to see more text simultaneously, or if you frequently click the mouse in the scroll bars by mistake, deselect these options until you need them again.

Wrap to window: If you're working in Normal view mode (see *Screen display*, later in this chapter), you won't see what the document will look like when it's printed. In Normal mode, selecting this option forces the complete line of text to remain visible (to *wrap*) when you resize the document window. This feature has no effect in Print or Layout view mode.

Edit settings

The Edit settings define how Word responds to your keystrokes when you insert, select, or delete text. Consider changing the following options:

Typing replaces selection

In this mode, selecting one or more characters and pressing another key replaces the selected text with whatever you type. This can speed up your edits because it lets you overtype and replace text rather than having to first insert new text, then delete the text that it is meant to replace.

When selecting, automatically select entire word

This option lets you apply changes to an entire word rather than simply to selected (highlighted) text. However, if you prefer to select and fix only parts of words rather than retyping the whole word (e.g., to correct a single mid-word typo) when revision tracking is enabled, this feature unhelpfully replaces the entire word. If that annoys you, deselect this option.

Drag and drop editing

This option lets you select a block of text, then hold down the mouse button and drag that text to a new position. This is very useful for moving sentences and juggling word order within a sentence without having to repeatedly cut and paste text.

Insert key pastes text

Because the Insert key lies right above the forward Delete key on many keyboards, it's easy to hit the Insert key by mistake. Doing so switches between insertion mode (in which typing pushes forward all characters to the right of the cursor position to make room for the new text) and overstrike mode (in which each new character that you type replaces the character to the right of the current cursor position). This behavior can be quite annoying if you're typing without watching the screen, as many of us do while copying text from a printout; it's easy to erase a fair bit of text before you look up and notice the problem. In overstrike mode, the OVR button at the bottom of the screen will be selected:

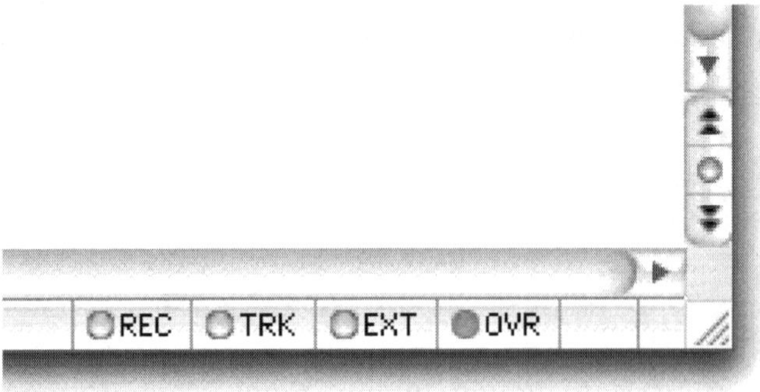

Selecting this option changes the behavior of the Insert key so that it pastes text that was previously cut or copied instead of switching between insert and overstrike modes. This makes it easier to insert copied text because you can press a single key (the Insert key) instead of two keys (Control + V in Windows; Command + V on the Macintosh) or opening the Edit menu with your mouse and selecting Paste to insert the text. The downside of this setting is that if you accidentally hit the key after you've copied a large chunk of text, that chunk gets inserted at the cursor position even if you didn't want to do that. Fortunately, this is usually easy to spot.

Print settings

This group of options lets you control what will appear in printouts. If you'll be working exclusively on the screen, these settings won't affect you, but if you or an author want to work on paper for at least part of the editing process, consider changing the following options:

Update fields and links

This option sets Word to update any fields, such as page numbers and cross-references, before it prints the document. If you want to check cross-references and other links on paper, this is a helpful option.

Print comments

In older versions of Word, this option appended any inserted comments at the end of the printout, with page numbers and the reference number of the comment included to help you find the corresponding text in the printout. You can also select this option in the Print dialog box by opening the "Print what" field and choosing this option. In Word XP/2002 and Word 2003 (Windows) and Word 2004 (Macintosh), the option to print comments is available only within the Print dialog box, and controlling what you see in the printout becomes much more difficult.

Fractional widths

This option is designed to improve the quality of printouts, and is thus automatically selected when you are viewing your document in Print or Layout viewing mode, where it's important to see exactly what the document will look like on paper. However, because this can make text more difficult to read on the screen, it is turned off by default in Normal view. Experiment with this setting to determine whether selecting or deselecting it makes it easiest for you to read text in Normal view.

Save settings

Because even the most careful of us occasionally makes mistakes, and because no software is ever as crash-proof as we might wish, it pays to learn how to fend off the worst consequences of such infelicities by configuring how our word processor saves files. Word offers the following useful options:

Always create backup copy

With this option selected, Word creates a copy of each file that you open, with a slightly different name: in older versions, the filename extension ".bak" is added to the name of the document, but in newer versions, the name becomes "Backup of..." followed by the name of the document. If you damage a file badly enough that you want to start over again from the version that existed when you first opened the document to start the day's work, simply open this backup file. However, each time you open a file, Word replaces any existing backup file with the current version of the file. Thus, this option does not by itself represent an adequate backup strategy. See Appendix I for more details on a sound backup strategy.

Allow fast saves

Never select this option. It's an antiquated feature from the days when computers and hard drives were so slow that anything capable of saving files more quickly was worth trying. Because this option inserts your changes at the end of the file rather than at the actual location of the change, Word must reconstruct the current version of the file by working through all of these changes each time you reopen the file. Eventually, this process will become so complex that Word will throw up its virtual hands in despair and give up, damaging the file and possibly losing all your hard work; this may not happen quickly, but a great many reports from the workplace confirm that it *will* happen. Moreover, files saved using this feature can be difficult for other software to open; it used to be possible to reliably crash WordPerfect and PageMaker by trying to open such files. If you've been using this feature, turn it off at once, then open the File menu and select Save As so you can save the file under a new name, which usually fixes any problems.

Save autorecovery information

This option instructs Word to automatically save a temporary copy of the current file at the specified time intervals. If Word crashes, you can generally recover some or all of the work you completed before the crash. (See the *File locations settings* section later in this chapter for details on where these files are saved and other important information on temporary files.) A good rule of thumb is to set the interval between saves short enough that you're willing to redo all the work since the last time you saved the file if Word crashes. Unless you're working under very tight deadlines or using a very unstable computer that crashes often, Word is generally stable enough that there's little reason to set the interval below 15 minutes.

Spelling and grammar settings

The spelling and grammar checkers built into modern word processors are sufficiently important that I've devoted all of Chapter 10 to this topic. Here, I'll only briefly review the most important options that govern how these tools work:

Check spelling as you type

With this option selected, Word reviews each word as soon as you finish typing it, and underlines the word if it can't find it in the relevant dictionaries (including your personal or custom dictionary). This option is intended more for writers than for editors, but it's of questionable value for both groups; most writers find it far more effective to write text first and revise it later than to interrupt their flow of thought to fix each typo as it occurs. Editors using revision tracking find that selecting this option adds yet another set of visual indicators on the screen, possibly increasing the amount of clutter to unacceptable levels. Nonetheless, the option is available in case you find it helpful.

Suggest from main dictionary only

With this option selected, Word uses only the main spelling dictionary and ignores any words you have added to your custom dictionaries.

"Dictionaries" button

This button lets you specify which dictionaries should be used with the current file. Using this function, you can set Word to use a specialized list of words (such as a medical dictionary) for the current document.

Check grammar as you type

This option is similar to the "Check spelling as you type" option, but highlights supposed grammatical problems. Unfortunately, Word's grammar checker is primitive at best, so I don't recommend using this option while you edit. (This statement is true of computerized grammar checkers in general, not just the one that comes with Word.) If you're going to use the grammar checker at all, select the option "Check grammar with spelling" in this tab of the dialog box and read Chapter 10 for details on how to use this feature productively.

"Settings" button

This button lets you customize which rules Word's grammar checker will enforce. By judiciously selecting the options that are both reliable and most likely to help you, you can make Word's grammar checker into a semi-useful tool.

"Check document" button

Word contains many shortcuts intended to help you work faster and smarter, but this isn't one of them. If Word has spellchecked a document, it sometimes decides to save you time by not checking text that it believes hasn't changed since the last spellcheck. To warn you that it's made this choice, it changes this button to read "Recheck document"—and too bad if you don't think to open the Spelling and Grammar settings to look for this warning sign. If you find Word skipping entire sections of a document, missing obvious typos, or refusing to even begin a spellcheck, click this button to force Word to start over again from the top of the document. That too will sometimes fail; see Chapter 10 for a few suggestions on what to do if it does.

Track changes settings

If you're performing onscreen editing, these settings are the key to defining how your changes will appear on the screen. Best of all, since these changes affect only your copy of Word, you can choose settings that are effective for you without worrying about whether those settings are equally effective for your authors. (If you have created two or more user accounts on your computer, each account can have different settings.) Because what you see won't necessarily match what your authors see, you'll occasionally have to teach your authors how to use these settings to customize the screen display to meet their own needs. (You'd be surprised how many of them never discover or learn to use these settings, and complain endlessly about the characteristics of the display that Word selects as its default behavior.)

The various options in this group of settings let you define the color and style that Word will use to display your insertions and deletions, as well as any formatting changes, and whether Word inserts lines ("change bars") in the margin to indicate any lines of text that contain your changes. Rather than exploring these four types of changes here, I'll instead concentrate on how these settings affect the screen display. For more details on the nature of these types of changes, see Chapter 6 (*Using revision tracking*), Chapter 7 (*Inserting and deleting text*), and Appendix III (*A summary of key changes since Word 2000*). In Word, you have the following options:

Color

Word provides a limited number of colors that you can use to highlight your revisions, including the classic editorial "red pen". However, there is no way to define a custom color if you don't like the available choices. If multiple editors or reviewers will be revising a document, you can select "By author" as the color, and Word will display each person's changes in a different color. Unfortunately, Word doesn't let you change the order in which the colors are assigned to each reviewer. Although primarily intended for onscreen use, the selected colors also govern how the document will print if you choose to review the edits on paper. If you or your authors expect to print documents for review and want the edits to be legible, pick a color that will be easily visible in the printout; this may require some experimentation.

> **Focusing on a reviewer:** Word 2002 and later (Word 2004 and later on the Macintosh) offer a useful feature for situations in which several people have reviewed a document. If you open the View menu, select Toolbars, then select Reviewing, you'll see that a "Show" option is now available in the Reviewing toolbar. Select that option, then select Reviewers. You now have the option to select the name of any individual reviewer so that you can examine, accept, or reject their changes independent of any other reviewer's changes. Other changes in how Word 2002/XP, Word 2003, and Word 2004 deal with revision tracking are described in Appendix III.

Mark (style of insertion)

This option lets you define the visual characteristics of the different types of edit so that each appears distinct. For example, you can set insertions to appear as boldface and set deletions to appear as strikethrough so that they stand out more clearly on the screen (or on the printed page if you choose to review edits on paper). These visual formats are applied only until a change is accepted or rejected, and won't permanently affect the underlying font characteristics. However, because this formatting is used only by the revision tracking feature, you cannot remove or change the formatting as you would for other text; for example, if you set Word to use underlining to display inserted text, you can't remove this underlining using the font formatting options available under the Format menu, nor can you find it by searching for underlined text.

Change bars

This option sets Word to display a vertical line (a "change bar") in the margin beside any line that contains an edit. If you edit as heavily as I do, this option is of little use because most lines contain at least one change and the resulting change bar stretches from the first to the last line of the document. But if you've already completed your heavy editing of a document and want a quick way to spot any final edits, this option lets you scan quickly down the screen or printed page to find them. (That being said, it's more effective to use Word's revision tools to find changes, since unlike us poor mortals, Word won't miss any changes. I'll discuss these tools in more detail in Chapter 6.)

User information settings

These settings define how Word will identify edits when authors review your edits and want to see who made each change. If you hold the mouse cursor over any edit performed while revision tracking was active, or over any comment inserted with or without revision tracking being active, Word will display the name and initials of the person responsible for that change in a small yellow popup. If Word won't display this information, select the "ScreenTips" option in the View tab of the Options (Windows) or Preferences (Macintosh) dialog box. The user information settings also define the creator information for a document. To display that information, open the File menu and select Properties, then select the Summary tab. Fill in as much or as little information as you consider to be necessary. There are two main situations in which you may need to revisit these settings after defining them for the first time:

Conducting anonymous reviews

In some circumstances, you'll be asked to review a document without identifying who you are; this is common for peer reviews of journal articles, in which the reviewers must remain anonymous to the author. The solution: Before you open the file and begin work, open the User information settings and change your name to "Anonymous reviewer" and your initials to "AR" (or create similar pseudonyms), then delete all other information in this tab of the dialog box that might identify you. After you've completed your review and closed the file, restore the original settings. If you do this often, it will be worthwhile recording a macro that makes all these changes for you. (See Chapter 11 for details on creating macros.)

Word forgets who you are

Many versions of Word have a pernicious bug in which the software suddenly and apparently randomly forgets who you are, even though the User Information settings appear to be correct and you know you haven't changed them. (My research has revealed no obvious cause for this bug, so it's not clear what you can do to avoid it.) Ordinarily, you can revise your own insertions and deletions with little difficulty, but when this bug bites, all such revisions are tracked as if some other person had made these changes, and if you change one of your own edits, Word tracks that change too. The only solution I've discovered is to save and close all files that are currently open, then retype your information in the User Information settings *exactly* the way it originally appeared. Then close and restart Word and hope this fixes the problem. Alas, it doesn't always.

Some versions of Word contain a bug in which changes to your User Information simply won't stick: you make the change, close the dialog box, and begin editing, only to discover that Word has somehow remembered your old name and is adding it to each of your edits. Before you get too busy editing a document after changing this information, try inserting a comment. If the comment displays your real name and initials instead of the replacement name and initials, you've encountered that bug. Try changing the settings again, save the file, then close Word and reopen the file.

If Word refuses to remember who you are and won't let you modify your own edits without insisting that someone else made the changes, try this desperation measure: Open the problem file, and save a copy under a new name, with all edits *accepted*. (See Chapter 6 for details on how to accept and reject edits quickly.) Reopen the file containing the edits, and save a copy with all those edits *rejected*. With this second file still open, open the Tools menu, select Track Changes, then select Compare Documents. When Word asks what file you want to compare, select the version of the file with all edits accepted. Word will now work through the two documents, line by line, and do its best to make the same changes that you originally made. When it's done with this task, you should have a version of the document containing all your edits, correctly attributed to you. You can now revise these edits without the changes appearing as if they were revisions made by a different editor.

Compatibility settings

Word has evolved quite dramatically since its early days, and the most recent versions may behave quite differently from older versions. In an attempt to fix this problem and let users continue working the way they were used to, Microsoft introduced a large and confusing array of "compatibility" settings that let you control, to some extent, whether your version of Word behaves like itself or, in some respects at least, like an earlier version. This seems like a great idea, but a quick glance at the list of available settings reveals dozens of inscrutable options, many of which interact in unpredictable ways. This kind of compatibility issue is something that advanced software should handle for you, but in the current state of Word's evolution, the problem is too complex for Microsoft to easily automate.

If you know that you'll be exchanging files with someone who uses a different version of Word, and you encounter problems with how the text displays on the screen, Microsoft has provided a series of predefined settings for most versions of Word, from the oldest to the current version. To access these options, look for the title "Recommended options for" in this tab of the dialog box, open the menu beside it, and pick the appropriate version of Word. Unfortunately, this won't solve all problems, and sometimes you'll have to go spelunking in the longer list of settings to solve certain vexing problems, most often related to garbled display of the text. If you examine the range of options, you'll quickly see that there are so many possible combinations of options that it would take the rest of your editing career to determine which combination works best in any given situation. Don't try; odds are good you'll only make the situation worse.

Nonetheless, a few of these options are reported by colleagues to occasionally come in useful when you're forced to troubleshoot display problems. When such problems arise, and the predefined compatibility settings don't help, try the following solutions:

Missing fonts

Although font mismatches are becoming much less of a problem, they still occasionally bedevil those of us who work across operating systems (Macintosh vs. Windows), across language barriers (e.g., Asian vs. North American versions of Word), or across both barriers simultaneously. If you don't have a font that the author used on your computer, Word does its best to choose a suitable temporary replacement font, and usually it does a good job. When it doesn't, clicking the "Font substitution" button provides better control over how Word should deal with the problem; selecting a different font installed on your computer may solve the problem. The cool thing about this trick is that the underlying font is untouched, so the author won't have to reapply that font when they receive the edited file.

Grid-based formatting in Asian versions of Word

If you're working with files produced by an Asian colleague, you'll sometimes discover that the actual spacing of characters or words doesn't match what you see on the screen. As a result, clicking to position the cursor will place the cursor in the wrong position, and dragging the cursor or double-clicking selects the wrong word. The problem occurs because the author created the file using an Asian version of Word that is designed to handle characters (such as Chinese ideographs) that should be aligned using a regularly spaced grid. Unfortunately, this setting also affects Western fonts that don't use this grid, and because the English and European versions of Word don't understand this approach to formatting, the display falls apart. The solution is to use the installation disk for Word or Office to install support for these languages; see the online help on "Asian language support" for details on how this works in your specific version of Word. You can then turn off the grid settings that are causing the problem. In older versions of Word, open the Format menu, select Document, then select the "Document Grid" tab to display these settings. In more recent versions, open the File Menu, select Page Setup, and select the "Document Grid" tab.

If you're not prepared to go to these lengths and possibly muck up a Word installation that has been working just fine up to this point, close the problematic file and try the following trick instead: Open a new blank document, open the Insert menu, select File, then select the problem file. Save the new file under a new name. If that doesn't work either, save the file in a format that doesn't support document grids. Only Word's .doc and .rtf formats support the document grid properties, so if you're having intractable display problems related to

Paging Dr. Adobe! As a last resort, here's something you can try if you own Adobe's InDesign software or know someone who does: Create a new InDesign document, then insert ("place") the problematic Word file in that document. Mysteriously, InDesign often does a better job than Word itself of handling troublesome Word files. You can now copy the text out of InDesign and paste it into a new Word document. Alternatively, open the text in the story editor, then open the File menu and select Export. Choose the "rich text format" (.rtf) option, open the new file in Word, then save it in Word's .doc format. Some reformatting may be necessary, but you'll at least have an editable document.

this grid, try saving a copy of the document in HTML or text format instead. You can then open the new copy of the document and resave it in Word's .doc format.

File location settings

The File Location settings tell Word where to store the various types of files that it uses. Spend a few moments defining where Word stores each type of file, since knowing these locations can make it much easier to find these files later should it become necessary to do so. At a minimum, define the following two file locations:

Autorecover

If you set a time interval for the "Save autorecovery information" option (see the description under *Save options* earlier in this chapter), Word periodically saves a copy of your document that it can use to recover the file if the software crashes. Rather than having to hunt down these files manually, it's easier to tell Word specifically where to save the files so you'll always know where to look. (I use a folder called "Autorecover files" on my main hard disk.) These files will let you recover most of the work you did up to the point of the crash.

Temporary files

Some versions of Word let you specify where Word stores the various temporary work files that it creates and uses while you're working on a file. When you save the file and close Word for the day, Word should politely erase these files. In practice, it often forgets—particularly in older versions of Word or after a crash. If Word crashes and you can't find the correct Autorecover file, try opening the temporary work files that were created most recently until you find one that contains most of your work. If your version of Word doesn't let you define where these files are stored, use the Windows or Macintosh operating system's search function to find them. See the sidebar for details on how to do this.

Autocorrect and autoformat

Word provides several useful automatic correction and formatting features, such as the ability to automatically capitalize the first letter of a sentence, or to change the second letter of a word to lower-case when you hold down the Shift key too long and accidentally capitalize that letter. Unfortunately, many of its automatic options are nothing short of annoying. Fortunately, you can turn off the annoying ones by changing the settings of the Autocorrect and Autoformat features. (In Chapter 11, I'll discuss how to use the autocorrection features to save yourself an enormous amount of typing when you insert comments or questions for the author.)

To change the automatic correction settings, open the Tools menu and select Autocorrect. The Autocorrect dialog box contains four tabs: two each for correction and formatting. The two "... as you type" tabs are the ones to focus on, since the other two tabs only come into play if you open the Format menu and select Autoformat. As a general rule, you can safely turn off *all* the "as you type" settings initially, then turn on a select few that suit the way you work.

When *temporary* is an oxymoron: If Word's temporary files accumulate in sufficient quantities, Word eventually gets confused and starts behaving erratically. The solution? Delete these files periodically—at least monthly if you find that they accumulate rapidly on your computer. Depending on which operating system you're using, you may be prevented from deleting files created on the current day. If so, no problem: delete them tomorrow instead. To find the autorecovery or temporary files when you haven't specified their location yourself, search for them using the search tools built into your operating system:

- **Windows:** Open the Start menu, select Search or Find Files (depending on your version of Windows), and in the Name field, type one of the two following search terms (without the quotation marks): "Autorecovery save of" for autorecover files, and "*.tmp" for temporary files. In some versions of Word, the files have the tilde (~) prefix, and you can search for that instead.
- **Macintosh OS 9 and OS X:** From the desktop, press Command + F, and in the search dialog box, set "Name contains" to the following (without typing the quotation marks): "Autorecovery save of" for autorecover files and "Word work" for temporary files. For the latter files, click the [+] button to add a second search field if one isn't already displayed, select "Visibility" as the search parameter, and select "Visible and invisible files" as the option for that parameter.

Screen display

Word offers three broad groups of options for customizing the aspects of the screen affected exclusively by Word. (See *Display settings* earlier in this chapter for a discussion of the main factors that affect the display for all programs on your computer.) The first involves "view modes", which represent collections of display options that have been grouped together for specific purposes, such as previewing what a print-out will look like. The second is a larger group of options that may be presented under the View menu or scattered throughout the software. Last but not least, the third group lets you rearrange the windows displayed by Word in a variety of useful ways.

View modes

Word offers considerable flexibility in selecting a display format best suited to your needs of the moment. Open the View menu, and you'll see the following options:

Normal view

In this mode, Word displays the text using the basic formatting that applies to words (e.g., boldface), sentences (e.g., indents), and paragraphs (e.g., spaces before and after paragraphs) but not formatting that applies to the page as a whole (e.g., headers and footers, margins). Thus, this view mode gives only the most basic impression of what the actual "page" (whether paper or online) will look like, but on the plus side, it's flexible and easy to use for editing.

Online (or "Web") layout view

In this mode, Word attempts to simulate what the file will look like if you save it in HTML format, as if you were creating a Web page. Word is *not* a good HTML editor or Web-authoring tool, so it doesn't do a particularly great job; if you need to really see what the page will look like, open it in a Web browser. But if you don't want to constantly switch back and forth between Word and a browser while editing, this mode offers a reasonable compromise.

Page, Print, or Layout view

In this view, Word shows you a good simulation of what the document will look like when you print it: all headers and footers, margins, page breaks, and other layout characteristics will be clearly visible. If you need to edit the document's layout as well as its content, such as when you're shortening a manuscript to fit within a specified amount of space, this mode is the one to choose.

Outline view

Outline mode is one of Word's lesser-known and more useful viewing options. A common criticism of onscreen editing is that it prevents you from seeing the structure of a document, but that's not a problem if you're using Word. In Outline mode, Word displays only the heading levels that you tell it to include in the outline, and you can expand or collapse the outline to show (respectively) more or less detail; at full expansion, you see the entire text. This provides an excellent way to review the structure of a document and rearrange text to produce a more logical and effective sequence or heading structure. (Of course, this assumes that the author has used heading styles to create the structure instead of manually boldfacing the text and changing the font size.) If you're responsible for ensuring that each heading has been formatted using the correct style name and verifying the consistency of capitalization, this is also a great mode to use. As a bonus, this mode lets you drag entire sections to new positions within the outline if you decide that another topic order would be more effective. Before doing so, turn off revision tracking so that the entire section isn't marked as a change; when you're done, turn on revision tracking again and insert a comment to explain what you've done and why.

Document map view

If you want an alternative to Outline mode that shows the entire document and its structure simultaneously, try this alternative. Unlike Outline mode, this option displays the document itself in a pane at the right side of the screen, using whichever of the other view modes you prefer (including Outline mode), beside a list of all current headings in a separate pane at the left side of the screen. Clicking on these headings takes you right to that part of the document, and you can collapse and expand parts of the "map" by clicking on the arrows beside the headings—without affecting the display of the full document on the right side of the screen.

Note: To turn off the document map and see only the main document window, open the View menu and select Document Map again.

Master document view

Word provides a Master Document feature that is intended to let you use a single "master" document to control formatting and other aspects of a series of subordinate documents, such as the chapters of a book. Unfortunately, this feature has been broken since at least 1997 and had not yet been fixed as I was writing this book. Very few people ever successfully use Master Documents without damaging files and losing hours or weeks of work, and those who do cannot reliably explain why everyone else is having so much trouble. To be safe, avoid using this feature.

Full screen view

This option displays only the menu bar and window title and menus at the top of the screen, with the text below it, thereby providing the maximum amount of space in which to display your document. (To return to the previous view mode you were using, simply press the Esc key.) In this mode, you can still display any toolbars that you use regularly; simply open the View menu, select Toolbars, then select the desired toolbar.

Ruler

This option lets you display (or conceal) one or more rulers as an aid in positioning text. In Word, you'll see only a horizontal ruler if you're working in Normal mode, but in Page Layout mode, a vertical ruler also appears.

Other view options

Word offers many other ways to customize the display until it suits your preferences. Experiment with each of the following options to see how they can ease the strain on your eyes:

Zoom

If the size of the type displayed on the screen is too small or large for your taste, open the View menu and select Zoom. This lets you specify an enlargement or reduction (typically up to at least double the actual size or down to half the original size) in any of the available view modes. Changing the zoom level is the fastest and easiest way to make onscreen text easier to read, and because it has no effect on the text properties (i.e., it does not change the font size), it is also the least likely to modify the contents of the file in a way that will subsequently re-

> **Positions of styles in the hierarchy:** To define where a given paragraph style will appear within the outline view, edit the corresponding style definition. (See *A primer on styles and templates* later in this chapter for details on how to edit styles.) The specific style characteristic you must edit is called "Outline level", and you can find it in the Paragraph settings.

quire repair. (Compare, for example, the discussion later in this section of what happens if you change the actual font or font size.)

Wrap to window

In Normal view, you can force the text to fit itself to the available horizontal space no matter how you resize the document window, which can be very useful if you prefer an unusually narrow or wide window. To do so, open the Options (Windows) or Preferences (Macintosh) dialog box, then select the View tab. Select the "Wrap to window" checkbox. This option won't work in any layout mode, since doing so would present a misleading impression of that layout.

Styles

If part of your editorial role will be to ensure that the correct paragraph styles have been applied to each heading and paragraph, it's helpful to be able to control which style names the software will display. Word allows you to display only the styles that are currently being used in a document, or the complete list of styles that are available for the template on which the current document is based and any global templates. To switch between these views, open the Format menu, select Style, then under the heading "List:", choose "all styles", "styles in use" (only the styles currently being used), or "user-defined styles" (ones that you have created yourself and stored in the current document's template rather than the styles that come with each version of Word).

Font name

Some authors have truly bizarre typographic preferences, and choose fonts that you simply can't read comfortably. Fortunately, there's no reason you have to live with their preferences. The best bet is to ask their permission to change the text to use a more standard font, and since this is a formal requirement of many publishers, you can generally persuade them to accept this change. If you can't do that and

Not sure what zoom works best? Try this trick: Open the View menu, and select Print or Layout mode. Next, open the menu again and select Zoom. In the Zoom dialog box, select Page Width. You can now drag the bottom right corner of the window to enlarge or shrink the window, and as you do, the type size will change. Stop when you reach a comfortable size. Open the View menu and select Zoom again to see what percentage you've chosen and use it in any other view mode.

you're willing to change the text into a new and more readable font, then change it back again when you're done, you can certainly do so:

- Record the current fonts used in the document.
- If the author has used any special characters, such as scientific or mathematical symbols from the Symbol font, note their locations so you can reinsert them if necessary; some fonts do not contain these characters and may replace them permanently with another character when you apply the new font. (For information on finding text formatted using a specific font, see Chapter 8, *Using the search tools (find and replace) to improve consistency*.)
- Optional: Turn off revision tracking. (In some versions of Word, the software records any font changes.)
- Select all the text (Control + A in Windows; Command + A on the Macintosh).
- Open the Format menu, select Font, and choose the desired font.
- Turn on revision tracking and continue editing.
- When you're finished, turn off revision tracking and restore the original fonts using the same approach.

Showing many pages at once: Word's zoom feature also lets you display multiple pages on your screen simultaneously, which is particularly useful if you need to examine page layouts quickly. To do so, switch to Print or Layout mode, select the "Many pages" option, and specify a small enough zoom percentage to fit the desired number of pages on the screen. To return to displaying only a single page, choose a zoom percentage of 100% or more.

Font size

If the problem is the size of the fonts, not the typeface, and the Zoom option described earlier in this section doesn't provide the desired degree of control over text size, it's possible to change type size for either the whole document in a single step, or for specific selected chunks of text. To make this change for any selected text, including the whole document:

- Carefully record the current font sizes used in the document.
- Optional: Turn off revision tracking. (In some versions of Word, the software tracks font changes.)
- Select the text that you want to resize. (Scc Chapter 5 for a lengthy discussion of different ways to select text.)
- Open the Format menu, select Font, and choose the desired font size.
- Turn on revision tracking and continue editing.
- When you're finished, turn off revision tracking and restore the original font sizes.

Juggling windows

In many editing activities, it's helpful to keep two or more windows open simultaneously; for example, one window may contain a manuscript, a second window may contain the style sheet you're using to impose consistency on that manuscript, and a third window may contain a checklist of editorial tasks or instructions from your client. In addition to resizing and repositioning these windows by dragging their borders, Word offers several other tools.

If you have several documents open, you can set Word to display all of them simultaneously so you won't have to manually resize and reposition each window. To accomplish this, open the Window menu and select Arrange All. Word resizes and rearranges the windows so that each window lies above the next window in the series. That's not very useful if you have a small monitor, and Word doesn't do a great job if you have many windows open; in that case, you'll have to resize each window by hand until it's the right size and at the right location. Displaying several windows simultaneously can be very useful if you have a short list of style conventions or other notes that you want to leave always visible while you work in the main document; simply re-

Change font sizes from the keyboard: Word offers a useful keyboard shortcut for changing font sizes. Select the text whose size you want to change, then use the following keyboard shortcut:

- **Windows:** Press Control + Shift + > to increase the size to the next available size (the next largest size specified in the Font size menu), and Control + Shift + < to decrease the size to the next smallest available size.
- **Macintosh:** Press Command + Shift + > to increase the size to the next largest available size, and Command + Shift + < to decrease the size to the next smallest available size.
- Repeat as often as required to produce the desired text size. If you overshoot, simply press the opposite keystroke combination: each undoes the other's effects.

size the window that contains these notes into a narrow vertical window that you can position beside the window containing the document that you're editing, then reposition the window so it doesn't overlap the narrower window. If you find that the text in one or more smaller windows is too small for easy viewing, simply change the Zoom settings for that window (as described earlier in this chapter).

In most programs and most operating systems, you can switch between open windows without using the mouse. In all Microsoft Office programs, for example, you can use the software's built-in window-switcher: On the Macintosh, use Command + F6; in Windows, use Control + F6. This shortcut lets you switch consecutively between windows without taking your hands off the keyboard. As of OS X, the Macintosh also offers system-wide window switching in any program using the keyboard shortcut Command + ` (the accent character to the left of the 1 on most keyboards). Word also helpfully displays a list of all open documents under the Window menu. Opening that menu (Alt + W in most software) and selecting the appropriate document provides a fast way to switch between windows.

What about when you want to be able to examine two or more parts of a single file simultaneously? This is helpful, for example, when you're checking literature citations against the bibliography or confirming that certain jargon words in the text have been defined in a glossary at the end of the document. If you prefer not to have multiple windows open into a single document and your goal is only to be able to refer to information elsewhere in the document, the simplest solution is to create a temporary copy of the document that you can work with. For example, when I check all literature citations in the text to ensure that they're present in the bibliography and are cited with the correct names and dates, I copy the bibliography into a new document and leave that window open while I edit the main document. Each time I encounter a literature citation, I switch to the bibliography window and confirm whether the citation matches the corresponding entry in the bibliography; if not, I insert a comment that explains the problem. I also add an * in front of the reference as a kind of checkmark that lets me confirm that every reference has been cited. When I'm done, any references that lack a checkmark haven't been cited and I can ask the author to either insert the missing citation or remove the reference from their bibliography if the publisher requires this for uncited references.

If you don't want to open a new document, Word offers a neat trick: split the current document window into two panes. To do this, open the Window menu and select Split. (On the Macintosh, Command + Option + S accomplishes the same effect and will also undo it; use Control + Alt + S in Windows.) This command splits the window into two panes, each showing a different part of the document, and you can move the cursor from one to the other with the click of a mouse—or press F6 if you don't want to take your hands off the keyboard. To resize the panes, simply drag the bar that marks the split (see the screenshot on the next page) until the two panes are the desired sizes. To restore the window to a single pane, repeat the keyboard shortcut, drag the split bar all the way to the top or bottom of the window, or open the Window menu and select Remove Split.

What a pane! Unfortunately, Word will not let you have more than two panes open in a window. Thus, if you open the Comments pane in a split window, the pane that does not currently contain the cursor will close, and when you close the Comments pane you will find yourself with a standard, single-pane window. Don't know about the Comments pane yet? Wait until Chapter 7.

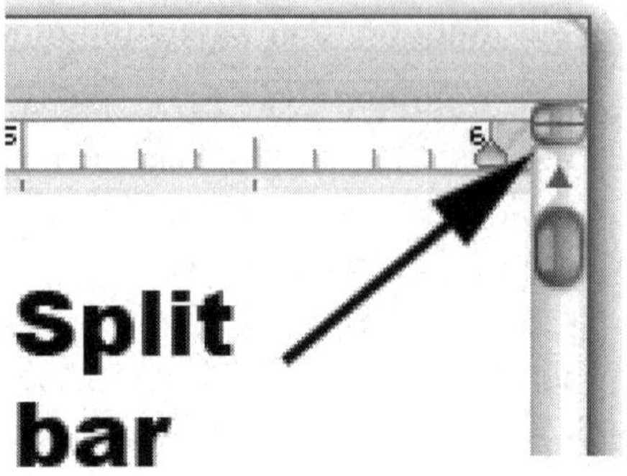

It's often useful to switch between programs on the same computer while you're editing. For example, you may be editing a software user manual by comparing the manual with the software it describes, or you may have your Web browser open to let you conduct Internet searches while you edit. Although both Windows and the Macintosh display icons for all open programs so that you can switch between them using the mouse (in Windows, in the status bar at the bottom of the screen; in Macintosh OS 9, in the Applications list at the right side of your menu bar; in OS X, in the Dock), you can also switch without ever taking your hands off the keyboard: use the program-switcher keyboard shortcut. On the Macintosh, the keyboard shortcut is Command + Tab; in Windows, it's Alt + Tab. If you hold down the modifier key (Command or Alt) after pressing Tab for the first time, both operating systems display a row of icons for each currently running program; while still holding down the Command or Alt key, press Tab again to highlight the next icon in the sequence, and continue doing so until you reach the desired program. (Holding down the Shift key reverses the direction of travel through the list.) When you release all these keys, the operating system switches you to the selected program. Repeat the keystrokes to return to your word processor.

Toolbars and keyboard shortcuts

If you prefer to work with the mouse, Word provides a range of special-purpose toolbars that hold buttons for performing common functions. In Word, these toolbars aren't locked in place below the menu bar; you can drag them around the screen to a more convenient position (they become tool "palettes" when they leave the menu bar area), and in some versions, you can even drag the bottom right corner of the

The more monitors, the better

The Macintosh has always supported the use of multiple monitors, and recent versions of Windows now permit this too. Given that monitors are increasingly affordable, you may find it helpful to purchase a second monitor that provides extra screen space; indeed, two 17-inch monitors provide more space than a single larger monitor, often at a lower cost. With multiple monitors, you can display different programs or different windows belonging to the same program on different monitors, saving you many keystrokes per day by eliminating the need to switch between programs or windows. Check the online help for your operating system to determine how to do this. Note that some CRT monitors don't play nicely together because the magnetic fields they generate interfere with the images on an adjacent monitor. (This is unlikely to be a problem with LCD monitors.) Modern monitors are better shielded than older models, but you may still need to experiment with positioning of the monitors to avoid decreasing the image quality.

toolbar to change its size and shape. Most of the functions available in Word's toolbars are also available using keyboard shortcuts or in the software's standard menus, but occasionally you'll find a feature that is only available in a specific toolbar. For example, in Word, the highlighter marker tool can only be accessed from a toolbar.

The highlighter marker tool

Two types of toolbar are particularly useful during editing: the first allows you to apply formatting (e.g., to change paragraph styles), and the second controls the software's revision tracking features.

Word doesn't limit you to the built-in toolbars that ship with the software. You can extensively customize existing toolbars to add or remove features, and you can create entirely new toolbars that contain only your favorite functions, new functions such as macros that you've recorded, or functions that apply only to a specific task, such as modifying pictures. Learning how to create a new toolbar is particularly useful if you find that you can never remember the location of a particular feature and want to place it where it's easily accessible, or if you prefer to use your mouse but find it awkward to reach a feature by navigating through several levels of menu and dialog box.

In Word, you can manage toolbars by opening the Tools menu and selecting Customize. At the bottom of the Customize dialog box, open the menu beside the text "Save in", then select the template that should store these changes. For example, choosing "Normal" makes the changes available in all documents on your computer; in contrast, if you create a toolbar in a template file that you're modifying, you can save the toolbar in that template and it will be available to all documents based on that template. You can do the following things with the Customize dialog box open:

- **Remove icons from a toolbar:** Click the mouse button on an icon, then drag the icon off the toolbar.
- **Change positions of icons within a toolbar:** Drag the icons into their new positions.
- **Add an icon to the toolbar:** Select the Commands tab in the dialog box, navigate to the desired command, and drag it into the toolbar.
- **Create your own toolbar:** Click the "New" button and name the toolbar. Then add features to the toolbar, as described above.

The same steps let you add new items to Word's menus, or remove them from the menus.

If you prefer to remove your fingers from the keyboard as infrequently as possible, menus and toolbars pose a challenge. Fortunately, Word rises to that challenge by letting you redefine the keyboard shortcut for almost any feature and assign keyboard shortcuts to features that don't already offer one. To change Word's keyboard shortcuts, open the Tools menu, select Customize, then click the "Keyboard" button:

- At the bottom of the dialog box, open the menu beside "Save in:" and select the template that should hold the customizations you're

> **Juggling toolbars:** In Word, you can display a new toolbar or tool palette and put away one that you are no longer using by opening the View menu, selecting Toolbars, then selecting or deselecting (respectively) the toolbar.

Customize with caution
Word offers a powerful but dangerous keyboard shortcut for Customize: Control + Alt + Hyphen (-) in Windows and Command + Option + Hyphen (-) on the Macintosh. This changes the cursor into a large minus sign (−) to remind you anything you touch will be "subtracted" from a toolbar or menu. Although you can use the Customize dialog box to restore deleted menu items or toolbar icons, you can't undo such deletions using the standard "undo" keystroke (Command + Z on the Macintosh; Control + Z in Windows). To escape this destructive function, press the Esc ("escape") key when you see the cursor change. To tame this feature and prevent it from destroying your menus and toolbars, open the Tools menu, select Customize, then assign this keyboard command to a useful or innocuous function. You can also open the Insert menu, select Insert Symbol, and in the palette of special characters, assign this keyboard shortcut to the em dash (—). Word displays the command already assigned to this shortcut (ToolsCustomizeRemoveMenuShortcut) so you have a chance to change your mind. The Customize feature itself remains available in the Tools menu should you need it. The biggest drawback? If you regularly use someone else's computer, you may wrongly assume you don't have to worry about this keystroke anymore. Beware!

about to make; select "Normal" if you want the changes to be available in all files on your computer.

- At the left side of this dialog box, you'll see a list of all menus; at the right side, you'll see a list of the typical commands that appear under a selected menu, including some you've never seen before.
- Select a command with the mouse, and Word displays the keyboard shortcut currently assigned to that command, if any. (This offers a good way to learn new shortcuts.) You can now type a new keyboard shortcut for the command, and Word will warn you if that particular shortcut has already been assigned to another command and give you a chance to change your mind. (This is also a good way to discover what a mysterious keyboard shortcut does. Open this dialog box and simply type the shortcut into the "Press new shortcut key" field, and Word will tell you what command, if any, that

shortcut is bound to. Then delete the shortcut from the field, so as not to rebind it to whatever command happens to be selected at the moment.)

- Keyboard shortcuts can be combinations of the Shift, Command, Option, Control, and Alt keys with most other keys on your keyboard, including the letters of the alphabet—Word won't let you use letters or numbers all by themselves based on the reasonable logic that you might some day want to use those characters again for typing.
- If you customize your keyboard to the point at which it becomes unusable, Word lets you restore the default settings. Simply click the "Reset All" button.

Even if you pick reasonably memorable shortcuts, it can be difficult remembering them all until you've used the shortcuts sufficiently often that your fingers remember them even when your conscious mind can't. You could certainly open the Customize dialog box and search for the command each time you forget a keystroke, but there are two alternatives that work better. The most effective is to record your list of customizations in a separate Word document; you can then read that document every time you need a refresher course in the shortcuts you created. This approach is effective because you can arrange the shortcuts in any order that makes sense to you, and use all of your word processor's powerful formatting tools to create an efficient layout that will help you to quickly find a command. (You can even use the Find or Search function to jump directly to a particular command if you re-

Remembering shortcuts: How can you remember all those cool shortcuts? Try using mnemonic devices such as the following to make the shortcuts a bit more memorable: the Control key (available for both the Macintosh and Windows) lets you control how the software functions, and its Macintosh counterpart, the Command key, lets you command the computer to do something. Similarly, the Alt key and its Macintosh equivalent, the Option key, let you choose an alternate (optional) way to do something. And the Shift key lets you shift things around. See Appendix IV for a handy list of the most commonly useful shortcuts for Word and for your computer's operating system as a whole.

member its name.) If all this seems like too much work, you can instead ask Word to produce a complete list of all shortcuts.

To print a copy of all keyboard shortcuts in Word, open the File menu, select Print, then in the field labeled "Print what?", select "Key assignments". Unfortunately, this printout is in Microsoft's order, not yours, and it will use up a ton of paper. But it can still be an effective tool for rapidly reviewing all the built-in shortcuts. For a more flexible approach, ask Word to generate an editable document containing these shortcuts using a macro kindly provided by Microsoft: First, open a new document. Under the Tools menu, select Macro, then select Macros. Under the heading "Macros in", select "Word commands", then type "listcommands" (without the quotation marks). Click the "Run" button to run this command, and Word will paste a complete list of all keyboard shortcuts into the open document. Save it and modify it to your heart's content.

A primer on styles and templates

One of our occasional editorial responsibilities is to impose consistency on the formatting of a document. Indeed, many copyeditors are responsible for tagging text using special codes defined by a publisher or using the paragraph and character styles defined in a particular document template. Performing this aspect of onscreen editing requires at least a basic knowledge of how modern word processors use templates to organize and apply collections of styles, not to mention an understanding of the styles themselves. In this section, I'll provide a whirlwind overview of the aspects of templates and styles that relate most directly to editing. As usual, I'll use Word to provide examples; most other software functions similarly, at least in broad terms, but you'll need to do a bit of research to learn the important differences. You'll also need to do a bit of research in Word's online help to learn some of the subtler points about using templates.

Styles

In the parlance of word processors and desktop publishing software, a *style* represents a collection of predefined rules that the software uses to format a chunk of text. Styles are a great tool for imposing visual consistency on documents if you use each style for its intended function, such as indicating that one chunk of text functions as a heading whereas another chunk functions as an item in a list. By gathering all the necessary settings into a single style, the software lets you apply them all in a single step, rather than having to apply them individually to each word, line, or paragraph governed by that style. Styles are most often managed and applied by means of templates, which I'll describe in the next section. Word's styles let you define the following aspects of text:

- **Typography:** the typeface, font size, justification (e.g., ragged right vs. centered), emphasis style (e.g., boldface vs. italic vs. underlined), spacing (within and between words, sentences, and paragraphs), and indentation (including tab settings) of the text.
- **Borders and shading:** ornamentation such as lines on any of the four sides of the text, or colors used to provide a backdrop for the text.
- **Language:** the primary dictionary that is used for spellchecks.
- **Numbering and bullets:** the style of numbering or bullet used for each level of heading or in lists of items.

Most software supports at least *paragraph* styles, which govern the appearance of entire paragraphs of text. In Word, a paragraph is defined as all the text between two carriage returns (that is, a block of text that ends when you press the Enter or Return key). Thus, from Word's point of view, paragraphs can range from one-line sentence fragments to page-long collections of unstructured notes. Word also provides *character* styles, which can be applied to individual characters, words, or sentences within a paragraph. Because character styles apply exclusively to parts of a paragraph whose formatting with respect to the page boundaries has already been defined using a paragraph style, they cannot override indentations and other spatial characteristics of the surrounding paragraph. Instead, they can do useful things like changing the font and language definition for the selected text; for example, you might create a character style called *Greek words* so that your word processor will format Greek words using a font that contains only Greek

More on consistency: For an overview of other forms of consistency, and the relevant word processor tools you can use to improve consistency, consult Chapter 8 (*Using the search tools (find and replace) to improve consistency*) and Chapter 9 (*Style sheets*).

letters and will use a Greek spelling dictionary (rather than the English dictionary used for the surrounding text) during spellchecks.

During editing, our main style-related role will typically be to apply or reapply styles in a document. For example, authors sometimes create headings by manually changing the font characteristics rather than using the correct paragraph styles or may fail to use a publisher-supplied template that would make the document appear visually similar to all other documents in a series (e.g., annual reports) or in a volume (e.g., the chapters in a book or the articles in a newspaper). Last but not least, substantive editing often reveals that the document organization created by the author is ineffective, and that it's necessary to add or remove headings or change the levels of certain headings to create a new, more effective structure. (See the discussion earlier in this chapter on the Outline and Document Map view modes for some tips on how to see this structure and revise it more efficiently.)

To apply a paragraph style in Word, you need only position the text cursor in that paragraph, then select the desired style from the list of available styles. To apply a character style to sections of text within a paragraph, you must first select the text before you apply the new style. (See Chapter 5 for details on a variety of ways to select text.) In Word, you can select the desired style from a menu, from a standard formatting toolbar, or from a custom toolbar. You can even use predefined keyboard shortcuts for certain common styles or assign your own keyboard shortcuts to these and other styles. To ensure that the correct styles have been applied, you can also set Word to display the styles that have been applied to each chunk of text. (For details, see the discussion of "style area width" earlier in this chapter.) If you display Word's standard formatting toolbar, Word will also display the name of the style attached to whatever text the insertion cursor is currently positioned in. There are three main ways to review and apply styles:

From the Format menu:

- Open the Format menu and select Style.
- At the left of the window, you'll see a list of all styles currently available.
- To reduce this list to a more manageable length, the field labeled "List:" lets you change the selection from "All styles" (the default setting, which displays every available style) to "Styles in use" (only

the styles that are actually being used in the document) or "User-defined styles" (only styles that you have defined for the template that controls the currently open document).

From the Formatting toolbar:

- If you are not already displaying this toolbar, open the View menu, select Toolbars, then select Formatting.
- Once this toolbar is open, you can apply styles directly from the dropdown list at the left side of the toolbar:

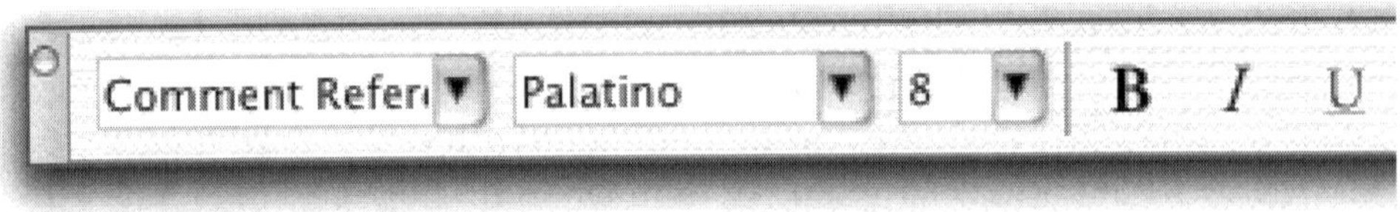

In this image, the "Comment Reference" style is shown.

- Either use the mouse, or press Control + Shift + S (Windows) to place the cursor in this field so you can type the style name or use the arrow keys to scroll through the list of styles. On the Macintosh, Command + Shift + S may accomplish the same effect in some versions of Word, but in other versions, this is the predefined shortcut for "Save As".
- If you change your mind and decide not to apply a style, press the Esc key to return the cursor to the text, or click anywhere in the text with the mouse.

From a custom toolbar that contains your own list of styles:

If you have created several custom styles and want to make those styles easily available, you can create a new toolbar that will hold buttons for applying them. To do so, see *Toolbars and keyboard shortcuts* earlier in this chapter.

Preserving manually applied formatting

Word has a significant style-related quirk that's a bit puzzling until you understand what it's doing. The software correctly assumes that if you manually applied a style such as boldface or a font change to a chunk of text, thereby overriding the paragraph or character style that was originally applied to that text, you *really* intended to do this. As a result, it won't automatically remove this manual formatting when you apply a new style to the surrounding paragraph. (Think, for example, how annoying it would be if each time you applied a style to a paragraph you had to reapply italics to all italicized words.) Unfortunately, this means that applying a new style to such paragraphs won't apply that style to all aspects of that paragraph: the manually applied formatting will be protected, including character styles. (It's not quite that simple, but that's a good enough description for most purposes.) The easiest way to eliminate this formatting is from the Formatting toolbar: select the paragraph containing the manually applied formatting, then select "Clear formatting" from the list of styles:

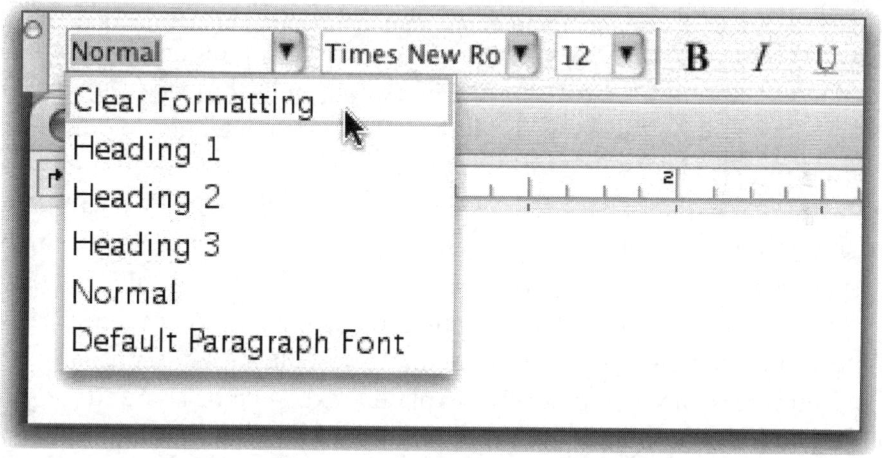

You can also do this from the keyboard: simply select the paragraph and press Control + Spacebar (Windows) or Command + Shift + Z (Macintosh) to remove the formatting and reapply the surrounding paragraph style.

Templates

In Word, the styles that are available for use in a given document can be found in three main places:

- Styles that are defined only within the current document are referred to as *local* styles.
- Styles that are gathered together so that they can be reused in other documents are stored in a file called a *template*. If the styles in that template are available for use in any document on your computer, the template is referred to as a *global* template.
- Templates can also be *attached* to specific documents, in which case only those documents can use the styles in the template. In point of fact, *attached* is a misleading word, because the template is not "physically" attached to the document in any way. If you want to e-mail a

file and its attached template to a client, you must remember to include the template file in your e-mail message rather than assuming it will automatically be sent along with the file controlled by that template. Thus, *linked* would be a better term.

Word's templates are separate files with the extension .dot added to their names. Normal.dot is the most familiar global template and a version of this template is present on any computer that has a copy of Word; in fact, if you delete this file, Word will automatically recreate it. Word's templates can define important aspects of the layout such as the margins and page orientation, can contain custom toolbars designed to facilitate the application of styles, can contain links to resources such as online style guides, and can be linked to custom spelling dictionaries. Moreover, templates can store shortcuts such as macros and automatic text (see Chapter 11 for details on both types of tool). This can be a useful trick because it lets you create sets of tools for specific tasks such as page layout or different types of editing work. (As described earlier in this chapter, you must specify which template should contain a keyboard shortcut when you first define that shortcut.)

Templates can also hold "boilerplate" text, such as standard copyright statements, that should appear in every new document based on that template. This concept deserves a bit more attention because judicious use of boilerplate text supports two goals of editing: to help authors write faster and to reduce the amount of editing required. A template that includes (for example) a complete outline of a typical document in a specific report series, such as all the required main headings and concise descriptions of what should be typed under each heading, helps the author to remember what information they must provide, and in what order, by specifying the requirements for each document and for each section of the document. This means you'll have less substantive editing to perform because if the author follows these instructions, all the required information will be present and in the right location. Because the template also formats the information it contains using the correct styles, the author can concentrate on writing rather than on remembering the style specifications for that report series. This will reduce your proofreading burden because most of the text will be properly formatted. Last but not least, longer chunks of boilerplate such as a complicated copyright page have already been edited, and won't have to be edited again.

This description illustrates how templates become a powerful tool for helping authors to write better and faster. But they can also improve our collaboration with authors. For example, creating a global template provides access to any shortcuts, such as macros and automatic text (see Chapter 11 for details), that we store in the template. The power offered by this feature is clear: rather than having to recreate these tools for each document, we can create them once in a template called "Editing tools", and attach that template to any document that we receive for editing or send to an author for review, thereby making those tools instantly available. Moreover, we can continually enhance the template as we learn new tricks or create new tools, and these changes automatically become available for each new job. Templates can also be linked to custom or third-party dictionaries, as described in Chapter 10 (*Spelling and grammar checkers*). By defining different dictionary settings for different types of projects, spellchecks become much more efficient. For example, if you edit some manuscripts related to a specific subject with its own jargon, and don't want to include that jargon in your main dictionary, you could attach a custom dictionary that contains only the jargon for that subject to the appropriate template.

Templates can also contain built-in links to writing and editing resources such as style guides and instructions. For example, one template I helped to create for a former employer contained links to planning documents produced jointly by the author, their supervisor, and the editor; these included an approved outline for the document, and a list of key criteria for the writer and editor to keep in mind while writing and revising the document, such as the intended audience and the communication goals. The template also linked to an online style guide, thereby providing one-click access to the most current version of our corporate style guide on the company's network. Some aspects of the style guide, such as a list of standard disclaimers, were included in the template so the author did not have to type them and the editor did not have to edit them; others could be easily copied from the style guide and pasted into the document. Making all these tools available via the template created what I've called a "dynamic" style guide: rather than being a static book that gathers dust on the editor's bookshelf, the dynamic style guide becomes integrated with the way authors and editors work. For more details, see my article on dynamic style guides (included in the bibliography).

There are two main ways you can use templates in your editing. If you can work with your authors before they start writing, create the initial document for them by opening the correct template, inserting any new text that's required in addition to the boilerplate that already exists in the template, and saving the results as a new file with the correct name. When you send the document to the author, they can start writing immediately, guided by the template toward the correct order of presentation, correct contents, and correct styles. Alternatively, if you receive a document that has been created by an author who didn't use the correct template, you can apply the correct template to the file.

To apply templates to a Word document:

In Word 97 for Windows and Word 98 for the Macintosh:

- Open the Style menu and select Style Gallery. Alternatively, open the Tools menu and select Templates and Add-ins.
- Select the desired template from the list.

In more recent versions:

- Open the Format menu and select Theme (Windows) or Style (Macintosh). Alternatively, open the Tools menu and select Templates and Add-ins.
- Click the "Style Gallery" button.
- Select the desired template from the available list.

One caution concerning templates: Word provides an option that automatically updates the styles defined in a template when you modify those styles as you edit. For example, if you select a paragraph defined using the Body Text style and change the font, Word will update the font information in the template, and all new paragraphs defined using Body Text will use the new font. You can control this behavior by editing the style definition: For each style, deselecting the checkbox labeled "Automatically update styles" prevents this automatic update

Where'd the template go? In Word, templates only define the style specifications that are available when you create a new document using that template, and are no longer required once you start working on the new document. Thereafter, the file is largely independent of the template, so if you move to another computer, the link to the original template is broken but the style definitions established when you first created the document remain in the document.

from occurring. In general, you should deselect this checkbox for each style to protect the template.

Features to avoid

All modern software contains a variety of ill-considered or poorly implemented features that can cause you considerable grief if you aren't aware of how to control the feature. This section describes two Word features you should avoid using, and how to repair and protect documents created using these features. Some of these problems exist in other software, in slightly different forms, and the specific details I've provided for Word may work in most other programs with appropriate changes. But if you're using different software, it pays to consult experts in that software to learn about the tricks and traps that are unique to that software. In the section *Helpful Internet resources* at the end of this book, I've listed several online communities where you can find these experts.

Fast saves and versioning

I described the "Fast Save" feature earlier in this chapter and recommended that you never use Word's version of it under any circumstances. As an editor, you need only be aware that some authors use this dangerous feature without knowing they're doing so because they selected it when they first installed and customized their copy of Word and long ago forgot that they made this choice. One symptom of a document created using Fast Save is that the document seems unusually slow to open and is far larger than you would expect given the actual contents. You'll be doing the author a great service if you fix the problem for them by using the tips presented later in this section under *Recovering a damaged Word document*. Many other programs offer an equivalent option for saving files. I haven't heard of any systematic problems with this feature in software other than Word, but if you have a reasonably modern computer, there's little need to take any chances. Disable this feature.

Word also offers a "versioning" feature (under the File menu) that provides the option of storing a new version of the manuscript in the same file each time you close the document. This function attempts to meet the needs of authors and editors who find it inconvenient to keep separate copies of each version of a document during the course of a long cycle of writing, editing, reviewing, and rewriting. Each time you reopen the document, Word stores all subsequent changes to the document as a new version, but in the same file rather than creating a new file. By opening the File menu and selecting Versions, you have access to each of these different versions of the document simply by clicking on the date and time of the desired version.

Although this would seem to be a useful tool for retaining each version of a manuscript produced throughout the review and revision process, there have been many reports that versioning is unreliable, and I've experienced enough suspicious behavior in files created using this feature that I don't feel confident recommending that you use it. (Since it appears to have been implemented using a variant of the Fast Save programming, that's not surprising.) To avoid any problems, it's wiser to simply save a fresh copy of each version of the file using a unique name that includes the date and time you completed that version. In Chapter 3 (*A standard process*), I described one simple variation of this method that you can use to keep track of the different versions of a file.

If you must use the Versions feature, perhaps because your employer or a client requests this, I recommend that you obtain permission to periodically delete old versions and save the resulting document as a new file that contains only the current version. (I used this approach for several years and, probably as a result of this precaution, encountered no problems with the Versions feature. This may be because the approach reduces the number of versions stored in a single file.) To eliminate versions from a file:

- Open the File menu and select Versions.
- Deselect the checkbox labeled "Automatically save a version on close".
- Select all the versions listed in this dialog box, then click the "Delete" button.
- Close the dialog box.
- Open the File menu, select Save As, and give the file a new name.

If more desperate measures are required, see *Recovering a damaged Word document* later in this section.

Master documents

The master documents feature was designed to offer a kind of super-template that allowed you to gather together a collection of Word documents and apply consistent formatting (e.g., running headings, page numbering) across the entire collection. Unfortunately, useful though such a feature would be, Word's implementation of it has been unreliable and likely to seriously damage Word files for many years, and Microsoft has not yet been able to fix it as of Word 2003, judging by reports from many colleagues. Thus, I recommend that you don't use this feature. Details on the nature of the problem can be found at the Word MVPs site (http://word.mvps.org). Search for the article entitled "Why master documents corrupt"; at the time of writing, this was located at http://word.mvps.org/faqs/General/WhyMasterDocsCorrupt.htm, but since online information tends to move around, you may need to search for it by title. The Word MVPs site also provides a detailed explanation of how to safely recover a series of files that have been gathered together using master documents. For details, see the article "How to recover a Master Document" (www.word.mvps.org/FAQs/General/RecoverMasterDocs.htm).

If you need the features provided by Master Documents, you can simulate these features by yourself, far more safely, as follows:

Create cross-references between files using Word's hyperlink function:

- Start by creating all the necessary bookmarks in each file. To insert a bookmark, open the Insert menu and select Bookmark.
- In the file that will hold the cross-references (i.e., the hyperlinks), type the text that will become a link or select existing text, then open the Insert menu and select Hyperlink.
- Select the Document tab, then click the "Select" button so you can specify the name of the file you want to link to.
- Click the "Locate" button to find the specific bookmark ("anchor") within that file that you want to link to.

Create a table of contents and an index for the information contained in all the files using "reference document" fields:

- Open a new document that will hold the table of contents and another that will contain the index; using separate files for each is generally more convenient.

- For each file whose contents (headings for the table of contents and index entries for the index) will be included in the new document, open the Insert menu and select Field.
- Under the heading "Categories", select "Index and Tables".
- Under the heading "Fields", select RD (shorthand for "reference document").
- Edit the contents of these fields so that they point to the correct file name, including the "path" to find that file on your computer. (Defining these paths is simpler if you store all the files in the same directory or folder.)
- Insert a table of contents and index as you would for any document: Open the Insert menu, select Index and Tables, then select the necessary options for the type of table of contents or index that you want to create.

For more detailed instructions on how to accomplish this, consult Word's online help. Alternatively, pick up a copy of Jean Weber's book *Taming Microsoft Word 2002* (listed in the bibliography). Jean has done an excellent job of researching the necessary information and has packaged it in simple, easy-to-use form.

Recovering a damaged Word document

If a Word document is beginning to develop a dangerous degree of corruption as a result of using Fast Save or a master document, you'll most often see this in the form of increasingly frequent crashes and other erratic behavior. When that happens, you have a few options to resolve the problem before it's too late:

- Before trying anything really complicated, try saving the file under a new name: Open the File menu, select Save As, and choose a new name. This solution solves only the simplest problems, and won't fix more serious forms of corruption, but sometimes it's all you need to do.
- If that doesn't work, try creating a new file, then open the Insert menu and select File. Choose the damaged file. The process Word goes through during insertion of the old document in the new one cures some forms of document corruption, but not the most serious forms.

Because Word stores a large amount of information about the structure and contents of a document at the end of the document, invisible to users of the software, it's that part of the document that is most vulnerable to damage. The solution is to copy the entire document, minus this hidden information, into a new document and continue working. Here's how to do this:

- Move to the last line of the document, and place the cursor immediately before the final paragraph marker. If you cannot see paragraph markers (the ¶ character), open the Options (Windows) or Preferences (Macintosh) dialog box, select the View tab, and select the checkbox beside "Paragraph marks". If you prefer not to work with these markers displayed, you can instead select everything but the last visible character in the file, then retype that character later.
- Press Control + Shift + Home (Windows) or Command + Shift + Home (Macintosh) to select all of the text except that final paragraph marker. (See Chapter 5 for details on a variety of other ways to select text.)
- Copy this text.
- Open a new document, then paste the copied text into that document.
- Save the new document and continue working.

If none of these approaches work, try saving the file in a different format, such as "rich text format" (RTF); RTF is often the best choice because it retains the most formatting information and thus requires the least rework after you have successfully recovered the file. To do so, open the File menu, select Save As, then under the heading "Format:", choose RTF or "Rich text format" (they mean the same thing, but the name that you'll see depends on which version of Word you're using). You can then open the RTF file and save it again as a Word document using the same Save As function.

Sometimes Word doesn't handle graphics so well, particularly if the author has been especially creative in finding incorrect ways to insert them, and particularly if you're using one of the Macintosh versions (which have great difficulty with Windows .emf and .wmf file formats). One of the most common problems you'll see is "file bloat": the file size grows much larger than you'd expect, and often becomes unmanageably large. Deleting the graphics will solve the problem, but before you do this, make sure the author has copies of the graphics stored outside Word so they can reinsert the graphics after you have returned the manuscript.

Other software stores its data differently, and thus develops different forms of document corruption. But in many cases, the same tricks described in this section can resolve the problem.

If you have a copy of Word 2003, or know someone who does, that version provides a useful but little-known tool for recovering corrupted Word documents: "Open and Repair". (This won't be available on the Macintosh until Word 2008 is released.) To use this function, close the problem document. Next, open the File menu, select Open, then select the problem file from the list of available files—but don't double-click the file or click the "OK" button the way you might usually do. Instead, look for a small triangle to the right of the "OK" button that indicates the presence of a hidden menu: click this to reveal a set of choices, and from that list, choose "Open and Repair". You may still need to try some of the other tricks described in this section, but this feature will generally make the document sufficiently stable that the other tricks have a chance of working.

Two other tricks may help once you've stabilized a problem document: open the File menu, select Save As, and set the format to "rich text format" (RTF) or "Web page" (HTML). In more recent versions of Word, the latter format may have its own entry under the File menu, such as "Save as Web page". Next, close the file, reopen it, and save it again as a Word (.doc) file.

Paging Dr. Adobe! As a last resort, Adobe's InDesign software can often do a better job of opening troublesome Word documents than Word itself. If you have a copy of InDesign, create a new InDesign document, then "place" the troublesome Word file in that document. Open the text in the story editor, then open the File menu and select Export. Choose the "rich text format" (.rtf) option, open the new file in Word, then save it in Word's .doc format.

Chapter 5. Moving around the document and selecting text

"There is a small steam engine in his brain which not only sets the cerebral mass in motion, but keeps the owner in hot water."—Anon.

"Motion or change, and identity or rest, are the first and second secrets of nature." —Ralph Waldo Emerson

One nice thing about mouse-driven interfaces is how easy it is to move around: simply scroll to the right location, then click the mouse in the text where you want to begin working again. If you've got a newer mouse with a scroll wheel, it's even easier: simply spin the wheel until you get to your new destination. Unfortunately, repeatedly moving your hands between the keyboard and the mouse wastes considerable time; it may only cost you a second or three each time you seize the mouse and a like amount to return your hands to the keyboard, but do that hundreds or thousands of times per day and the wasted time adds up. This is doubly true if you're using the awkward and unergonomic pointing devices found on most laptop computers. Since most of us are skilled typists, it's generally more productive to keep our hands on the keyboard and use that to move around. Yet many writers and editors never master this skill and remain ignorant of the many navigation shortcuts available in most word processors.

In this chapter, I'll present the most useful keyboard-based tricks for moving around a document during editing, plus a few tips on non-keyboard or hybrid (keyboard plus mouse) tricks for moving more efficiently through a document. Once you've mastered those tips, the last part of the chapter will teach you how to use these tricks to select text more efficiently. Because both Windows and the Macintosh have increasingly standardized their keyboard commands across programs, these tips will work in most software with only minor variations. If your software doesn't support a particularly useful shortcut, consult its documentation to discover the equivalent command, or consider recording a macro that achieves the same results (see Chapter 11, *Automating your edits*).

When all else (including your mouse) fails, you can access any menu command from the keyboard. In any Windows program, press the Alt

> **Same keystrokes, mostly:** Rather than always presenting keystrokes for both the Macintosh and Windows, I've presented primarily the Windows version in this section; Macintosh users should substitute Command for Control and Option for Alt unless otherwise noted. There are few cases where this won't work, and I've noted them in the text.

key to activate the menus (i.e., to tell Windows that you want to scroll through the menus using the keyboard), then press the underlined letter in a menu name or command to select it, or scroll through the menus using the arrow keys. The Macintosh OS 9 operating system doesn't offer such a standard shortcut, but Word 98 does: you can activate the menu bar by pressing F10, then use the underlined letters in the names to move between and within menus. Unfortunately, this shortcut was eliminated in Word X and 2004, which run under OS X, making keyboard-based menu navigation considerably less efficient. Fortunately, OS X offers a partial solution: Open the Keyboard preferences panel, and select the Keyboard Shortcuts tab. Under the heading "Keyboard navigation", select "Focus on menu"; by default, this shortcut is Control + F2, but if you don't like that option, double-click on that line and press a new keyboard combination. With this keystroke, the operating system lets you begin scrolling through the menus using the arrow keys.

Small jumps

Most cursor movements during editing occur between words, sentences, or paragraphs. You'll make these jumps so often during an editing session that it makes no sense to be constantly interrupting your work to grab the mouse. Try learning the following keystrokes instead:

Next or previous word

Control + → / ←, respectively.

Beginning or end of line

Home and End keys, respectively.

Beginning or end of sentence

There's no universal keyboard shortcut for doing this, so you'll have to research the solution for each program that you use. (To do this in Word, see the sidebar on the next page.)

Beginning or end of paragraph
Control + ↑ / ↓, respectively.

Bigger jumps

Sometimes you need to jump farther, such as between screens, pages, or sections. Try learning the following keyboard commands:

Next or previous screen
PageUp or PageDown, respectively.

Section break or manual page break
Open the search dialog box (Control + F) and search for the appropriate special character used to define the break. This varies among programs. Different versions of Word use either ^m or ^k ("m" for a *manual* page break; "k" for a *breaK*) or ^b (section *break*).

Keystrokes for the start and end of a sentence in Word: In Word, you can do this by combining the mouse with the keyboard: Hold down the Control key, click anywhere in the sentence to select the sentence, then release the Control key and press the left or right arrow key to move to (respectively) the beginning or end of the sentence. However, unless it's an unusually long sentence, that's not very efficient. Instead, try defining a new keyboard shortcut:

- Open the Tools menu and select Customize.
- Click the "Keyboard" button.
- In the field labeled "Save changes in", choose the template that should store these customizations. (The change will subsequently be available in all documents based on this template. Using Normal.dot allows you to make the customization available in all documents.)
- Under "Categories", select "All Commands", and scroll until you can select "SentLeft" (the command to move to the beginning of a sentence).
- Position the cursor in the field labeled "Press new shortcut key", then press the desired key combination (e.g., Control + Alt + Left Arrow).
- Repeat this process to select "SentRight" (the command to move to the end of a sentence), then press the desired key combination (e.g., Control + Alt + Right Arrow).

Other special formats or contents (such as graphics)

Most software lets you search for various special formatting codes, such as those used to indicate the presence of a graphic or a table. In Word, for example, click the "More" button in the search dialog box (this has been replaced by a downward-pointing triangle in some recent versions), then click the "Special" button to display a list of the special characters that can be searched for.

Beginning or end of a document

Control + Home or Control + End, respectively.

A specific section

Open the search dialog box (Control + F) and enter a word or phrase that you know will be found in the desired section. For example, if you want to move to the next chapter and each chapter title begins with the word *Chapter*, type that as the search term. Alternatively, you can type part of the heading text as the search term.

A bookmark

Software that provides bookmarks also lets you jump to any named bookmark using a "go to" or "jump to" function. If your software doesn't provide bookmarks, you can accomplish the same result by typing marker words at the desired locations and searching for those words. An ideal marker word won't appear in the file, because you don't want to have to skip repeatedly over normal uses of the word in the text. Typing special characters around a marker makes it stand out and makes it easier to find; consider, for example, *[continue here]* or *&check this&*. Such phrases are good choices because they clearly identify the bookmark's role. If you use such bookmarks in your editing, always add an item to your checklist of editing tasks: remove them during your final edit.

A specific page

Most "go to" functions also let you jump to a specific page; in Word, Control + G (or Control + F, then clicking the third tab) opens a dialog box that lets you specify the page number. If you're willing to use the mouse, many programs that provide a page number at the bottom of the screen offer another option, there's often a popup menu beside the page number that lets you select a page; this is the case in InDesign, for instance. Alternatively, double-clicking the page number may open a dialog box that lets you enter a new page number; this is the case in Word, for instance.

> **Finding a section by its title:** In Word, you can search for words appearing at the start of a new paragraph by typing *^p* (the code for a carriage return) before the word. There are a few exceptions: If you need to find a word that has been forced onto the next line using a soft return (holding down the Shift key and pressing Return or Enter), type *^l* (lower-case L) instead. If the word has been forced to the beginning of a new line by inserting a page or section break, type *^m* or *^b* instead.

Your previous position

If you need to temporarily pause your editing so you can move elsewhere in the document (e.g., to confirm a chapter title for a cross-reference), it's easy to leave a bookmark in the file and use the search function to find that bookmark once you're done. I've standardized on <> (two angle brackets) because this is short, easy to type, and unlikely to occur in anything that I edit.

Really big jumps

Sometimes you actually want to jump much farther than within a document—between files or programs, for example. Try the following:

Recently used files (across all programs)

Windows and the Macintosh both let you display recently used documents or favorite documents under the Apple () and Start menus,

> **Bookmarks in Word:** Word offers a bookmark function. To use it:
>
> - Position the cursor at the desired location, then open the Insert menu, select Bookmark, and name the bookmark.
> - To move to the bookmark from anywhere in the document, open the search dialog box (Control + F), click the third tab (labeled "Go to"), and enter the bookmark name; if you're willing to memorize yet another keyboard command, Control + G gets you to this dialog in one step.
> - The "Go to" dialog box also allows you to go to several other things in a single click, such as sections, lines, comments, and tables.

respectively. In Macintosh OS X, the Apple menu may only show recent "items", which are limited to programs by default. To add recently used documents such as word processor files under the Apple menu, open the Appearance preference panel, and under the heading "Number of recent items", select the desired number from the menu beside Documents. In Windows XP, modify the My Recent Documents setting if you don't see recent files under the Start menu: right-click the taskbar, choose Properties, click the Start Menu tab, and select Start Menu (not Classic Start Menu). Click Customize, then click Advanced. At the bottom of the dialog box, select Recent Documents.

Recently used files (within the current program)

Most software now provides a "Recent files" or "Recent items" option under the File menu that provides access to the files you most recently worked on.

Getting back to where you started: Word offers a nifty shortcut (Shift + F5) that steps you backward, one jump at a time, to each of several previous positions where you changed text. Clicking the double arrows at the bottom of the vertical scroll bar accomplishes much the same purpose:

Unfortunately, Word occasionally gets confused (particularly if you insert a comment) and loses track of these positions. This means that it's wise to use another strategy, such as manually inserting a bookmark, to ensure that you can easily return to your starting point.

Frequently used files

It's often helpful to place shortcuts to frequently used documents in convenient locations, such as on your desktop. To create shortcuts (Windows) or aliases (Macintosh) that point to a file:

- **Windows:** Right-click the file and select "Create Shortcut". Drag the shortcut to some convenient location. To make it appear under the Start menu, which you can open using the Windows key, place the shortcut in the folder "Startup items". (The location of this folder varies among versions of Windows, so use the search function to find it.)
- **Macintosh:** If you're using OS 9, select the file and press Command + M ("make alias"), then place the alias in the folder "Apple () menu items". In OS X, the keyboard shortcut is Command + L, and you cannot add items to the Apple () menu; instead, drag the alias into the Dock or the Sidebar of a Finder window.
- **Libraries:** Some software also offers a "library" function that provides fast access to frequently used files.

Other open windows in an application

With two documents open, you can switch between them via the Window menu in most software. In Windows, there is no standard keyboard shortcut for switching between these documents; the shortcut may be Control + Tab or (if each open document appears independently in the task bar) Alt + Tab. In Macintosh OS X, all software lets you switch between windows using the keystroke Command + ` (the accent character to the left of the number 1 on most keyboards). If you don't like that shortcut, change it in the Keyboard preferences panel.

Other open applications

This is a particularly useful shortcut if you're editing software documentation or researching something on the Web and must switch repeatedly back and forth between the software and your word proces-

> **Recently used files:** In Word, you can choose how many files to display (up to nine): Open the Options (Windows) or Preferences (Macintosh) dialog box, click the General tab, and enter a number in the field "Recently used file list". Word will then list the most recently opened files at the bottom of the File menu, each prefixed with a number so you can access it from the keyboard.

sor. The shortcuts are Alt + Tab in Windows and Command + Tab on the Macintosh.

Experiment!

Some of these shortcuts can be expanded or customized with a little creativity. For example, if you frequently have to move to the next instance of a particular heading style, record a macro that opens the "Find" dialog box and defines the search target as that heading style, then create a keyboard shortcut for that macro. (For details on finding special text properties, see Chapter 8. For details on recording macros, see Chapter 11.) Pay enough attention to how you work that you can identify the kinds of jumps you do repeatedly, then find or develop a keyboard shortcut that lets you make those jumps quickly and easily. The time savings can be enormous. Plus, as a bonus, you'll impress the heck out of your friends and colleagues when they see you doing this.

Selecting text

"Far too often the choices reality proposes are such as to take away one's taste for choosing."—Jean Rostand (1894–1977), *The Substance of Man*

The tasks we perform during editing often involve selecting blocks of text, whether to change the format, delete the text, copy it, or move it. Understanding how to efficiently select text prior to taking any of these actions is particularly important when we're reorganizing a document to improve the effectiveness of its structure, which is a common task for developmental editors who must help authors to organize their thoughts before they actually begin writing and for substantive editors who must fix the problems that result when authors skip the developmental edit.

Most computer users know at least one way to select text, but it may not be the most effective way for them or for certain specific tasks.

Moving between Word documents: Word's Control + F6 shortcut lets you cycle sequentially between all open documents without opening the Window menu.

Word's Work menu: Word's version of a library function is called the Work menu. To add this menu to your menu bar:

- Open the Tools menu, select Customize, then select the Commands tab.
- Under "Categories", select "Built-in Menus".
- Under "Commands", select "Work".
- Drag this menu out of the dialog box and onto your menu bar.

Henceforth, you can add open documents to the Work menu by opening this menu and choosing "Add to Work Menu". To remove files from this menu:

- Press Control + Alt + Hyphen to turn the cursor into a large – sign.
- Open the Work menu and click on the file you want to delete.
- Press the Esc key to return the cursor to its normal pointer shape before you do *anything* else; otherwise, you risk deleting icons or menu choices from Word's interface.

For more information, check out the Microsoft MVPs (http://word.mvps.org) article on this topic: "How do I use, and what is, the Work menu?" Apple's Safari browser won't reliably open most pages on the MVPs site, but the Firefox browser displays the pages with no problems.

In this chapter, I'll present a range of alternatives that you should experiment with until you find the one that works best for you in each situation. I'll start with keyboard-based methods, since most editors eventually find that using the keyboard is faster and more effective, then conclude with mouse-based methods because (my beliefs about the efficiency of the keyboard notwithstanding) the mouse may be more effective for some tasks and for some people.

Selecting with the keyboard

One of the most useful keyboard tricks involves extending the selection from the cursor's current position by holding down the Shift key and scrolling in the desired direction using the arrow keys. What's less well known is that you can combine many other keys with the Shift key to select text more quickly. For example, to select from the cursor's current position to another position:

The beginning or end of the line
Shift + Home and Shift + End, respectively.
The start of the document
Control + Shift + Home
The end of the document
Control + Shift + End
The previous screen
Shift + PageUp
The next screen
Shift + PageDown

Earlier in this chapter, I listed many keyboard shortcuts for moving around within a file, and many of them can be combined with the Shift key to select large chunks of text quickly. So long as you hold down the Shift key, you can use most of these keystrokes to continue extending the selection. For example, let's say you just used Shift + PageDown to select a full screen of text, but need to select one more line to reach the end of a paragraph: to do so, continue holding down the Shift key, then simply press the down arrow key to move to the next line, and (if necessary) the End key to move to the end of that line.

Selecting with the mouse

Most computer users quickly learn the basics of selecting text with the mouse: you simply hold down the mouse button and drag the cursor across the text. For example, if all you want to select is a single word or paragraph, the most obvious way to select text with the mouse is to drag the mouse cursor across that text: Click at the start of the text you want to select to position the cursor at that point, then hold down the mouse button and drag the cursor to the end of the selection. You can drag the cursor in any direction from that starting point. In most software, double-clicking will select a specific word, and in some software triple-clicking will select an entire sentence, so it's worth trying these options in whatever program you're using. If your fingers aren't fast enough to double-click or triple-click easily, see Chapter 4 (*Personalize how your software works*) for information on how to customize mouse and keyboard speed.

Selecting text with the mouse works well if all the text that you want to select lies within a single screen, but if the text spans multiple screens, continuing to drag past either the top or bottom edges of the window

Extending selections from the keyboard: Word also lets you quickly extend a selection from the keyboard without wearing out your Shift key:

- To begin, position the cursor at the start of the text, and press F8.
- If you press the left or right arrow, the selection expands to include (respectively) the previous or next character; pressing the up or down arrow keys extends the selection by one line of text. Similarly, pressing PageUp or PageDown extends it to the previous or next screen. If you instead press F8 a second time, you'll select the next word; press it a third time and you'll select the next sentence; press it a fourth time and you'll select the entire paragraph.
- If you made a mistake, press Shift + F8 to reduce the selection to the previously selected chunk of text.
- When you're done, press Control (Windows) or Command (Macintosh) plus the period key [.].
- You can now do whatever you like with the selected text (e.g., delete it, copy it).

typically scrolls the document too fast, often overshooting the desired endpoint and selecting more text than you intended. In some word processors, there's nothing much you can do about this, but in others, scrolling moves faster the farther outside the window you drag the cursor; try dragging only just as far as necessary to begin scrolling, then move the cursor farther until the text scrolls at a suitable speed. If your mouse has a scroll wheel, most current software lets you use it to provide greater control over the selection speed.

If you can't control the scrolling speed to your satisfaction, either because your software won't cooperate or because your reflexes aren't fast enough, you can achieve similar effects by combining the mouse with the keyboard:

- Click the mouse once to position the text cursor at the start of the text you want to select.
- Click the mouse in the vertical scroll bar (or use the scroll arrows) to scroll forwards or backwards through the document. In most soft-

ware, each click in the scroll bar moves the display one screen at a time without changing the position of the text cursor. Clicking on the up or down arrows at the top and bottom of the scroll bar and then holding down the mouse button will cause the document to scroll continuously at a manageable rate.

- When you reach the end of the text that you want to select, hold down the Shift key and click the mouse button at the end of the text that you want to select.

If your software lets you display style names beside paragraphs of text (usually in a separate column to the left of the text), you can use this feature to select several paragraphs with a series of mouse clicks. (To use this feature in Word, see the description of customizing the style area width in Chapter 4.) Clicking on any one style name selects the associated paragraph; holding down the Shift key and clicking on a style name elsewhere in the list selects all paragraphs between the initial paragraph and the paragraph selected with your final click. As described above, you can also click with the mouse in the scroll bar or hold down the mouse button on one of the scroll arrows to move to the desired point in the document without losing your initial selection.

If your software provides a full-featured outline view, you can achieve a similar effect in that mode. Outline views let you expand the displayed text to include subheadings and paragraphs, or collapse the displayed text to show only higher levels of headings. You can then select individual components of the outline (e.g., all text from the current level 1 heading to the next level 1 heading) in exactly the same way as using the list of styles: click to select the initial section, then shift-click on the final section. The advantage of using the outline view is that you can collapse the outline to show only the headings, letting you display

Selecting sentences and paragraphs: In Word, you can select an entire sentence by holding down the Control key (Windows) or the Command key (Macintosh), then clicking the mouse in that sentence. Word also lets you select an entire paragraph by triple-clicking. Holding down only the Shift key and clicking again anywhere in a subsequent sentence or paragraph (respectively) will extend the selection to include the entire sentence or paragraph and all intervening text.

more of the document simultaneously than would be possible when displaying all the text. This is obviously an efficient tool for quickly reorganizing entire documents, particularly if your software lets you select a heading and drag it to a different position in the sequence to move the entire section to that position.

Undoing a selection

If you select a large chunk of text and decide that this isn't what you wanted to do, you can easily undo the selection: simply press any of the arrow keys or click once with the mouse anywhere in the text. In most cases, you'll want to press the left or up arrow keys or click at the start of the selection, because this puts you back where you started so you can try again.

Because it's easy to inadvertently hit a key and delete all the selected text, particularly if you're working on a laptop, pay careful attention to what you're doing whenever you prepare to select text. One helpful strategy is to save the document immediately before you perform any potentially disastrous action; that way, if you cause a problem that you can't easily solve, simply close the document without saving it, then reopen it to begin work again with the last good version of the file. If you haven't done this, disaster strikes, and you inadvertently delete a large selection, immediately press Control + Z (Windows) or Command + Z (Macintosh) to undo that deletion so you can try again. If you've cut text and pasted it in a new position, pressing the undo command twice will restore the text to its original condition (the first press undoes your insertion of text; the second press undoes the deletion).

Selecting noncontiguous text

Noncontiguous text means two or more chunks of text that are not touching, such as the first and last sentences of a long paragraph. Most software does not let you select noncontiguous text. The solution is to make each selection independently, perform the necessary work on that selection, move it to its new location, then repeat the procedure for the next chunk of text. For example, if you wanted to move the first and last sentences of a paragraph to the start of the next paragraph, select and move the first sentence, then select and move the second sentence.

There are occasionally other useful workarounds, such as using the "spike" in Word (for details, see the next section, *Spiking text in Word*).

> **Selecting in Outline view:** In Word, open the View menu and select Outline. In this mode, you can expand or collapse the outline to show only the levels of heading and text that you currently need to work with. Click the [+] button to expand the outline to include more levels, and the [–] button to show fewer levels.

If you're not using Word, some software accomplishes the same effect using multiple clipboards. "Clipboard-replacement software" is available for both the Macintosh and Windows to provide similar features; search the Tucows site (http://tucows.com/) using the search word "clipboard" and you'll turn up a variety of options.

Before Word X and 2004 on the Macintosh and Word XP and 2003 for Windows, you could not select noncontiguous text. With these versions, you can now select the first block of text as usual, then for the second and subsequent blocks, hold down the Command key (Macintosh) or the Control key (Windows) before you use the mouse to make additional selections. When you finish selecting the noncontiguous text, you can format the selected text or do anything else you want to it (e.g., copy the text, apply a format such as boldface or a style). If noncontiguous text remains highlighted when Track Changes is enabled, simply click anywhere outside the highlighted text to deselect it, then continue working.

"Spiking" text in Word

As of Word 97 for Windows and Word X for the Macintosh, it was not possible to select noncontiguous blocks of text, but you could accomplish something similar using a feature called the "spike". Given how bad a job Microsoft did with Clippy the Paper Clip in Word's online help, it's probably a good thing that this isn't a sly reference to everyone's favorite character in *Buffy the Vampire Slayer*. Instead, think of this feature as a large metal spike onto which you can impale pages of paper, face down, with each new page added at the end of the pile. When you remove the items from the spike, they come off in the same order in which you placed them there.

To use the spike:

- Select the first chunk of text using any of the methods described previously.

- Hold down the Control (Windows) or Command (Macintosh) key and press the F3 key at the top of the keyboard. The text disappears from the screen and is now stored on the spike.
- Repeat these two steps (select plus spike) for each additional selection that you want to place on the spike.
- When you're done, position the text cursor at the desired destination, hold down the Control (Windows) or Command (Macintosh) and Shift keys, then press F3 again. Unlike regular copy and paste operations, which leave copied text on the clipboard, this approach empties the spike, so you can't paste the same spiked text repeatedly. However, you will now have all the formerly noncontiguous text in one place, and can easily reselect it for reuse.

The spike also lets you move text containing tracked changes without losing the tracked changes. In versions of Word older than Word XP for Windows (Word 2004 on the Macintosh), cutting or copying text that contains tracked changes and then pasting it somewhere else in the document would paste only the results of your edits. To move both the original text and your edits to a new location in these older versions, turn off Track Changes before you cut text to the spike, then turn it on again after pasting the text so you can continue editing. In newer versions of Word, the cut and paste feature won't lose your tracked changes so long as you turn off revision tracking before you move the edited text.

Chapter 6. Using revision tracking

"Elinor agreed to it all, for she did not think he deserved the compliment of rational opposition."—Jane Austen, *Sense and Sensibility*

Thus far, I've focused on providing a firm grounding in the nuts-and-bolts tools that will let you efficiently use Windows and Macintosh software for onscreen editing. This is clearly important knowledge, since you can't edit productively if you don't know how to use the basic tools. In this chapter, I'll begin to discuss the actual meat of this book: editing. The most effective approach relies on revision-tracking tools built into the software that let you communicate your changes (*revisions*) to the author so the two of you can work together to implement the changes and revise your suggestions when necessary. (I have not used the term "editing tools" in this book because the documentation for most word processors refers to changing a document in any way as "editing", and searching through user manuals or online help for advice on editing inevitably turns up the wrong information. For better or worse, we're largely stuck with "revision tracking" or its cousin, "tracking changes".) If you've skipped the previous chapters because they didn't seem to relate directly to onscreen editing, I urge you to at least skim those chapters before continuing. You'll be glad you did.

Because a discussion of software tools is inevitably somewhat specific to a given program, it's not possible to provide a completely generalized description of the overall process of onscreen editing. To fully understand how a feature works, you need to experiment with that feature *as it is implemented in your software* until you understand how it works—or at least until you reach a suitable *modus vivendi* in which you may not really understand how the feature works, but can at least use it to predictably accomplish the desired results. In this chapter, I'll focus on the revision-tracking tools provided by Word. Since these tools changed dramatically when Microsoft introduced Word XP for Windows and Word 2004 for the Mac, I've summarize these changes in Appendix III. Between the two descriptions, you should be able to figure out the tools provided by other software, including the increasingly popular OpenOffice suite (www.openoffice.org).

As a general rule, all effective revision-tracking systems allow us to clearly mark insertions, deletions, and comments or questions, so that we and the author can easily locate them. In addition, most programs provide an automated way to find and review (accept, reject, or temporarily skip) each edit.

Although it's possible to simply go through a manuscript, make all the changes you feel are necessary without identifying them, and leave it to the author to figure out what you've done, this is both unreliable and unwise from a human perspective. The *unreliability* comes from the fact that authors have generally seen their manuscript so many times before it reaches you that they are too familiar with it, and can no longer force themselves to concentrate on the text. In my experience, this is true of most authors—including me, when I was revising this book for the final time. This means that authors inevitably miss small or subtle changes that perhaps we shouldn't have made. The solution is to find a way to ensure that they can see each change. The *unwise* aspect arises from the fact that it's always more difficult to examine a fully revised manuscript that provides no evidence of what was done (think "forensic science"!) than it is to examine each individual change and ensure that it's correct. Authors naturally resent the extra work, and resent it even more if an editorial error escapes their review, makes it into print (or is published on the Web), and embarrasses them. The solution? Again, make sure they can see each change. Tracking your changes turns the review and revision from a hunt for unpleasant surprises into a collaborative dialogue, and that's a very good thing indeed when it comes to working productively with authors.

In the present chapter, I'll focus on the mechanics of using the revision tracking tools provided by Word. Chapter 7 (*Inserting and deleting text*) provides some general principles on how to handle insertions, deletions, comments, and questions whether you're working on paper or on the screen, but with an emphasis on the main quirks related to onscreen editing. Chapter 12 (*Editing in special situations*) describes how you can use your word processor's revision tracking feature for types of files that you wouldn't ordinarily think you could edit in a word processor, such as spreadsheets and Web pages. Last but not least, Chapter 13 (*Coping when revision tracking isn't available*) provides some advice on last-ditch methods for clearly communicating your changes when you don't have the luxury of using revision tracking. Think of the latter chapter as the "clay tablet plus stylus" approach to onscreen editing: it ain't pretty, but it works.

Enabling and disabling revision tracking

There's no point in using any tool that makes our lives easier if it makes the author's life significantly more difficult. For onscreen editing to be truly effective, it must also make the author's life easier. The key feature that makes revision tracking so useful is that once we turn it on, any changes that we make will be highlighted in such a manner that the author can see exactly what we've done, and can approve or reject our changes or suggest a compromise solution. (For details on how to customize how revisions appear on the screen, see *Track changes settings* in Chapter 4.)

Word offers several ways to turn on revision tracking:

From the menus:

- Open the Tools menu.
- Select Track changes.
- Select Highlight changes.
- Select the checkbox for "Track changes while editing".

From the keyboard:

Windows versions of Word provide the Control + Shift + E keyboard shortcut to switch between tracking and not tracking changes. If that doesn't work on your computer (and it *doesn't* in the early Macintosh versions of Word; Command + Shift + E works in Word X and Word 2004), create your own keyboard shortcut:

- Open the Tools menu.
- Select Customize.
- Click the "Keyboard" button.
- Under the heading labeled "Categories", select "Tools".
- Under the heading labeled "Commands", scroll down until you find ToolsRevisionMarksToggle.
- Specify a keyboard shortcut that you can remember easily. In an older version of Word on my Macintosh, I chose Command + Shift + E on the logic that I'm *commanding* the software to *shift* between editing (*E*) and not editing.

From the status bar:

If you've set Word to display the status bar at the bottom of the document window (in the Options or Preferences dialog box, select the View tab, then select "Status bar"), you'll see four small buttons towards the right edge of the status bar. (If you can't see them, drag the bottom right edge of the window to enlarge the window until you do.) To enable or disable revision tracking:

- Click the button labeled TRK. On the Macintosh, the circle beside TRK turns green to remind you that Word is now tracking your changes; in Windows, there's no circle, but TRK is boldfaced to indicate that Word is tracking your changes.

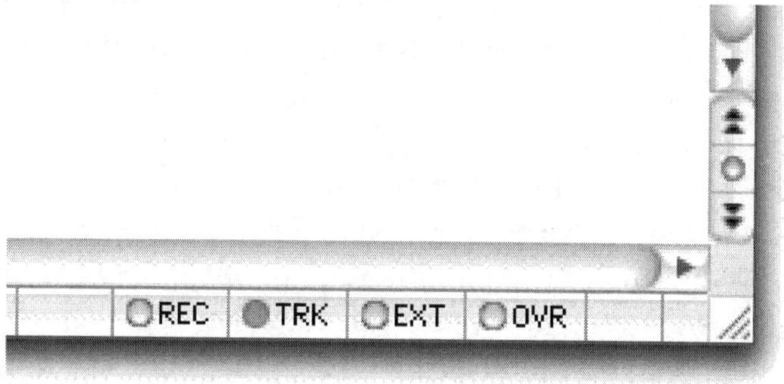

- Click that button again to turn off revision tracking. The circle beside TRK will no longer be highlighted (or TRK will no longer be boldfaced) to remind you that Word is no longer tracking your changes.
- **Tip:** Right-clicking on TRK (or Control-clicking if your mouse has only one button) pops up a small menu that lets you change how revision tracking works and offers several other useful options related to revision tracking.

You can turn tracking off again, in the same way, whenever you need to make changes the author shouldn't have to deal with (such as replacing all double spaces with single spaces) or doesn't have the authority to reject (such as applying the correct paragraph styles to a document). Use this power judiciously! Although authors generally appreciate not having to confirm every trivial change, it's dangerous to create the impression that you're doing anything behind the author's back. Our goal should always be to build a trusting relationship with our authors, and the smallest hint that we're trying to sneak something past them can completely undermine that trust. Often, it's wise to begin your discussion with an author by obtaining permission to make certain kinds of changes without tracking these changes. If you receive such permission, remind the author that you've done this when you return the document, or insert a comment directly in the manuscript to explain what you've done; authors often forget this kind of detail. (See Chapter 7 for more details on inserting comments.) If the author spots a change that you haven't tracked, they'll understand why you made that change rather than wondering what other changes you might have made without their approval.

Most authors will also learn that they can turn off change tracking, and this can be a very bad thing indeed if they use this knowledge to make changes behind *your* back. Ask them to offer you the same courtesy that you have offered them: a commitment to not make any changes without tracking the change or discussing it with you before they proceed. Remind them that if they rewrite any text without tracking those changes after you've already edited the manuscript, you'll have to work your way through the entire manuscript one more time just to find the changes before you can even begin to review them. In contrast, if they track their changes, you can find the changes quickly, edit only the text that has changed, and return the manuscript far faster than would otherwise be possible. In my experience, many authors never understand this until I've explained it to them, but after hearing the explanation, they quickly realize that they can save time and money by tracking their own changes. So make sure you discuss this aspect of editing during your initial negotiations with the author.

In some cases, it may be necessary to make it impossible for the author to make changes without tracking them or to disregard our changes. Some publishers, including one university press I'm familiar with, have experienced enough problems that they no longer even return the edited files to their authors, and instead require authors to review printouts of the edited manuscript; the editor then transfers the author's responses from the printout into the edited file and accepts all the edits that remain after incorporating those responses. This is clearly effective, but may be too draconian a solution when we're working with professional writers and have an established, trusting relationship with them. In that case, a compromise solution may be to protect the document so that authors cannot make any changes without tracking them and cannot accept or reject our changes (i.e., they can only comment on the changes, whether positively or negatively).

Document security in Word: In Word, you can protect a document as follows:

- Open the Tools menu.
- Select Protect Document.
- Select "Tracked changes". (In more recent versions of Word, you have more control over exactly what types of changes you will permit.)
- Enter a password, if so desired. (If you don't specify a password, the author can use the Protect Document feature to turn off the protection. If you use a password, only someone who knows the password can change the level of document protection or make changes without tracking them.)
- Note that this feature provides only weak protection. A sufficiently persistent author will find it fairly easy to disable the protection, including downloading "password cracker" software from the Web. Fortunately, most authors won't make the effort to do so. Conversely, unless you're willing to be that persistent yourself, make sure you don't lose the password! There is no way to recover it from within Word.

Displaying or concealing changes

While you're editing, there are times when it helps to see what you've done by having your software display your changes and other times when you'd rather see only the results of those changes. (See Chapter 4 for details on how to customize the display of tracked changes.) For example, I usually edit a manuscript for the first time with the changes displayed so I can monitor my progress and quickly find specific changes that I've already made. During my second pass, I conceal these changes so I see only the results of my edits—a great way to eliminate all the visual clutter created by myriad additions and deletions so I can focus on any remaining errors, as well as any errors that I introduced myself. Even if you choose to always work with edits displayed or concealed, you'll need to know how to switch quickly between displaying and concealing changes because this setting is saved with the file rather than specified for your computer as a whole. If someone sends you a file with the edits concealed and you want to see what they've done, you'll have to switch back to displaying the edits. Conversely, you should always send edited files to your authors with changes displayed to ensure that they can see what you've done. Many authors are inexperienced with revision tracking, and if you don't display the changes, you'll have to answer scared or angry questions about why they can't see your changes.

Word offers several ways to switch between displaying and concealing edits:

From the menus:

- Open the Tools menu.
- Select Track changes.
- Select Highlight changes.
- Select the checkbox for "Highlight changes on screen". (There's a companion setting for "Highlight changes in printed document" if you want the changes to be visible in print.)

From the keyboard:

Word provides no keyboard shortcut to switch between displaying and concealing changes. However, you can record a macro (see Chapter 11) that performs the necessary commands, and assign a keyboard shortcut to that macro:

- Open the Tools menu.
- Select Macro.
- Select "Record macro".
- Pick a memorable keyboard shortcut for the new macro. On my Macintosh, I chose Control + D to display changes and Control + Shift + D to conceal changes.
- Record the menu-based approach described earlier to display changes.
- If your version of Word does not use the same command to toggle between displaying and concealing changes, repeat this process to record a macro for concealing changes.

From the status bar:

If you've customized Word to show the status bar at the bottom of the document window, you'll see four small buttons towards the right edge of the status bar. (If you can't see them, drag the bottom right corner of the window to make it wider.) To display or conceal revisions:

- Right-click the "TRK" button. In Word XP (Word 2004 on the Macintosh) and later, you'll need to do this using the "Show" button on the Reviewing toolbar. See Appendix III for details.
- In the popup menu that appears, select Highlight Changes.
- Select the checkbox for "Highlight changes on screen" to show your revisions; deselect this checkbox to conceal your revisions.

There's one important quirk you need to be aware of if you're editing a document with your changes tracked but concealed: Even though you can't see the changes, they're still present in the file and Word must still deal with them—in particular, the cursor may need to move through this invisible "ghost" text. This can lead to surprises in some versions of Word, such as when you press the Delete or Backspace key and nothing happens. Here's what's going on: You see the cursor sitting next to text that is ripe for deletion, but Word sees the cursor next to text that has already been deleted. As a result, Word helpfully moves through the deleted text, one character at a time, each time you press the Delete key until it reaches the first undeleted character that you can see on the screen; *then* it deletes that character. If you've already deleted several words or sentences at that point in the document, this will clearly take a long time. Unfortunately, you can't see this happening because you've concealed your edits, including the deleted text; displaying your tracked changes makes it clear what is happening, and lets you move the cursor directly to where it needs to be to make the desired changes. Other similar forms of surprising behavior occasionally occur, such as deleted words suddenly becoming visible again as you type over them. If you edit with changes concealed, and something odd seems to be going on when you make a change, set Word to display your changes again; you can now see what's happening and revise your approach accordingly.

Accepting or rejecting changes

Once someone receives an edited document, they must find a way to review all of our changes and accept, reject, or comment upon each change. Authors perform this task more often than we do, but we may still be called upon to review an author's responses to our edits or to teach an author how to use revision tracking to incorporate our changes. Fortunately, Word provides a variety of ways to review changes.

One change at a time

When you're just learning how to work with revision tracking, it makes sense to review each change individually, one at a time. The problem with this approach is that it requires one or more keystrokes or mouse clicks to deal with every single change in the document. With a heavily edited manuscript, this can take a long, long time. Nonetheless, the approach is effective and a good way to begin your work with revision tracking. (I'll discuss a faster way to proceed in the next section, *All at once*.) Here's how the process works in any software that provides tools for reviewing changes:

- Use the software's tools to find the next change.
- Decide whether the change is acceptable.
- Accept or reject the change. If necessary, insert a comment to explain your decision. If you're not sure how to deal with a change, skip it and move on to the next change. Subsequently, you can discuss the problematic change with the person responsible for it.
- Repeat this process until you reach the end of the document.

You can perform each step in a few different ways. Here are your options in Word:

From the Reviewing toolbar:

There are two menu-based ways to display this toolbar (illustrated on the next page):

- Open the View menu, select Toolbars, then select Reviewing.
- Open the Tools menu, select Track changes, then select Accept or reject changes.

If you've customized Word to show the status bar at the bottom of the document window (in the Options or Preferences dialog box, select the View tab, then select Status Bar), you'll see four small buttons towards the right edge of the status bar. (If you can't see them, drag the bottom right corner of the window to make the window wider until you can see them.) Then you have a third option:

- Right-click the TRK button.
- In the small popup menu, select "Accept or Reject Changes".

The toolbar offers icons that allow you to move to the next (or previous) change, accept or reject the change, or enter a comment.

Using the mouse:

- Scroll through the document, with the changes displayed.

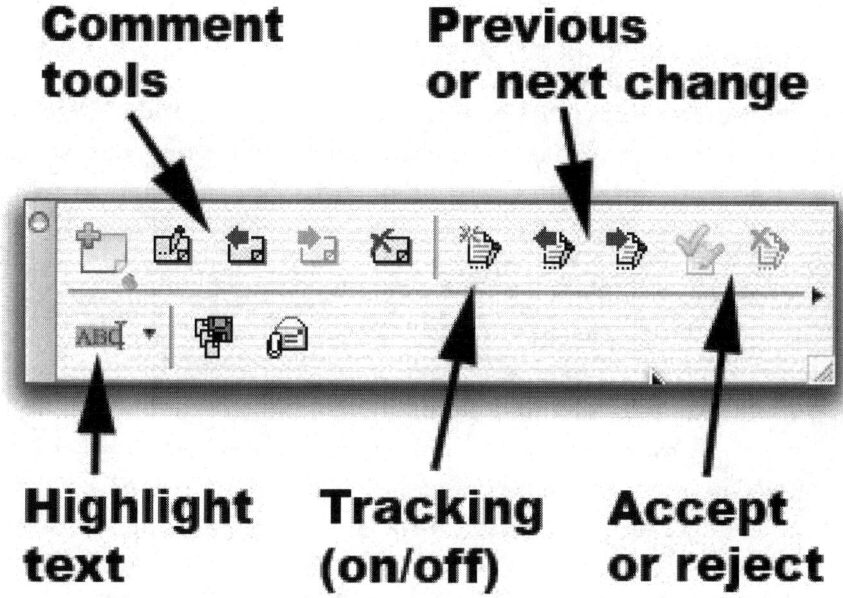

- When you encounter a tracked change, right-click the changed text. (If your mouse has only one button, Control-click on the text.)
- From the popup menu, select Accept Change or Reject Change, then move on to the next change.

From the keyboard, using only keystrokes:

Word provides no default keyboard shortcuts to find, accept, and reject changes, but does provide hidden commands that you can customize to use your own keystrokes. To attach these commands to a keyboard shortcut:

- Open the Tools menu.
- Select Customize.
- Click the "Keyboard" button.
- Under the heading labeled "Categories", select All Commands.
- Under the heading labeled Commands, scroll down to find the commands for finding the next and previous revisions: these are named *ToolsRevisionMarksNext* and *ToolsRevisionMarksPrev*. Select each of these commands and define a keyboard shortcut that you can easily remember.
- Under the heading labeled "Commands", scroll down to find the commands for accepting and rejecting changes: these are named *ToolsRevisionMarksAccept* and *ToolsRevisionMarksReject*, respectively.

Select each of these commands and define a keyboard shortcut that you can easily remember.

A combination approach:

With the Reviewing toolbar visible, you can click the Previous Change and Next Change icons to move quickly to the previous or next change that you'll review, then use either the mouse or the keyboard to accept, reject, or skip that change.

All at once

Clearly, a more efficient approach would minimize the number of keystrokes required to review and incorporate all the changes. The solution is to review all the changes, reject any that are erroneous and insert a comment to explain the problem, then accept all other edits (because you agree with them). In more detail, here's how this approach works:

- With changes displayed, scroll through the document and examine each change, one change at a time. (You can also use the Reviewing toolbar to move through the document if you prefer.)
- If a change is acceptable, move on to the next change.
- If a change is unacceptable, insert a comment to explain the problem. (Open the Insert menu, then select Comment, or use the comment icon in the Reviewing toolbar.) One easy way to do this is to select and copy the suggested change, paste the copied text into the comment pane, then revise the comment, perhaps as follows: "You suggested [pasted text]. Unfortunately, this doesn't work, because [explanation]. Could we do [suggestion] instead?" Then reject the change.
- Continue in this manner until you reach the end of the document.
- Accept all the remaining changes in a single step: Open the Tools menu, select Track Changes, then select Accept or Reject Changes. In the reviewing toolbar, click the "Accept All Changes" button and confirm that you really want to do this by clicking the "OK" button.
- Any comments that you inserted will be easy to find so you can discuss them with the author. In the Find and Replace dialog box, type *^a* (short for "annotation") in the "Find what" field to find the next comment. (This code is no longer listed in the list of special codes for Word 2003, but still works just fine in that version.)

Some authors come to trust our editing so much that they'll be tempted to perform only the final step and accept all our changes without reviewing or discussing them. Instead, they review only the final document that results from implementing all our changes. In general, I strongly recommend that you avoid this approach and teach your authors to avoid it, because even the most careful editor occasionally makes mistakes, and by the time a document arrives on our desk for editorial review, the authors have revised it so many times that they're too familiar with the manuscript's contents to pay careful attention anymore. Inevitably, authors who adopt this approach will miss one of our editing errors, leading to embarrassment for everyone concerned—if we're lucky. In the worst-case scenario, someone may get hurt or even killed as a result of following instructions that contain a serious editing error. The only way to have a good chance of catching such errors is for the author to review each of our changes individually. Even then, if the consequences of error are severe, this author review is no substitute for having a third person (another editor or a technical expert) perform a final review of the document after all our edits have been incorporated.

Other authors prefer to read the entire document that results from our edits to see whether anything looks wrong. To do so, they turn off the display of our changes (as I described earlier in this chapter), and only display the changes again if something looks wrong and they want to know what we did to introduce the error. This approach works better than simply accepting all changes outright, but it doesn't eliminate the problem of overfamiliarity: an author can never review their own document as well as someone else can. For authors who prefer this approach, try to arrange a final review by a third party if there's any risk of someone getting hurt if an error slips through the review process.

However you proceed, the last step in reviewing the edits should always be to search through the document using the Reviewing toolbar (or the keystrokes that you created to find changes) so you can ensure that no tracked changes were left behind to amuse, offend, or endanger the reader. This is particularly true for comments, some of which can be embarrassing or even legally suspect. If you're using revision tracking, any inserted comment is tracked as an insertion, and this means that an author can accidentally accept that insertion, thereby making the comment marker part of the text, without actually making the changes requested in the comment. The comment marker now remains behind, invisible to the revision tracking tools because it has been accepted. To ensure that all such comments are found and dealt with, simply open the pane that displays the comments. (In Word, open the View menu and select Comments; if there are no comments to be found, this menu choice will be grayed to indicate it is unavailable.) In most versions of Word, clicking the mouse to position the text cursor in the comment text will scroll the pane containing the manuscript itself to the position where the comment was inserted. You can then modify the text and delete the comment. If you won't have a chance to examine the final reviewed document to detect these forgotten comments, remind the author to do so and explain how to do this if they don't already know.

Multiple reviewers

Most traditional review and revision processes require a great many different review stages. These include:

- editorial review (by an editor) or peer review (by one of the author's colleagues)
- technical review by an expert
- management review, often by managers at several levels in the organization's hierarchy
- review by the marketing and sales departments
- review by the legal department

In many workplaces, all these reviews proceed in sequence, with the author reviewing all the edits made at each stage before the next edit occurs. As you can imagine, such a process consumes enormous amounts of time, and by the end of it, the author may be so fed up with re-reading their manuscript that they simply accept all changes and hope the reviewers did a good job. This is inefficient in terms of time requirements, and ineffective in terms of ensuring that the author can devote enough attention to the task to ensure that each proposed change is correct.

If a document must be reviewed by several reviewers, it's generally more efficient to send out multiple copies of the document simultaneously. This process won't work when some people must review documents that already incorporate edits made by other reviewers, but where that isn't necessary, you can greatly reduce the number of review stages by performing parallel (simultaneous) reviews. This is most com-

Updates for newer versions of Word: If you're using Word XP, 2003, or 2004, see Appendix III for details on dealing with comments.

mon when two or more peer reviewers must simultaneously perform a technical review on an early draft of a manuscript. In such cases, each reviewer works on a different copy of the document. When the author receives the reviews, they then copy all the edits into a single document. It's certainly possible to do this manually, by manually copying each change made by a reviewer into the author's copy of the manuscript, but this can take far too long if each reviewer has many changes or if there are several reviewers.

Some software offers utilities that can make this process more automatic, usually by "merging" two documents to create a third document or using a "compare documents" feature. In theory, all the review comments will then end up inside the same file, ready for review. In practice, multiple conflicting edits of the same passage of text can be difficult or impossible for the software to handle and even more difficult for the author to disentangle. If you're willing to experiment with this approach, here's how Word handles the process when each of the reviewers has tracked their changes in their review copy:

- Open a *copy* of the original document that was sent out for review. (Always keep the original document safe in case you need to return to it. In addition, retain a copy of each reviewer's edited document so you can examine it if necessary.)
- Open the Tools menu, then select Merge Documents (or Compare and Merge Documents in more recent versions of Word).
- Select the document containing the first reviewer's edits.
- When Word finishes the merge, save the document. (You can continue merging additional documents without first saving the open document, but if anything goes wrong, you'll have to start over again.)
- Repeat the merge process for each additional reviewer's document.
- When all documents have been merged, review the edits in the final version of the resulting file.
- For quality control, someone should then read through each reviewer's document and ensure that the requested changes have been

made in the final document, or that a satisfactory rebuttal has been made wherever the author did not accept a change.

Word's similar Compare Documents feature does not require that the documents being compared have been reviewed using revision tracking. Rather, it uses revision tracking to summarize the differences between any two documents so you can review the differences more easily. To compare two Word documents, open the first document, then open the Tools menu, select Track Changes, and select Compare Documents. Select the second document. After comparing the documents, Word will use revision tracking to mark up the first document to show how it differs from the second one.

Those who have used the Merge Documents and Compare Documents features in Word (and similar features in other software) report that they don't always work reliably, and sometimes miss or misinterpret changes, particularly when those changes are complicated. (The biggest problems arise when two reviewers produce contradictory recommendations or when one reviewer edits another reviewer's revisions.) Thus, I recommend that you use both features with considerable caution. Still, when this process works, it's far more efficient than having to review the edits separately in each document and manually copy them into one final document. But given that it doesn't necessarily work perfectly, I don't recommend that you rely exclusively on this approach for important jobs unless you add a final quality control stage in which someone (usually an editor) confirms that each edit has been satisfactorily addressed.

Comparing documents in Word: The Compare Documents feature can be an excellent way to recover edits if a reviewer inadvertently performs their review without using revision tracking, or if the author accidentally accepts all of a reviewer's edits before reviewing them. It's also a useful way to quickly check a revised document to see which of our edits an author ignored and to find any new text they may have inserted without tracking the change. Here's how:

- Open a copy of the document containing your edits. Accept all the changes (as described earlier in this chapter in the section *All at once*), then save the file under a new name (e.g., "Geoff--all edits accepted.doc"). Don't close this version of the file.
- Open a copy of the revised document returned by the author, accept all changes, then save the file under a new name (e.g., "Author--all edits reviewed.doc") and close the file.
- The version of the edited document with all your edits accepted is still open, and you'll now use it to see what changed—and what didn't. Open the Tools menu, select Track Changes, then select Compare Documents.
- Select the copy of the revised document that contains all the accepted revisions (in this example, "Author--all edits reviewed.doc").
- The resulting document will (or at least should) display all differences between the two files. Use the revision-tracking tools to find the differences and determine whether any follow-up is necessary.

Chapter 7. Inserting and deleting text

"He that wrestles with us strengthens our nerves, and sharpens our skill. Our antagonist is our helper."—Edmund Burke (1729–1797)

"If you give a man a fish he will eat for a day. But if you teach a man to fish he will buy an ugly hat. And if you talk about fish to a starving man then you're a consultant."—Scott Adams

As editors, we spend most of our time inserting missing punctuation, letters, words, phrases, and sentences, and deleting redundant or incorrect punctuation, letters, words, phrases, and sentences. All these insertions and deletions represent changes to what is already present, and in most cases, the reasons for these changes will be sufficiently obvious to the author that they require no explanation. But sometimes the reason for a change isn't obvious, or we're not sure how to solve a problem, and when that's the case, we must explain what we've done and why, or ask the author questions designed to help them clarify their thinking and help us find a way to make that meaning clear. These explanations or questions are generally referred to as "comments", since we're commenting on what we've done or what has not yet been done. Writing comments requires a certain amount of tact, so that the author will want to respond appropriately, but any insertion must also be done so as to minimize the amount of work required by the author. Where possible, the comment should also minimize the risk of error when responding to our revisions.

Since editing a manuscript can be a lot of work, it's important to learn how to make our revisions in a manner that's efficient for us, since we don't always have the luxury of sufficient time to edit as thoroughly as we'd like, but we must also strive to make the revisions easy for the author to handle. I can't emphasize the latter point strongly enough: If you edit in a way that makes the task of reviewing your edits unnecessarily difficult, authors will look for shortcuts to simplify their task, and these shortcuts often lead to significant errors. Moreover, if you're a freelancer (as I am), it's sobering to remember that a client who is sufficiently upset with your approach to editing won't provide any additional work in the future. In this chapter, I'll explain how to make the process as painless as possible for you and your authors.

There are two main philosophies concerning how best to modify a manuscript. The "teach them how to write" school of editing believes that we should enter each correction directly where it occurs, no matter how complicated the resulting changes may appear to the poor author. For example, if a single word contains three typos, philosophers from this school would recommend correcting each typo rather than simply retyping the whole word. This approach follows the rationale that by seeing each minute change, authors will learn from their mistakes and gradually learn to write cleaner manuscripts. Less charitably, this approach could be described as the "demonstrate how good we really are by pointing out every correction we made, no matter how small" approach, since it makes the results of our edits seem more complicated and demanding than they might actually be, thereby impressing the author with our technical merit and attention to detail.

This approach may indeed by useful for students who are learning to write or for unusually picky authors who want to see every tiny change rather than the results of those changes. But in my experience, most authors are more interested in reviewing our edits as efficiently as possible than in learning how to write (most believe that they already write well enough!), and even picky authors quickly lose patience if the complexity of our edits exceeds their tolerance threshold. That being the case, I recommend adopting a second philosophy—the one taught by the school of editing for maximum efficiency for both editor and author. Efficient editing *does not* mean that you should attempt to minimize the number of keystrokes you must type to make a given change, though it may indeed have that salutary result. Instead, it emphasizes techniques for quickly entering changes in the file while still helping authors quickly review and approve those changes. In addition, because changes are clearer and easier to see, the risk that an author will miss a small correction is reduced.

Fortunately, the same techniques can improve life for both editors and authors.

Insertions and deletions

There are only two things you must remember to insert or delete text efficiently. The first is that it's inefficient to move the text cursor painfully to each of several positions within a word to enter missing letters or delete superfluous letters. For longer words, it's more efficient to retype the entire word; most editors are sufficiently fast typists that we can retype the word faster than we can individually correct multiple errors within it. After typing the corrected word, we can then delete the original word with a single keystroke: Command + Delete on the Macintosh and Control + Delete in Windows to delete the word that follows the cursor, or substitute Backspace for Delete to delete the word that precedes the cursor.

The second is that a retyped word is easier to understand at a single glance than a puzzle word that contains several tiny corrections; in the latter case, the author must reconstruct the final word by assembling and integrating those corrections. For example, compare:

Puz**<u>z</u>**l~~**le**~~e words

<u>Puzzle</u> ~~**Puzllee**~~ words

Puzzle sentences that result from such edits in every second word can be similarly difficult to untangle, and retyping (or copying and pasting) a sequence of several words produces a result that is much easier for the author to understand. The resulting changes are also simpler for the author to accept: one click to accept the deletion of the incorrect word or phrase, and one more to accept the insertion of the correct word or phrase, for a total of two actions rather than one action per correction.

This approach makes increasing sense for the author as the number of corrections increases, because each insertion and each deletion requires one action to accept or reject. As soon as the number of insertions and deletions exceeds two, retyping makes reviewing faster for the author. You'll see this most clearly with phrases and sentences, which more often contain several words that must be changed or replaced by new words. In that case, it makes more sense to retype the entire chunk of text that contains a series of corrections. It may seem that retyping a long phrase or an entire sentence becomes difficult for us, even though it clearly makes reviewing more efficient for the author, but there's a shortcut that can make it nearly as efficient for us as correcting individual words: select the problem text, use the "copy" command (Control + C in Windows, Command + C on the Macintosh) to copy the problem text, then without touching any other keys, use the "paste" command (Control + V in Windows, Command + V on the Macintosh) to paste the copied text on top of the original. Because the original text is still selected (highlighted), this lets you accomplish both the insertion and the deletion in a single step. You can now fix the individual problems in the pasted text. (Alternatively, make your changes first, then copy and paste the entire resulting text. Both approaches work equally well.) This is particularly efficient when the corrections involve juggling word order, since most software lets you select words with the mouse and drag them around the sentence until they're in the right locations.

I generally recommend that editors place inserted text *before* the deleted text that it replaces. This approach lets the author read clean text, which is often self-explanatory, rather than encountering an unexplained deletion and pausing to figure out whether the deleted text is simply gone or has been moved somewhere else. That eliminates one stumbling block in the process of understanding and approving our edits. If the authors are truly interested in figuring out what we did (most aren't), they can still compare the inserted words and phrases with those we deleted; if not, they simply agree that the edited text is correct and move on to the next edit. Other editors prefer to insert new text *after* the deleted text, in part because if you select the text you want to delete and start typing, the new text may appear after the selected text, as it does in Word. I'm not convinced there's any hugely significant difference between the two approaches, and in any event, authors will quickly learn your style. As long as you're consistent in how you do this, neither approach should pose a significant obstacle to the author. Of course, if your author expresses a preference, it's wise to accommodate that preference as much as possible.

A bit more explanation may be in order when it's necessary to move whole sentences or larger chunks of text to a new position. If the text will be moved to a position later in the document, you can simply delete the text and insert a comment explaining the move so the author won't have to wonder where the deleted text disappeared to and why. For example: "I moved this text to the next section because it is easier to understand after you've explained the context, which you do in that later section." Conversely, if you move the text to an earlier position in the manuscript, add a comment at the new location to explain the sudden and otherwise mysterious appearance of the new text. For example: "I moved the following paragraph here from the end of the instructions because warnings should always *precede* the procedures that require them." You can also add a note where the moved text originated to explain its absence. For example: "As noted previously, I moved the text that was originally here to the Methods section." This is particularly useful when you moved the text so far away that the author may have forgotten it by the time they reach its original location. (Authors really are this forgetful sometimes.)

If you need to both edit text and move it somewhere new, you have two options:

- Leave revision tracking enabled, and use the "cut" command (Control + X in Windows, Command + X on the Macintosh) to remove the text from its original location. Insert a comment to explain the deletion (e.g., "I moved this paragraph to page 10"), paste the text in its new location, then accept this change so that your subsequent edits to the moved text will be clearly visible. If you don't accept the change (the insertion) before you begin editing the text, the software will track all of the inserted text as a single insertion and all your changes will become part of the same insertion, forcing the author to examine it carefully, looking for changes. As noted previously, this is not a good solution. A careful author will successfully review your changes, but not all authors are sufficiently meticulous for us to rely on their skill. Even if the author is meticulous, this is still more work for the author.
- Because a careless author may reject the deletion and accept the insertion, there's a risk of leaving two copies of the same text in the manuscript—embarrassing at best, and sometimes problematic too. To avoid this problem, it's safer to simply move the text to its new location *before* you edit it. The easiest way to do this is to temporarily turn off revision tracking, cut the text from its original location, insert a comment to explain the disappearance of the text (i.e., its move to a new location), paste the text in its new location, insert a comment to explain the sudden appearance of the new text, then turn on revision tracking again so you can edit the moved text.

What if you belatedly discover that you'll have to move a chunk of text to a new and more effective location after you've already edited that text extensively? In some programs (including most versions of Word), that's a problem: If you cut and paste the edited text, the software will delete the original text, including your edits, then insert only the results of your editing at the new location; as a result, the author will see only the results of your edits, not the edits themselves. (This problem has been fixed in Word XP for Windows and Word 2004 for the Macintosh and in later versions. In these versions, all you need to do is turn off revision tracking before you move the text.) You could, of course, insert a comment that tells the author where to move the text after they've reviewed your edits, and that's an acceptable approach in many cases, particularly if you insert another comment ("yes, paste it here!") at that destination. Unfortunately, that risks having the author introduce an error during the move. For this reason, it's more effective to move the text yourself, eliminating both the extra work for the author and one more opportunity for introducing an error in the document.

If you're using software that won't let you move text containing tracked revisions without losing track of the revisions (as is the case in older versions of Word), try the following trick:

- Save the current version of the file to preserve your most recent changes.
- Save a temporary copy of the file under a new name (e.g., "Temporary").
- In the temporary copy of the file, delete all the text except the chunk that you want to move. (You can either turn off revision tracking before doing this, or leave revision tracking enabled and simply accept these deletions.)

  Tip: Position the cursor before the text you want to retain and press Control + Shift + Home (Windows) or Command + Shift + Home (Macintosh) to select all the text before that point in the file, then press the Delete key. Then move the cursor to the end of the chunk of text you want to retain, and press Control + Shift + End (Windows) or Command + Shift + End (Macintosh) to select the remainder of the document, then press the Delete key.
- Save and close the temporary file.
- In the original file, insert a comment to explain the proposed deletion, then turn off revision tracking and delete the text that you want to move.
- Move the cursor to the position where the edited text should appear.

- Open the Insert menu, then select File.
- Select the temporary file, then click OK to insert it.
- With the text now inserted at the correct location, turn on revision tracking and continue editing.

A brief digression about efficiency

As I noted previously, making the author's job easier goes a long way towards making the task of reviewing your edits more palatable. That's a good investment in a happy long-term relationship with the author. Moreover, if you're working in a corporate setting, it may be considerably more important to minimize the *total* time spent reviewing a document than it is to minimize your editing time. This is particularly true when the author works more slowly than we do, which is often the case; if we're working with "occasional" authors such as engineers and scientists rather than professional writers such as journalists or technical writers, we tend to do much more onscreen editing than they do, and thus, practice our skills enough that we write and edit much faster than they do. Helping authors work faster will produce a greater net benefit than focusing on our own needs, even if helping them actually costs us time, and this sacrifice is often a good one to make in that context.

In any event, I'm hoping that reading this book will teach you so many techniques for working faster and better that you'll be able to afford to spend a bit more time pampering your authors. Much of this pampering comes in the form of inserted comments and questions, which will be the topic of the next section in this chapter. Sometimes

Spiking text in Word: If your version of Word does not allow you to move text containing tracked edits and retain those edits, you can try using the "spike" instead:

- Turn off revision tracking.
- Select the text you want to move, then press Control + F3 (Windows) or Command + F3 (Macintosh) to copy the text to the spike.
- Position the text cursor where you want to insert the text and press Control + Shift + F3 (Windows) or Command + Shift + F3 (Macintosh) to paste the text in its new place.
- Turn on revision tracking and continue editing.

our edits are so instantly clear that no explanation is necessary—as is generally true for corrections of simple typos. Other times, it may take a bit of thinking for the author to figure out what we did and why. Although encouraging authors to think is an inherently good thing (society benefits every time we encourage someone to improve their powers of reasoning), that's not necessarily a goal we can afford to support: editing is an inherently adversarial relationship, since every edit says clearly "your writing is poor and this edit proves that I'm a better writer than you are". Increasing our own efficiency must never come at the cost of emphasizing this message, and forcing authors to repeatedly stop and figure out the subtle brilliance of our editorial reasoning does little to take the edge off this adversarial relationship. Because cryptic, telegraphic comments are more difficult to understand, it's preferable to write full sentences with easily understood explanations, even though these take longer to craft. (See Chapter 11 for some tips on how to automate the creation of certain oft-repeated comments.)

It pays to remember that authors wrote something in a specific way because that way made sense to them; thus, our changes are rarely as obvious as we might hope.

Comments and questions

"Have you actually read your own paper?"—Ernie Heidersdorf, Research Director

In an ideal world, editing becomes a dialogue between editor and author in which each learns from the other and we work together to produce the best possible result: a document that communicates clearly with the reader, while still retaining the author's own unique voice. One problem with onscreen editing, particularly when you will rarely or never meet the author (as is the case for many modern freelancers), is that it can eliminate this dialogue. Over the years, I've found that it's possible to mitigate the distance between author and editor that is created by onscreen editing by recreating the dialogue in the form of inserted comments. The dialogue never reaches the level of a post-work chat over beers, but it can at least approach the epistolary dialogue of traditional handwritten letters and modern e-mail conversations.

In this section, I'll describe some of the "best practices" and learned wisdom relating to comments. A comment may be a simple statement that explains a change, a question that indicates that we can't understand something, a list of possible alternative wordings for the author to choose among, or a short essay that describes a problem with the text and proposes at least one solution. Most comments involve explanations of some sort, even when that explanation takes the form of a question such as "Do you mean...? If not, please reword this text to make the meaning clearer."

Deciding when to explain what we've done rather than leaving the reason implicit is more of an art than a science. As a general rule, it's safer to insert too many comments than too few comments because being misunderstood has more serious consequences than over-explaining; if an author can't understand the problem that prompted us to make a change, they may arbitrarily reject that change and leave the problem to trip up the next reader. Explanations also help remove a common obstacle in the author–editor relationship: the perception that our edits are arbitrary and done purely to impose our style on the author. (This attitude is widespread, particularly among authors who have worked with bad editors and haven't yet learned to trust *us*.) Good explanations persuade the author that we have a sound reason for everything we do, and over time, that perception establishes a feeling of trust in our expertise. Similarly, demonstrating that we understood the message the author was trying to communicate and that we tried to make that communication more effective establishes both our authority and the feeling that we're trying to help the author, not criticize them. In a sense, comments simulate the kind of dialogue with the author that we'd strive to achieve if we were working in the same office and discussing writing problems and how to solve them. If we *do* work in the same office, that dialogue is possible but may not happen as often as we'd like. When we're working at a distance with authors we'll never meet other than through e-mail, it's vital that we attempt to bridge that distance through good communication.

Over time, an author will learn to trust our judgment and understand how our edits make them look better. This changes the relationship from one of criticism or confrontation to a more friendly collaboration, and results in more effective communication between us and the author and between the author and their audience.

Long-distance collaboration in real-time: When it's truly necessary to discuss something with a distant author, a telephone conversation is always an option. For authors who live in the same city, a visit to their office may sometimes be in order. But where phone calls or visits are impractical, possibly because the author works in a different country, there are always alternatives. The most obvious alternative is to use one of the various forms of chat or instant messaging, in which you and the author open a session (i.e., establish a link between your computers) and take turns typing messages back and forth to each other. If you have a sufficiently modern computer, it may be worthwhile investigating the Skype internet telephony service (www.skype.com), which is free or inexpensive (depending on what options you choose), reliable, and easy to use. More sophisticated solutions combine instant messaging with a dynamically updated Web page that author and editor can both edit together. As such programs are still in their early stages of development, and are generally quite expensive, I won't discuss this option in any detail here.

Is a comment necessary?

The main risk of overexplanation is that the author, wearied by our solicitude and numbed by the consistent correctness of our changes, may come to trust our judgment so implicitly that they simply accept our edits without carefully reading each comment and without fully considering the possibility that we might be wrong. We can take a few simple steps to minimize this risk:

- Explain something once, early in the manuscript, rather than repeating the explanation each time the problem arises. We can then highlight future occurrences of the problem with a cryptic comment that says "see my previous comment on this point" or that contains only the proposed correction. Sometimes we can even make the change without further explanation.
- Write concisely so as to minimize the amount of text authors must read. However, don't create telegraphic sentence fragments; take the time to write clearly.
- Obtain the author's permission to make certain changes (e.g., applying the correct styles to headings and text) without explaining them. This can eliminate the need for many comments.

- Only insert comments if they're truly necessary.

The last of these suggestions seems at first glance to contradict my statement that it's better to overexplain, but I've added it to the list to remind you to never insert a comment without carefully considering whether the comment is truly necessary. Don't waste the author's time explaining obvious points of grammar such as subject–verb accord or the use of articles such as *the*, but do explain why the verb the author used was wrong or the different implications of articles that might both seem correct but that communicate different meanings (*the* vs. *a* is a particular problem for authors whose native language doesn't use articles). That being said, there are several situations that suggest the need to insert a comment:

Introduction

If this is your first time working with an author, consider inserting a comment right at the start that *briefly* explains who you are and makes it clear that you want to work with the author to come up with mutually satisfactory solutions. This is also an opportunity to remind the author not to reject an edit out of hand simply because *you* misunderstood the text; remind the author that if you misunderstood, someone else may misunderstand too. Offer the chance to discuss alternatives if the author doesn't like your solution. This can also be part of your cover letter when you return a manuscript to the author, but placing it directly in the body of the manuscript makes it harder to ignore.

Explanation

Sometimes the author's original text appears quite reasonable, but ignores a problem you have encountered before, such as a particular phrase that journal peer reviewers object to. Other times, your edit clearly represents a better solution once the author understands why. In such cases, a brief explanation is the spoonful of sugar that makes the medicine go down more easily.

Confirmation

Sometimes we're only 90% confident that we've correctly understood the author's mangled prose, and that our rewording is clearer and correct; this is often true when we attempt to fix unclear antecedents or pronouns. It's the 10% of the time when we're wrong that can destroy all the good will we've earned through our skillful edits up to that point. Specifically asking the author to confirm this edit—when no such

Working with Word's comments: In older versions of Word, you can insert comments in a document by opening the Insert menu and selecting Comment. This opens a Comments pane at the bottom of the main document window, into which you type an explanation or question. To indicate which chunk of text the comment applies to, select that chunk of text *before* you insert the comment. Doing so will highlight both the selected text and the comment marker in yellow so that it's clear which specific words the comment applies to; holding the mouse cursor over the final comment will then display a pop-up balloon containing the full text of the comment. (In some cases, you may first need to click inside the highlighted text; there's a bug in several versions of Word that sometimes prevents comments from being displayed if the text cursor isn't inside the highlighted text.) If you can't see the comment marker, open the Options (Windows) or Preferences (Macintosh) dialog box, select the View tab, then select Hidden text and ToolTips (or ScreenTips).

You can also insert comments in two other ways:

- Click the Insert Comment icon on the Reviewing toolbar. (To display this toolbar, open the View menu, select Toolbars, then from the submenu, select Reviewing.)
- From the keyboard: Record a macro (see Chapter 11 for details) that records your actions as you open the Insert menu and select Comment. Choose a keyboard shortcut for this macro that you can remember easily.

Unfortunately, Microsoft crippled the Comments feature in Word XP for Windows and Word 2004 for the Macintosh, and only partially fixed the problem in Word 2003 for Windows, which lacked a corresponding Macintosh version when I was writing this book. (See Appendix III for details on the nature of these changes and how to deal with them.) For this reason, some editors prefer to avoid using Word's Comments feature, and instead insert their comments directly in the text, using symbols such as brackets to separate each comment from the main text.

request accompanies the other edits—emphasizes the need to pay more attention to this particular edit to ensure that we got it right. If you prefer, you can instead use the comment to remind the author that they should contact us to discuss alternatives.

Collaboration and options

Offering the author a choice of two or more wordings demonstrates whether we have understood or misunderstood the original wording, and provides the author with an opportunity to collaborate in picking a solution that we both like, rather than imposing our choice on the author each time. Even if we guessed wrong, we've at least provided the author with a starting point for understanding why we might have misunderstood so they can develop better wording. Of course, if we guessed right, they can simply copy our solution into the text, and that's one less thing for us to edit during the next pass.

Sometimes a sentence may have two or more possible interpretations, and we can't edit the sentence to clarify it until we know which the author means. Since we can't insert all possible clarifications in the text, it's helpful to instead insert a comment that explains the problem and offers solutions. For example: "In the current wording, the highlighted text could refer to either A or B. If you mean A, say [suggestion] but if you mean B, say [suggestion 2] instead". If we're reasonably certain that one option is correct, we can replace the original wording with that option, then add a comment that presents an alternative in case we got it wrong: "My revision means [explanation]. If you mean Y, say [suggestion] instead."

Question

Sometimes we don't have the faintest notion of what the author is trying to say, or have some vague notion but aren't sufficiently confident that we're correct to make any changes. In that situation, just about the only option left to us is to gently explain the problem and ask the author to propose a solution. Try something like the following wording: "I'm afraid that I don't understand what you're trying to say here. Please e-mail me an explanation so I can help you choose clearer wording."

Explanation of a global problem

For recurring problems that are relatively easy for authors to fix, you can simply report the problem once and leave it to the author to resolve. For example: "This author's name (*Smith*) is spelled as *Schmidt* in the references. Which is correct? Please make the necessary corrections everywhere in the manuscript." This type of question avoids the need to insert the same comment at each of many locations where the problem occurs. However, this approach relies on the author to find and fix all those problems, and that may not always be a wise choice. In that case, it's more effective to repeat the comment concisely each time. For example, the previous comment might subsequently be condensed to "Schmidt?" where the text says Smith, or "Smith?" where the text says Schmidt. In this case, the comment is telegraphic and terse, but the conciseness and clarity of meaning makes that terseness acceptable.

Explanation of an error of omission

Sometimes authors omit necessary definitions or create logical *non sequiturs* by leaving out a few key words. In that case, explain the problem and propose the solution. For example: "Because readers of this journal may not be experts in your field of study, I recommend adding a brief explanation of [a key concept readers must understand before they can understand the rest of the manuscript]." Sometimes the existing text is adequate, but could be made more effective by other means. Suggesting those methods helps the author communicate better. For example: "A photo or illustration would make this much clearer."

Explanation of an error of commission

When authors blunder, bring the error to their attention—but tactfully. Error-prone authors grow progressively more frustrated as they deal with repeated reminders of their fallibility, so you must be particularly diplomatic. For example, the annoyed editor's "Can't you even add three numbers correctly? Try again!" should become "I calculate an average of 4.55 (or 4.6 to one decimal place) for these three numbers, not 4.8. Please confirm that there are no typographical errors and change either the data or the calculated result, as necessary."

Explanation of ineffective organization

Authors sometimes gather all the necessary information and describe it clearly, but present it in seemingly random order. Explain the problem and provide a solution. For example: "Because readers must learn basic concepts before they can understand an advanced concept, I recommend moving these definitions to the Introduction, before the procedural information begins. You could also create a glossary to contain these definitions."

Explanation of mandatory change related to the publisher's style guide

If some of your edits are mandated by a publisher's style, it helps to explain why you've made a change to text that superficially appears correct. For example: "this magazine places captions *below* figures" or "this journal only uses metric units".

Pointer to relocated text

As I noted earlier in this chapter, it's often easier to move sentences or paragraphs to a more effective or appropriate location without a lengthy explanation, but you should still at least alert authors to this move.

Effective comments and questions

As the sample comments that I've provided indicate, there's something of an art to creating an effective comment. Despite the facetious quotation with which I began this section, comments should always be professional, tactful, and designed to encourage dialogue and collaboration rather than to increase the natural resistance to being edited. Editors often joke that the real reason we make a second pass through any document is to eliminate snarky comments and reword what we were really thinking in a manner more likely to encourage the author to adopt our suggestions.

An effective comment has the following characteristics:

It's polite

Most of us don't say *please* nearly often enough. In a comment, this magic word turns the comment into a request rather than a demand and thereby changes how the author will perceive the comment. A demand increases resistance, whereas a request encourages the author to think about what you're asking.

It focuses on our needs as readers rather than attacking the author

Comments should always focus on our difficulties rather than criticizing the author. Such comments explain why *we* are having difficulty understanding. The author clearly still failed to communicate successfully, and is thus a bad writer, but at least we're not rubbing their nose in this fact.

It's tactful

It should be obvious that we can't establish a collaborative working relationship with an author if we repeatedly criticize or demean them—even if they deserve such criticism by any objective standard. (It *is* obvious, right?) Yet you'd be surprised how often editors slip and let their frustration show, particularly under deadline pressure. *Always* make time to edit your comments to ensure that they focus on the problem and its solution, not on criticizing the author.

It explains the problem

By explaining a problem (e.g., "*Editor* is more commonly used than *Mutilator of Text*, in my experience"), we emphasize why we misunderstood something or felt obliged to correct it, and thereby emphasize the fact that other readers are likely to encounter the same problem. Understanding the problem also lets the author see how our proposed solution solves the problem, or leads them to think about how to solve the problem in another way, in their own words.

It offers an effective solution

Rather than just stating that you don't understand something, make the extra effort to propose a solution to the problem you've explained. Provide full replacement phrases or sentences rather than fragments so the author can adopt a solution, perhaps after modifying it a little, rather than having to come up with one of their own. It's always easier to accept an editor's carefully crafted solution than it is to develop a wholly new solution.

An example

Here's an example of an effective comment that illustrates all these points:

> "In this sentence, *them* refers grammatically to your colleagues, but I suspect you mean the lab equipment. If you mean *your colleagues*, reword the sentence to read 'unpleasant odors from my colleagues'; if not, say 'unpleasant odors generated by the lab equipment'. If neither is correct, please rewrite the sentence to clarify the meaning. Please e-mail me an explanation so I can propose a better rewording you could use."

This comment explains the problem in a tactful way, focuses on the problem (an unclear antecedent) rather than on the author, offers instantly usable solutions based on each possible interpretation, asks the author to choose one of these alternatives, and reminds the author of the opportunity to collaborate.

To make your proposed solutions even more effective, teach authors how to cut and paste text from your comments into the main document window. In Word:

- Double-click on the comment marker to open the Comments pane.
- Select the replacement text and copy it.
- Close the Comments pane by clicking on its "Close" button.
- Paste the text at the desired location in the text.

If your word processor preserves the formatting of copied text, and inserts that formatting when you paste the text into the document, you can use this behavior to your advantage. To do so, set the attributes of the comment's style (e.g., font name and size) to match those of the main body text. (See the sidebar below for details.) Since the author will be pasting text into paragraphs more often than into headings, redefine the characteristics of this style so that they match those of the most common paragraph style used in the document.

Controlling the typography of comments: Word formats comments using the Comment Text paragraph style. Since the most common paragraph style in a Word document is typically either Normal or Body Text, edit the properties of the Comment Text style to match whichever of those styles the author has used most often so that copied and pasted text will have the right format:

- Open the Format menu.
- Select Style.
- In the list of available styles, scroll down and select Comment Text.
- Click the "Modify" button.
- If the author has used styles correctly: In the field labeled "Based on…", select the style whose characteristics you want to apply to the comment text (e.g., Normal).
- If the author created all formatting manually rather than using styles correctly: Open the Format menu of this dialog box, select Font, then enter the correct typographic information (font name and size).

Inserting and removing comments

As I noted earlier, in Word it's helpful to select the chunk of text that the comment refers to before you insert a comment. (See Chapter 5, *Moving around the document and selecting text*, for an explanation of the various ways you can select text.) When you actually insert the comment, the highlighted text changes to have a yellow background, as if you'd used a highlighter marker on a paper printout, and holding the cursor over the yellow text causes Word to display a popup balloon containing the comment text. (This feature works differently in Word XP and 2003 for Windows and Word 2004 for the Macintosh. See Appendix III for details.) Highlighting the text this way lets the author see both the comment and its context (what the comment applies to).

If the comment applies to a large chunk of text such as an entire paragraph or section, highlighting the entire block of text is likely to prove ineffective because that context is too broad to be meaningful. Moreover, any additional comments you insert related to smaller parts of that text will be obscured by the original highlighting, making it difficult to see which comment applies to which part of the text. In that case, select only the first word in the block of text, so as to associate the comment with that word.

Word offers an actual highlighter pen tool:

I don't recommend using it. Finding the tool is difficult, and many authors never learn where it's hidden and thus have no way to remove the highlighting. (In contrast, the highlighting associated with inserted comments disappears as soon as you delete the comment. We'll come to that shortly.) I mention this tool here primarily because many editors also never learn where the highlighter tool is hidden, and thus never learn how to remove this form of highlighting when it appears in a manuscript. To display this tool:

- Open the View menu.
- Select Toolbars, then from the submenu, select Reviewing.
- Select the text that you want to highlight or from which you want to remove the highlight.

- To apply the currently specified highlight color, click the icon for the highlighter pen; click the arrow to the right of the icon to select a different color.
- To remove the highlighting, select the highlighted text, then click the arrow to display the color choices; select "None" or "No Highlight".

If you find yourself endlessly repeating the same comment, perhaps with minor variations, it's easy to type it once and then copy it from that previous comment each time you need to reuse it, but there's a faster way: create a short keyword or phrase that your software will automatically expand into the full sentence. (See Chapter 11 for details.) If your editing software doesn't provide this feature, you can fake it easily enough: create a file called "Standard comments" that contains all the comments you routinely make while editing, then keep this file open in the background while you're editing. You can then quickly switch between the manuscript and your comments (see *Window juggling* in Chapter 4 for details), copy the required comment, switch back into the manuscript, and paste the comment into the text. If you're a gadget geek and love adding new programs to your computer, there are many clipboard-replacement utilities that let you store several different items on the clipboard for easy pasting, and system-level utilities that allow you to insert standard text in any program. There are many reliable sites where you can download these utilities safely. The Tucows site (www.tucows.com) provides a wide range of software for Windows, Macintoshes, and Linux.

Here are some examples of comments that I found myself repeating so often that some kind of shortcut was clearly necessary:

- This reference is not cited in the text. Either insert a citation at the correct location or delete the reference from your bibliography.
- This reference is missing from your bibliography. Please add it there, or correct the current citation to match one that is already present.
- This date does not match the date elsewhere in the text (i.e., 19XX). Please confirm the correct date, then make the necessary changes everywhere.
- If that's not what you mean, please change the wording to make the meaning of [phrase] clearer.

- Do you mean… If not, please reword the highlighted text to make the meaning clearer. Or feel free to e-mail me an explanation so we can discuss alternatives.

And so on. Pay careful attention to the kinds of errors you encounter most frequently or that require the most typing when you encounter them. The last two examples refer to wording problems that are so common in the work my authors do that I may insert dozens of these comments in even a short manuscript. And *all* my authors have great difficulty matching their literature citations to the entries in the bibliography, so even in short manuscripts, I may have to enter the first three comments a dozen or more times each. Note that creating such shortcuts accomplishes two goals: First and most important, it allows me to communicate concisely with the author, but in full sentences that both describe the problem and propose a solution. Second, it saves me from having to type these long explanations myself (my word processor does it for me), so I have the time to use longer, author-friendly explanations instead of cryptic sentence fragments. In addition, because I carefully checked the comments when I first created them, there are no typos to correct.

Once a comment has been inserted, removing it becomes considerably trickier than you might expect. It's easy to delete comments that you yourself inserted: select the comment marker, then press Delete or Backspace. Because you are editing your own edits, Word simply removes the comment marker. The real problem arises when revision tracking is turned on and authors try to delete your comment. In this case, Word does precisely what it should do, even though that isn't what the author wants to achieve: it marks the comment marker as having been deleted, just as it would mark any other text they delete while revision tracking is enabled. As a result, the comment marker remains in the file, just as any other deleted text would. The solution should be obvious (i.e., accept the deletion), but I've seen authors driven nearly to tears trying to figure out how to remove a deleted comment with revision tracking still turned on. (**Tip:** This problem goes away if you turn off revision tracking, delete the comment, then turn on revision tracking again. However, you may not want to teach authors the trick of disabling revision tracking until you're confident that they won't abuse this knowledge.) Nonetheless, some editors prefer inline queries, typed directly into the text and set off with brackets or other special characters, because working with this type of comment is far more intuitive and avoids the whole problem.

There are two other ways to delete comments that use the mouse:

- Right-click on a comment, then in the popup menu that appears, select Delete Comment.
- If you're using the Reviewing toolbar, simply position the cursor before the comment marker or anywhere in the highlighted text, then click the Delete Comment icon.

Printing comments

Sometimes authors want a printed copy of your comments. In current versions of Word, it's easy enough to print a list of comments by selecting "Comments" from the Print What? menu in the Print dialog box. Should that feature ever disappear, there are two other ways you can accomplish this:

First, in the most recent versions of Word, you can save a temporary copy of the document, and accept all the changes: the comment markers will remain in the file, since you have accepted them. Next, open the Print dialog box, and under the Print What? menu, select List of Markup.

Alternatively, in any version of Word, you can open the Comments pane, copy all the comments, paste them into a new document, then select all the comments. Open the Format menu, select Bullets and Numbering, then select a number format. The numbers will now match up with the numbers of the comment markers in the text, though you'll lose the page and line references.

Cleaning up

After a heavy edit, a document will be littered with insertions, deletions, and comments. Even the most well-intentioned author is likely to grow weary dealing with the editorial carnage, and is likely to miss

> **The Office clipboard:** Word XP for Windows and later versions (including Word 2004 for the Macintosh) offer a feature called the "Office Clipboard" that lets you cut or copy several chunks of text for future reuse.

an occasional correction. Less well-intentioned authors, and careless authors, are likely to miss more comments or introduce errors in responding to our edits and comments. And even with relatively straightforward edits of short documents, human nature ensures that some errors will still slip through. For this reason, someone must always take responsibility for reviewing the final manuscript.

Ideally, this person will be you, since you know what problems you asked the author to solve and are thus best suited to confirm that they actually solved the problems. In corporate settings, it's quite common for the editor to be given a chance to review the document after the author incorporates all the edits and responds to all questions and comments. But in many cases, particularly for freelancers whose clients live halfway around the world, we may never see the document again. In that situation, it's important to remind the author that someone must read carefully through the final manuscript to ensure that nothing was missed and that no new errors were introduced by responding to questions or editing the edits.

Deleting comments can require some persistence: In Word, placing the cursor before the comment marker and pressing the Delete key or positioning the cursor after the comment and pressing the Backspace key doesn't work—at least, not immediately. You'll have to press the key twice instead of once. This is actually a design feature, not a bug: comments usually contain significant amounts of text, and should not be allowed to disappear as a result of a single injudicious keystroke. Word provides partial protection against this problem by only selecting the comment marker with the first keystroke. The second keystroke confirms that this is really what we wanted to do, and deletes the comment marker as we intended. To accomplish this slightly faster, select the comment marker, then cut it (Control + X in Windows or Command + X on the Macintosh).

Chapter 8. Using the search tools (find and replace) to improve consistency

"Do I contradict myself? Very well, then I contradict myself, (I am large, I contain multitudes)."—Walt Whitman (1819–1892), *Song of Myself*

"I don't necessarily agree with everything I say."—Marshall McLuhan, cultural historian and communications theorist (1911–1980)

As editors, we are responsible for imposing consistency on manuscripts. At times, authors are bemusingly and amusingly inconsistent: they may use several words to mean the same thing, may make contradictory claims in different parts of the manuscript, and may provide cross-references to the wrong section or even to sections that no longer exist as a result of previous revisions. The text may contradict the accompanying graphics and tables of information, or may cite the wrong graphics and tables. Literature citations in an academic work may not match their corresponding entries in the bibliography, or may be wholly missing from the bibliography. As a result of careless application of styles, headings at the same level may differ so wildly in appearance that chapter titles look like the names of subsections, whereas headings at different levels may end up appearing identical. The most creative authors commit all these sins simultaneously, as well as offering surprisingly clever combinations of several other different types of inconsistency.

Individually, none of these problems may be fatal, but taken as a whole, they undermine the reader's confidence that the author knows what they're doing, and can sabotage the reader's ability to make sense of what the author is trying to say. To help readers receive the intended message as painlessly as possible and to help the authors look like they've really sweated over the details, it's our job to identify and resolve inconsistencies. When we edited on paper, we did this in two ways: First, we relied on a capacious memory for detail to let us remember a specific date or how a specific word had been spelled several hundred pages earlier. Second, we kept notes on this type of information on various scraps of paper, and consulted those scraps whenever we spotted a possible discrepancy. (I'll discuss these notes in more detail in

Chapter 9, *Developing style sheets: a tool for consistency*.) Unfortunately, large manuscripts with many inconsistencies tended to overwhelm our memory and led us to miss some of these problems. Worse still, discovering on page 400 that, say, the spelling of a name that we'd been using consistently for the previous 399 pages was wrong, and had to be corrected, meant a tedious rereading of the entire manuscript in an attempt to find and fix each of those problems. Or, on seeing the author say "white" on page 200, we might feel a terrible suspicion that they had said "black" somewhere earlier—but we didn't know where. Or it might have been a subtler contradiction, such as changing 90% grey to 80% grey. In hindsight, it's amazing that we were ever able to make manuscripts self-consistent.

Fortunately, computers are great at performing such repetitive, memory-intensive tasks. I've already discussed how using styles and templates correctly can impose consistency on the visual appearance of the text; for example, if your software offers an outline view, you can see at a glance whether headings have been formatted correctly, and if it offers the ability to display style names in a style area, you can quickly scan these names looking for inconsistencies. (See Chapter 4 for details on how to use both tools.) These tools offer one of the more compelling advantages of onscreen editing. The more broadly useful advantage, which you can use even in software that doesn't provide styles and templates, is the ability to quickly confirm a previous statement or search for all occurrences of a problematic word or phrase, its synonyms and variant forms, and its preferred replacements. Each time a suspicious statement appears, we can immediately check that statement against previous statements. After finishing our first pass through the manuscript, we can run through the style sheet one line at a time, using the search tool to find any inconsistencies in the manuscript that we missed during our first pass. This approach isn't foolproof either, but it does move us considerably closer to that elusive goal of perfection—once we know how to use the word processor's search tools to find inconsistencies. In this chapter, I'll show you how to use those tools effectively.

Searching for variations on a theme

In this chapter, I'll use the phrase "search term" to describe the thing that we're searching for and that we'll type into the "Find what" field of the "Find and Replace" or "Search and Replace" dialog box. Search terms can be a single letter or number, a complex description of a pattern to be matched (including text styles or formats), or a simple but long chunk of text—perhaps even one or more sentences. (The limitation on the length of the search term varies among programs.) What goes in the "Replace with" field of the dialog box can be new text, a new format (such as boldface), a new paragraph style, or some other property that we'll apply to whatever the software finds, whether to change the wording or the properties of the text.

"Elegant variation" (Henry Fowler's term) is one of the things that makes literature so potentially interesting, even though Fowler used the term to critique those who did not understand what true elegance involves, namely that clever and judicious—*elegant*—use of synonyms lets writers communicate subtle or dramatic shades of meaning that using a single word everywhere could never hope to communicate. In so doing, the author creates a complex mosaic of meaning that is far more interesting than a simpler verbal palette. (Moreover, it stretches the reader's vocabulary, and I'm enough of a word geek to believe that this is a good thing.) However, inappropriate use of this strategy creates what I call "inelegant variation"—variation that becomes awkward because it interferes with rather than enhancing comprehension. This is a particular problem in technical writing and other forms of nonfiction. In these genres, changing a word solely to appear creative forces readers who may already be struggling with impenetrable jargon or difficult concepts to determine whether that change conveys a special meaning. For example, does the instruction to "click" a button somehow differ from the instruction to "select" a button, and is there any difference between "click" and "click on"? If there's no difference, this variation has forced the reader to waste time figuring out that the author was more interested in showing off their vocabulary than in communicating clearly—or was just careless. Of course, even in fiction it's important to be consistent in some ways. Character names, for example, must be spelled consistently everywhere—and the same person must not have two different names unless they've been given an alias to advance the plot.

Imposing consistency on long manuscripts can become one of our more tedious and error-prone tasks. In short manuscripts, it's relatively easy to ensure that the author wrote "user manual" everywhere instead of an occasional "reference book", but book-length manuscripts pose a considerably greater challenge. There may be tens or even hundreds of terms that we must help the author to use consistently, and we must keep that list in mind throughout our editing so we can spot changes in usage and replace those changes with a single preferred wording. You can see the problem: as the number of terms to juggle grows, we're increasingly likely to miss important but sometimes subtle inconsistencies.

The search function, combined with a style sheet that we build as we go, solves this problem. If we see the author using a new term, it's easy to consult our style sheet to check what term the author used previously. Unlike on-paper style sheets, an electronic style sheet can be quickly rearranged to suit our needs of the moment. If the style sheet grows too long for us to scan it at a glance, we can use the search tool to locate items of interest. I'll discuss these strategies in more detail in Chapter 9.

The search function also permits *ad hoc* consistency checks. For example, let's say that late in a manuscript, we see a date of 1067 for an event but are reasonably certain that the date was 1066 earlier in the manuscript—only we're not sure where. On paper, we'd have to skim through the entire printout, hoping to find that one previous reference and any other repeated references to that date—a daunting and time-consuming task that leaves open the possibility of missing other points where the dates diverge. In contrast, the search function lets us seek out all references to 1066—or even to "106" if we're only confident that we've remembered the decade right. If using the year as our search term doesn't turn up the necessary previous reference to that date, we can always try one or more related terms, such as "Norman conquest" and "French invasion", to see what dates emerge.

The same approach works any time we suddenly feel the need to check up on something. One of the unfortunate general rules in editing is that we can't trust our authors to get anything right more than once; references to figures or tables, literature citations, and cross-references are all easy to get wrong, and authors usually do. (It's not that they're stupid. Really. It's just not their area of expertise or primary interest; only editors are truly obsessive about these details.) The solution? Learn to immediately check any cross-reference, whether to a previously stated

> **Returning to where you started:** Before departing on such a wild Norman chase, it's helpful to have a way to return quickly to our point of departure so we can continue editing where we left off. See *A brief word on distractions and "getting lost"* later in this chapter for some tips on how to only interrupt our train of thought rather than derailing it completely.

fact or to a specific part of the text, to confirm that the reference is correct. If we're reasonably confident that we know what we're looking for, we can immediately search for the item each time we encounter a reference to it. This lets us confirm that the cross-reference is correct or that a statement is consistent with what the author said elsewhere in the text. If we can't understand what they're asking readers to look for sufficiently well that we can find it quickly, then that's also clearly a problem that needs fixing.

One of the most common problems of this type in nonfiction editing involves the need to confirm that every publication cited in the body of a manuscript appears in the bibliography with the same author and date information—and conversely, to ensure that every bibliographic reference has been cited somewhere in the text if that's part of the publisher's style guide. (You'd think this would be easy, but in nearly 20 years of editing, I've seen no more than one in ten of my authors manage this feat, and usually far fewer.) Working on paper, the traditional approach was to separate the reference list from the remainder of the printout, set it aside, and check the citations against this section as we encountered them. This was time-consuming and difficult to do without disrupting the flow of our editing—which can pose problems during substantive editing, when we're struggling to grasp the complexities of a subtle argument and ensure that the author has explained the subtleties clearly and without contradiction. But it was still better than waiting to check the citations only after we'd completed our editing on paper: doing so meant rereading the entire text for the sole purpose of finding the citations, and time for that additional read-through wasn't always available. Workarounds such as using highlighter markers or marginal notes were typically ineffective; it was easy to forget to label an occasional reference, and even when we remembered, it was a distraction to put down the editorial red pen and grab a highlighter.

When we're working onscreen, the search tools let us ignore literature citations until we've completed our editing, then complete the reference check in a single pass. I'll describe the process in some depth because it's easy to generalize the approach to checking other types of recurring elements. In this approach, the search tools let us reliably find each citation without having to scan through the document ourselves—a tedious and error-prone process. We could print out the bibliography and use that as our reference for each citation, but that wastes paper, and in any event, this isn't a book about on-paper editing. If we want to work entirely on the screen, the first step is to copy all of the bibliography into a separate document so we won't have to scroll down to the bibliography each time we find a literature citation. Instead, we can switch between windows (using the keyboard shortcuts described in chapters 4 and 5), confirm the details of that reference, and add a checkmark to confirm that the reference has been cited somewhere.

The trick in all such searches is to recognize the recurring element that will be present in each of the things we're looking for. If the author has used the author–date style of citation, in which the citations resemble "Poe (1850)", the recurring pattern is that of a four-digit year. Of course, if we're editing a text that cites older documents, we might also encounter dates with one, two, three, or four digits. (This might occur, for example, when the author is citing an old manuscript based on its supposed date of creation rather than citing an archival source.) In that case, the things that remain constant in each citation are the "("

You *could also* print the references: I've recommended that you *not* print out your references, but by no means does this mean that you shouldn't do this if it works for you. If working partially on the screen and partially on paper proves most efficient or comfortable, then by all means, do it. Onscreen editing should be a tool for making our lives easier, not a dogma that we embrace to the point of foolishness. For example, even though I'm clearly an advocate of onscreen editing, I usually print out figures and tables so I can consult them as I work without having to constantly switch windows.

character that comes before the year and the ")" that follows the year, and we could search for either of these characters. (However, if the author likes parenthetical comments as much as I do, that could rapidly become tedious. I'll discuss a more efficient approach when I discuss pattern matching later in this chapter.) Another common citation style numbers the references in the bibliography sequentially, and cites the number in square brackets in the text: "[42]", for example, rather than "Adams (1995)". In this case, the search term could be either of the two square brackets.

To make the search process more concrete, let's consider the details involved in checking literature citations. Here's how this might work:

- To start the process, we'd copy the bibliography into a new document and save that document.
- Next, we'd move the cursor to the start of the main document, and search for the first reference. For example, if the manuscript uses the author–date style of citation, and we know that all references are in the first decade of the 21st century, we would specify "20" as the search term. (There are much more sophisticated search strategies, but for now, let's stick with simple patterns.)
- When we find a match, we can close the "Find and Replace" dialog box, then switch to the document containing the bibliography to check whether the found text matches the bibliographic entry. The names of all authors must be spelled identically in both places, the year must match, and the title must seem reasonable; for example, if the citation states that "*The Raven* (Poe 1846) is a touching tale of found love", yet the Poe (1846) reference is for *The Cask of Amontillado*, then clearly the author cited the wrong reference. (Note that you can't always perform this check; some citations refer to details that aren't evident from a publication's title.)
- We can now insert any required comments or make any necessary edits in the text. For example, if there's an error, we can insert a comment that describes the problem and proposes a solution. For example: "Should this date be 1845? The 1846 reference is for *The Cask*, not *The Raven*. In any event, please confirm your statement; "a touching tale of found love" is probably not the most accurate description of either *The Cask* or *The Raven*."

- If the publisher's guidelines require that each item in the bibliography must be cited somewhere in the text, we can add a checkmark of some sort (any character will do) in the bibliography at the start of the reference to indicate that it has been cited. Later, we'll check the bibliography to find any items that haven't been cited.
- We continue the process by searching for the next term in the main document that matches the "Find what" pattern, using the appropriate keyboard shortcut. (See the sidebar *Searching without the dialog box* on the next page for details on how to do this. In most software, it's not necessary to repeatedly open and close the "Find and Replace" dialog box.) We then check the new citation, as we did before.
- This process continues until we reach the end of the manuscript.
- If necessary, we can then scroll through the bibliography to find any entries that lack a checkmark. For each one, we should then search for the author's name or the year of publication in the text to verify that the item truly wasn't cited; the search function can occasionally skip past an instance of the search term if we inadvertently hold a key down too long or click twice with the mouse, and sometimes we simply forgot to add a checkmark in the bibliography. If the reference truly hasn't been cited, we should inform the author and request that they add a citation at an appropriate location in the text or delete the item from the bibliography.

You can use the search tool in this manner to find anything that has or that should have a predictable pattern. I'll discuss more sophisticated ways to find specific patterns of characters in the section *Advanced searches* later in this chapter. Here are some examples of the kinds of things you can search for in an effort to make a manuscript consistent:

- You can confirm that every term in a list such as a style sheet (see Chapter 9) has been used correctly throughout a document.
- You can check for minor variations in spelling, such as whether a compound word is set solid, hyphenated, or left open (e.g., *onscreen*, *on-screen*, and *on the screen*).
- You can search for all headings that have been formatted using a specific paragraph style (see *Advanced search and replace operations*, later in this chapter, for details), to confirm that the style has been implemented correctly. For example, authors often seem to capital-

Searching without the dialog box: Most software hides the search function under the Edit or Tools menu, and the function itself may be named "Find" or "Search". Increasing standardization of software interfaces over the past 20 years means that in most software, you can invoke this function from the keyboard, usually with Control + F (Windows) or Command + F (Macintosh). Similarly, most software offers a "find again" or "find next" function under the same menu. Where the software offers this function, you can generally close the "Find and Replace" dialog box as soon as you find the first occurrence of a term and use the keyboard shortcut to find all subsequent occurrences. Unfortunately, the keyboard shortcut for this function varies. Control + G (Windows) and Command + G (Macintosh), in which the "G" serves as an odd mnemonic device for *aGain*, is one common variant. In Word, Control (Command on the Macintosh) plus the PageUp or PageDown keys will also find (respectively) the previous and next instances of the term. If you prefer mouse shortcuts, Word lets you click (respectively) the double-up arrows or double-down arrows at the bottom of the vertical scroll bar:

More monitors merrier: This kind of task is easier if you have a very large monitor or two monitors. In that case, you can keep the bibliography window open beside the document window, and only switch to the bibliography when it's necessary to add a note or scroll in that window. This can save enormous numbers of keystrokes in a long document such as a book.

ize headings randomly, and searching through the document one heading at a time quickly reveals any inconsistencies.

- You can confirm the correctness of any sequence, such as the numbers assigned to chapters, figures, and tables. For example, search for each occurrence of the word *figure* (or its abbreviation, *Fig.*), starting at the beginning of the document, to ensure that the author has cited every figure and that there are no gaps or duplications in the figure numbering. Then repeat this process for all tables, using "table" as the search term.
- In a statistics or mathematics manuscript, most style guides require that variables and parameters be italicized. When you encounter any variable, you can immediately search the manuscript to find all occurrences of that variable and italicize any that are not already italicized.
- If your style guide requires the use of serial commas (i.e., "A, B, and C" rather than "A, B and C"), you can search for the word "and" (preceded by a space so you won't also find all occurrences of *candy*, *bandaids*, and *pandemonium*). Where necessary, add the missing comma.

And so on. Anywhere your author has used a predictable pattern to state something or format part of the text provides an opportunity to search for and confirm the consistency of that pattern. Doing this one instance of the term at a time can be tedious when the term is used very commonly, but it's the only way to ensure consistency if two or more

Don't trust Word's automatic numbering: You might expect that modern software would let you automatically number items that follow a simple sequence, and for the most part, you'd be right. However, Word's automatic numbering has a well-known, long-standing bug in which Word occasionally restarts numbering when it shouldn't or forgets to restart numbering when it should. Searching for each style that is defined to use automatic numbering is a great way to spot and fix these problems. For a simple and elegant fix (until Microsoft comes up with a better solution), see David Knopf's article on this topic (www.knopf.com/tips/autonumber.html). Ignore the references to RoboHelp, which is a Word-based tool for creating online help files; the solution works equally well in Word by itself.

potentially correct alternatives exist and these alternatives might confuse the reader. The section *Global search and replace operations* later in this chapter describes a more efficient way to perform such changes when you are absolutely certain that the same change must be made in every single instance—and describes the necessary precautions.

Where we only need to compare the text with a short list that could fit in one small window, we can display that list beside the main document window. Most software lets us automatically line up documents side by side or one above another (called "tiling" in many programs); if not, it's easy to manually resize and reposition the windows. (See *Window juggling* in Chapter 4 for details.) As we work through the main document, we can simply glance at the reference document each time we come across something that must be checked against that reference. This won't work as well for a bibliography, which is usually too long to display in a single screen, but it's a wonderful tool when we're dealing with a limited number of things that we need to look up occasionally. For example, in some of the scientific manuscripts that I edit, the author may introduce a dozen or more acronyms that are unfamiliar to me. To understand what the author is saying, I need to look up each acronym each time it appears until the meanings begin to make enough sense that I've got them memorized. I could use the search tool to repeatedly find the original definition of that acronym, or jot down notes on a scrap of paper, but it's easier to list those acronyms in a second window that remains constantly visible as I edit the manuscript.

A brief word on distractions and "getting lost"

The temptations offered by the search tool carry two serious risks: first, the risk of distraction (losing our train of thought), and second, the risk of getting lost and forgetting where we began our search. Indeed, if you have a high-speed Internet connection and include the Web in your repertoire of search tools, it's easy to be carried entirely away and forget to return to the actual work—particularly for those less intellectually stimulating jobs. (For more details on using the Web productively, see Chapter 14, *Using the Internet to improve your editing*.)

The first risk is arguably the greater, at least if you have more self-discipline than I do. When we're focusing on substantive editing, whether we're following a complex argument through to its conclusion to confirm whether it makes sense and is consistent with the rest of the text or whether we're simply massaging a single phrase until it communicates efficiently, we should carry that process through to the end. Interruptions can force us to start the whole process over or can make it take longer than necessary. Interrupting substantive editing to fix relatively minor consistency problems disrupts our concentration and makes it harder to return to that previous mental state. At worst, it can make us lose a subtle yet important point dangling right at the edge of our perception, and thereby prevent us from gaining a sudden understanding of that point (*satori*, or perhaps a slowly developing *gestalt*) and using it to improve the communication. Thus, if you're going to use the search function to begin a consistency check through a document, force yourself to complete your current thought process first. If necessary, jot a note on a scrap of paper to remind you what aspect of consistency you suddenly felt a need to check.

Ideally, if the issue is as simple as a question of spelling rather than as complex as the correct use of a word in two different contexts, add it to your style sheet and move on; you can always check it later. It's more efficient to do certain kinds of checks, such as the literature citations discussed in the previous section of this chapter and the style sheet entries discussed in Chapter 9, in a single step after you've completed the main edit. However, sometimes we really do need to stop editing and do a consistency check. If the issue that we've suddenly perceived is complex and will affect subsequent editing, it may be useful to complete the current task and then perform the consistency check immediately, so we'll have a solution ready the next time we encounter the problem.

If that kind of distraction happens with any frequency, it's important to be able to return quickly to where we left off. Getting lost (the second type of problem) is a relatively minor risk, since it's always possible to remember (perhaps with some effort) the last section we were

Don't rule out paper: Even though I'm a strong advocate of on-screen editing, I keep a pad of paper and handful of pens beside my keyboard for jotting notes. Sometimes, as in the case of building a style sheet, it's more appropriate to type these notes in a word processor file—but sometimes there's simply no substitute for paper.

working on and return there, but it's better to get there with a minimal waste of time and effort. There are a variety of ways to do this:

- We can scroll through the manuscript, one page at a time, until we find our starting point. That's clearly a slow process, but it does work *in extremis*.
- If we remember the last few words we were editing before beginning our search, we can search for those words. (This works most efficiently if the particular search phrase is relatively uncommon in the document. Searching for *and* is rarely productive; searching for *it is the beating of his hideous heart!* is more likely to prove useful.)
- If we remember (or have recorded on a scrap of paper) the page number where we left off editing, we can use the "go to" function to return to that page. See the section *Really big jumps* in Chapter 5 for details on how this function may work in different programs.
- If our software offers a "bookmark" feature, we can use that instead. The section *Really big jumps* in Chapter 5 provides details on how this feature may work in different programs. As these bookmarks are generally invisible unless we explicitly instruct our software to display them, we'll need to remember to remove them before returning the manuscript to the author. Add a note on your pad of paper or in your style sheet so you won't forget!
- The simplest method of all is to manually insert a few special characters, such as <>, as a bookmark. This eliminates the need to use any of the software's menus (you can initiate a search by pressing Control + F in Windows or Command + F on the Macintosh), and the shortcut can be typed quickly and found quickly using the search tool. Because most software highlights the search term when it finds the term, you can simply press the Delete or Backspace key to remove your bookmark from the document as soon as you return to your starting point. Moreover, because these simple bookmarks are unlikely to legitimately appear anywhere in the text, even a careless proofreader will spot and remove them if you forget to do so before returning the document to the author. Still, it's wise to leave yourself a reminder to check.

All these methods use the computer the way that technology should be used: to make life easier. Each option has its advantages and drawbacks, so the key is to try each one to find out which best suits your work style. Sometimes comfort is far more important than sheer theoretical efficiency, since you'll naturally use something comfortable more readily than something that is extraordinarily efficient but uncomfortable to use.

For most consistency checks, I recommend starting at the top of the manuscript, since this lets you see the search term in its first context and that context sets the tone for all subsequent instances of the word. However, that's by no means the only way to proceed. If the search term appears in the current sentence and you use the search tool to begin making changes from that point onwards, the search function will eventually reach the end of the file and ask whether you want to continue from the start of the document. If you choose to do so, the software will eventually return you to your starting point and stop the search.

Options for refining your search

Most software offers myriad options that can help you do more than match a specific sequence of numbers or letters. Unfortunately, many of these options are hidden where you'd never think to look for them. For example, in more recent versions of Word, the basic "Find and Replace" dialog box has been streamlined to show only the most basic options, presumably to avoid intimidating new users. Unfortunately, my experience as a teacher suggests that this approach also conceals the options from many experienced computer users. If the full range of possibilities isn't visible, click the "More" button or the small downward-pointing triangle (which valiantly attempts but fails to communicate the concept "click here to expand this dialog box") to display more options.

In this section, I'll present the options most commonly available in a range of software. Later in this chapter, in the section *Advanced search*

Watch where the cursor is: Powerful software such as Word lets you specify sophisticated options for both the "Find what" field and the "Replace with" field. To ensure that you specify these patterns correctly, make sure that the text cursor is in the correct field before you define the options for that field; it's easy to inadvertently set the options for the wrong field, and have to repeat the search or undo a search and replace operation.

and replace operations, I'll discuss some extremely sophisticated (but correspondingly complex) options for narrowing your search to an exquisite degree. The most common searches fall into two main categories: matching text patterns or properties, and finding special characters.

Matching patterns

The search tools I first learned to use were hopelessly literal, and if you didn't precisely specify the search term you were looking for, you wouldn't find it, even if it was clear to the human eye that the search term was present in the manuscript. Modern software is far more sophisticated. Among other things, it typically provides some or all of the following options:

Wildcards (variants)

When you select this option, you can ask the software to seek variants of a word or phrase that contain *any* single character or range of characters at one or more specific positions within the search term. Most commonly, you'll see *?* used to stand in for a single character and * used to represent a series of characters. For example, searching for *s?ng* would find *sing*, *song*, *sang*, and *sung* (i.e., the question mark would be replaced with the single characters *i*, *o*, *a*, and *u*), whereas searching for *s*ng* would find these words plus *stetting* and *searching*. In some software, including Word, you must select a checkbox with a name such as "use wildcards" so the software knows that you're not searching for ? or *.

Matching case (capitalization)

Depending on which software you use, this option may find only text that has a capitalization pattern identical to that specified in the "Find what" field (so that you could search for *Red Death* without also finding instances of *red death* and *RED DEATH*), may change the capitalization of the replacement text to match the pattern of the found text (so that if you are replacing *black* with *red*, the software will also replace *Black* with *Red*), or may replace the text using the capitalization specified in the "Replace with" field (replacing *red death, Red death,* and *RED DEATH* with *Red Death*). Spend a few moments learning the idiosyncrasies of how your software handles this specific option.

Homonyms ("sounds like")

This option instructs the software to look for phonetic misspellings. It isn't particularly accurate, but when it works, it can work surprisingly well; for example, searching for *masque* would also find *mask*. It's worth trying this option if you only vaguely remember the spelling of a word.

"Whole words only"

This option lets you narrow your search to include only whole words rather than parts of words. For example, using this option to search for *beat* would not find *beating heart*.

Word variants ("Find all word forms")

This option lets you find related word forms, such as *laugh*, *laughed*, *laughing*, and perhaps *laughter*. For example, if you're trying to use a particular verb in the present tense throughout a manuscript, this option would find most other forms of the verb and give you a chance to decide whether to change each to present tense.

Location ("Find where")

This option allows you to constrain the location in which the search will take place. For example, Word lets you search only within the main document or only within the comments pane. Some software will let you define the direction of a search—forward from the cursor position to the end of the document, or backwards from the cursor position to the start. More powerful search tools, including those in Word, will let you select "All open documents" to extend your search if you have several windows open (e.g., different chapters of the same book) and want to perform the same search in each document. If your version of Word supports this feature (it seems to have disappeared some time around Word XP/Word 2004), you'll find it in a dropdown menu below the "Find" or "Find Next" button, above the checkbox for "Match Case"; by default, this displays "Current Document All".

Some software, including Word, also lets you select text before you start the search. The software then confines the search to the selected text instead of searching the whole document. This can be very useful if (for example) you only want to search within a section such as the bibliography.

Formatting

Most software also lets you search for characteristics of the text such as its font (e.g., Times New Roman 12 point), format (e.g., boldfaced), style (e.g., the Body Text paragraph style), alignment (e.g., flush right), and language (e.g., Canadian French). In Word, these options are available by clicking the "Format" button to display the various categories of formatting that can be searched for; each of these categories has many options. For more information, see the section *Advanced search and replace operations* later in this chapter.

Finding special characters

Most software makes it possible to search for a range of special characters, ranging from symbols and letters from foreign languages to some of the specific codes that the software uses to define formatting or provide special features such as cross-references that update automatically when their destinations change. In general, you can search for these characters by selecting them from a special menu or by typing codes that represent them (referred to as "control codes" in Word) into the search box. If you're not sure what a character is or how to type it yourself, try copying it from the text and pasting it into the "Find what" field; depending on the software you're using and how special the character is, this may or may not work.

In Word, you can access many special characters from the list of available options by clicking the "Special" button at the bottom of the "Find and Replace" dialog box. This displays a popup menu of the

Using "Go to" to find something: In Word, some of these control codes can be searched for by name, type, or number. For example, the find and replace function offers an additional "Go to" tab that lets you go directly to a specific instance of some code (e.g., a footnote) rather than simply finding the next instance. Word lets you specify which instance to find:

- **By name:** bookmarks and other named objects such as embedded spreadsheets
- **By type:** fields
- **By number:** comments, endnotes, equations, footnotes, graphics, headings, lines, pages, sections, and tables. For these items, you can also move ahead two or more instances at a time by adding a plus or minus sign followed by a number. For example, +2 would skip ahead to the second item following the cursor position, whereas −1 would skip backwards to the previous item before the cursor position.

options that are available in the current context. (If you can't see this button, click the "More" button or the downward-pointing arrow to expand the dialog box and reveal your other options.) Selecting a special character inserts that character into the "Find what" field (or into the "Replace with" field if you place the cursor there first), but in the form of a control code. In Word, control codes are represented by the caret character (the ^ that appears above the 6 on most keyboards) plus a letter or symbol that defines the specific control code. Once you know these shortcuts, you can type them yourself without making a separate trip to the Special menu. If you're convinced, as I am, that it's faster to work from the keyboard than to constantly reach for the mouse, spend some time exploring this menu and learning the codes for the special characters you most often need to find.

The available options change if you make different selections elsewhere in the dialog box. For example, with none of the checkboxes selected, Word lets you choose from the following special characters or type the associated control code:

Special character	Control code
any single character	^?
any single digit (number)	^#
any single letter	^$
carets	^^
column breaks	^n
comment markers ("annotations")	^a
contents of the clipboard	^c (not available in all versions of Word)
em dashes (—)	^+
en dashes (–)	^=
endnote markers	^e

Special character	Control code
fields (used to perform certain automated functions)	^d
footnote markers	^f
graphics	^g
manual line breaks	^l
manual page breaks	^m or ^k, depending on your version of Word
non-breaking hyphens	^~
non-breaking spaces	^s
optional hyphens	^-
paragraph markers	^p
section breaks	^b
tab characters	^t
text box	There doesn't appear to be one, though ^001 may work in some instances (e.g., for inline text boxes).
white space (multiple spaces and tab characters)	^w

Note that the letters in these shortcuts must all be lower-case; you cannot, for example, search for *^P* if you want to find the end-of-paragraph marker. It's possible to combine these control codes with other search terms, including other control codes. For example, if you wanted to search for the word *editing* at the start of a paragraph rather than in the middle of a paragraph, you would search for *^pEditing*; this pattern tells Word to search for the end of a paragraph (*^p*), then check whether the first word at the start of the next paragraph is *Editing*.

Be extremely cautious when you try to *replace* any special characters that the software uses to perform a calculation, look up information, or insert information from another location. For example, you could delete all graphics in a document by specifying ^*g* (any graphic) as the "Find what" pattern, and leaving the "Replace with" field blank; this translates as an instruction to "find all graphics and replace them with a blank (i.e., with nothing)". You could also apply specific formatting to each graphic (e.g., spacing around it) in a single step. You could not, however, replace all current graphics with updated versions of the same graphics—at least, not without some fairly complicated programming. (See Chapter 11 for more information on creating macros.) That kind of limitation may be frustrating, but it's not fatal. In contrast, you can wreck a document beyond hope of recovery by replacing things like comment markers and footnotes. These are numbered, and the numbers are recalculated by the software each time you insert or delete a new marker; interfering with that automation is rarely wise.

Word also lets you search for (but not replace) many of the characters that you can't see on your keyboard but that are part of the Unicode character set. To do so, type ^u followed by the number assigned to the character. For example, you can find the Greek letter alpha (α) using the search text ^u945 (where the 945 represents the Unicode decimal value of this letter). You can find the complete official list of these codes for most known languages at the Unicode Organization's Web site (www.unicode.org/charts/), but unfortunately, the codes are provided in hexadecimal format, which Word won't recognize. To convert them into decimal format, search the Web using the keywords "hexadecimal to decimal conversion utility" (without the quotes). For example, try EasyCalculation.com's Hexadecimal to decimal converter (www.easycalculation.com/hex-converter.php).

Replacing text one instance at a time

It's generally possible to replace all instances of a search term in a single step—an operation called a "global" search and replace. (For details, see *Global search and replace operations* later in this chapter.) The problem with doing this is that if you haven't specified the search term sufficiently carefully, you may end up replacing many instances of that term that shouldn't be replaced, such as when it appears inside a larger word, a quotation, or the title of a bibliographic reference. (Yes, I've done all of these. Oops!) Such a "blind" approach doesn't provide a chance to confirm whether each instance of the search term should in fact be changed. Thus, many types of search and replace are best handled one instance at a time. This clearly takes considerably longer than replacing every instance in a single step, but it's safer and often more effective, and effectiveness is more important than raw speed.

When the search function finds a term, it highlights the term so you can find it more easily, but this highlighting also means that the term is selected. (Remember: you can now close the dialog box and use keyboard shortcuts to find the next occurrence of the term.) This has a consequence that can be turned into a major tool for efficiency: If you start typing, most software replaces the highlighted term with whatever you type. If you need to delete the highlighted term, this saves a single keystroke (you don't have to manually delete the whole term) but you can take that small efficiency one large step further: if you copy the most likely replacement text (a word, phrase, or sentence) to the clipboard before you begin your search (Control + C in Windows, Command + C on the Macintosh), you can paste this copied text into the document (Control + V in Windows, Command + V on the Macintosh), instantly replacing the highlighted text. If you didn't think of this before you began the search, you can instead copy the replacement text the first time you type it and use it in subsequent replacements. This is a great way to work your way through a document one instance of a search term at a time and replace some, but not all, instances.

This approach also makes it quick and easy to perform a series of minor changes that might otherwise require considerable cursor movement and mousing around or that might be difficult to elegantly perform using a global replace operation. Consider, for example, a mistake I must often correct in the science manuscripts that I edit. Many of my authors cite multi-author works as follows: "Poe, et al., 2005". The comma before the year is required by many journal style guides, but I've never seen a journal that wants a comma after the author's name. I could certainly do a global search and replace to fix this problem everywhere (i.e., to replace ", et al." with " et al."), but if I'm tracking such changes, that would delete the entire search phrase (starting with the comma after the name and ending with the period after "al") and create much more red ink (or its onscreen equivalent) in the document than is necessary. In fact, I could also turn off revision tracking, do the search and replace, turn on revision tracking again, and leave the author a small note explaining what I've done. (This is precisely the kind of change that it's not necessary for authors to approve.) But there's an alternative that not only produces the minimal amount of change (i.e., deletes only the comma) but that also has wider application:

- Search for the recurring pattern that you want to fix, but start the search term with the first character of the text you're looking for or end it with the last character. In the comma example, that search term could be ", et al" (without the quotes).
- Find the first occurrence of this error, then close the "Find and Replace" dialog box.
- Because the search function highlights the entire phrase, pressing the left or right arrow key moves the cursor to (respectively) the beginning or end of the highlighted text. You can now perform the necessary correction—insert text, delete text, or, in this specific example, delete the problem comma with a single keystroke.
- Use the "Find next" keyboard shortcut to move on to the next occurrence of the problem and repeat your edit, if necessary.

A little thought will reveal many other ways to use this approach to speed your editing those times when a global search and replace isn't safe; it's particularly useful when you need to turn a word into a phrase by adding one or two more words before or after the search term. Combined with the technique of copying replacement text to the clip-

Pasting with minimal fuss and bother: Some versions of Word exhibit an annoying behavior if you try this approach. When you paste text beside the cursor, Word helpfully does a "smart paste" that inserts space around the pasted text. Many times, this saves you the effort of inserting that space yourself. But if you're trying to fix a word (e.g., by adding a suffix), this feature actually creates more work because you then have to delete the space. You could perform another search operation to find all the erroneous spaces and delete them, but it's easier to disable this spacing feature: open the Options (Windows) or Preferences (Macintosh) dialog box, select the Edit tab, and deselect "Use smart cut and paste". The problem will mostly disappear, though there are a few exceptions you'll still have to deal with manually.

board before you begin the search, this can be a tremendous productivity booster.

Global search and replace operations

Thus far in this chapter, I've discussed how to search through a manuscript to find individual instances of a search term so you can decide what to do about each instance. This technique is always useful, but sometimes it's not nearly as efficient as performing the replacement throughout the manuscript in a single step. If you're fortunate enough to encounter a situation in which the author has used two words to communicate the same concept, neither word is used in any other context, and only one of the words is actually permitted for that concept (perhaps because of a publisher's style preferences), you can replace the incorrect word with the correct word throughout the file (globally) in a single step. You can do this by clicking a "Replace all" or "Change all" button in the "Find and Replace" dialog box.

For some kinds of global corrections, such as correcting obvious typos or replacing all double spaces after a period with single spaces, there's no need to force the author to review and approve each such change. When you're confident that this is the case, and have the author's permission to do so (there's that "dialogue" concept again!), you can turn off revision tracking, then click "Change all" in the "Find and Replace" dialog box. But far more often, you should make all global changes with change tracking enabled, since this makes it easier for you to spot any errors in a subsequent pass through the manuscript, and gives the author a chance to correct any errors you may not have noticed. If you collect a list of all likely search and replace operations, you can do the global change before you begin your first or final editing pass; this gives you a chance to spot any problems that resulted from the changes. For example, if you have created a style sheet (as described in Chapter 9) for previous chapters in a book or have been given a style sheet by the client, you can use this approach.

If you decide to replace a word or phrase everywhere, be exquisitely careful, whether or not you track your changes! Never attempt a global search and replace at the end of a long and stressful day or at any other time when you're too tired or stressed or otherwise preoccupied to think straight, as might be the case if your name is Fortunato and you're completing a rush edit over a cask of Amontillado; at those times, concentrate on more mechanical forms of editing that you can do safely with little conscious effort. Injudicious choices for the "Find what" part of the find and replace operation can lead to replacing far more words than you'd anticipated and create a huge problem for you (worse yet, for the author) to correct. These problems arise from what's called *stemming*: when you specify a search word that forms the root (i.e., the *stem*) of other words, the search word *and all other words that contain the stem* will be changed by a global replacement operation. For example, a colleague once replaced all instances of *day* with *night* to correct a timing problem, but forgot to type a space in front of *day*. (In Word, selecting the "Whole words only" option would also work.) As a result, she changed all days of the week to nights (e.g., *Friday* became *Frinight*). This kind of accident suggests that as a general rule, you should never try a global search and replace if you won't have time to read through the document one last time to spot such problems.

These problems can be quite subtle at times. For example, I once caused myself a fair bit of unnecessary work when I decided to fix page ranges globally in a bibliography. The author had formatted the ranges without a space after the "p.", so that they appeared as, for example, "p.1-3". I chose to add that space globally, forgetting that many of the author names in the bibliography looked something like "E.A. Poe", where a space between the initials would be wrong in this particular style. That left me to search through the bibliography to find all such

Testing whether a global replacement is safe: Want to do a global search and replace, but need a way to quickly check whether you were perhaps too ambitious? Use the trick described in the sidebar on the next page to highlight all the newly inserted words, and skim quickly through the document looking for possible problems. Alternatively, use the formatting options described in the section *Advanced search and replace operations* later in this chapter to change the color or size of the replacement text so that it stands out from the background. For example, if you're tracking changes in red, change the inserted text to bright green. After you've fixed any problems introduced by the global search and replace, do a global search and replace to replace all green text with text of the usual color.

names and correct my error. If I'd been less fortunate, and had changed another type of abbreviation ending in a period, I might also have had to search through the entire text to find additional problems.

A similar problem can occur if you perform a global search and replace in a document that includes a bibliography or extensive quotations from the works of other authors, which must not be changed. If the search text might conceivably be present in either the bibliography or the quotations, it's generally unsafe to do a global replacement. Though you can sometimes exclude portions of a document from the operation, it's easy to forget this step. Moreover, most software won't

Highlighting all occurrences of a search term

Word offers a nifty shortcut that can quickly reveal whether a global search and replace operation would be safe. Type the search term in the "Find what" field. Then select the option "Highlight all items found in", immediately below this field, and use the dropdown menu to specify where Word should search for that term (e.g., the main document, headers and footers, comments). Clicking the "Find All" button will highlight all matches in the text in a single step. If you click in the document window or press any key, the highlighting disappears and you have to start over again. But so long as you only use the scroll bar to move through the document, you can scan one screen at a time, examining each highlighted term. If any of the terms requires special treatment, don't use a global search and replace.

If you refined your search sufficiently, you can format all the highlighted terms in a single operation (e.g., change the font, italicize the selected text) by using the mouse to open the appropriate menu and select the desired option. You can't type replacement text, however, since pressing any key or clicking in the document window deselects the highlighted terms. If you cleverly copied the replacement word or phrase to the clipboard before you highlighted all occurrences, you can replace all the terms simultaneously by opening the Edit menu with the mouse (don't use the keyboard!) and selecting Paste. However, if you're confident enough to try this trick (i.e., no obvious exceptions require special treatment), it's easier to do a global search and replace, as described later in this chapter.

let you exclude multiple sections of a document simultaneously. In that case, performing the replacement one term at a time is a wiser approach.

If you do opt to "Replace all" despite these cautions, there are several steps you should take to protect yourself from potential problems and recover more easily if you err:

- Look for patterns that let you constrain your search and replace operations. For example, if you don't want to make any changes in titles or quotations and know that all titles and quotations appear in italics, you can specify that the "Find what" pattern match only search terms that are *not* formatted as italic. I'll discuss some possibilities, including this specific example, in the next section.
- Consider waiting until after you've completed your first pass through the document before you attempt the global replacement. The knowledge you've acquired after reading the whole document permits a better-informed decision about whether a search term is being used consistently and will not appear anywhere that a global change would cause problems. If you're not finished your first edit, record the potential problem in your style sheet or on a scrap of paper, and wait until you've finished.
- Find and examine many instances of the search term in the text in order to decide whether a global change is safe. (For example, use the "Highlight all" option that I described earlier.) This is time-consuming, but it does offer a chance to spot instances where the replacement would cause problems; if you don't spot any after a brief search, you can then boldly decide to try the global replace.
- If you see a significant problem after the global replace operation, undo the operation immediately. Most word processors let you do this if you haven't yet typed anything else, usually by opening the Edit menu and selecting Undo; the usual keyboard shortcut is Command + Z for the Macintosh or Control + Z in Windows. How-

Deleting all occurrences of a search term: Here's a useful trick for deleting a specific search term throughout a manuscript: To remove the characters that you find, leave the "replace with" field empty. In effect, you're telling the software to replace what it finds with a blank (i.e., with nothing).

ever, that doesn't always work, particularly with older word processors with less robust undo functions. Thus:

- *Always* save the document *before* you make any global change, especially before attempting a complex replacement operation. If you've made a mistake you can't easily undo, and don't notice it for a few minutes, you can immediately close the document without saving your changes, then reopen the saved version and try again more carefully.
- After you make the change, examine the number of changes that the software reports. Sometimes the reported number of changes is considerably larger than you might expect, and this suggests that you might have chosen the wrong search term. If so, stop editing for a few moments to search through the document for the replacement text to see whether any of the changes are incorrect.
- Because search and replace errors often become obvious during final read-throughs or spellchecking, *always* leave time for a final pass through the manuscript whenever you replace one or more terms globally.

There's one more *gotcha!* to beware: capitalization and formatting. Most software is very literal about following your instructions, and will use exactly the capitalization pattern that you specified when you typed the replacement text. For example, Word replaces the original text with

Constraining searches to part of a document: Most software lets you constrain search and replace operations to a specific part of the document, most often by selecting that part before you open the "Find and Replace" dialog box. This is useful if you want to replace a search term only in one section of the text but not elsewhere. For example, you may want to correct a spelling in the main text but not in the bibliography, where the incorrect spelling may actually appear in the titles of one or more references. When the software completes the global replacement operation, it usually displays a dialog box asking whether you want to extend that operation to the rest of the text. Don't. It's very easy to reflexively press Enter or Return and accept this option if you're tired or working under deadline, thereby undoing all your careful work in selecting the relevant text before you began.

the new text, but retains the capitalization pattern of the text that it replaces (e.g., all caps, all lower-case, only the first letter capitalized). This is generally a good idea if you consider, for example, that words found at the start of a sentence or within an all-caps heading should retain their original capitalization after being replaced: if the software used the capitalization pattern that you specified for the replacement term rather than the original pattern, you'd have to hunt down each of the changed words to see whether you need to fix the fix. Where it's necessary to use your specified pattern rather than the existing pattern, the solution in Word is to select the "Match case" option at the bottom of the "Find and Replace" dialog box. (You may need to click the "More options" button or a downward-pointing triangle to expand the dialog box to reveal the "Match case" option.) Word will then use the capitalization that you specified for the search term, excluding instances of the search term with different capitalization, and will replace any search terms that it does find with the capitalization that you specified for the replacement term. If you opt to "match case", think carefully about your choice to ensure that you won't be creating more work than you saved.

Advanced search and replace operations

Earlier in the chapter, I provided some general guidance on how tools built into the software's search and replace functions can help you narrow down your search; for example, I described searches for sound-alike words and variant spellings, and the use of wildcards to find words that differ in only a single character. However, these tools are designed to be somewhat generic solutions because the programmers cannot anticipate every possibility. For those cases when they did not correctly anticipate our specific needs, it pays to learn some of the more advanced tools that are available. These tools may be referred to using terms such as "advanced search and replace", "pattern matching", or "regular expressions", depending on the software, so have a look at your software's online help for details on how the search and replace tools have been implemented. All of the options that I'll discuss in this section are available through Word's "Find and Replace" dialog box, and have more or less powerful equivalents in other software.

A word of warning: The details of advanced search and replace operations can be quite complicated because the designers of Word didn't go out of their way to make things easy for us—but more importantly, because it can be difficult to correctly define the pattern that you're searching for. Don't worry if you don't understand the details. You can survive quite well as an editor by learning nothing more about search and replace than what I've already described in this chapter. But when you're ready to tackle really difficult challenges, the details I've provided in the rest of this chapter will help.

Find and replace options

One powerful tool for refining searches is the ability to specify the formatting that has been applied to a search term and the formatting we want to apply each time we replace that item with new text. For example, in a book that contains a search term both in the text and in many quotations that have been formatted in italic type, you might want to find only the terms outside the quotations. (This follows the general rule that we should never alter the wording of quotations other than to correct transcription errors.) Similarly, it might be necessary to find all instances of a given foreign word and italicize them—a common style choice for non-English words. Word's search tool can perform these and many other formatting changes. To do so, click the "Format" button at the bottom of the "Find and Replace" dialog box to display the available formatting options. These fall into the following categories:

Really powerful searches: Grep, the "general regular expression parser", is a standard UNIX program that permits remarkably complex (and correspondingly powerful) search and replace operations. Versions are also available for the Macintosh and Windows. If a job requires large amounts of complex text twiddling, you may save considerable time by obtaining the author's permission to convert the document into a format compatible with your operating system's version of grep, perform all the necessary cleanup, then restore the text to your word processor for the remainder of the editing. Alternatively, look into Jack Lyon's MegaReplacer utility for Word (www.editorium.com/14843.htm).

Font characteristics

These options let you search for any formatting characteristic you can specify using the Font dialog box (e.g., typeface, point size, and the use of boldface, italics, and underlining). For example, these options would let you find all occurrences of the company name Microsoft and apply italics, the correct corporate font, and the correct corporate color to each one.

Paragraph characteristics

These options let you specify any characteristic available in the Paragraph dialog box (e.g., alignment, spacing, initial indent). For example, you could use this to find any paragraph that had a hanging indent of 0.5 inches instead of a first-line indent as a result of incorrectly applied paragraph formatting.

Tab settings

If you encounter a spacing problem related to any of the tab settings that can be defined in the Tabs dialog box, you can find and fix the problem. For example, you could find all decimal-aligned tab stops so you could check whether a right-aligned tab stop is required instead.

Language

This lets you confine your search to text defined using any language (e.g., U.S. English) that is available in the Languages dialog box, or change the language definition for certain words. For example, in a document containing many foreign words, you could globally replace their language setting with the correct language each time you encounter such words. Subsequently, Word will use the correct dictionary for that language during spellchecks. (See Chapter 10, *Spelling and grammar checkers*, for more details on language options.)

Learning the complexities of search and replace: Although all of these options are available in Windows versions of Word, not all are available for certain Macintosh versions. The only way to know for sure is to try them—or to download Jack Lyon's excellent (though complicated) discussion of advanced search and replace (www.editorium.com/ftp/AdvancedFind.zip), which lists most of the exceptions and some workarounds.

Frames

This option allows you to find frames (borders around text or a graphic) that have specific characteristics, or to change those characteristics. For example, this option would let you set a consistent style and size of text wrap for all graphics in the document in a single operation.

Styles

This option finds text formatted using any of the paragraph or character styles (e.g., Body text, Heading 1) available in the Styles dialog box. For example, you could use this option to work through the document, one heading style at a time, to ensure that the capitalization of each was correct (e.g., only the first letter and proper nouns capitalized vs. "title caps" with all main words capitalized). Or you could replace all Heading 1 headings with your own custom heading style in a single step.

Highlighting

This option lets you find any text that has been highlighted using the highlighter marker tool (available in the Reviewing toolbar):

Word's highlighter marker tool

Although you could certainly scroll through a long document to find this easily visible highlighting, then manually remove the highlighting using the Highlight tool in the Reviewing toolbar, it's much easier to do so in a single step using the search and replace tools.

Adding power to wildcards

Most software offers at least a basic "find something that looks like..." function, but this function becomes quite sophisticated in some programs. Earlier in the chapter, I introduced basic wildcard functions that are present in most software (?, $, #, and * to find, respectively, any single character, any single letter, any single number, and any group of characters). Though you can accomplish quite a bit with these options, more powerful options are usually available for complicated matching of patterns. If you select the "Use wildcards" checkbox that Word offers, the following additional options become available:

To search for	Type	Description and example
Grouped characters	( )	The round brackets let you specify that the enclosed text should be treated as a single unit. This is most useful in replacement operations (see the next section) in which you want to treat each group separately or in defining search terms that appear at the start or end of a word. • Example: Searching for *(copy)(editor)* would let you globally change *copyeditor* to *substantive editor* without affecting *copyediting*. This example is a trivial one because you could perform the same change without using grouping. For more sophisticated examples, see the next section, *Replacement options*.
Any character in a list	[ ]	The search will find words containing one of the characters listed between the brackets at the indicated position. Note that these characters are not separated by any spaces or punctuation inside the brackets. • Example: Searching for *wr[io]te* would find both *write* and *wrote*.
Any character in a range	[-]	Ranges must be defined between the square brackets in ascending order (i.e., smallest number first, or in alphabetic order). These ranges are case-sensitive, so *A-Z* would find only capital letters, whereas *a-z* would find only lowercase letters. • Example: Searching for *[1-3]* would find any instance of *1, 2,* or *3* in a document.
Beginning of a word	<	• Example: Searching for *<copy* would find *copyeditor* but not *photocopy*.

To search for	Type	Description and example
End of a word	>	• Example: Searching for *write*> would find *rewrite* but not *writer*.
Exclusion ("not")	[!]	When the "not" character occurs inside square brackets, it means that words containing any of the characters inside the brackets will not be found by the search. • Example: Searching for *[!copy]edit* would find *editor* and *creditor* but not *copyeditor*.
At least one occurrence of the pattern	@	Finds any text in which the character or group of characters before the @ occurs at least once. • Example: Searching for *(ing)@* would find both *sing* and *singing*
A specific number of occurrences of a pattern	{ }	This search pattern specifies how often the character or group of characters preceding the brace brackets should occur. You can search for: • an exact number of occurrences of a character: For example, *i{2}* would find both *Hawaii* and *skiing*. • at least the specified number of occurrences of a character: For example, *9{2,}* would skip *9*, but would find *99* and *1999*. • a range of occurrences of a character: For example, *0{1,3}* would find *0*, *0.01*, *0.001*, and *0.0001*, but not *1.00001* • **Note:** This pattern doesn't work in Word 2001 and Word X for the Macintosh, but should work in previous and later versions.

To search for	Type	Description and example
Special characters used in wildcard searches	\	Special measures are required to find characters such as *, #, and ? that are themselves defined as a wildcards; to do so, type a backslash (\) before the character in question. • Example: Typing *\?* will let you find question marks as part of a wildcard search—a useful trick when you're editing one of those authors who insists on using !!! to exclaim loudly or ??? to indicate extreme puzzlement.

Replacement options

Most of the patterns or formats or special characters that you can find using the search tools can also be specified as the replacement pattern or format in the "Replace with" field—in theory, if not always in practice, as there are occasional frustrating exceptions. For example, you can find all underlined text and change it to italicized text in a single search and replace operation, and you can replace parts of words or phrases with different words or phrases, and change their formats. However, there's a major quirk in how this replacement occurs: some software requires you to retype the "Find what" text in the "Replace with" field to apply a format change (rather than replacing the search term with new text), but other software doesn't—or does so only part of the time. You'll need to test your software to find out how it handles this issue. In Word, for example, you run into the following discrepancy:

If you want to simply change the search term's formatting, there's no problem: leave the "Replace with" field blank, and simply apply the new formatting option (e.g., italics) in that field. However, if you want to replace text that you found using wildcard options, you'll have to be more specific. To replace whatever search term the software finds with the same characters, but formatted differently, you must type *^&* (the control code that means "use the text that was found by the search") in the "Replace with" field. For example, to boldface all numbers in a document, you would do the following:

- Select "Use wildcards".
- In the "Find what" field, type *[0-9]*.
- In the "Replace with" field, type ^& and then, with the cursor still in that field, click the "Format" button, select Font, and set the style to Bold.

This extra step of typing *^&* would be unnecessary if you were using a specific search term (e.g., only the number *9*) rather than a range of values or other pattern that must be matched. Whenever you define the specific text to be found, it's easy for the software to figure out what you want to do, but as soon as you multiply the possibilities, you need to be more specific so the software will understand your intentions. The problem is exacerbated somewhat by quirks in the way the pattern matching is implemented; for example, Word distinguishes between an ordinary carriage return (¶) character, which means nothing more than "begin a new paragraph", and the special paragraph marker that it uses to store formatting information. Many of these distinctions are represented using a series of standard (ANSI) character codes; I won't present those here, but if you're intrigued by the possibilities inherent in these advanced search and replace tools, download Jack Lyon's excellent discussion of the subject (www.editorium.com/ftp/AdvancedFind.zip). In addition to summarizing all of the search tips I've listed in this book plus many more, Jack presents a series of examples that show explicitly how you can use these tools to solve some remarkably thorny problems and provides a useful macro for discovering the ANSI code for any character. Jack's Web site (www.editorium.com) also provides

An exception for the Macintosh: On the Macintosh, certain ANSI characters differ from those used in Windows, and wildcard searches don't always work properly. If you need to use an ANSI code, try enclosing it in square brackets and adding a \ before the caret; for example, ^p becomes [\^013]. Depending on which version of Word for Macintosh you're using, you may need to specify a four-digit version of the ANSI code, often by adding an extra zero at the start of the code; for example, 013 would become 0013. Confused yet? Blame Microsoft. They could have made this much easier, and could have matched the capabilities of Macintosh versions of Word to the Windows versions. They didn't choose to.

a range of powerful tools for editors that can greatly facilitate many editorial functions; most work on the Macintosh as well as in Windows, and best of all, some of them are free.

In the remainder of this section, I'll present only the basics of how to use advanced pattern matching to control replacements using wildcards. There are two additional control codes that it's useful to know for replacement operations in the "replace with" field:

Replace what was found with itself

Use the ^*&* code. For example, to replace all instances of *file1, file2, file3, …* up to *file9* with *oldfile1, oldfile2, … oldfile9,* select "Use wildcards", type *file[1-9]>* in the "Find what" field, and type *old^&* in the "Replace with" field. You can change their formatting in the same step by choosing the desired formatting while the cursor is in the "Replace what" field. (It isn't necessary to use ^*&* if you're not using wildcards and are only applying formatting to each search term that is found.)

Replace the found text with the contents of the clipboard

Use the ^*c* code. If you want to replace a search term with a chunk of text that is too long to fit in the "Replace with" field, copy the replacement text to the clipboard, then use the search tool to find and replace each instance of the search term with the contents of the clipboard. Unfortunately, this feature hasn't been implemented for the Macintosh. On the Macintosh, you'll have to use the Find function all by itself, then manually paste the copied text over top of the text that is found and selected.

A real-world example illustrates how we could use this approach productively in combination with a placeholder. Consider a situation in which, while revising a manuscript, some repeated standard wording has not yet been finalized. For example, we might want to use the placeholder *[warning]* to mean "when the Legal department finalizes the words of the warning, I'll insert them here and many other places". Note that the word "warning" might legitimately occur elsewhere in the manuscript, so I have formatted the placeholder text differently from those legitimate uses of the word by adding brackets around the word. Note, however, that we could not easily use *[warning]* if we wanted to perform a more complicated wildcard search, because the *[* and *]* characters are special characters in wildcard searches; if we selected "Use wildcards", we would have to add a \ before the *[* and *]* characters so that Word would know we mean the actual characters rather than their special wildcard meaning.

Assuming that we chose an appropriate placeholder, the *^c* control code would let us insert the final warning statement in only two steps. First, we would copy the replacement text to the clipboard (select the text and press Control + C in Windows or Command + C on the Macintosh). Second, to replace each instance of the search term with the text we just copied, open the "Find and Replace" dialog box, type the placeholder text in the "Find what" field, type *^c* in the "Replace with" field, then click the "Replace all" button.

What if the text we're seeking comprises two or more groups of characters and we need to perform a separate action on each group? To do so, we must first distinctly identify each group in the "Find what" field. We can accomplish this using parentheses (round brackets) and two special codes that define the groups:

- In this context, *group* can mean a single character, a range of characters, or a specific pattern of characters—the word means only that they are enclosed in brackets (are *grouped*) so that Word can recognize them as something we want to handle as a unit.
- We can also use *[ ]* to indicate ranges and { } to indicate numbers of occurrences of a character in a group.

Here's an example: If we were looking for all combinations of a lower-case letter followed by a number so we could swap their positions, we would specify the search pattern as *([a-z])([0-9])* so that the first set of parentheses defines group 1 as the letters and the second set defines group 2 as the numbers.

To identify each group to the software in the "Replace with" field, we would use a backslash (\) followed by the group's number (its position in the list of groups); thus, *\1* would represent the first group (in this particular search, the letters) and *\2* would represent the second group (in this example, the numbers). If we defined a third group in the "Find what" pattern, that group would become *\3* in the "Replace with" field.

To switch the position of the letter and number, we would type *([a-z])([0-9])* in the "Find what" field and type *\2\1* in the "Replace with" field.

Note the lack of any space or other characters between the two group designators: any characters that we type in addition to the group codes will be added to the text during the replacement operation. For example, let's say that we are once again looking for letter–number combinations, but this time, in addition to reversing their order, we want to add text. We might need to do this in a manuscript in which the author used only letter–number combinations to refer to each graphic, even though the publisher's guidelines require authors to add the word "Figure" in front of these combinations and to place the number before the letter. Here's how we'd accomplish this:

- Type *([a-z])([0-9])* in the "Find what" field.
- Type *Figure \2\1* in the "Replace with" field (note the single space after the word *Figure*).
- This instruction translates into the following instruction: Find any letter (group 1) followed by a number (group 2), reverse their order (*\2\1*), then add the word *Figure*, followed by a space, in front of the two groups.

Unfortunately, groups can't be formatted separately in the "Replace with" field: the settings we define for that field (e.g., italics) apply to all groups that we include in that field. For example, we could not use the search pattern *(copy)(edit)* to change *copyedit* to *copy*edit in a simple search. We could, however, accomplish this in two steps:

- Search for *(copy)(edit)* and replace it with *\1^&*, formatted in italics. In this example, the *\1* refers to the first group, namely the word *copy*, and the *^&* refers to the entire search term, namely *copyedit*.
- Click the "Replace all" button. The result is that every instance of *copyedit* in the document will be replaced with *copycopyedit*. The entire "Replace with" phrase has been italicized.
- We can now search for all occurrences of *copyedit* and change those to *edit*, with the replacement formatting specified as "no italics".

This is only a brief introduction to wildcard searches and pattern matching. To learn more, download a copy of Jack Lyon's detailed discussion of advanced search and replace in Word (www.editorium.com/ftp/AdvancedFind.zip).

Chapter 9. Developing style sheets: a tool for consistency

"A foolish consistency is the hobgoblin of little minds."—Ralph Waldo Emerson, *Self-Reliance*

Consistency is something readers never notice—until they trip over an inconsistency. That's why our efforts to impose order on chaos don't belong to Emerson's category of *foolish* consistency. As I noted in Chapter 8, we often face a considerable challenge when we attempt to impose consistency on manuscripts. Many authors don't understand why consistency is important, and note with some justice that readers are pretty good at detecting and resolving inconsistencies. And after all, they note, "shouldn't challenging material be challenging to read?" No, it shouldn't. Neither the assumption that readers can easily detect discrepancies nor the assumption that they can easily resolve the problem stands up to careful analysis. At best, it's a discourtesy to force our readers to do this extra work; at worst, we may do more than provide a minor intellectual challenge—we may confuse readers and fail to communicate. Texts should be challenging because the concepts are difficult, not because the writing makes them more difficult than necessary. Consistency is important, and sometimes even crucial, because it removes one more obstacle between the reader and understanding.

That being the case, part of any editor's responsibility must always be to impose consistency on occasionally chaotic manuscripts. The important consistencies—those that would significantly inconvenience a reader—must be established even in a fast-turnaround edit. Other consistencies remain important, but if they don't significantly inconvenience the reader, and particularly if they're the kind of thing the average reader would never notice, then perhaps they can wait for our second pass through a manuscript, if time permits one.

Long or complex manuscripts often introduce myriad things that must be kept consistent, and the more of these things we must keep in mind, the harder the task becomes and the more likely that some inconsistencies will escape our vigilance. The solution, on the screen as well as on paper, is to create a quick reference guide to the decisions we've made and the things we must watch out for—in short, an editorial *style sheet*. Each time we encounter a possible inconsistency, we can refer to that style sheet to see how we've decided to handle that situation previously, rather than having to search backwards through the manuscript to find this information. Recording our decisions relieves a large and growing burden on our working memory by letting the style sheet do the memorizing for us; our task then becomes one of staying alert to the kinds of things that are likely to be inconsistent, and remembering to look them up in the style sheet each time we encounter them.

Style *guides* versus style *sheets*

Before diving into an exploration of the topic of consistency, it's worthwhile understanding a key distinction: that between style *guides* and style *sheets*. A style *guide* represents a compilation of "best practices" and proven solutions for the common problems encountered by editors working in a specific genre. In this context, genres represent fields of study or discussion, such as journalism, literature, and science. Each genre faces problems that are common to all forms of English communication, but also has its own unique set of problems that may not arise in any other genre. As a result, most editors use a different primary style guide for each genre in which they edit. For example, the Associated Press guide is a preferred resource for journalists, the Sun style guide is a common alternative to the Microsoft style guide for those who edit computer manuals, the Council of Science Editors style guide is a common reference for science editors, and the Chicago Manual of Style and the Modern Language Association (MLA) style guide are common references for academic publishing. (I've listed each of these in the bibliography.)

Unfortunately, it's not possible to cover every conceivable quirk of the English language in any style guide. To do so, the authors would have to include an entire unabridged dictionary, a dictionary specific to the genre, a reference book on modern usage, and several other book-sized collections of reference material. This would no longer be a style guide so much as it would be a library. As a result, creators of style guides attempt to summarize their genre's most common problems and leave us to extrapolate from those few examples to the entire marvelous diversity of problems we'll encounter within a genre. For large or complex projects, we must often consult several additional guides in search of guidance, and most of us have a full shelf of reference material to

> **Rules, *schmules*!** A careful perusal of the titles of the guides I've included in my bibliography (and many others) will reveal a curious consistency in naming: few use the word "rule" or its synonyms in the title. This is not an accident. Most guides are written by editors who are experts in their chosen field and who recognize that few rules apply universally throughout a genre—there are exceptions to any proposed rule. As a result, the authors consciously present their books as *guides* that are designed to help editors find solutions, not as bodies of law. Astute editors will keep this in mind, and will remember that in the end, it's our job to use our judgment to come up with a workable solution appropriate to each unique situation. Style guides should be used as guidelines that help us make informed decisions, not as corsets that squeeze text into artificial and uncomfortable shapes.

support our research. But despite these tools, each manuscript presents unique problems that require judgment calls—possibly because we must choose between conflicting advice provided by two style guides or must develop a solution on our own because no style guide provides a solution to the particular problem we're facing.

In this case, we must use our judgment to reach a decision that is broadly compatible with the overall patterns in the genre and the advice in our style guides. But then, to ensure that we won't have to repeat the research and thinking process several hours later, after we've forgotten that decision, we record these *ad hoc* solutions in a style *sheet*. In effect, style sheets represent our supplements to the published style guides and become the functional equivalent of a style guide for the smallest genre of all: an individual manuscript. They in no way replace the larger guides, but rather summarize the key exceptions and supplements to those guides that we have decided on for a given manuscript. With small manuscripts, these exceptions and supplements may be sufficiently rare that a few cryptic notes on scrap paper will be enough to jog our memory as we edit. But with larger texts and more complex subjects, recording the exceptions becomes considerably more challenging because the number of elements we must keep consistent can grow far beyond our ability to keep them all in our head simultaneously.

There are three compelling reasons to create a style sheet:

- It provides a reference we can use to remind us of the decisions we've already made rather than forcing us to reinvent a solution in each case. This allows us to make the same changes (i.e., to be consistent) at each subsequent occurrence of a particular problem. When a new problem arises, we can research a solution, then add it to the style sheet.
- It provides a checklist that clients can use to review our editorial decisions. Sometimes they'll reject a decision, for good reasons or bad, and a good style sheet presents enough information for them to quickly and easily undo any changes they disagree with.
- It helps a publisher's proofreader confirm how to handle any seeming inconsistencies they encounter while doing their work. A good proofreader will consult our style sheet before making a change, so as to avoid inadvertently contradicting one of our decisions and introducing an inconsistency.

Onscreen style sheets offer many advantages over their handwritten ancestors. Large or complex projects, and particularly those involving multiple authors, typically force us to create and maintain correspondingly large or complex style sheets. If we record these notes on paper, the style sheet soon becomes impossible to use efficiently: a tidy list of spellings that starts out in alphabetical order quickly accumulates a great many marginal notes for newly encountered words that must be penciled in between previous words in the list. The resulting mess makes it difficult to quickly find any given word. Paper, by its nature, prevents us from efficiently fitting new information in the middle of existing information and makes it difficult to reorganize and retrieve information; each such reorganization requires recopying the entire style sheet from scratch. Moreover, paper doesn't expand automatically to make room for new entries, and if your handwriting is as bad as mine, skimming becomes neither easy nor fast.

Onscreen style sheets make it easy to repeatedly insert new, legible entries in alphabetical order, and to swiftly reorder the list to suit our needs. Keeping the style sheet open on the screen in a second window makes it instantly available and frees up desk space for our dictionary and other reference books. Best of all, we can find specific entries quickly using the word processor's search function. If these entries are long phrases or even entire paragraphs (e.g., for a standard warning message

> **Why not print your style sheet?** If you prefer to work on paper, you can still take advantage of an onscreen style sheet: simply print a fresh copy that you can refer to and annotate whenever you need to add new entries. When the printed version becomes unmanageable due to the abundance of annotations, or needs to be reorganized to suit a new task, enter your annotations into the onscreen version and print a fresh copy. This is also a helpful solution for those days when the cat knocks the coffee over on the printout. And when you need to use the onscreen version (e.g., to copy text or search for something), you can do that too.

that must accompany every procedure), we can simply copy and paste the text from the style sheet into the document instead of having to retype it from scratch. Last, and by no means least, a neatly typed word processor document can be spellchecked and sent to the client—unlike a handwritten style sheet, which must either be recopied completely or typed into a word processor. On the whole, it's much simpler and more efficient to eliminate the paper version and work entirely on the screen.

In the rest of this chapter, I'll describe the many kinds of inconsistencies we must watch for, and provide some tips on how an onscreen style sheet can help you deal with these inconsistencies.

Kinds of consistency

There are two main kinds of consistency any editor must confront: internal consistency within a document (defined in a style sheet), and external consistency with the real world or the conventions of a larger genre (defined in a style guide). Of course, style guides also ensure consistency within a document; the distinction I'm making is between overall general-purpose guidelines and document-specific guidelines. However, there are a great many flavors of inconsistency within each of these categories. In effect, any statement that refers to something the author already said or may yet say again somewhere else in the document represents an opportunity for inconsistency, and that's as true for simple word choices as it is for references to specific statements elsewhere in a document. Similarly, any style decision that must be made at one point in a manuscript should be made consistently everywhere else in the manuscript.

The kinds of things we must help our authors to keep internally and externally consistent fall into several broad categories:

Spelling (including hyphenation)

Spelling must be consistent both with the publisher's preferred dictionary and within the document. For example, both *onscreen* and *on-screen* are correctly spelled as adjectives; I have chosen to use the closed-up spelling consistently in this book.

Use of synonyms

As I noted in Chapter 8, elegant variation is most appropriate in literature and becomes inelegant variation in most nonfiction works. In scientific and technical communication, there is usually a preferred term for each concept, and that one term should be used everywhere, with no synonyms allowed unless the goal is to alert the reader to the existence of synonyms in that genre. In the humanities, other rules apply, and use of synonyms may be acceptable, particularly when there is no one standard term.

Verb tenses, voice, and points of view

In nonfiction, verb tenses are relatively straightforward: for the most part, what happened in the past requires the past tense, what remains true in the present or is happening now requires the present tense, and what is expected or hoped to happen in the future requires the future tense. Similarly, the voice may be active or passive, but is always the voice of the author speaking directly to the reader, and that voice defines a consistent viewpoint. In fiction, the problem becomes much more challenging, as authors can forget what they're doing and unintentionally shift tenses, voices, and points of view. It's our job to bring them back on course.

Implicit references

An *implicit* reference occurs when the author refers to something presented elsewhere in a document without naming that location, whether in the form of "as I noted previously" or the repetition of a previous conclusion. Each such statement must be examined to confirm that it does not contradict statements elsewhere in the manuscript.

Explicit references

Conversely, an *explicit* reference occurs when the author names another location in the document. These references include cross-references, literature citations, page references, and citations of figures or tables. In each case, the cited content in the reference must match the actual content; in the latter two cases, the number of the figure or table must also be correct.

Definitions

Wherever an author has explicitly defined a term, we must carefully check all subsequent uses of that term to ensure that they comply with the definition. Particularly where interpretations of a term differ within a field, it's easy for authors to inadvertently depart from their own definition and begin using someone else's.

Shortcuts

Authors often create shortcuts, such as acronyms and initialisms, to avoid having to repeat long phrases. Unfortunately, so many TLAs (three-letter acronyms) and longer shortcuts exist that authors occasionally slip up and use someone else's shortcut. This can be confusing if the reader has learned to instinctively replace the TLA with one meaning, but the author means something different. The problem wears many faces. For example, scientists often present equations gleaned from multiple sources; in this case, the shortcuts are the letters or symbols used to represent specific concepts encapsulated in the equations (i.e., the names of the variables or parameters in the equation). Occasionally, different sources use the same letters or symbols in different ways or use different letters or symbols for the same concept. This creates a situation in which a single variable has two or more definitions, or a single concept is represented by two or more variables.

Formatting

Although formatting is most often a problem for the publisher's proofreader, most editors are also responsible for imposing at least a basic level of consistency on the manuscript and some are completely responsible for formatting. In such cases, we must ensure that headings are consistently styled (checking their capitalization, use of imperative or descriptive syntax, etc.), and that recurring elements, such as headers and footers, appear correctly throughout. Consistency issues may also arise at smaller scales. For instance, we must ensure that bullet points are either complete sentences or sentence fragments—or decide when one or the other should be used—and that numbered lists either do or do not use a period after the numbers.

Sequences

At a broader scale, consistency in sequence means that the manuscript follows the same sequence of all similar manuscripts in the series; in many journals, for example, each paper begins with a title, author information, and an abstract. At a finer scale, we must ensure that anything numbered (whether figures or numbered headings) follows an uninterrupted sequence, with no gaps or repetitions, and that anything presented alphabetically (such as a bibliography) has been correctly alphabetized.

Numbers

The presentation of numbers can pose some interesting consistency challenges. For example, most editors are aware of the common style guideline that numbers smaller than 10 should be spelled out whereas larger numbers should be expressed using numerals. But there are numerous exceptions; for example, when you are mixing large and small numbers, you should use numerals for all numbers rather than blindly following this rule, and in the sciences, all measurements are presented as numerals irrespective of the size of the number. In the sciences, there are additional consistency issues related to the number of mathematically significant figures that should be presented and which units of measurement to use.

Learning to be consistent

As our editorial experience increases, we gradually internalize the need to check each of these types of consistency and begin making such checks without being consciously aware that we're doing so. Until we reach that level of skill, it's helpful to keep this list in mind and consciously try to check each item on the list. A good style sheet can be used as a checklist for each of these types of consistency. It's perhaps a bit facetious to say that we should never trust an author to get anything right, but it's also a conservative statement that serves as a good guide for all editors to keep in mind when checking for consistency. Authors err through simple human inattention more often than through outright incompetence, but whatever the reason, err they do, and frequently.

Components of a style sheet

An effective style sheet should contain three main components:

- Identification of us and the project.
- A list of the standard references that we followed.
- A list of our decisions where the standard references provided no guidance.

A client may have specific requirements for a style sheet, including a list of standard references (e.g., the Chicago Manual of Style instead of the Council of Science Editors style guide; U.S. instead of British spelling). Add these to your style sheet too.

Identify yourself and the project

Start every new style sheet with information that identifies you and that defines the various components of the project. Provide at least the following information:

- the name of the project
- any necessary reference numbers (e.g., a contract code or report number)
- the date, particularly if you will be editing different editions of the same document, such as an annual report, over a period of several years
- the name of your contact person (e.g., the author of the manuscript, the manager who awarded you the contract)
- your name and complete contact information
- a list of file names (and formats, if necessary) for each manuscript in the project

Without this information, a busy client juggling multiple projects, such as a university press or a journal, can't easily determine which style sheet accompanies which project. Worse yet, authors who work with you through an intermediary, such as a publisher's acquisitions editor, may not know whom to contact with questions. This information also remains important for smaller projects and less busy staff; if the project staff changes, as often happens due to maternity or sick leave, long vacations or sabbaticals, mergers and acquisitions, layoffs and promotions, or other inconvenient facts of corporate life, the new project manager will need this information to understand what was done and by whom.

If you do many jobs that require style sheets, use your word processor to create a standard style-sheet template that contains all the information you'll submit to each client. This includes a list of any of the standard information described in the remainder of this chapter; you can always delete items that don't apply to a specific project when you create the initial style sheet for that project. This approach eliminates the need to retype this information for each project, and ensures that you won't miss anything important when you begin a new style sheet. (But be careful: the problem with this kind of boilerplate is that it's easy to forget to remove things that aren't relevant if you've grown overfamiliar with your template. Editors need to be edited too!)

List the standard references that you followed

List any standard references, including specific style guides and dictionaries, that you used for the overall project. Don't forget any non-traditional references that you plan to consult; nowadays, these are most often Web sites that contain useful information, such as online glossaries, library databases, government legislation, and so on. If you will be consulting a human expert, such as a subject-matter expert working for the client or a colleague who is a recognized authority in a field, add their name and contact information too.

Clients often specify such references when they first negotiate a contract with you, but when they don't, you must choose appropriate references that are suitable for the manuscript's genre (e.g., science vs. literature) and propose these choices to the client. Once the client has accepted your choices, or has proposed their own alternatives, add them to the style sheet so that everyone is working based on the same understanding. This process of discussion and negotiation is a specific example of a broader principle: it always helps to subject your style sheet to a reality check with the client. After you've spent enough time working on a document to get a good feel for the types of issues you'll be facing, send the client a working draft of the style sheet containing your proposed solutions. If they accept these decisions, you can continue to use them; if not, you've saved yourself the unpleasant discovery at the end of the project that you'll need to make yet another pass through the manuscript to undo many of your changes and redo the edits according to the client's preferences. Although you should certainly confirm major additions to a style sheet, you shouldn't send overly frequent updates. Ask your client what frequency they desire.

Even when a client specifies the style guide you should use, they may be working with a publisher whose production staff is unaware of this choice. Find out early whether this is the case. If a different organization will be doing the final production work, including proofreading, they need to know what guidelines they should follow when they perform final quality control on your work. Because some publishers have rigorous standards that they expect their authors to follow, you should always try to communicate with the author's contact person at that publisher to learn their requirements. If they already have a style guide, you can adopt this as one of your references and thereby avoid the need to redo much of your work when you belatedly discover that you didn't follow the publisher's style guide. (Other publishers have no preferred style guide, and only insist that a document be internally consistent, not necessarily consistent with the publisher's other publications.) And just as you confirmed the acceptability of your style sheet with the client, you should also run it past the publisher for a reality check. Better by far to resolve any disagreements before you get too far into the work, and to avoid problems from the start, than to be forced to fix these problems later. Even if the publisher will fix them, you don't want to gain a reputation as someone who creates extra work for others.

List your decisions

The heart of any style sheet is a comprehensive list of all decisions you made that are not inherently obvious (e.g., correcting typos) or that aren't covered by the standard references that you agreed to use during your edits. For example, routine spelling decisions can generally be handled by consulting the dictionary specified in your reference list. Once the client has agreed to use that dictionary, you no longer need to itemize the spelling of any words that appear in that dictionary. When you encounter an exception, however, you should add that exception to your style sheet. As I noted in the previous section, it's important to have your client confirm your choices early in the editing process so that you won't have to undo your changes or revise your approach late in the project, when deadlines are approaching.

The types of decisions you'll need to add to a style sheet typically fall into several broad categories:

- Always include a list of problem words or phrases that appeared in the manuscript, listed alphabetically and with each entry followed by an explanation of how you handled the problem. This list should include hyphenation decisions and formatting issues, such as the use of italics for certain foreign words and phrases or the use of a different font to indicate menu choices in a computer manual.
- You may need to explain how you treated unusual spellings. For example, words may be transliterated from Chinese either in the modern *pinyin* system of Romanization, or the older Wade–Giles system. In a manuscript containing such words, you may need to indicate both which system you used as your first choice, and how you handled situations such as quotations from multiple authors who used different systems.
- Provide a list of your choices in situations where there were two or more valid approaches, perhaps because the author was inconsistent and different style guides or authorities recommended different approaches. In each case, you should explain the choice, concisely justify your decision, and cite any relevant authority to support that decision.
- Add sections for various special purposes that are unique to each document. For example, if a document contains complex footnote, endnote, or citation schemes, deals with large amounts of foreign text, includes many quotations, or uses a variety of numerical values or symbols, a brief explanation of the approach you took in formatting or styling each of these elements can be very helpful. Computer books often require a moderately complicated list of formatting and spelling choices for menus, dialog boxes, and the like.

Indicating the locations of specific problems and inconsistencies sometimes proves helpful to the author, but a comment inserted in the text generally accomplishes this more effectively because it eliminates the need to search through the manuscript to find that problem. Page and line numbers work acceptably well for editing on paper, but work poorly for onscreen editing. Even today, with increasing standardization, different computers and word processors and operating systems may include fonts with slightly or significantly different *metrics*—the parameters that define character size and spacing—or may deal with these metrics differently, causing the cited page and line numbers to drift out of synch with the actual position. Moreover, page and line numbers will differ depending on which view mode the user has chosen (e.g., Normal vs. Print Layout in Word) and whether they are displaying or concealing tracked changes; moreover, if they are accepting tracked changes as they work through the manuscript, the page and line numbers will drift increasingly out of alignment between the style sheet and the manuscript. As a result, page and line numbers can be outright useless in longer manuscripts. Thus, style sheets tend to be most useful for describing your solution to generalized problems; specific problems are best described directly in the text.

As your list of decisions lengthens, add simple and helpful navigation aids such as headings and use white space effectively to facilitate skimming; for example, add space above headings, indent text below subheadings, use bulleted lists, or group information in tables. This is particularly true if you don't know what will happen after a manuscript leaves your hands. Clients whose manuscripts will be subsequently revised by a publisher and the publishing staff working to prepare a manuscript for a client sometimes receive printed copies of your style sheet rather than the onscreen version, and your simple courtesy in trying to make their lives easier is greatly appreciated. (It pays to remember that such small kindnesses help clients and colleagues see you as someone who cares about their needs, and the more they appreciate you, the more likely they are to hire you again or refer other clients to you.)

The lists of decisions in a style sheet tend to lengthen as we work because of an odd aspect of human (or perhaps just editorial) psychology. Many editors and writers report that the longer you stare at something familiar, such as an often-repeated word or phrase, the greater the likelihood that it will suddenly begin to look wrong to you. In addition, we sometimes tolerate certain problems rather than solving them immediately so that we have time to figure out a solution, or use a temporary solution that suddenly and dramatically stops being tolerable. On the other hand, we sometimes encounter a problem relatively late in a manuscript that has implications for parts of the text we've already edited. When this happens, it pays to take a break to add the new decision to the style sheet, then decide which of two strategies has become necessary:

- If pausing to fix this problem in all the previously edited text would seriously interrupt our editing, we should simply record the problem in our style sheet and plan to fix it in a subsequent pass through the manuscript. When we're performing substantive or developmental editing, for instance, our focus during initial edits should be on issues of logic and clarity, and stopping to fix a style problem would disrupt this focus.
- If fixing the problem will solve more problems than it creates, we should note our current location in the file and pause to fix the problem everywhere before continuing our edit. This might be the case when, for example, we encounter a definition of a word or phrase that has been used previously in a more generic sense. Upon encountering that definition, it's worthwhile returning to the start of the manuscript to correct any misleading uses of the word or phrase—and sometimes to move the definition we've just encountered to the first use of the word or phrase, so it can provide context for everything that follows.

Pausing to make a change globally can save considerable time if we're editing with changes tracked and visible. Because all the changes we make in response to a style decision will stand out from the original text (typically in a different color), we can see at a glance whether we have already fixed a particular problem. (This both spares us a trip to the style sheet to decide how to handle the issue—because we can see how we handled the issue in earlier edits—and gives us a second chance, when we see each change, to decide whether the change was truly necessary or appropriate.) If you prefer to edit with changes concealed so you can focus on the text that results from your edits rather than on the details of each edit, it's still possible to send yourself a clear message that you've already fixed a particular problem by changing the color of any text that you insert.

For example, let's say we've decided to replace almost every occurrence of *icon* with *button*. If the change is relatively simple, and you're confident you can make it everywhere in a single step, you have the option of making the change using a global search and replace operation, as I described in Chapter 8. If you do this, always leave time to ensure that you haven't introduced any errors. At least during your first pass through a manuscript, it's safest to display your tracked changes as you work so you can confirm that you haven't introduced any errors later in the manuscript as a result of your global change. However, if you prefer to edit with changes concealed, you can still make your global changes visible by defining a new color for the replacement text in the "Replace with" field.

If you're concerned that a global replacement might cause problems, make the changes one instance at a time instead:

- Start by using the search tool to find the first occurrence of *icon*. (The word will now be selected.) Close the search dialog box to get it out of your way.
- Type *button* to replace the selected word.
- Select the word *button*, then open the menu choice that allows you to change font colors. (In Word, open the Format menu and choose Font. Word also includes an icon for changing the font color in the standard Formatting toolbar, so you can use the mouse to apply a new color without having to open any menus.)
- Under the heading that defines font color, select a color such as red that will make the inserted word stand out from the background.
- Copy the selected text. The word *button*, now colored red, is available for pasting elsewhere else in the manuscript that you must make this change.
- Using the search tool, work through the rest of the document using any of the techniques described in Chapter 8 to find each instance of the inconsistency and paste the copied text to replace the original text if necessary. If not, skip ahead to the next instance.

Continue until you reach the end of the file, and if you're working on a multi-file project, continue in each of the other files. Whenever you subsequently encounter changes that you made for the sake of consistency, you'll know from the color change that you've already addressed the problem and won't need to consult your style sheet, but you'll also see a clear visual clue that it's time to "edit the editor" and decide whether you made the right decision. If your software's revision tracking tools define the color of tracked changes automatically (as is the case for Word) rather than using a paragraph or character style to set the color, you can remove all these colors in a single step. When you're finished editing, turn off revision tracking, select the entire document, and use the Font menu choice or the toolbar icon to change the text color back to the default value for that manuscript. After all, you don't want to send your client a manuscript filled with (for example) "words in woad" because you colored your consistency checks blue.

You can use this approach for many other types of consistency check, such as determining whether an acronym has already been defined. If you encounter an acronym that doesn't look familiar, consult your style sheet to determine whether you've already defined it in the manuscript—or move to the start of the document and use the search function to look for the acronym earlier in the manuscript. (If the author hasn't yet defined it, the first result of your search will be the use that prompted your search.) If the acronym doesn't appear earlier in the manuscript, define it in the current location and add that definition to your style sheet. Next, you can replace all other instances of the longer text with the corresponding acronym throughout the file—either one at a time or with a global replacement—and use either revision tracking or a color change to remind yourself that you've made the change. Similarly, if you've confirmed the spelling for (say) a complicated foreign word or technical phrase that you're having difficulty remembering, change all instances of that name to use the same color you've used to highlight other changes. Should you encounter any similar wording that *isn't* colored, you'll know that something is wrong with the spelling or that you haven't yet checked that term and added it to your style sheet. You can expand this trick to help you spot other problems, such as lookalike word pairs: simply color each of the two words in a different color using the search and replace function so that each word stands out when you do your final pass through the document.

Using a style sheet

As I've noted previously in this chapter, a style sheet provides an ongoing quick reference while you're editing a manuscript for the first time. But its true power becomes apparent when you perform your final edit: You can now use the list of decisions, supplemented by your word processor's search tools, to ensure that you haven't missed any instances of a particular problem.

To support you in this final consistency check, create a table that lists all the consistency checks you must do based on your style sheet. This table is exclusively for your own use; because it's intended to help you ensure that you have applied all your style decisions consistently, there's rarely any need for the client to see it. The table should include one row for each consistency check, and one column for each file, such as the individual chapters in a textbook or the individual manuals in a documentation suite, that must be subjected to that particular check. The table on the following page provides a highly simplified example of what one such table might look like.

Once you've completed the preliminary editing, use the table as a checklist that reminds you of each item or category of items that you must check in each file. Note that in my example, I've included two headings (for terminology and formatting) that correspond to typical headings you'll see in just about any style sheet, and a third heading (structure and sequence) that only applies to documents that contain tables and figures. Each section in your style sheet should have a corresponding heading in the table. Although the table is not essential, using it helps to structure your approach to working through the manuscript and thus helps to protect you from inadvertent omissions. It also provides a clear record of what you've accomplished thus far, and of what remains to be accomplished before your deadline.

To use this approach, work through the table one row or one column at a time. For example, the first line in my example table reminds me to replace *click on* with *click*. To ensure that I've made this change consistently, I would search for the word *click* throughout the current file to ensure that the word *was not* accompanied by the word *on* but *was* accompanied by the name of the object being clicked. (Note that if I had only searched for *click on*, I would not find instances of *click* that were not followed by the object being clicked. These should be rare, but moving text around and cutting and pasting in a hurry can often cause words to appear or disappear as a result of human error.) I would continue searching through the entire file until I had confirmed that there were no exceptions to this rule, then check off the corresponding box in the table and repeat this process for the next style decision in the list. It's also possible to move across the rows instead; that is, you could check the use of *click* in all files before moving on to the next item in the table.

That's more monotonous than the approach I described, and requires more opening and closing of files, but it may be more efficient for you. Try both approaches to see which you prefer!

It's certainly possible to print the table and work with only the file being edited open on your computer, but you may find that you're more productive if you keep the table open in another window. Here are a few advantages that may persuade you that juggling windows is more effective than using paper:

Simplified example of a table that can be used in consistency checks.

	Chapter 1	**Chapter 2**
Computer terms		
"Click on" becomes "Click" for buttons	✓	✓
"Right mouse button" becomes "Right-hand mouse button"	✓	✓
"Select the [name] menu" becomes "Open the [name] menu"	✓	✓
Formatting	✓	✓
Heading 1: all caps	✓	✓
Heading 2: initial caps only	✓	✓
Heading 3: only first letter capped	✓	✓
No punctuation at end of headings	✓	✓
Structural/sequence		✓
All tables are numbered sequentially	✓	✓
All figures are numbered sequentially	✓	✓

> **A useful redundancy**
> You can also accomplish more complicated tasks, such as redefining an acronym at the start of each chapter in a long document such as a book. (Doing so ensures that someone who first enters the book at a particular chapter, instead of reading all the previous chapters, still has a chance to understand the acronym.) You can then copy the definition from your style sheet, find the first occurrence of that acronym in the new chapter, and add the definition at that point. Whether you choose to do this or choose to define acronyms only once per manuscript, add this decision to your style sheet.

- Where desk space is limited, it may be difficult to find room for a large style sheet or table, and placing it off to the side of your keyboard may cause neck strain from repeatedly turning your head to consult the list.
- You can copy the search term from the style sheet and paste it into the search dialog box, thereby avoiding the need to retype it each time. For longer style sheets, for unfamiliar foreign words (including a genre's jargon), and for longer phrases, this can save substantial amounts of time and finger strain.
- Copying the recommended replacement text out of the style sheet also lets you immediately paste that text into the document, where necessary, without retyping it. Better still, if you specify the search term properly, the found text is highlighted automatically and pasting the replacement text into the document replaces the original text in a single keystroke. This too can save substantial amounts of retyping.

Always conclude your final editing pass with a spellcheck. None of us is perfect, and any changes we make during our final edit may introduce typos and other errors. That's doubly true when we're working through the consistency table, since that's usually the last major step in cleaning up a document before we return it to the client. A single typo may be forgivable, but if you've changed words using a global search and replace or if you're typing a correction once and then pasting it into the text many times to replace individual instances of a problem, a single error can potentially propagate hundreds or even thousands of times in a long document.

Simplifying style sheet checks: Checking every single word choice in your style sheet across a long document or multiple styles is tedious work. Wouldn't it be much nicer if you could automate this process? Fortunately, you can! Jack Lyon's MegaReplacer macro suite for Word (http://editorium.com/) will do most of the hard work for you.

Clean it up before the client sees it

Even on the computer, style sheets can become quite messy. Cleaning up the style sheet as you work through it will make your job easier, but more importantly, will make things easier for the client when they receive it. A happy client is a repeat customer, and a clean style sheet is just one of those little details that contributes to their happiness. So run through the style sheet and do a quick edit to ensure that your own cryptic notes will be clear to the client, contain no typos, and contain no notes to yourself or miscellaneous philosophical musings that seemed worth recording at the time but that aren't appropriate for the client. In addition, take one last look at your decisions; what seemed logical at 2 AM the morning before you return the manuscript to the client may seem less reasonable now that you've caught up on your sleep. Spotting the problem now lets you fix it so the client will never see your flub.

Going beyond style sheets

Not all style sheets resemble the style sheets I've described thus far in this chapter. Some take different forms and take advantage of different tools. But each has the same purpose: helping you to impose consistency on the document. Here are a few examples that most editors find useful at one time or another:

Memory aids and other tricks

As I noted in Chapter 8, keeping several windows open simultaneously is a good way to quickly look up certain things or leave yourself useful notes. I find this particularly helpful when I'm way over my head in a complex scientific manuscript. When a term or phrase or complicated process simply refuses to stay in my mind, I pause and do my best to understand the logic—then I type an explanation or summary into a second document so I can quickly consult that explanation and refresh my understanding whenever necessary. Similarly, I can record the author's conclusions or key points as I encounter them, and refer back to those points. This is a great way of ensuring that the author's conclusions at the end of the manuscript match the results they reported earlier in the manuscript, and that all the key results appear in the conclusion. You'd be surprised at how often this trick reveals inconsistencies ranging from minor differences in numbers to major contradictions or omissions in the conclusions.

A little creativity will quickly reveal other uses of this trick. For example, if you need to consult half a dozen Web sites to look up various categories of facts (e.g., one site to do a literature search in a library database, another to confirm the correct names of metric system units of measurement), why not copy their URLs into a separate document and click on each one to take you right to the correct site? (Modern Web browsers all support tabbed browsing or multiple open windows, so you can open each page in its own tab or window and accomplish the same result more effectively.) Why not create a list of standard terms that you'll need to use repeatedly so you can simply copy them into the main manuscript rather than retyping them from scratch? Anything you may need to quickly look up or copy can be stored in this manner.

Consistency through concordances

Using style sheets is neither automated nor error-free, and is thus vulnerable to our human failings. For example, we must not only remember to insert a term into our style sheet, but must also remember to correct the problem it represents everywhere in the manuscript. The advantage of onscreen editing is that we can enlist the computer to automate tedious tasks and protect us from ourselves. Concordances represent one way you can harness the computer for such tasks.

In its most basic form, a concordance is a list of all the words that appear in a document, possibly including the number of occurrences of each word. The advantages of using a concordance in editing become much more obvious if you consider what is probably the world's biggest concordance: the database used by Google. (Or any other Internet search engine, for that matter.) Such concordances are particularly useful for those of us who prefer a descriptive approach to language over the prescriptive approach embodied in many dictionaries. Textual researchers use a more constrained version of this approach when they examine a *corpus*—a collection of works in a specific language or subject area, or by a specific author.

The most basic form of a concordance is wholly free of context. For example, the concordance for a 1000-page biography of Benjamin Franklin would probably list the word *Franklin* on every page, with no indication of which instances referred to his birth, death, or other key events in his life. Similarly, the concordance for a software manual would reveal the word *menu* on most pages, with no indication of which menu each instance referred to. But if you look at the search results generated by most Web search tools, you'll see that each search result contains a title and a few words that reveal the context of that result—an enormous help in deciding whether the result is likely to be useful. Depending on our goal in creating a concordance and the software we use to generate the concordance, we can also obtain the locations of each word in the document and the surrounding text—a "keyword in context" (KWIC) concordance. KWIC concordances resemble the results of Web searches and the indexes of books because they provide enough of the surrounding words to provide the missing context. Unlike indexes and Web searches, however, concordances don't group the keywords according to their context or provide synonyms.

Concordances can help us to improve a manuscript's consistency in two important ways:

- A basic concordance lists all words used in the manuscript, in alphabetical order, so we can quickly detect variant spellings that were permitted by our spellchecker. If the concordance indicates the frequency of each spelling, this can also help us decide which form is most likely to be correct.

Display multiple windows simultaneously: If you have a single large monitor or have two monitors connected to your computer, open your style sheet and any other memory aids in a new window, then reposition the windows so that they're all visible simultaneously. Often, the things you need to check will already be visible without scrolling; if the reference window were open but obscured by the manuscript window, you'd have to manually switch to that window each time you wanted to consult the style sheet.

- A KWIC concordance lets us see the multiple contexts in which a word or phrase appears, and thus what contexts we must address in our style sheet.

Consider, for example, how we might use the basic concordance. Jack Lyon, author of the wonderful *Editorium Update* e-newsletter (www.editorium.com), provided the example of *manger* and *manager*: unless the author is satirizing the eating habits of managers, *manger* probably doesn't belong in the same manuscript, but it's an easy typo to miss during editing and the spellchecker won't find the problem—unless you've added the word to an "exclusion dictionary", as described in Chapter 10. Similarly, consider the example of a large manual on Internet technical specifications. In such a book, we might expect to find TCP (the Internet's "transmission control protocol") in our concordance, but not necessarily TCL (a "tool command language", used for rapid prototyping, conceivably to simulate TCP software). Are both legitimate acronyms in this context, or is TCL a typo? (After all, P and L are very close together on the keyboard. Could happen!) Scanning the concordance reveals the potential problem, and using the search function lets us quickly find each occurrence of TCL and, if necessary, change it to TCP—perhaps by means of a global search and replace if TCL truly has no place in the manuscript.

This suggests some effective tricks that improve our consistency. For example, most software lets us sort the concordance by the frequencies of words. In the resulting list, words with the lowest frequencies may represent errors such as *manger* that we can find and correct using the search function. To detect subtler problems such as the TCP vs. TCL difference, we could instead sort the word list alphabetically; as in this example, typos that would slip past the spellchecker often occur sufficiently close together in the concordance that they're easily visible.

A simple concordance also provides a useful tool for generating and editing an index, particularly if you're not a professional indexer. Such a concordance cannot itself be used as an index, since it lacks the most useful feature of a true index: the human indexer's insights into the context of each use of a word. But the concordance can help us to ensure that the indexer covered every important word. We can do far better than that: we can use a KWIC concordance to substantively edit an index by confirming that the index covers all the contexts of a keyword.

A KWIC concordance presents all the main keywords in the document alongside the contexts of these words. We can examine the concordance to ensure that all the contexts we expect to see are in fact there. In the Franklin example, we might find that we have no index entry for his invention of the Franklin stove.

Concordances can also help us check statements for consistency. Let's say we're working on a really long geography manuscript in which the author made inconsistent statements in two or more places—for example, about the size of a certain region. We know one word associated with that detail (the region's name), but we don't want to use the search function to work through hundreds or thousands of instances of that keyword to check each one. But if we generate a KWIC concordance, that concordance will concisely display all instances of that keyword alongside the accompanying context. We can now scan through the list to identify each mention of the size of that region and verify that it is correct, or correct it if necessary. If there are many discrepancies, we can insert a comment at each location to report the contradictory statement and ask the author to confirm which alternative is correct.

Those of us who occasionally work with translators can use a concordance to check the quality of the translations, even if we don't know the second language particularly well. (Ideally, clients should hire an editor who has expertise in the second language to do the checking, but I've heard many technical writers complain that this isn't possible.) In this case, a different form of KWIC concordance can help. "Parallel" concordancing shows the two documents side by side so you can compare the wording at each location; for example, Biblical scholars may use this approach to compare an English version of the Bible with the source of that translation in its original language (e.g., Hebrew, Greek, or Aramaic). By examining each instance of a word or phrase and its corresponding translation, we can identify inconsistencies in which the translator used different wordings for the same concept. This kind of accuracy check is less necessary for translators who are using mature translation memories (which are lists of preferred translations for standard phrases), but remains useful for "free" translations in which no such list exists. Even when we don't know the second language, this technique can reveal seeming inconsistencies that we can ask the translator to check.

Speaking of foreign languages, concordances are a useful tool for anyone who strives to improve consistency in software—both in the interface and in the underlying programming code. Teams of programmers can use concordance tools to track all the references to a particular entity (such as the name of a variable or a subroutine) within a single long program or across the many files of a complicated project. This is clearly useful for documenting the program code and eliminating certain kinds of errors (e.g., using the same variable name to mean different things in two places, or calling the wrong subroutine). But the approach is also useful for editors: if we can gain access to the text labels included in the software's user interface, from dialog box titles to button names, a concordance will reveal terminological inconsistencies in the interface so we can fix them.

Concordances have also been used to teach the subtleties of English. For example, prepositions and adverbs pose a challenge for many writers, such as engineers and other folk who have English as their second language. (The engineer's first language? "Tech".) A concordance can reveal the many different variations in preposition use with a given word or within a specific phrase, as well as variations in the positions of adverbs. An editor could use this list directly as a tool to correct any exceptions to the word patterns, but authors themselves can use it as a learning tool to help them write better. Two researchers (Gaskell and Cobb; see the bibliography) recently reported that concordances summarized sentence-level errors in a way that helped less-skilled writers learn to recognize patterns of errors in their own writing. Better still, the students they tested generally found this approach helpful.

For documents of any substantial length, creating and reviewing concordances is clearly a time-consuming way to improve consistency, since the resulting word lists can be huge. But concordance tools can solve consistency problems that are beyond our ability to easily solve by more traditional means, such as the creation of style sheets. For example, a concordance would be particularly useful when many of the words are unfamiliar to us or difficult to recognize; examples might be (respectively) a programming language reference with many code words and a Chinese history text with many Chinese names. (If you're unfamiliar with Chinese nomenclature, which bears little resemblance to English, spelling errors are difficult to recognize.) Moreover, after reading the original article on which I based this chapter, one colleague gleefully reported his plans to use a concordance to impose consistency on the kind of nightmare editing job many of us dread: a government policies and procedures manual containing hundreds of thousands of pages of text.

If concordances interest you, they have many theoretical uses in textual research and education, many of which are discussed at the ICT4LT Web site (www.ict4lt.org/en/en_mod2-4.htm). As for software, Jack Lyon's *WordCounter* utility for Word (www.editorium.com/counter.htm) provides a simple way to create a tabular concordance in Word. However, this process can be slow, even on a fast computer. It's not that building a concordance is inherently computationally intensive; rather, the problem is that Word isn't optimized for this work. Justus-Liebig University's Web page on concordance software (www.uni-giessen.de/~ga1007/ComputerLab/concordance.htm) is worth a visit if you'll be doing a lot of concordancing. For example, have a look at the Simple Concordance Program (SCP; www.textworld.com/scp), which is available for both Windows and the Macintosh, or the Macintosh-only program Conc (www.sil.org/computing/conc). Such dedicated tools will be much faster than any word processor, and will offer considerably more flexibility.

Chapter 10. Using spelling and grammar checkers

"I suppose we all have our foibles. I like the exact word, and clarity of statement, and here and there a touch of good grammar for picturesqueness; but that reviewer cares only for the last mentioned of these things. His grammar is foolishly correct, offensively precise. It flaunts itself in the reader's face all along, and struts and smirks and shows off, and is in a dozen ways irritating and disagreeable... I write good grammar myself, but not in that spirit... This reviewer even seems to know (or seems even to know, or seems to know even) how to put the word 'even' in the right place; and the word 'only,' too. I do not like that kind of person. I never knew one of them that came to any good. A person who is as self-righteous as that will do other things."—Mark Twain, *Comment on Tautology and Grammar*

Ask anyone you meet on the street what an editor does for a living, and you'll almost inevitably be told that we fix spelling errors and correct faulty grammar. Ask an *editor*, on the other hand, and you'll be told that we do a great deal more than that, particularly if we work primarily as substantive editors rather than copyeditors; indeed, most editors are insulted by the assumption (made by many authors) that we are nothing more than glorified spellcheckers and grammar technicians. The grey area between these contrasting perceptions is, as is often the case, the most interesting place to explore. We do indeed add much more value to the publishing process than simply removing typos and dangling participles, but it's also true that no editor's work would be complete without careful efforts to eliminate spelling errors and fix both obvious and subtle grammatical problems.

Spellcheckers are the most obvious of the computer tools that help us with this task—in fact, they're so obvious that many editors take them for granted, and never go beyond learning how to launch the spellchecker. Some even forget the limitations of these tools—in particular, that no spellchecker can tell which of two or more correctly spelled words is the correct one to use in a given context. The grammar checkers provided with most word processors should help resolve this difficulty, but their usefulness remains limited because linguistics researchers haven't yet figured out how to successfully transfer their analyses of the semantics of text into software. (Much of the problem lies in the quantity of data that is required to cover every eventuality, but the problem is exacerbated by the fact that English is such a uniquely slippery language.) Nonetheless, like spellcheckers, a grammar checker can be a useful tool once you understand its capabilities and its limitations.

In using either tool, remember to retain an appropriate skepticism. These tools can strongly *support* our own sense of what is right—but can never *replace* that sense, at least not in their current incarnations. Both tools miss many errors that only a human mind will catch. The biggest problem is that neither tool *understands* the words that it checks and thus, neither can evaluate the use of the words in their current context; this means that both tools remain incapable of finding problems other than those that can be described by means of simplistic pattern matching. (This is why Word's grammar checker is often harshly criticized: it relies on pattern matching, rather than a deep understanding of the text, to reveal potential problems.) Moreover, these tools cannot distinguish among errors related to incorrect positioning of a word, homonyms, idiomatic misspellings, and so on. (In short, they can't identify legitimate words that are used incorrectly or seemingly illegitimate words that are used correctly.) Most seriously of all, they cannot perform the kind of consistency checks that I described in Chapter 9: they cannot tell when a word that is used correctly in a given context is also used correctly in a different context elsewhere in the manuscript. Neither can they tell whether two correctly written statements present contradictory or misleading meanings (or no meaning at all).

Still, both tools can assist our efforts to improve the readability and consistency of manuscripts. Moreover, modern word processors offer additional language tools that can support these efforts. Understanding how these tools work will let you increase the power of a simple spellcheck and let you take advantage of grammar tools you may have dismissed without much thought. First, though, you need to understand a bit about how language tools are implemented by most word processors.

A small efficiency note before we begin: It may seem most productive to perform a spellcheck before you begin editing, since this would let you quickly fix typos that would otherwise interrupt the flow of your editing and break your concentration. It took me many years to learn that this is often not the case. Even the best of us inevitably introduces an occasional typo into a manuscript, and that means we'll need to perform a spellcheck as the final step in any edit. It's the only way to catch our own typos. That being the case, why perform this spellcheck twice? Do it only once, at the end, and use the time you saved for more demanding work.

Defining languages

Just as spellcheckers cannot recognize the meanings of words, they cannot recognize the language that a word belongs to. That's particularly true for English, which has adopted words from most living languages and a good many extinct or obscure ones, and which has developed several distinctive and somewhat incompatible dialects around the world. (One version of Word came with spellcheckers for 13 different dialects of English alone, plus a large selection of other languages, many with their own dialects.) To perform an effective spellcheck, you must therefore have some way of telling the software which dictionary it should use when it checks each word. There are two common ways in which this is done. Older or less sophisticated word processors define the language once for an entire document, and if the author included many words from other languages in the document, author and edi-

Word X spellcheck crashes: In early releases of Word X for the Macintosh, using the spellchecker seems guaranteed to cause Word to crash. This appears to happen most often when you click the "Ignore all" button too many times within a given spellcheck. For example, this happens to me when I work on documents created by Asian clients. In many of their manuscripts, it would take too long and provide too little benefit for me to add all the Asian words to a custom dictionary for that job, so I simply confirm the word is correct, then click the "Ignore all" button. At some point, the spellchecker can no longer add to its list of words to ignore, and once it reaches that point, the software crashes. My solution: Save the document before I begin the spellcheck, then record any typos I missed on a scrap of paper so I can make the changes manually if Word crashes. Not even I claim that you have to do everything on the screen! The problem was mitigated but not entirely eliminated by the latest patches, so visit the Macintosh downloads portion of Microsoft's Web site (www.microsoft.com/mac/downloads.aspx) to download and install the latest patches.

tor must simply resign themselves to forcing the spellchecker to ignore those words, or to adding them to a supplementary custom dictionary.

More modern word processors, including most current versions of Word, provide considerably more flexibility by building language definitions into their system of styles. (See Chapter 4 for a primer on styles and templates and a discussion of how Word implements styles.) Most word processors offer at least two types of style that govern how each chunk of text will be handled:

- *Paragraph* styles affect an entire paragraph, and cannot be used for smaller chunks of text. Note that in word processing terms, even a single-line heading counts as a paragraph: paragraphs are defined as the text between two carriage returns (¶), regardless of its grammatical completeness.
- *Character* styles govern smaller sections of text such as words, phrases, and sentences that are subsets of a chunk of text formatted using a paragraph style. Even if your word processor lets you apply character styles to entire paragraphs, it's wiser to use paragraph styles for this purpose and avoid any surprises.

Word provides an excellent example of how these language definitions work: both paragraph and character styles allow you to define the language applied to all text formatted using that style. The spellchecker uses this setting to determine which dictionary it should consult when it checks the spelling of words, phrases, sentences, or paragraphs defined using that style. If you position the text cursor inside a paragraph, Word's Formatting toolbar will display the name of the style that has been applied to the text:

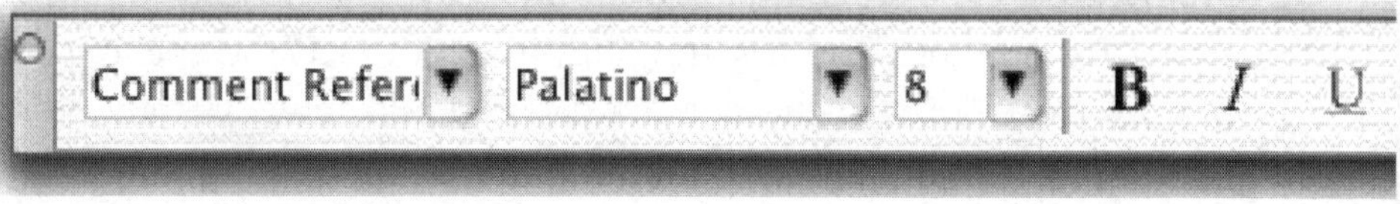

Character styles: Word assumes, by default, that any new style you create will be a paragraph style. To create a character style, open the Format menu, select Style, then click the "New" button. Name the style, then in the field labeled "Style type", select "Character style".

(If you don't see this toolbar, open the View menu, select Toolbars, then select Formatting.) If you scroll the text cursor through text that has been given a character style, the style name displayed in the Formatting toolbar will change to reflect the name of that character style.

The ability to use multiple languages in a document by defining styles with different language settings lets us include multiple languages in a manuscript without tearing out our hair during spellchecks. (Even the sanest editor will go slightly mad after hitting the "ignore this spelling" button for the thousandth time.) Where there are full paragraphs or sections written in a second or third language, which is a common occurrence in bilingual or multilingual regions such as Canada and much of Europe, we can create parallel paragraph styles for each language; for example, we might use "Body Text French" and "Body Text English" for French and English paragraphs. Conversely, if we will be working primarily in a single language, with only occasional words or phrases in a second language, we could instead create character styles that are only used for the isolated chunks of foreign text. During subsequent spellchecks, the software will check the spelling of foreign words using the dictionary we have specified for them rather than treating each foreign word as a spelling error—thereby preserving our receding hairlines.

Not using styles in this way can waste an unacceptable amount of time and energy: we must repeatedly tell the spellchecker to ignore all the words that are correctly spelled in the other language. Furthermore, defining the correct language for each word offers the advantage of checking the foreign text for spelling errors even if we don't know that language. Of course, in that case, it's wiser to simply report the potential misspellings and ask the author to confirm the spelling than to blindly trust the spellchecker when we don't actually know which alternative is correct. Unfortunately, most spellcheckers won't let us pause in mid-check to insert a comment in the file without forcing us to start the spellcheck over again from the beginning of the file. In that case, it's simplest to record any questionable words on a scrap of paper or type them into another file, then insert a comment about the spelling when the spellcheck is complete.

If you'll be working on a long manuscript, invest a moment in reviewing the language settings for all styles used in the document. Then

> **Autocorrect or *autocorriger*?** Most current software also uses a specific paragraph style to govern inserted comments. (In Word, this style is called "Comment Text".) Many of my foreign clients carefully redefine the main styles in the document to use U.S. English, but forget to make this change for the comment style. My first clue that this is the case comes when several of my Autocorrect shortcuts, which are bound to English paragraph styles, stop working. The problem arises because language settings also govern how Word's Autocorrect feature works (see Chapter 11 for more details). For example, when you type text in a paragraph formatted as French, Word automatically changes English quotation marks (" ") to French ones (« ») and inserts a space before each colon (:) and percent symbol (%). That's great if you're editing a document in French, but not so pleasing if you're editing a translation of that French document in which the translator forgot to change the style definitions to use English.

confirm (if you don't already know) which language or languages should be used to check spellings. Authors rarely know how to use the language features correctly, and occasionally apply a variety of bizarre language settings in an attempt to be helpful; many of my overseas clients send me manuscripts set to use two or more different English dialects, making it impossible to use the same dictionary for the entire manuscript without first fixing this problem. To ensure that your spellchecker works properly, edit the properties of all paragraph and character styles used in the manuscript so that they use the correct language. Although it's tempting to select all the text in a file (Control + A in Windows, Command + A on the Macintosh) and apply a single language setting to all the selected text, resist that temptation. Doing this overrides the language settings defined by the paragraph and character styles, and if anyone (you, the author, or the author's colleagues) changes any of the properties of these styles and reapplies the changed styles to any of the text, the language that you applied manually will be replaced by the setting defined in the style. This problem can also occur in software that has been configured to automatically update the styles to reflect changes in the underlying template whenever you open the document.

Another trick authors sometimes pull—usually inadvertently—is to change the language of some of the text to a setting that Word calls "No proofing" (other programs use similar wording)—a setting that tells the spellchecker to ignore that text. Although this is a useful trick for text such as mathematical equations that should not be spellchecked, sometimes authors get overzealous and inadvertently apply this setting to text for which it's inappropriate. To find such text, you can use the software's search tools and specify this language choice. For example, here's how you'd do that in Word:

- Open the "Find and Replace" dialog box. If necessary, click the "More" button or the downward-pointing arrow to expand the dialog box and display additional search options.
- From the Format popup menu, select Language.
- Select "No proofing".
- Begin your search. If you find any text formatted in this way, reapply the correct paragraph style by selecting the affected text and choosing the correct style from the list of available styles.

Special dictionaries

If you use the spellchecker without modifying its settings, you're only taking advantage of the standard dictionaries provided by the software. These are the ones that you'll use most heavily during a typical spellcheck, because even in a jargon-heavy genre of writing, these dictionaries contain the words that bind the jargon together. But there are less-obvious spelling features many editors never discover, or use without taking full advantage of them. Two spelling options in particular offer considerable power once you learn how to use them: *custom* or *personal* dictionaries and *exclusion* dictionaries. In general, most spellcheckers first look for a word in the main dictionary for a language (the language defined in the paragraph or character style of that word), then check the other kinds of dictionaries to see if the word can be found there too.

Custom or personal dictionaries

Most word processors and most desktop publishing programs ship with generic spelling dictionaries for each language that are adequate for a general audience, most typically defined by the software's devel-

What dictionary am I using? During spellchecks, Word displays the dictionary being used for each highlighted word in the title bar of the spellcheck dialog box.

oper as "office workers". Unfortunately, such dictionaries have limited vocabularies that are hopelessly inadequate for most editors, particularly if we work in obscure genres filled with jargon that is little known outside the author's field. (Of course, obscure is a relative term. Word's spellchecker, for instance, contains a good selection of Microsoft jargon that might be familiar to every Microsoft employee but mysterious to the software's target audience.) If there were no way to teach the spellchecker new words, we would rapidly grow frustrated with having to force it to ignore the jargon of a particular genre every time we edited manuscripts in that genre. Worse yet, without being able to teach the software new spellings, we would have no way to check and automatically correct the spelling of important new words.

Fortunately, most software provides the option of custom dictionaries that can solve this problem. Custom dictionaries are also called *personal* dictionaries. The distinction depends largely on the wording chosen by the designers of the software, but it's worthwhile making an important distinction: software such as Word allows us to maintain both a personal dictionary, which works for all documents written in a specific language, and additional custom dictionaries that can be used for specific documents. During a spellcheck, the software identifies each word that is not present in its standard dictionary for the language specified in the paragraph or character style definition that governs that word. In addition to the usual "ignore this" or "change the spelling" options, software that supports the use of custom dictionaries also offers an "Add" button that lets us add correctly spelled words to a supplementary custom dictionary. Gradually adding these words as we encounter them will eventually add an entire specialized vocabulary, such as the jargon of a particular genre, to the list of words that the spellchecker considers to be valid. This can save us increasingly substantial amounts of time because it eliminates the need to constantly tell the spellchecker to skip those words; moreover, it also lets the spellchecker propose a correct spelling whenever it encounters a typo in one of these words.

Most editors already know about the "Add" button, but may not know that we can do far more than simply add words to a single massive repository. For example, software that permits the use of multiple custom dictionaries allows us to create a dictionary for each genre in which we edit, and lets us add these dictionaries to the spelling resources at our disposal each time we work on a new document. How to define and use a custom dictionary varies among programs. Let's use Word as an example. To accomplish this in Word, open the Options (Windows) or Preferences (Macintosh) dialog box:

- Select the Spelling and Grammar tab, then click the "Dictionaries..." button.
- In this dialog box, Word displays a list of all dictionaries that are available for use, and places a checkmark beside any of the available dictionaries that are currently being used with the current document. To activate a dictionary so that it will be used with the current document, click its checkbox, which places a checkmark beside its name; to deactivate the dictionary, click the checkmark again to remove it.
- If you don't see the dictionary you need, click the "Add" button and navigate through your hard disk until you find the correct dictionary. To remove a dictionary that you no longer want to make available to Word, select the dictionary's name and click the "Remove" button. (Removing a dictionary here does not actually delete the dictionary; it only makes it unavailable until you add it once more to the list of available dictionaries. This is most useful when you reach the software's limit on the number of dictionaries you can add for use with a given manuscript.)
- The default custom dictionary is named, logically enough, *Custom dictionary*. To create additional custom dictionaries (e.g., one for marketing campaigns and another for software documentation), select the language that you want the custom dictionary to be used with (e.g., English U.S. rather than French Canadian), then click the "New" button. Name and save the dictionary—in a common location where you keep all your custom dictionaries if you want to use that dictionary in multiple projects, or in the directory containing the project files if you only want to use the dictionary for the current project.

> **Hiding the dictionaries:** Since Word 97, Microsoft seems to have changed the names and locations of all its dictionaries roughly once per version. The guidelines I'm providing in this section are broadly applicable in most versions of Word, but with sometimes significant differences in the file names and locations. Since it wasn't possible for me to provide separate instructions for each version of Word on each operating system, I've instead chosen to provide a broad overview of how the system works. To learn the details, consult the online help for your specific version of Word.

- To change which custom dictionaries are currently available, add and remove dictionaries through this dialog box, as described earlier in this list of steps. To activate any dictionary that is listed as being available, click the checkbox beside its name.
- To correct errors in a custom dictionary or manually enter a list of words to get the dictionary started, select the dictionary, then click the "Edit" button. (You can also open the file directly in Word and edit it that way.) If you inadvertently include an incorrect word in your custom dictionary, you can remove it by editing the word list in that dictionary.

If your software only lets you use a single custom dictionary, you can probably trick it into letting you use separate custom dictionaries for specific purposes. To do this, you'll first need to find the custom dictionary. (Check the online help to learn where your software stores this file.) Then try the following steps:

- Copy that dictionary and store the copy somewhere safe, such as a folder on your hard drive named *Dictionary backups*. For the sake of this example, let's call the custom dictionary used by your software *Custom.lex* and the copy you just made *Custom backup.lex*.
- Next, spellcheck your jargon-heavy document and add any words not already present to the custom dictionary.
- When you're done, close the software and change the name of the custom dictionary you've been using to something memorable, such as *Editing jargon.lex*. Again, move it somewhere safe.

- Now all you need to do is make a copy of *Custom backup.lex* in the correct location for the custom dictionary, and rename it *Custom.lex* so that your software will recognize its name.
- Whenever you need to use the *Editing jargon.lex* dictionary, simply repeat this process: move *Custom.lex* back to the safe directory, then rename a copy of *Editing jargon.lex* as *Custom.lex* and move it into the correct directory. Awkward, but it works.

Custom dictionaries typically have a size limit, which was around 10 000 words for Word at the time when I was writing this book. In any software that has such a physical limit, you may eventually run out of room to add new words to the custom dictionary, particularly if you don't bother creating a separate dictionary for each genre. When you reach this limit, the results vary from program to program. Word, for example, simply stops the dictionary at that point and prevents you from adding any new words. Although you could manually edit the dictionary to remove the least-useful words and create space for new ones, it's more effective to create additional dictionaries if your software allows this. Here's how this works in Word:

- Open the Options (Windows) or Preferences (Macintosh) dialog box.
- Select the Spelling and Grammar tab, then click the "Dictionaries" button.
- Select your current custom dictionary, then click the "Remove" button. (Remember, this doesn't actually delete the file. You'll restore that original custom dictionary later in this procedure so you can continue to use it during spellchecks.)
- Select the language for which you want to create the custom dictionary.
- Click the "New" button, then enter an appropriate name for the new dictionary. For example, if you're going to be editing software documentation, call the dictionary *Software.lex* or something similar.
- Click the "Save" button, and select the location for the custom dictionary. What to do next depends on the version of Word and the operating system that you're using, so consult the online help for details using the search term "creating custom dictionary" (without the quotes). In more recent versions of Word, you can simply save the custom dictionary in the same directory as the project you'll be

working on or in a standard directory where you store all your custom dictionaries. In other versions, you may need to select the directory that holds your main language dictionary.

- If your version Word asks you to specify the format for the dictionary, select "Speller custom dictionary" if this option is available; if not, try the "text only" or "plain text" format, and add ".lex" as the filename extension.
- If the custom dictionary does not already have a checkmark beside its name to indicate that it has been activated, click in the checkbox beside the name to activate it for the current document.
- To restore your old custom dictionary, click "Add", select the old dictionary, then click "OK". New words will be added to the first dictionary in the list (the newly created custom dictionary), but so long as both dictionaries are selected (i.e., both have a checkmark before their names), Word will use both to check the spelling in your document.

You can also create a custom dictionary that will only be associated with a single document or a series of documents. This is particularly useful for large projects, such as books, that use a vocabulary that you won't use again in your other editing projects. In that situation, you won't want to use up valuable space in your main custom dictionary by

Finding your dictionaries: Finding the main dictionary for a given language can be tough, since its name and location varies among versions of the software and between operating systems. The easiest way to find it is to check the online help. If that doesn't tell you what you need, you may need to go spelunking in the depths of your hard drive looking for files with likely names. If the online help provides the actual name, you can use your operating system's search feature to find it. If not, you need to be a bit trickier. Instead, create a new document, type a new word that you want to add to your dictionary (such as your name), then do a spellcheck. Instruct the spellchecker to add that word to the custom dictionary. Search for the custom dictionary by specifying "all files modified after..." and pick a time a few minutes earlier than the current time. One of the files found by the search will be your custom dictionary, since you've modified that file by adding the new word to it.

adding these words but will still want to ensure that you can spellcheck these unusual words. Here's how to do this in Word:

1. Create the dictionary

To create a new custom dictionary:

- Open the Tools menu, then select Spelling and Grammar.
- Click the Options button.
- Select a language (e.g., English U.S.) that the custom dictionary will be used with, then click New.
- Name the dictionary (e.g., *Jargon*), and save it in the directory (folder) for the current project so that you can find it easily.

2. Enable the dictionary

To enable this dictionary for use with the current document:

- If the checkbox beside the new dictionary is not already selected, select it. (Without a checkmark, this dictionary won't be used in the current document.)
- If *Custom dictionary* (the overall custom dictionary for all your editing projects) is selected, deselect it before you do your first spellcheck on the current project. This ensures that any words you add will go into *Jargon* rather than into *Custom dictionary*.

3. Add new words

As you spellcheck the document, you'll find correctly spelled words you may want to add to the dictionary. To do so, click the "Add" button each time you encounter such words. In this example, they'll be added to the new dictionary (*Jargon*).

4. Edit the dictionary

If necessary, edit the new custom dictionary to correct typos and other problems:

- Open the Options (Windows) or Preferences (Macintosh) dialog box.
- Select the Spelling and Grammar tab, then click the "Dictionaries..." button.
- Select the new custom dictionary and click the "Edit" button.
- Make the necessary changes, then save and close the dictionary file.

Limitations on dictionary number

There is usually a limit to the number of custom dictionaries you can have active at any time; when I was writing this book, that limit was 10 files for Word. If, for some reason, you need more than this num-

Word's dictionary quirks: As you might expect, Word has a series of quirks related to dictionaries. For example, in older versions you may be unable to add certain foreign words to the dictionary, or may be able to add them but not use them in spellchecks. This is generally because the accented characters in these words require a Unicode font that isn't supported by the spellchecker in those versions. While researching this book, I found no easy solution to this problem other than to upgrade to a newer version of Word.

ber of custom dictionaries, you'll have to do some careful planning to ensure that you can activate the 10 most relevant dictionaries for a given project. If it's necessary to remove one or more dictionaries to make room for new ones, use the procedures described earlier in this section to remove the least relevant dictionaries and add the most relevant ones. If you expect to do this kind of dictionary shuffling fairly often, using different sets of dictionaries for different projects, learn how to record a macro that will do the hard work for you. (See Chapter 11 for more information on macros.)

Exclusion dictionaries

Correctly spelled words that are perfectly acceptable in certain contexts can be embarrassingly inappropriate in other contexts. For example, *pubic* is one of those words that cause nightmares for newspaper editors because it's a common typo for *public* and is likely to appear in inch-high type in headlines, where only the poor copyeditor could possibly have missed it. In software that offers an exclusion dictionary, you can force the software to highlight such words and give you one last chance to confirm their correctness. Indeed, the word *exclusion* comes from the fact that the spellchecker will exclude these words from the list of correct spellings and identify them as potentially incorrect.

Even if we have a higher embarrassment threshold than most, we can take advantage of this feature in other useful ways. For example, exclusion dictionaries let us compensate for personal blind spots related to certain words or to frequently confused word pairs. Once we've added them to the exclusion dictionary, doing a final spellcheck will offer us one last chance to confirm that we used them correctly. What kind of words might be useful to add to an exclusion dictionary? Consider the following categories:

Category	**Reason to add to exclusion dictionary**
Personal preference	Sometimes, for reasons good or bad, we each have preferences for certain spellings. For example, I prefer to use the spelling *metre* rather than *meter* for the unit of length in the metric system; it is, after all, the metric system, not the *meteric* system. So even though *meter* is correct in U.S. English, I want my spellchecker to give me the option of changing that spelling.
Variant spellings	If, like me, you often edit in environments where there are two possible correct spellings for a word, you don't want to add both to your custom dictionary, because then both spellings would be treated as correct. For example, when I'm editing manuscripts about international research, I may encounter research centers both in the U.S. and in countries that use British spelling. Thus, I may want to permit the Great Lakes Forestry Centre to coexist with the Center for Science in the Public Interest in the same document. Adding *center* and *centre* to my exclusion dictionary lets me confirm that I've used the correct spelling in all such names.
Pairs of similar words with different meanings	This category includes words such as *economic* and *economical*; the first refers to the science of economics, but the latter means inexpensive or cost-effective. Adding these to the exclusion dictionary helps me remember to check whether I've used the right word in each case.

Exclude or exclusion? In Word, the exclusion dictionary is referred to as an "exclude" dictionary in the online help, and that's the name you'll need to look for if you want to learn more about how your specific version of Word handles this dictionary.

Category	Reason to add to exclusion dictionary
Pairs of dissimilar words with different meanings	Adding words such as *which* and *that*, which many editors use to distinguish between non-restrictive and restrictive clauses (respectively), offers a second chance to confirm that you've used the correct word for the job.
Overused words	Some words, such as *very* and *really*, are meaningless filler that should generally be removed from text where precision is important; there, it's better to use a more precise term that explains the magnitude of the *very* or *really*. Similarly, each of us has certain favorite words that we tend to overuse (one of mine is *wonderful*); as a result, we may have a blind spot when other people use these words. Adding such words to an exclusion dictionary provides a reminder to delete these words from the text in most cases.

Details vary among programs

As with everything else in software, details of how to create and manage exclude dictionaries vary among programs, and sometimes among versions of a given program. Here's an overview of how to work with them in Word:

- Create a new document.
- Enter the list of words that you want Word to highlight. Press the Return or Enter key after every word, including the last one.
- Open the File menu, and select "Save As".

Exclude excludes single characters: Unfortunately, single-character words aren't permitted in a Word exclusion dictionary. For example, when I'm writing, I often find words such as *I* that are completely legitimate, but that are actually typos for short words such as *In* and *Is* at the start of a sentence. It would be nice to include *I* in the exclusion dictionary, but that's simply not an option.

- Select the file type in the field labeled "Save as type" or "Format". The correct format depends on which version of Word and which operating system you're using. (Consult the online help for details.) In more recent versions of Word, the format is likely to be named "Speller exclude dictionary".
- Name the file. If Word doesn't automatically add the correct filename extension (.exc or .dic, depending on the version), type this yourself. (This shouldn't be necessary in most Macintosh versions of Word.)
- Navigate to the directory that holds the main dictionary that your exclude dictionary will be used with. To learn this name, you must first find where Word stores that dictionary—a challenge, since this directory has changed from version to version. In older versions of Word, these obscurely named files end in .lex or .dic, and the easiest way to find them is to search from the Desktop for all files that end in these extensions. More recent versions of Word store the dictionaries in a more obvious location such as a directory named "Proofing tools" and use more obvious names.
- Click "Save", then quit and restart Word so these changes will take effect. (Restarting may not be necessary in some versions of Word.)

Various problems can prevent exclude dictionaries from working properly. Microsoft provides some solutions on their Web site (http://support.microsoft.com) if you search using the keywords "exclude dictionary". Typical problems include:

- Words need to appear in each of their various forms, such as both lower-case and capitalized, and both singular and plural.
- On the Macintosh, the file may need to be saved in the folder *your home directory*/Library/Preferences/Microsoft, where *your home directory* is the name you used to log into your computer. (Mine is *Geoff*, for instance.) Note, however, that exclusion dictionaries don't appear to work reliably in Word 2004.
- Only one exclude dictionary can be active at a time for any given main dictionary.

Build your own exclusion dictionary

The exclusion dictionary in Word 2004 for Macintosh doesn't work reliably, or perhaps at all according to some, and this tool can be difficult to get working properly even if you're using another version of

Word. If you're having trouble with this function, here's a useful trick you can try instead: highlight the words yourself. You can do this with or without revision tracking turned on; however, it's simpler to apply and remove the highlighting with revision tracking turned off because then the author will never see what you've done. Since the highlighting is purely for your own use, this is an acceptable example of doing something without informing the author.

First, create a list of the words that are giving you trouble (i.e., the same words you would want to place in a true exclusion dictionary). Next, record a macro that will work through the file, one word at a time, and use the search and replace feature to find every instance of those words, and in the "replace with" field, set the format to whichever highlighter color or font color you prefer. To do so, expand the dialog box so you can see the Format menu at the bottom, then open that

Forcing Word to recheck a document: What can you do when Word doesn't want to recheck spelling in a document, even when you click the "Recheck document" button? Here are a few things that have worked under various circumstances:

- Save a backup copy of the file you're working on. Create a blank new document, then open the Insert menu, select File, and select the backup copy. Save the new file using the original name of the file you were working on.
- Select all the text (Control + A in Windows or Command + A on the Macintosh), then open the Tools menu, select Language, and choose a new language. Then repeat this process, but change the text back to the desired language. The double change often tricks Word into resetting the spellchecker. However, this can cause problems when the resulting language definition conflicts with the definitions used in the paragraph or character styles.
- Sometimes the problem is that text has been set to "no proofing", which is Word's way of telling the spellchecker to ignore the text. Try doing a global search and replace, as follows: in the "Find what" field, set the language to "no proofing", and in the "Replace with" field, set the language to "English (U.S.)" or whatever language should be used.

menu. To use the highlighter marker, select Highlight; to change the font color, choose Font. You can then set the desired color. (Details on how to do this once, for one word, and then edit the macro to add additional words, are provided in Chapter 11, where I discuss my own translation macro.) Once you've highlighted all the problem words in your list, edit the way you would usually do, but pay particular attention to the highlighted words.

When you're done, you should remove the highlighting so that the author doesn't have to see what you've done. If you've used the highlighter tool, select the whole text (Control + A in Windows, Command + A on the Macintosh), and click the highlighter marker's dropdown menu; select None as the highlight color. If you've used changes in font color, select the whole text, open the Format menu, select Font, then change the font color to "Automatic" (i.e., to the font defined by the underlying style).

Jack Lyon's Megareplacer utility (www.editorium.com/14843.htm) offers an easier way to accomplish much the same effect; the current version allows you to define a list of words that will have the "CheckMe" character style applied to them, and you can edit the properties of that style to apply whatever formatting you prefer. Once again, you can use this tool with revision tracking turned on or off. When you're done, you can remove the character style using the search tool, as described in Chapter 8: find all text that has been styled with the "CheckMe" character style by selecting this style in the "Find What" field, select the "Use wildcards" checkbox, select the "Highlight all items" checkbox (which only appears after you have selected "Use wildcards"), then click the "Find all" button. In the Formatting toolbar, select "Clear Formatting" at the top of the list of styles to restore the underlying formatting. (To display this toolbar, open the View menu, select Toolbars, then select this toolbar.)

Third-party dictionaries

Although you can gradually build your own custom dictionary for each genre that you work in, this can take quite some time. Fortunately, many software developers have already invested this time for you, and you can find a range of special-purpose dictionaries for fields such as medicine and law. Searching the Internet for *Microsoft Word* plus *dictionary* turns up thousands of options, and you can narrow your search further by adding keywords such as *medical* or *legal*, or the name of a standard dictionary's publisher (e.g., Merriam-Webster, Dorland). Some examples that colleagues have recommended over the years:

- Spellex (http://spellex.com) offers medical, legal, and scientific dictionaries.
- Merriam-Webster offers an English spellchecker that you can invoke directly from Word (www.m-w.com/help/support/w3_30.htm).
- Stedman's offers a well-respected medical and pharmaceutical spell-checker (www.stedmans.com), which also works with WordPerfect.
- The American Geological Institute offers a dictionary for Earth and environmental science that also works with WordPerfect (www.agiweb.org/pubs/pubdetail.html?item =300200).

These dictionaries usually come with clear instructions for making them available to your word processor. If not, you can try installing them yourself, then making your software aware of their existence. For example, here's how you do that in Word:

- Open the Options (Windows) or Preferences (Macintosh) dialog box.
- Select the Spelling and Grammar tab, then click the "Dictionaries" button.
- Click the "Add" button.
- Navigate to the directory containing the new dictionary, and select it. If the new dictionary does not already have a checkmark beside its name, select it.

If you're willing to work outside Word when you need to research a term, the Internet is a superb resource. For example, the OneLook multi-dictionary search www.onelook.com), claims to offer access to more than 7 million words in nearly 1000 dictionaries. I'll discuss this and other Internet tools or editors in more detail in Chapter 14.

Spelling surprises

Most spellcheckers have their own unique idiosyncrasies, and we must simply learn to live with them. For example, older versions of Word won't recognize single-character "words" and thus won't protect you from typing O instead of I as a personal pronoun. You can fix some of the oddities by changing the default spelling settings directly in the spellcheck dialog box, but it's often more effective to change settings in the Options (Windows) or Preferences (Macintosh) dialog box. In Word, select the Spelling and Grammar tab and try the following options:

- **Suggest from main dictionary only:** Word won't consult any custom dictionaries you have created.
- **Ignore words in UPPERCASE:** Acronyms won't be checked.
- **Ignore words with numbers:** Word won't highlight text such as 1nd (a typo for 2nd).
- **"Recheck document" button:** If this button appears at the bottom of the Spelling and Grammar tab (instead of the "Check document" button), Word won't recheck any portions of a document that it believes it already checked. Click this button to force Word to start the spellcheck over from the beginning of the document. Most times, it will.

Grammar checkers

The fact that you're reading this book means that you understand something important about human languages: they're sufficiently complex that mastering them requires specialized training and lots of practice. As a result, only language professionals can reliably spot and fix typical language problems, and sometimes only experienced editors can figure out what to do with the most serious problems—rewriting a sentence from scratch, for instance, rather than trying to patch fatal flaws. Given that most *humans* require editors to straighten out their prose, it's hardly surprising that nobody has yet come up with truly effective grammar-checking software for personal computers. As a result, the current options generally work poorly and provide bad advice about as often as they give good advice. Most editors, after briefly experimenting with a grammar checker, give up in disgust.

That's a shame, because once you've suitably disabled various options, even a bad grammar checker can improve your editing effectiveness if it's able to highlight certain specific problems you have difficulty spotting on your own. (Each of us has our blind spots.) Once you recognize that you have such a problem (e.g., overusing passive voice), try customizing the grammar checker's settings so that it will seek out and highlight only that specific type of problem. This strategy can help you learn to detect the problem on your own by drawing your attention to instances of the problem you may have missed. Of course, you'll still have to closely examine the grammar checker's recommendations to confirm that they're correct, but when this trick works, it provides a nice safety net until you learn to overcome your blind spot.

To access the relevant settings, open the Options (Windows) or Preferences (Macintosh) dialog box, then select the appropriate section of the settings. In Word, for example, these settings can be found in the Spelling and Grammar tab. If you click the "Settings" button under the "Grammar" heading, the dropdown menu beside "Writing style" offers five different groups of grammar settings (Casual, Standard, Formal, Technical, and Custom), each of which has its own set of options. Exploring each of these styles will reveal various options that you can try out. For example, if you select the Custom style, here are some things that can be checked:

- Serial commas: whether a comma is required before the "and" in a list (A, B, and C).
- Punctuating quotes: whether the punctuation belongs inside the quotation marks (American style), or outside (British style, with some exceptions).
- Capitalization errors.
- Commonly confused words.
- Hyphenated and compound words.
- Misused words.

There are many other settings, most of which look less helpful, but one editor's hindrance is another's help. If something seems like it might prove helpful, try it. If it proves ineffective, you've only wasted a few minutes and you can quickly disable that option; if it proves helpful, you can use that option to save you time or reduce the frequency of errors from that point onwards. By focusing on only those problems that you need assistance with, you can not only improve your accuracy but also eventually learn to recognize and solve some classes of problems by yourself.

As an alternative to the standard grammar checker built into your word processor, you might want to investigate tools designed to check the language structure of a document. One of the more advanced forms of structured language is the standard for AECMA Simplified Technical English (www.simplifiedenglish-aecma.org/). For example,

Boeing offers a Simplified English Checker (www.boeing.com/phantom/sechecker/) that can work through text to check its compliance with the standard. This type of tool has the same limitations as other grammar checkers (i.e., it applies rules mechanically rather than by truly understanding sentences), but does offer some useful tricks, such as identification of missing articles and problems with participles. On the negative side, it's designed to work with the AECMA standard, which is more rigorous and restrictive than most forms of writing, so you'll still have to use this tool for what it does well, and ignore the parts where it doesn't work so well.

Of course, as I noted above, the best grammar checkers are human. Online communities such as copyediting-L (www.copyediting-l.info) and techwr-L (www.techwr-l.com) are great ways to meet human experts who can help when all else seems lost. For other useful Internet resources, see Chapter 14.

Chapter 11. Automating your edits

"I have always wished that my computer would be as easy to use as my telephone. My wish has come true. I no longer know how to use my telephone."—Bjarne Stroustrup (originator of the C++ programming language)

"The probability that a given program will conform to expectations is inversely proportional to the programmer's confidence in his ability to do the job. When a programmer tells you 'no problem', you have a serious problem. No system is ever completely debugged. Attempts to debug it invariably introduce new bugs which are even harder to find."—Brasington's laws of programming

One of the underused advantages offered by computers is their ability to automate tedious tasks. Though computers have yet to achieve anything like their full potential as labor-saving devices, there are several promising developments you can take advantage of right now. Scripting languages built into your operating system, such as Applescript for the Macintosh (and "Automator" in OS X 10.4) and the Windows Scripting Host for Windows, let you automate many of its tasks. With a little research, you can even figure out how to control other software. As the details of scripting languages vary dramatically among versions of the operating systems, and as application software varies greatly in its ability to be scripted, I won't go into details on these tools here. (See the bibliography and list of Web resources for pointers to useful reference material.) The system-level tools are less useful for editing *per se*, but can be very useful for managing associated tasks, such as backing up your files and returning files to the author via e-mail. If you're a real programming whiz, you can even use these tools to develop complete workflow solutions.

In this chapter, I'll focus specifically on the tools built into your word processor, as these are the tools that most directly support onscreen editing. Most word processors offer at least two groups of automation features:

- "Macros" (sometimes called "scripts") are simple programs that you can record by setting the software to watch what you do, or that can be programmed from scratch using the software's built-in programming language.

- "Automatic text" features (also called "autocorrections") watch what you're typing and automatically perform certain actions, such as replacing a short keyword with a longer chunk of text, as soon as you reach the end of a word or type a specific shortcut.

In this chapter, I'll discuss both sets of tools. To simplify your editing work, you should consider creating a macro for any multi-step operations that you perform frequently (more than a couple times per manuscript or per day) as well as for any operations that you perform infrequently but that take considerable time to complete because of the number of steps or their complexity. Similarly, you should create autocorrections for any kind of text that you type repeatedly over the course of a day, or for long text that you may only type occasionally but that takes lots of time to type. Spend a few moments each day monitoring the kind of work that you do repeatedly or that is costing you time, then spend a few more moments pondering whether this might be something you could automate. If you're not sure, consider asking the question in a forum such as copyediting-L (www.copyediting-L.info), where many experienced editors are available to answer your questions. This small investment of your time can repay you with enormous time savings over the course of the work week—and even greater savings over the course of a long project.

It's also important to spend some time researching how each different program that you use handles these features, since that will deter-

A warning for Macintosh users: Microsoft has officially announced that Word 2004 is the final Macintosh version of the program that will run VBA macros. The next version of Word, due out in 2008, will not allow you to record new macros or run old ones. Microsoft has stated that it should be possible to recreate most existing macros using Applescript, but it remains to be seen how well this will work, and it's going to require considerable work to rewrite all your old macros. Moreover, it means you won't be able to run any macros required by your Windows-using clients. If this pisses you off as much as it pisses me off, write to Microsoft and (*politely!*) complain. Don't hold your breath expecting a response, but if enough of us complain, just maybe they'll do something about this situation. Until then, keep your old version of Word available to run macros.

mine how you implement and use them. Macintosh and Windows versions of Word, for example, both store macros in templates, so that the macros are available to all files based on the template that contains them. However, autocorrect entries can be more difficult to pin down; depending on the version you're using, these may be stored in a surprising range of places. More recent versions of Word store the autocorrections in separate files with the name extension ".acl" (Windows) or with a name that contains "MS Office ACL" (Macintosh); both names include the language for which those shortcuts apply. Other software stores these shortcuts "communally", in a common folder available to all software. As in previous chapters, I'll focus on Word's implementation of these technologies to provide a concrete example of how you can use them, but most modern software provides comparable features. If your specific software does not provide these features, you may be able to emulate them using Applescript or Automator on the Macintosh or the Windows Scripting Host for Windows. There are also third-party automation solutions such as Macro Express for Windows and QuicKeys for both Windows and the Mac. (See *Helpful Internet resources* at the end of the book for details on each of these options.)

Using macros effectively

Macros are ideally suited for capturing multi-step procedures such as selecting menu items, customizing certain settings in the dialog box for that menu choice, then closing the dialog box. They're even more effective for more complex multi-step procedures, such as performing a long series of consecutive search and replace operations to correct a variety of problems or reformat a document to follow a publisher's style guide. Best of all, you don't need to be a programmer to use macros: As a general rule, you can set the software to watch you and record what you do as a macro. Recorded macros can typically capture any menu selection, button click, and typing that you can do using the mouse or keyboard. You don't have to learn a new skill (computer programming) to record macros, although you can develop far more sophisticated and powerful macros if you're willing to learn the programming language that comes with your software. That knowledge lets you subsequently edit the macro by hand to fix any small glitches or to fine-tune the macro for improved performance. But the important point is that you don't *need* to do this. You can achieve surprisingly good results just by recording your actions, and that's a whole lot less intimidating than trying to learn programming.

Creating macros

The easiest way to create a macro is to record one. For this to work, you need to spend a few moments understanding what you're trying to accomplish and practicing that action or series of actions so that you won't make mistakes that would require you to edit or re-record the macro. This is more a question of effectiveness (understanding how to accomplish what you're trying to achieve) than one of speed; the software will wait patiently for as long as it takes you to complete the series of actions, so you can take your time and not feel pressured to work fast. (The macro will not record and reproduce the time you spent thinking.) Some software also offers a "pause and resume" feature that lets you stop recording your macro, do a bit of work without recording those actions, then continue recording.

Word provides a simple, unintimidating example of how to record macros:

- Open the Tools menu and select Macros, then select Record New Macro.
- Give the macro a memorable name so you'll remember what it does. (At least in older versions of Word, the name had to be a single word, but you can use internal capitalization to make the meaning clearer. For example, AcceptAllDeletions is a valid name.)
- Click the "Assign to Toolbar" or "Assign to Keyboard" buttons to specify how you will subsequently access the macro (respectively, via an existing toolbar or via a keyboard shortcut). Since I'm a keyboard advocate, I generally assign my macros to the keyboard so I can run them with a single keystroke, without ever lifting my hands from the keyboard. If you choose this option, choose a memorable keyboard shortcut to run the macro; Word will warn you if that shortcut has already been assigned to another command so you can choose another shortcut or reassign the old shortcut to your new command. (I've listed my personal shortcuts in a separate Word document that I can easily consult if I ever need to refresh my memory.)
- Define where the macro will be stored. In Word, this defines how widely available the macro will be. By default, macros are stored in

the Normal.dot document template, and are available in all open files. But you can also store a macro in another template, so that it will only be available in files based on that template, or in a specific file, so that it is only available in that file. This approach lets you create groups of client-specific, genre-specific (e.g., science vs. literature), or task-specific (substantive editing vs. proofreading) suites of macros.

- Optionally, add a description of what the macro does. This description (which defaults to your name and the creation date of the macro) can provide useful information such as the conditions under which the macro works—or doesn't work. This description will be included in the program code that Word uses to implement the macro, and you can edit it later if necessary.
- Click OK to close this dialog box, then perform all the steps that you want the macro to repeat for you: open menus, select options, type text, click buttons, and so on. You can even run through several menu choices and dialog boxes to record long, involved processes such as mail merges. There is a practical limit to how long a macro can be, but unless you're automating a long process with scores of menu choices, you'll probably never reach that limit. If you do, you can usually break the macro into two or more parts and run those parts separately, in sequence. (I'll provide an example of how to do this later in this chapter.)
- Click the Stop Recording button to save the macro:

- To run the macro, type the keyboard shortcut you defined at the start of this process, or open the Tools menu, select Macro, select Macros from the submenu, then choose the correct macro from the list that appears in the "Macros" dialog box.

That's as complicated as you need to get. When you're done, the software translates your actions into program code that Word will understand, and stores this information for future reuse as a macro. Even though the actions you've performed are stored as program code, you need never see or interact with that code in most cases. (If you need to or want to do so, see the next section, *Editing macros*, for a primer on how to do so.) Word offers an unusually powerful programming language called *Visual Basic for Applications* (VBA for short) that actually underlies many of the program's features. Because VBA provides access to just about every function that Word can perform, including some that are not at all obvious from Word's menu system, you can use this programming language to invoke these features, alone or in combination. In this chapter, I'll focus on Word's macro language, but my suggestions generally apply, with appropriate modification, to other word processors.

VBA is such a powerful programming language that Word expert Woody Leonard claimed, "Anything you can do in Word… [and many] things you *can't* do in Word, you can do with a VBA/Word program." Unfortunately, the documentation on VBA isn't always exactly in synch with the reality, so it may take a bit of experimentation to make VBA programs run the way you expect them to. In the bibliography, I've provided information on Leonard's classic discussion of this subject, *Word 97 Annoyances*, as well as a more comprehensive reference (the book by Hart-Davis). Jack Lyon's Editorium site (www.editorium.com) offers a range of free macros if you want to learn more about how macros work, plus some more powerful tools for sale.

Most programs provide considerable flexibility in how you can run a macro:

- If you assigned a key combination to the macro when you first created it, you can type that keyboard command to run the macro without ever lifting your hands from the keyboard. Assigning macros to keyboard shortcuts tends to be most productive for skilled typists.
- If you prefer to use the mouse, you can run the macro directly from the appropriate menu. In Word, open the Tools menu, select Macro, select Macros from the submenu, then select the macro of your choice and click the "Run" button. This approach works well if you've reached your memorization limit and don't want to memorize yet another keyboard shortcut.

- If you assigned the macro to a toolbar, this offers a good compromise between the efficiency of the keyboard shortcut and the ease of use of the menu approach. So long as the toolbar is visible, you can run the macro with a single mouse click. This approach is particularly useful if you create your own custom editing toolbar that contains a suite of useful macros related to onscreen editing.

Editing macros

Although I've said that you can automate almost anything you want to simply by recording a macro, it's still helpful to know how to edit macros. This editing may be as simple as changing the macro's name to something more memorable if you forgot to assign a good name when you created the macro and thereby ended up with a powerful macro with an obscure name such as Macro0127. (Indeed, if you develop many macros, particularly complicated ones that require lots of de-

Adding a keyboard shortcut for a Word macro: Already recorded a Word macro but forgot to assign a keystroke or store it in a toolbar? No problem. You can always do this later:

- To assign a keystroke, open the Tools menu, select Customize, and click the "Keyboard" button. Under the "Categories" heading, scroll down and select "Macros". Select the desired macro from the list of options, and type a keyboard shortcut in the field labeled "Press New Shortcut Key". Word will warn you if that shortcut has already been assigned to another command, so you can choose another shortcut or reassign that shortcut to your new command.
- To assign a macro to a toolbar, open the View menu, select Toolbars, then select the toolbar that will hold the macro. Next, open the Tools menu, select Customize, and select the Commands tab. Under the "Categories" heading, scroll down and select "Macros". The available macros will have an intimidating name such as *normal.newmacros.[name]*, where the first part of the name identifies the template that holds the macro (in this example, Normal.dot); the *[name]* part is the name that you gave to the macro when you recorded it. Simply select the desired macro and drag it out of the dialog box and into the toolbar.

> **Making macros accessible in other documents:** If you need access to a particular Word macro in a new document but that macro is stored in another template, open the Tools menu, select Templates and Add-ins, click the "Add" button, and select the template containing that macro, so that a checkmark appears beside it. This makes its contents available in the current file. Alternatively, open the Tools menu, select Macro, then select Macros from the submenu. Click the "Organizer" button to display a dialog box that lets you open the file containing the macro on one side of the screen and the current file on the other side. From here, copy the macros into the current file. (In more recent versions of Word, you can't select individual macros and copy only them; instead, you have to copy all macros in a single operation, then use the Macro editor to delete any that you don't want.) You can also use this dialog box to delete macros once you no longer need them in the file. However, even if you delete all macros from a file, older versions of Word may still believe that there are macros in the file, and this may trigger Word's warning that the file contains a macro virus. The easiest way around this problem is to insert the file into a new document based on a template that contains no macros.

bugging and revision, you may want to add a suffix such as "-beta" or "-testing" to remind yourself which macros are ready for full-time use and which ones are still works in progress.) Editing may also be as complex as fine-tuning the specific steps in a macro to improve their performance or correct a small error; for example, you may have inadvertently selected the wrong checkbox midway through a long procedure, and would rather fix that selection than re-record the entire procedure.

Depending on the software you used to create the macro, you may open the macro for editing directly in that software or in a text editor, or you may need to use a specific macro editing program. The VBA editor provided with Word, for example, is a full-featured professional programming environment that offers a raft of features (including debugging tools) that you'll probably never use for simple macro editing, and some that you will definitely benefit from using, including online help that describes the commands and how to use the editor. For simple ed-

> **Escaping the VBA editor:** In Word, you must actually close the entire VBA editor by opening the File menu and selecting Quit, or by clicking the close button at the top of the window. This is a bit intimidating the first time you do this, because it seems like you're about to quit Word itself. Don't worry; you're not.

iting, all you need to do is type directly in the window that contains the macro, save your changes, and close the file.

To edit a macro in Word, open the Tools menu, select Macro, then select Macros. Select the desired macro, then click the "Edit" button. You'll find yourself amidst a complex-seeming series of windows, but for the moment, concentrate on the one at the right that contains the actual programming code. Here's what the code of a typical macro (in this case, one that replaces double carriage-returns with a single return) looks like:

Program code	Explanation
Sub Cleanup() ' Cleanup Macro ' Macro recorded 8/7/05 by Geoff Hart '	In the first line, *sub* refers to a *subroutine*, which is programming jargon for an entire set of commands performed by a specific macro. This keyword is accompanied by *end sub* (at the end of the program code) to mark the end of the macro. The single quote (') character at the start of the line indicates that this text is a comment (i.e., information for you rather than an instruction to Word). In this case, the macro is named *Cleanup*. One simple edit might be to remove the line that describes when the macro was recorded.

Program code	Explanation
Selection.Find.ClearFormatting Selection.Find.Replacement.ClearFormatting	These lines clear any formatting specifications left over from a previous search.
With Selection.Find .Text = "^p^p" .Replacement.Text = "^p" .Forward = True .Wrap = wdFindContinue .Format = False .MatchCase = False .MatchWholeWord = False .MatchWildcards = False .MatchSoundsLike = False .MatchAllWordForms = False End With	These lines define the properties of the text that will be found by the search and replace operation (between *With* and *End With*). As explained in Chapter 8, *^p* is the code for a carriage return; this macro searches for two carriage returns in a row and replaces them with just one. The other lines define various settings, such as the fact that the search should continue from the current cursor position forward to the end of the document, then "wrap" back to the start and continue from there. The several *Match* options define what criteria should be used to find the search term; the various options set equal to *False* represent search parameters that aren't relevant to this particular macro.
Selection.Find.Execute Replace:=wdReplaceAll	This line says what to do with the found text: replace every instance of this text with the replacement text defined above.
End Sub	This line concludes the macro.

You can copy and paste macro text that you want to reuse in another macro; this trick requires little or no programming skill. For example, I've written one macro that helps me perform translations much faster than would be possible without the macro's assistance: the macro performs several hundred search and replace operations for groups of nouns and other parts of speech whose meaning is fixed (so I can translate them without knowing their context), thereby eliminating the need for me to repeat each of these search and replace operations or type each individual word while I'm doing a translation. When I first created this macro, I didn't record each of those hundreds of search and replacement operations, nor did I re-record the entire macro each time I needed to add a word pair. Instead, I simply recorded a single search and replace operation, then copied and pasted the resulting code for each new word pair. What did I copy and paste?

- The necessary code begins with the line *With Selection.Find.*
- It ends with the lines *Selection.Find.Execute* and *Replace:=wdReplaceAll.*
- Whenever I needed to expand this macro to include new word pairs, I simply copied the existing text for my first search and replace operation, and pasted it into the editor immediately above the *End Sub* line.
- The last step was to replace the search term following *.Text* with the new search term, and the text following *.Replacement.Text* with the new replacement text.

I haven't studied VBA enough to learn how to identify the minimum instructions necessary to create an efficient macro, so I suspect that not all the code in this macro is necessary; for example, I could probably delete all of the lines ending in *false* with little harm, greatly shortening the macro. The important point is that such editing isn't necessary! However, because I didn't do this editing, I eventually added enough word pairs to my list that the macro would no longer run: it was simply too long. The solution was to break the macro into several parts, then run each part in sequence. Here's the macro code that accomplishes this solution:

Program code	Explanation
Sub Translate1() [long list of search and replace operations] End Sub	This is the code for part one of my translation macro, named *Translate1* (the round brackets after this name are required syntax in this programming environment). This part of the larger macro ends with the words *End Sub*. There are four more subroutines (*Translate 2* through *Translate 5*) that hold the remainder of the search and replace operations. I haven't shown them in this example, as they're essentially identical to *Translate1*.
Public Sub Translate() Call Translate1 ... Call Translate5 End Sub	This is the code that appears after all five parts of my translation macro, and is the actual macro (*Translate*) that I run to implement all five individual parts (1 to 5). The *Call* command instructs the macro software to run each named part of the overall translation macro.

If you need to change user identities frequently, as might be the case if you need to do "blind" (anonymous) reviews in which your identity is concealed from the author (a common procedure for peer-reviewed journals), you'll have to change the name you entered in your User Information settings (in the Options or Preferences dialog box) often enough that it's worthwhile recording a macro to accomplish this. However, *recording* such a macro includes a fair bit of unnecessary overhead in the resulting code. Here's the irreducible minimum you can get away with (substitute your own name and initials for mine, and enter the words you want to use to identify yourself as the anonymous reviewer):

Task	Macro code

To change to a "blind review" identity	Sub Blind()
	   Application.UserName = "Journal Reviewer"
	   Application.UserInitials = "JR"
	End Sub

Task	Macro code

To restore your original identity	Sub Geoff()
	    Application.UserName = "Geoff Hart"
	    Application.UserInitials = "GHT"
	End Sub

To add this to your list of macros, open the Tools menu, select Macro, then select Macros. For each macro in turn, type the name of the new macro (*Blind* and *Geoff*, respectively), then click the "Create" button. Copy (or type) the macro text from this table into the VBA editor software between the *sub* and *end sub* lines for the macro you're creating. (Note that you don't need to type the *Sub* and *End Sub* lines of each macro, since the VBA editor will create them for you as soon as you click the "Create" button.) To assign these macros to a keystroke or toolbar, open the Tools menu and select Customize. Follow the instructions I presented earlier in this chapter (*Creating macros*) on using the Customize dialog box.

That's as far as I'll go with my explanation of macro editing, since this brief description covers some of the main aspects you need to know, and more detailed explanations would require a separate book—many of which already exist. If you enjoy programming and want to learn more, you'll be able to develop far more sophisticated macro routines as you gradually master the software's programming language and learn to directly type the various commands in the VBA editor. For Word users, I highly recommend Leonard et al. (1997) for a sound basic introduction to VBA and its many quirks. If you want to delve more deeply into the subject, Hart-Davis (1997) includes copious examples and a CD-ROM full of the sample code from the book.

There are also many free resources available. Start with the online help in Word and in the VBA editor, which contain detailed information on creating macros. The Electric Editors run the *Grapevine* discussion list (www.electric editors.net), and their web site provides many Word (Macintosh and Windows) and WordPerfect (Windows) macros free for the downloading, each contributed and tested by working editors. Jack Lyon's Web site (www.editorium.com) is another excellent macro resource that provides many free macros and several powerful macro suites you can purchase that have been designed specifically for editors. While you're visiting, have a look at his newsletter archives (www.editorium.com/euindex.htm) for a large selection of free, well-explained macros that also explain many of the details and teach you how to do a better job of writing your own macros. In particular, have a look at his article on *Using "found" macros* (http://lists.topica.com/lists/editorium/read/message.html?mid=1706922855). In case that link breaks, look for the 30 May 2001 issue of the newsletter.

Typical macros

Each time you run a macro, the software re-enacts all the steps you performed when you first recorded the macro—or follows all the instructions you typed if you wrote the macro yourself using the software's own programming language. The longer the sequence of steps and the more often you use them, the greater the savings of time and effort: instead of repeating all these steps, you can run the macro with a single keystroke, menu choice, or mouse click. That description—replacing many keystrokes with one—holds the key to deciding what things you should automate via a macro: any task that involves many keystrokes or mouse clicks. The more often you perform that task, the more important it will be to create a macro that will do the work for you, and the faster you'll repay the effort involved in creating the macro.

Most editors eventually develop at least a few basic macros to meet their unique needs. Just as customizing your word processor's screen display requires close attention to how you work, paying attention to what you do while editing a manuscript will reveal various types of actions that you perform frequently, or that you perform less frequently but that take considerable time to accomplish via the menus. Here's the key question: Will you repeat any of these activities sufficiently often that the time you spend developing a macro will be less than the time you'll save using the macro? Surprisingly often, a small investment of time spent watching your own editing behavior and identifying repetitive tasks can produce enormous paybacks in time savings later on.

If no repetitive tasks come to mind, find a simple way to record every activity you perform during a day of editing—for example, create a two-column table on a sheet of scrap paper that lists the activities in the left column, and the frequency in the right column. Each time you do something, add a checkmark in that row of the table. At the end of the day, the activities that you've done most often are things you should consider automating first. The results of this simple survey of your working habits may well surprise you, since it's human nature to ignore boring things that we do repeatedly.

The specific macros you develop will obviously depend on your work habits and the nature of the work you do most often. For example, paying close attention to the kinds of edits I do revealed several multi-step tasks I was performing dozens of times per manuscript, and sometimes even dozens of times per hour. Here are a few examples:

- Authors for whom English is a second language often reverse the order of word pairs, such as nouns and adjectives, when they write in English. Switching the word order manually takes several keystrokes: select the first word, cut that word out of the manuscript, move the cursor to the space after the second word, then paste the word into its new location. By recording these steps as a simple macro, without ever having to learn anything about VBA, I made this into a one-keystroke operation.
- Many authors never learn how to format their documents using styles, and use multiple spaces or even tabs to indent text; even writers who don't do so often inadvertently introduce spaces at the beginning or end of paragraphs (e.g., by splitting an existing paragraph into two new ones) or hold down the space bar too long and enter multiple spaces. To resolve this problem, I recorded a macro that searched the entire document for all these types of errors and made the necessary corrections. Each of the search and replace operations required to perform this cleanup only takes a few keystrokes, but I need to do them several times per day—once per manuscript, in fact. That's sufficiently tedious that it eventually proved easier to simply record the macro to do all the dirty work for me.
- When I translate one client's French reports into English, the most *important* part of the job is to convert clear, idiomatic French into clear, idiomatic English, but the most *time-consuming* part is to repetitively replace standard French technical terms with their standard English equivalents. To improve my turnaround times, I created the translation macro that I described earlier in this chapter. This macro also does basic cleanup unique to converting French typographic rules into their English equivalents (e.g., it removes the spaces insert-

ed before colons and percentage symbols), and sets the Language property of all the text to English so I can spellcheck the document using the correct dictionary once the translation is complete. After running the macro, I need only edit the resulting text so that it flows smoothly and fix any glitches introduced when I added a pair of words to the macro without carefully constraining the "find" or "replace" part of the pair. (When that's the case, I edit the macro, as described in the previous section.)

- Many editors work for publishers that use highly specialized typesetting systems to generate page layouts. To prepare a manuscript for production by these systems, the word processor's proprietary coding scheme for describing formats such as headings must be converted into a series of tags, similar to those used to define the structure of Web pages. Making these changes manually for long documents such as books would be prohibitively time-consuming; as a result, many publishers have developed powerful macros for automating the work.

When it comes to developing truly magnificent macros, I'm strictly an amateur. For a glance at the true wizards in action, check out the following sites:

- The Editorium (www.editorium.com): As I noted earlier in this chapter, Jack Lyon offers a range of powerful editing aids, many of which are available for free or as a "try before you buy" evaluation copy before you purchase them. Jack's free newsletter, *The Editorium Update*, provides regular examples of useful macros that can make life with Word much easier.
- The Electric Editors (www.electriceditors.net) offer many Word (Macintosh and Windows) and WordPerfect (Windows) macros free for the downloading, each contributed and tested by working editors
- Allen Wyatt's free WordTips newsletter (www.vitalnews.com/wordtips) offers advice on all aspects of bending Word to your will, as well as a reader forum that allows you to write in with questions.

Why wait until spring? I'm my own worst enemy when it comes to reducing my workload: I usually wait until I'm completely fed up with some task before I force myself to make time to automate it. Don't be like me!

Industrial-strength automation: If you handle really large jobs, particularly in the medical domain, you'll be interested in the automation tools created by Rich Adin of Freelance Editorial Services (www.freelance-editorial-services.com/). The site describes these macros and provides videos of the macros in action. Currently, they're scheduled for release in the first quarter of 2008.

"Automatic text" features

I'm a fast typist, and for longer than I care to admit, I simply repeatedly retyped the same questions or comments over and over and over again when I edited manuscripts. When I worked under significant deadline pressure, I often copied previous comments and modified them slightly to address the specific problem that prompted a new comment, but that sometimes involved hunting through the existing comments to find text I could copy—in hindsight, a remarkably inefficient way to work. Although this approach worked acceptably well for the small projects that represent the majority of my work, the first large book that I edited made all that retyping prohibitively time-consuming. Fed up, I finally took my own advice and began looking for a way to eliminate the need to manually perform such repetitive tasks.

Most software offers automation features that can do much of the work for you. (Where they don't, you can often create a macro to do the work, as described earlier in this chapter.) In Microsoft Word, the software's "automatic text" features are called *autoformatting*, *autocorrect*, and *autotext*. In other software, these features may be referred to as glossaries, library items, or shortcuts. In this section, I'll focus on how Word implements these features and suggest how you can use a similar approach to lighten your workload in other software.

Why automate the simple things?

If some small action takes little time to perform, there seems little reason to consider automating that action. Yet when you perform simple edits repeatedly, the cumulative number of repetitions adds up fast, and you may be wasting a considerable amount of time over the course of the day. For example, when I edit scientific articles destined for journal publication, I compare the literature citations within the text against the contents of the bibliography at the end of the manuscript. In nearly 20 years of this work, I've found that perhaps one author in twenty successfully matches all citations to the references—and many editors report much lower success rates. With the other nineteen authors, many citations in the text are missing from the bibliography, others are present in the bibliography but have not been cited in the text, and many citations contain errors such as mismatches between the names of the authors or the publication dates. Even those rare authors who avoid these glaring mistakes still often err by omission or commission when they type the reference details into their bibliographies. Publisher details (name, city, or location) are commonly missing, authors often use "et al." to avoid typing a long list of authors even if the journal they're writing for requires that all authors be identified, and so on.

In each case, I need to insert a comment that explains the problem and proposes a solution. (I could be far more cryptic, of course, but as I noted in Chapter 7, terse, telegraphic writing is less effective and less clear than complete, clear sentences. That's particularly true for authors whose native language isn't English.) With some manuscripts, I may retype the same comment dozens of times. Fast though I type, all this repetition wastes time better spent on more important things—such as having a life beyond the keyboard. To solve the problem, I created a batch of autocorrect shortcuts that do the typing for me. I'll discuss how Word implements these features in the next section. Other software provides comparable features.

Automatic formatting and text insertion

Word's text automation tools come in two flavors: *Autoformat* and *Autocorrect*. The Autoformat feature applies certain types of formatting automatically as you type, such as capitalizing the first letter of the word that starts a new sentence, and although some of these features are quite useful, most cause Word users considerable grief because they work behind our back and have an unfortunate tendency to undo some of our work or introduce changes we don't want or need. Since Autoformat offers little in the way of useful editorial assistance, most editors find it more effective to simply disable all these features and only selectively enable them for their own writing rather than for editing. However, Autocorrect and its close cousin, Autotext, more than compensate for the evils of Autoformat. If you don't use Word or dislike how these

> **Automatic text depends on the language setting:** In Word, automatic text settings are defined independently for each language. This means that any autocorrect shortcuts that you defined for your English documents will stop working in text controlled by a paragraph style that has been defined to use another language. Moreover, shortcuts defined for that other language may seem to appear out of nowhere; for example, if you're working on an English translation of a French document but failed to notice that your French author defined all the document styles to use French as the language, you'll notice that every time you type a % symbol or a colon, Word will insert a space before it. The clue that solves the mystery? This is correct formatting *in French*. Fortunately, the solution to both problems is simple: Change the language definition for each style to the correct language (English, in this case). *Voila*! Problem solved.

features work in Word, see the next section for details on how to develop your own solution.

Autocorrect monitors your typing, and as soon as you hit the end of a word, it scans its list of rules to find a match for what you've just typed; if it finds one, it follows the instructions specified by that rule to replace what you've typed with the specified text. For example, you could add the shortcut *]mr* (short for "missing reference") to your list of autocorrections rather than repeatedly typing "This reference is missing from your bibliography—please add it there." As soon as you type this shortcut and press the spacebar, Word replaces the shortcut with the full sentence. If an automatic correction isn't what you intended, undo the change (Control + Z in Windows, Command + Z on the Macintosh) as soon as you notice what happened. Note that I've used a closing square bracket as the first character of the shortcut for missing references; since I'll almost never type a closing square bracket followed by a word, I can be confident that I'll never inadvertently type this particular shortcut and have to undo it. Autocorrect is very useful for both short phrases and long explanatory paragraphs that you must type repeatedly. I wasn't able to determine the exact maximum length of an Autocorrect entry in my research for this book, but experimentation suggests that it's around 255 characters. If you need more space, the simple solution is to create two Autocorrect entries and use them sequentially or even to include an Autocorrect entry inside another autocorrect entry. For example, if my "missing reference" query were much longer, I could define the Autocorrect entry *]mr*, which contains the following text: *]mr1]mr2*

Typing *]mr* and pressing the spacebar would cause word to automatically insert *]mr1]mr2* for me; moving the cursor after the 1 and 2, respectively, and pressing the spacebar would expand each shortcut into the text that I defined for that shortcut.

The kinds of shortcuts you'll want to create depend on careful study of the types of comments or insertions that you perform most frequently, and you'll need to monitor your editing habits for a day or more to learn what these are. After a bit of observation, I discovered that I needed the following shortcuts just for fixing problematic literature citations:

-]mr = This citation is missing from the References section. Please add it there.
-]rnc = This reference has not been cited in the text. Please insert a citation.
-]aw = The spelling of this author's name (spelling 1) differs from the spelling (spelling 2) in the bibliography. Please confirm the correct spelling.
-]wd = The date for this citation (date 1) differs from the date in the references list (date 2). Please confirm which date is correct.
-]ce = If you accept this suggestion, make the same change everywhere in the document.

I have additional Autocorrect entries for many other comments and queries, including comments where I'm not sure about the meaning and want to propose two alternatives, comments that ask the author to check a particular edit more carefully than the other edits (because I wasn't confident in my solution), and so on. Periodically, I notice that I'm wasting a lot of time retyping some phrase, and after ruefully reflecting on my inattention, I make the time to add a new autocorrect entry for that text.

To create a new Autocorrect shortcut, simply type the text into your document, select the new text with the mouse, then:

- Open the Tools menu and select Autocorrect.
- Select the Autocorrect tab.

- The field labeled "With" should already contain the selected text that you want Word to type for you. Simply type the desired shortcut in the "Replace" field.
- Click the "Add" button.
- Note that you can also open the Autocorrect dialog box from the menu and work directly in that dialog box to enter new shortcuts.

Once this shortcut has been recorded, Word will replace it with the longer phrase as soon as you type the last character of the shortcut and press the spacebar. Be careful to choose shortcut text that you'll rarely if ever type; for example, because *mr* is also used as a shortcut for *mister*, I've added the *]* character at the start of the shortcut to ensure that I'll only get the missing reference admonition when I really want it. Although you can undo undesired replacements easily enough using the undo command, this rapidly grows tedious, particularly if you've already typed several words before you notice the problem.

To remove a shortcut you no longer need:

- Open the Tools menu and select Autocorrect.
- Click the Autocorrect tab.
- Scroll through the list of entries, select the unnecessary item, then click the "Delete" button. (Another good reason to prefix your custom Autocorrect entries with a character such as *]* is that this groups

Turn off the Autoformat feature: Word's Autoformat feature often causes strange things to happen to text without any intervention by you; for example, e-mail and Web addresses suddenly become hyperlinks, sentences begun with a hyphen suddenly become bulleted lists, and a series of three dashes (often typed to replace an em dash) suddenly becomes a line across the width of the page. To tame this feature, open the Tools menu, select Autocorrect, and turn off the settings on both Autoformat tabs. "Autoformat as you type" specifies changes that Word should make each time you reach the end of a word or sentence or paragraph; "Autoformat" specifies changes that are made only if you open the Format menu and select the Autoformat option. (You can also apply the Autoformat command to a selected block of text rather than the whole document. That's generally more useful.)

all your shortcuts together in the alphabetical listing, thereby making it easier to find them.)
- Click the "OK" button to close the dialog box.

Autotext (formerly Word's *Glossary* function) is designed to work better for larger blocks of text, such as the multiple sentences in a standard warning message. Here's how to use Autotext for these longer texts:
- Select the long chunk of text that you want to create as an autotext entry.
- Open the Tools men and select Autocorrect.
- Select the Autotext tab. The text will appear in the bottom of the dialog box under the heading "Preview". You can't edit the text here, so if it's wrong, close the dialog box and revise the text in the main document window before you try again.
- Word will propose the first few words of the selected text as a shortcut. Replace this with a shortcut such as *[warning]* that will be easier to remember and use.

When you begin typing the shortcut that you've defined, Word scans through its autotext list, and if it finds the word you've typed, it displays a popup balloon that contains the first few words of the replacement text; to insert that text, simply press the Tab key. If you have several similar Autotext entries, keep typing until you've displayed enough text in that popup balloon to distinguish between them, *then* press the Tab key.

To remove an Autotext entry that you no longer need:
- Open the Tools menu and select Autocorrect.
- Click the Autotext tab.
- Select the shortcut you want to remove, then click the "Delete" button.
- Click the "OK" button to close the dialog box.

Is there any reason to select Autocorrect over Autotext? Not really. Autotext is better at accommodating long passages of text, but is slightly more awkward to use because you have to remember to use the Tab key. In practice, the choice mostly comes down to a matter of personal preference. Choose whichever of the two tools best suits your work style; the more comfortable it is to use, the more often you'll use it.

To print a list of all autotext items you've created, open the File menu, select Print, then in the field labeled "Print what?", select "Autotext entries". Better still, make a backup of these entries in a separate Word document, as described in the last section of this chapter.

Build your own automatic text features

If your software lacks a specialized autocorrect function or if you don't want to deal with the potentially confusing manner in which Word stores these shortcuts, you can build your own autocorrect function. The easiest solution involves recording a macro that (only on demand) uses the software's search and replace tools to replace one or more of your shortcuts (such as the *Jmr* shortcut that I described previously) with the desired text. In this approach, you simply type all those shortcuts without bothering to replace them instantly, then at a convenient moment, run the macro to do the replacements for you.

If you prefer more control over the replacement process or don't like macros, simply create a file that stores all the shortcuts you plan to use, along with the associated text. Then type all the shortcuts into the manuscript as you edit. At the end of the edit, open the file containing your shortcuts and use it as a checklist to guide a manual search and replace operation. For each item in the checklist, copy the replacement text to the clipboard, then manually do a global search and replace for the shortcut, using any of the approaches described in Chapter 8.

If even this is too much work, create a word processor document that contains all your standard chunks of text, grouped nicely under headings and arranged in a logical order so you can find them easily. Keep this file open in the background while you're editing a manuscript, and whenever it's necessary to insert a long comment, switch to that file. (The keyboard shortcuts for switching efficiently between files are described in Chapter 5.) You can now copy and paste the comment into the manuscript.

Back up your hard work

If you've gone to all the trouble to create the time-saving shortcuts described in this chapter, you won't want to risk losing them to a computer crash, a lightning storm, or a thief who runs off with your computer. Thus, you should make a point of including the files that store this information in your ongoing backups. In this section, I'll help you understand which files to include and where you can find them.

Some software stores its macros in a special directory, where they become accessible from within any new or existing document. In contrast, Word stores macros in its template files and makes those macros available for use in any documents based on those templates. (You can also copy macros between templates or from a template to a document file to make them accessible more widely, as discussed earlier in this chapter.) By default, Word stores its macros in the Normal.dot template, but as I noted earlier in this chapter, you can also store macros in other documents.

The advantage of storing macros and other shortcuts in Normal.dot is that they automatically become available in any document on your computer. That's more convenient than having to manually load them for each file that you work on. The drawback is that if anything bad happens to Normal.dot, you've lost all the hard work that went into creating them, and it may take a very long time indeed to restore them. Unfortunately, Normal.dot is a major target of virus writers, and is vulnerable to irreversible damage if Word or your computer crashes while the template file is in use. Some Word experts recommend not storing macros in Normal.dot for these reasons, but storing them in another template doesn't protect your macros if Word crashes while those templates are in use. Thus, it's crucial to include all your template files in your backups.

The location of the template files varies among versions of Word. In current versions, you can find them in a directory named (logically enough) "Templates", most often found in the Microsoft Office directory that stores Word and the other Office programs. To find this directory quickly, use the search function provided by your operating system to find all files that end in the ".dot" extension (Windows); on the Macintosh, search for a file named "Normal" (with no extension) or for the Templates directory itself.

If your software stores macros in a separate directory on your hard disk, learn the location of that directory and include it in your backups. Consult the online help for details, or ask other people who use the same software.

Backing up your templates and any directories that contain macros means that if anything happens to the originals, you can replace them in a matter of minutes. (I've presented more details on a complete back-up strategy in Appendix I.)

Automatic text information can be considerably trickier to back up, as the location of this information is not always clear or easily accessible. Current versions of Word stores automatic text in so-called "ACL" files. In Windows, these files have the filename extension ".acl", and you can find them easily using the Windows search tool. Information on how to work with these files can be found on Microsoft's "How to move autocorrect entries between computers" Web page (http://support.microsoft.com/?kbid=207748). The Word MVPs site also provides information on how you can export autocorrect files for use on another computer (http://word.mvps.org/FAQs/Customization/ExportAutocorrect.htm).

On the Macintosh, ACL files are stored in your Preferences folder, and have names such as "MS Office ACL [language]", where [language] indicates which language the autocorrect entries apply to. To back up these files or move them to a different computer, simply copy them and move them to the desired location.

For additional protection, you can copy the text of all your macros (e.g., the VBA programming code) and all other shortcuts (e.g., automatic text) into a separate word processor document and include that document in your backups. This is less necessary if you have a good backup strategy for the other files, but it provides a measure of additional security.

Other programs work differently, but the principle remains the same: take the time to learn where your software stores all your customizations so you can make backup copies of this work. All it takes is one virus or hard disk crash and you're back where you started, endlessly typing and retyping text manually and manually performing all those tedious tasks you used to perform in a single step with a macro.

More efficiency tips

Efficiency is about more than just learning the intricacies of your software so you can bend your computer hardware and software to your will. The best way to steadily increase your productivity is to spend a few minutes each day paying attention to things that frustrate you or that take too long, and trying to learn a new trick that will make your editorial life easier. Most of this book is designed to help you identify these tricks, but each of us works differently and will find different areas that need streamlining.

Efficient use of your computer is not restricted to onscreen editing alone. For a source of a great many additional insights into how you can force your computer to make your life easier, make a point of periodically checking out the tips and tricks at the "lifehacker" Web site (www.lifehacker.com).

Chapter 12. Editing in special situations

Hocine bibo aut in eum digitos insero? (Do I drink this or stick my fingers in it?)
—Henry Beard, *Latin for all Occasions*

It might seem that your word processor is only useful for editing word processor files, and that statement is indeed true so far as it goes: by definition, you can't open a file for editing in your word processor if your word processor can't open it. However, the circularity of that definition is a clue that something's wrong with the logic, and the error is subtle: when we think of word processor files, we tend to think only of files created in that word processor. The key to opening our eyes and widening our horizons is the following: most applications, in addition to saving files in their own proprietary format, can also save their files in a range of other formats. These alternatives include rich text format (RTF), the Web's HTML format, and "text" (ASCII) format. As I'll show in the rest of this chapter, you can easily open files in these formats in most word processors.

The realization that your word processor can open more than its own files opens up a whole new world of editing opportunities. So long as a given program can save stored information in text (ASCII or HTML) format or in a word processor format such as RTF, you can open the file in your word processor, save it again in your word processor's native file format, and edit it on the screen with all your changes tracked. (I'll explain the procedure in more detail later in this chapter.) If you're really lucky, the author can simply review your edits, then re-import the edited file into the original software. But even in the worst-case scenario, it's still possible to manually copy your edits into the original software. In that case, you're still using your word processor as a powerful tool for editing more effectively and consistently, and for clearly communicating your edits to the author.

In this chapter, I'll discuss several broad categories of information that pose difficult editing challenges:

- Web pages (HTML files) and other files created using a "markup" language
- desktop publishing files
- databases and spreadsheets

But first, a brief digression into the history of publishing to provide some important insights into how editing fits within any information creation and publishing process.

Edit twice, publish once

In the traditional publishing business, it was always much easier, faster, and less expensive to change manuscripts *before* layout, and most publishers ensured that the heavy-duty editing was performed before the manuscript was sent for layout. This practice has its origins in the days when it was extremely difficult to create layouts with the available tools: When you had to haul a new 10-ton block of marble from the quarry because you screwed up the wording and had to redo several days of hammer-and-chisel work, you had a powerful incentive to figure out what you were doing before you actually tried doing it. The offset printing revolution made things better because the quarry was no longer part of the picture, but you still didn't want to have to manually reinsert thousands of lead slugs into dozens of wooden galleys to redo the layout of an entire book because the author omitted a paragraph. Early desktop publishing software, though far more flexible than galleys

A new Word format: When they released Word 2007, Microsoft reverted to its old bad ways and adopted a new file format (.docx) completely incompatible with previous versions of Word. The good news? You can still save files in the old format (.doc). The bad news? Versions of Word older than Word 2000 won't open .docx files. Microsoft released a conversion update for newer versions, and to find out whether one is available for you, visit their Web site (www.microsoft.com/downloads) and search for "Microsoft Office Compatibility Pack for Word, Excel, and PowerPoint 2007 File Formats". Microsoft won't fix the problem for older versions, and Macintosh converters were "in the works". If you use these versions, you'll have to ask your client to save the file in the old doc format, or rely on third-party conversion utilities. For the Macintosh, try the Docx Converter software; search for it Apple's downloads site (www.apple.com/downloads/macosx/). Unfortunately, you must be using OS X 10.4 (Tiger) or later to use this utility.

of lead type, was still quite primitive, and major changes at the layout stage remained difficult and expensive until quite recently. When I began working with peer-reviewed journals in the mid-1980s, it was still common for a journal publisher to charge the author as much as US$10 *per line of type affected by an author's correction* after the article had been laid out by their production staff; if inserting a word changed the word wrap in the next ten lines of type, that insertion cost the author US$100.

To a lesser extent, these problems persist today. Today's desktop publishing software is far more powerful than the software available even a few years ago, and is often integrated with word processors so that editors and designers can work simultaneously on the same texts, but complex layouts still require considerable time and effort. All this time and effort may be wasted if major changes are subsequently required in the text. Even seemingly minor changes, such as renumbering a figure caption or deleting a figure, can have major repercussions that ripple like falling dominoes through the rest of the layout. The difficulty of redoing layouts has led to a standard workflow in which the bulk of the review and revision (including editing) is done long before a manuscript is sent to the layout staff.

Given that it can still be difficult to redo layouts and republish information, despite the advances made by modern publishing technology, it remains most productive to edit information heavily before you go to all the effort of creating a layout for printing. The same is true to differing extents for any other file type, whether a Web page, a database, or a spreadsheet, but in these cases, it's even more important to do the editing first. Because of the ease of publishing a Web page or database or spreadsheet, it's tempting to publish the material instantly, then clean it

More sophisticated tools: The expensive software used by high-volume publishers who produce weekly magazines and daily newspapers lets them avoid many of these problems. In addition, technical writers often work with modern single-sourcing tools that separate the layout or display of information from the information itself. (If you've ever designed a Web page using cascading style sheets, you understand how this works.) Both groups of tools automatically redo layouts in response to editing changes—even major ones. But most editors only occasionally work with such tools.

up later. This leads to considerable embarrassment when the inevitable errors are discovered by the audience. This kind of embarrassment is entirely unnecessary; it's not rocket science to plan for an editing stage between the writing and publishing stages.

Apart from the embarrassment of making your stupid mistakes visible to the whole world, there's another good reason for editing material before laying it out or structuring it in a database or spreadsheet: current Web authoring, database, and spreadsheet software offer revision tracking and editing tools that are primitive at best and completely inadequate in many cases. (There are some promising signs of change, but it'll be several years before the tools currently in development have been refined to a point at which they can compete with the revision tracking features in Word and WordPerfect.) The result is that the collaborative process of editing and revision becomes far more difficult and time-consuming than necessary once information is moved into these tools and prepared for publishing. This is particularly true when the editors and designers use different and incompatible software.

The solution is simple: just as carpenters proverbially "measure twice, cut once", information creators should edit twice and publish once. Often, the easiest way to do this is to work within a word processor that offers good revision tracking tools. If the information originates in another program such as a spreadsheet, it may still be helpful to export the information into a word processor and edit it there before importing the information back into the original program. Unfortunately, it isn't always possible to do so, and this leads to many situations in which we can't edit material before it is laid out, entered into a database or spreadsheet, or published online. In these situations, the guidelines in this chapter can help you cope while minimizing the amount of work required of everyone involved in the review and revision process. Chapter 16 goes into considerably more detail about onscreen *proofreading* of documents that have been laid out in desktop publishing software. In the present chapter, I'll focus mostly on the more major tasks of developmental editing, substantive editing, and copyediting that precede the proofreading stage: proofreading should ideally involve only the kinds of minor changes that are left to perform after a document has already been heavily and carefully edited. Because graphics represent a special class of problem, I'll deal with them separately in Chapter 13. In this chapter, I'll focus on Web pages, markup languages, databases, and spreadsheets.

Sometimes light editing is possible

Sometimes authors have followed the traditional process described in the previous section, and we're fortunate in only having to do light copyediting—work that is almost at the level of proofreading. In that case, it doesn't really matter what software is being used to produce the material that we'll edit; we don't have to work in that software or import the information into another program. We can simply give the author a list of comments.

For a really light edit, sometimes all that's necessary is a simple e-mail message containing such editorial gems as "you spelled my name wrong—it's *Geoff*, with a *G*" and "In the first sentence of the second paragraph under the heading *Editing*, change *revsion* to *revision*." We don't have to retype all the problematic text: we can simply copy it into the e-mail message so the author can focus on the specific problem. After copying the text, we can explain the problem and how to fix it.

However, as the number of problems we must report increases, the author's job of deciphering and carrying out our instructions becomes increasingly tedious and error-prone. To facilitate this process, consider sending a word processor document containing a table that organizes and presents the information more clearly. For example:

Heading	Paragraph	Sentence	Error	Correction
Title	1	1	Jeff	Geoff
Editing	2	1	Typo: revsion	Revision

Note that the table works better than the simplistic e-mail message for two reasons: First, it groups information into logical navigation aids such as headings that help the author find the problem. Second, it eliminates the need to repeatedly retype the location information. If we're working with a paginated PDF document, alternative column headings might be Page, Column, and Line number; if we're working on a spreadsheet or a database, the corresponding headings might be the cell coordinates (e.g., row 12, column C) or record numbers, respectively. In each case, the goal must be to efficiently and clearly communicate the location of the problem and provide enough information that the author can decide how to fix the problem. If the resulting table of edits extends over more than one page, we should repeat these column titles on each page—and most word processors can do the hard work for us, by automatically repeating table headings at the top of each new page.

Because clients must still incorporate our edits manually, with the attendant risk of introducing new errors while fixing the old ones, someone must take responsibility for ensuring that our edits have been correctly incorporated in the file. Ideally, that someone should be us, since we're most familiar with the problems we asked the author to solve, and thus best qualified to decide whether they solved those problems. But another advantage of using a table is that we can easily add a column for checkmarks to indicate that a change has been made. Whoever has the responsibility for confirming that the changes were made correctly can simply write a checkmark on a printout of the table or type a checkmark in the word processor file. This makes it easier to ensure that all changes have been made, and have been made correctly.

The increasing availability of Acrobat PDF files provides another good option for light edits. For example, Macintosh OS X offers the ability to produce PDF files from the Print dialog box of any program. (A similar capability is planned for Windows Vista.) We can therefore create a PDF file from just about any information and use Adobe Acrobat (the PDF-creation software, not Adobe Reader) to annotate the information using commenting tools. If you're not willing to purchase the full version of Acrobat, there are many alternatives, such as PDFPen for the Macintosh (www.smileonmymac.com/PDFpen/index.html). Acro-

Repeating table headings: To repeat table headings on each new page in Word, select the first row of the table, open the Table menu, and select Table Properties. Select the Row tab, then select the checkbox for "Repeat as header row at the top of each page". The details may vary slightly from version to version of Word, but the basic idea is the same.

bat itself offers a Web Capture tool that can convert entire Web pages into PDF files (as shown below).

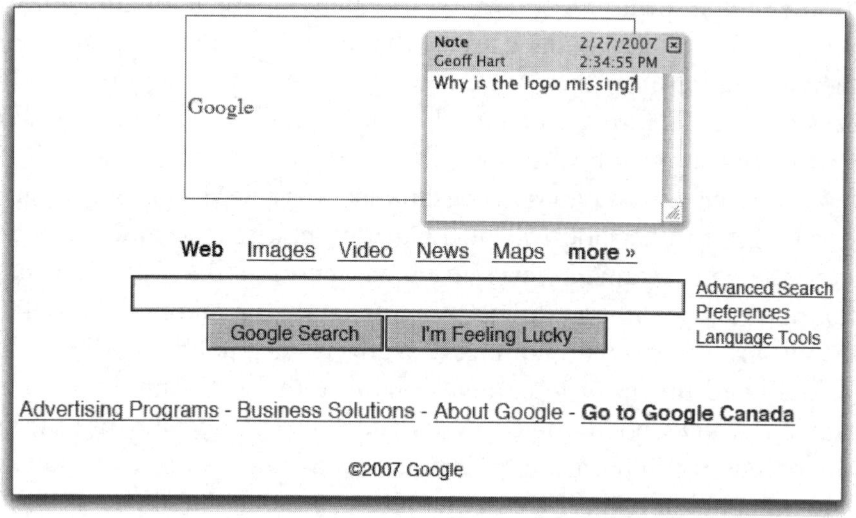

Unfortunately, clients must still manually integrate our revisions into the source document and confirm that the changes have been made correctly.

There may also be specialized tools for dealing with certain types of files. For example, tools that let visitors annotate Web sites were briefly popular a few years ago. The best known example of these tools was ThirdVoice (now seemingly disappeared), which let its users annotate a Web site so that anyone using the ThirdVoice software could view the annotations, which were stored on the ThirdVoice server. The software could be used as a "graffiti" tool for posting comments (polite or otherwise) about a Web site without the owner's permission, or as an annotation and collaboration tool that allowed designers and users of Web sites to collaborate at a distance to improve the design. More recently, Quadralay stepped into the gap created by the departure of ThirdVoice with a truly professional tool for annotating Web sites: WebWorks ePublisher for Word and FrameMaker (www.quadralay.com). Although this software doesn't permit true substantive editing, it is excellent for both light editing and heavy commenting on a document, using an approach similar to Acrobat's.

However, more often we find that managers who are inexperienced in the fine art of information creation have published their information without any editing. That's a particular risk on the Web, since—in contrast with having to recall an entire print run of a publication and pay for a new printing—there's no perceived cost for fixing errors. (Never mind the irreparable damage that can be done to corporate and other reputations!) In these cases, significant editorial surgery may be necessary, but we face a problem: the information is usually now stored in special-purpose software, probably a Web authoring tool such as Dreamweaver or a database program such as FileMaker. Simply listing changes to be made will no longer be efficient because incorporating the edits manually takes too long, increases the risk of missing important edits, and risks introducing new errors—all of which defeat the purpose of onscreen editing. Starting from scratch by editing the original word processor document might be the best solution in some cases, but won't work if you don't have access to that document or if (as is increasingly common) the information was never in a word processor document in the first place (e.g., if it was created in a Web authoring tool). In that case, it would be far more useful to edit the information using effective revision-tracking tools to communicate our changes to the author. If only that were possible!

Fortunately, it often is.

Many file types, one approach

In many cases, it's possible to edit information using your word processor even if that information didn't begin its life in a word processor. The trick is to find a way to export information from a program (i.e., save it in a different file format) so that you can open the resulting file in your word processor, edit it there, and return it to the creator so that they can import the edited information back into its original software. The good news is that most modern programs can export their information as a text (ASCII) file or using formats such as the Web's HTML language. The bad news is that this isn't always easy, and that it isn't always easy to reimport the edited information. But with patience and persistence, you can accomplish much more than you might expect. In the rest of this chapter, I'll discuss several examples of this process.

There are three things to keep in mind before you use your word processor to edit material created in a different category of software:

- Some software relies heavily on calculation formulas or other special codes that are indissociably attached to the words and numbers that you'll be editing. For example, many numbers stored in spreadsheets are not actually numbers, but are instead defined as calculation formulas such as *sum(c1:c15)*. (That's the instruction in Microsoft Excel that tells the software to add up the contents of cells *c1* to *c15* and place the result in the cell that contains this formula.) Much of this hidden coding will disappear during the conversion into a format that is editable in a word processor; depending on the software and how the coding has been implemented, the formula will either be replaced by the results of the formula (here, a single number), thereby losing the formula, or will be replaced with static information that may be impossible to correctly translate into a formula again. If the coding is not stored separately from the information that you'll be editing, the author will have to recreate the coding manually when they reopen the edited file in the program used to create it.
- The original creator software should ideally be able to reimport the edited file so that editorial changes don't have to be manually copied into the original copy of the file. Unfortunately, some software does a much better job of exporting information into a specific output format than it does of reimporting that information. If the software can't reimport the edited file efficiently *and accurately*, the author must instead transfer the edits manually, and that sacrifices one of the biggest benefits of onscreen editing.
- Ideally, the format of the information should be defined for each category of information as a whole (e.g., for an entire spreadsheet column) rather than for each individual piece of information. Where formatting has been applied to each item, that formatting may disappear during the conversion into a format that is editable in your word processor, and must then be reapplied manually; if the formatting is applied to a collection of information as a whole, this step is no longer necessary. The RTF file format is often a good choice because it preserves most formatting and is read accurately by most word processors. However, it does not preserve formulas and special codes.

You can still edit files in your word processor despite these problems, but you'll have to recognize that the problems exist and develop ways to detect and solve them. With these caveats in mind, the approach to editing files that did not originate in a word processor is the same in each case. It comprises the following steps:

1. **Extract the information from the software.**

   Open the File menu, and select Save As or Export.

2. **Choose the new format.**

   In the file format options, choose an appropriate format. "Rich text format" (RTF) is a good choice for information that is primarily textual, since it retains formatting information such as paragraph styles, whereas "text" (ASCII) is better for primarily numeric or unformatted information. HTML or XML are better choices for structured (hierarchical) information such as Web pages. Where text format is your only option, typical formats include *text only*, *text with line breaks*, *MS DOS text*, and *MS DOS text with line breaks*. Try them in that order to see which one works best for your specific combination of software.

3. **Open the file in your word processor.**

   Most word processors are set by default to list only files that have been stored in their own special format (e.g., .doc files for Word, .wpd files for WordPerfect). If you don't see the file containing the information that you'll be editing, you'll have to change this setting. In the "Open File" dialog box, set the options for "Display files of type" to "All documents" (or equivalent wording).

4. **Save the file in your word processor's native file format.**

   This step is necessary so you can use the software's version of revision tracking. The codes used to describe revisions are usually only available in the software's native file format (e.g., .doc for Word), but a subset of these codes will usually be preserved in other formats such as RTF.

5. **Edit the file.**

   Edit the file using revision tracking so that the author can see and review your edits.

6. **Return the edited file to the author.**

   The author can now review your edits. Ideally, they should use the same word processor that you used to perform the edits. Because most computers now ship with some version of Word or WordPerfect, editing in these programs is generally a good choice. OpenOffice (www.openoffice.

org) is another good choice because free versions are available for Windows, Macintosh, and Linux.

7. **Save the final file in a suitable format for reimport by the original software.**

   After reviewing your changes and ensuring that no unimplemented edits remain in the file, the author saves the file again in whichever format (e.g., RTF) is easiest for the original software to reimport.

8. **Restore the information to its original format.**

   The author opens the file or imports it into the original software used to create the information, then performs any necessary cleanup. Careful inspection of the result is necessary to detect any problems such as lost codes or formulas.

In any such approach, the author or someone else with sharp eyes must always examine the information carefully to ensure that nothing has been lost, imported into the wrong location, or otherwise messed up. Where the software performs programmed actions, such as the calculations in a spreadsheet or links between tables in a database, these actions must be carefully tested. This step cannot be neglected if you expect to avoid unpleasant surprises. As we'll see in the section on spreadsheets later in this chapter, however, storing information separately from the codes and formulas that use that information may largely eliminate this problem. If you know that you'll be doing large amounts of editing for an author, it's worth discussing whether that approach to design is possible.

If you're using a relatively recent version of your word processor, you may be able to import files such as spreadsheets directly, without going through the export process I've described. For example, Word 2000 and later versions can directly import Excel spreadsheets and convert them into Word tables. To do so:

- Open the File menu and select Open.
- Under the heading "File of type", select Excel worksheet.
- In the "Open File" dialog box, choose "Entire workbook".
- When the import is complete, the contents of each worksheet will become a separate Word table.

Many authors import files such as spreadsheets and graphics into a word processor document as *embedded objects*. Although this offers certain efficiencies (e.g., the numbers in the word processor document are automatically updated as the contents of the spreadsheet change), it is not

> **Be careful with exports and imports:** If you plan to try this kind of editing (i.e., export, edit, then reimport the edited information) for the first time, test this process scrupulously to ensure that it works and to identify any potential problems. This requires a quality-assurance phase in which someone with sharp eyes and good knowledge of the expected results reviews the final version of the information in the final software that will publish that information. (Think of this as the equivalent to proofreading text after importing a word processor file into desktop publishing software.) For example, I've edited simple Microsoft Access databases in Word with little problem, but more complicated databases with large text fields (paragraphs rather than sentences) resulted in erratic and unpredictable data loss. I suspect that this resulted from errors in the database design (a single large table rather than a proper fully relational design with multiple tables), but could not confirm this.

a useful approach for editing. Why? Because you generally cannot edit the embedded object using the word processor's revision tracking tools. When you click inside the object, the application that created it (here, spreadsheet software) opens. At best, you are restricted to the editing tools provided by that application. At worst, you cannot edit the object at all.

While you edit a Web page or any other kind of document that has been laid out and structured, pay attention to more than just the individual numbers or words and phrases. The effectiveness of such documents relies on both the information and its presentation, and the two are sometimes inseparable. This is also true in print publishing, but for more dynamic documents such as Web pages, we must also test things such as links and scripts, as well as special effects such as responses of the page to mouse movements (e.g., displaying popup balloons or changing the appearance of a button). Since you're already acting as the reader's advocate when you edit the text, make the extra effort to report usability or comprehensibility problems for the Web page as a whole. Point out problems such as:

- Unclear links or links that go to the wrong destination.
- Illegible portions of the layout.

Revision tracking in Excel: Excel also offers its own revision tracking tools, but although they are effective for small editing jobs, they are clumsy and inefficient compared to the tools provided by a modern word processor. Nonetheless, you can use them for small spreadsheets that contain relatively little text, for small amounts of editing, or for spreadsheets in which it is impossible to separate the editable text from the calculation formulas. The section on editing spreadsheets later in this chapter provides some additional options.

- Unclear visual structure and navigation schemes.
- Mismatches between the text and any accompanying graphics, whether the problems are objective (outright contradictions) or subjective (an inappropriate style or tone).
- Ineffective or illogical sequences of information.
- Inconsistency (visual or textual) with other pages that serve similar functions.
- Incomplete content, such as missing contact information or links back to the home page.

These general principles apply to any situation in which you'll be using your word processor to edit information created in another type of program. In the remainder of this chapter, I'll present several specific examples of how this approach to editing works.

Simple markup languages: Web pages and HTML

Web pages are the most familiar kind of files formatted using a markup language—specifically, the HyperText Markup Language (HTML)—but markup languages were also used way back in the dark ages of personal computing. Most people who were using personal computers to write in the 1980s (me, for instance) used word processors such as WordStar and AtariWriter, in which writers manually applied formatting codes that greatly resembled those used in modern HTML. For example, to boldface a word, you might surround it with codes marking the beginning and ending of boldface format: <b>boldfaced</b>. WordPerfect represented something of a breakthrough in its approach to writing: the software hid these formatting codes until you explicitly chose to reveal them, at which point the markup language suddenly appeared in the form of more or less cryptic tags. The ability to inspect these tags was a godsend when it came time to troubleshoot problems with what you were seeing on the screen. Then along came Microsoft Word and ruined everything by hiding the codes, by refusing to reveal them, and by storing the codes in a convoluted proprietary format that only a computer could understand and love.

Unfortunately, Word is more typical of modern software. Just about any computer file requires some variant of a markup language to describe and structure the data it contains, though that markup language may be impenetrably obscure and next to impossible to read without using the software that created it. HTML differs from these proprietary formats in two significant ways

- The files are saved in text (ASCII) format and thus can be edited without first converting them from a proprietary format that is understood only by the software that created them.
- The formatting tags are simple enough that anyone can learn them with a little effort. (Even if you don't want to learn how to code Web pages in HTML, you can quickly learn to recognize the tags.)

Both of these points are important, because they reveal how we can edit seemingly uneditable files such as Web pages while still tracking our revisions for the author to review. First, we must convert the files from their native text format into a format that allows our word processor to use revision tracking; this is usually no more complicated than saving the files in the word processor's standard format (e.g., .doc files for Word). Second, we must be able to sort through all the tags and present the information in such a way that we can focus on the content. (Here,

Other markup languages: HTML is the naïve kid brother of two more powerful markup languages: XML and SGML. We'll discuss those two languages in the next section. If you work with scientists and mathematicians, you'll occasionally get requests to edit files produced in TeX or LaTeX, which are specialized word processors designed for typesetting manuscripts that are heavy on the mathematics. Because these programs use markup languages in much the same way that HTML files do, you can use the approach described in this section to edit them too.

I'm assuming that as editors, our job is to edit the content, not the tags that describe how that content should be displayed. If you're an HTML geek, you may be asked to edit the tags too.) Third, we must find a way to minimize the risk that we'll damage any of the tags, and thus prevent the edited Web page from displaying properly.

With that in mind, here's how to proceed.

Save the file on your hard disk

If your client has sent you a Web page via e-mail or on CD, simply save a working copy on your computer. If you must instead work with a page already published on the Web, open that page in your Web browser. With the page displayed, open the File menu and select Save As. The options will vary among browsers, but typically you should select "Web page, HTML only (*.htm, *.html)" to save just the text components of the page. If you will be editing the graphics as well, select "Web page, complete (*.htm, *.html)" or the equivalent option, then edit the graphics separately, as described in Chapter 13.

Although HTML files are standard ASCII text, most word processors will recognize the filename extension (.htm or .html) and do their best to interpret the HTML codes. This means that, left to their own devices, they'll open and display the file as if it were a Web page (e.g., words meant to be italicized or boldfaced will actually appear that way) and you won't see any of the HTML tags. That's not a good thing, because most word processors will attempt to apply their own formatting and conversion rules to the HTML tags, and you run a high risk of damaging the original contents of the file by rewriting existing tags or inserting new ones. (Word is particularly notorious for this.)

To avoid this problem and ensure that you'll be able to see the tags, rename the file so that your word processor will treat it as an unformatted text file rather than as a "formatted" HTML file. To do so:

- Make a copy of the file.
- Replace the .htm or .html filename extension of that copy with .txt so that your word processor will treat the file as a simple text file. (That's what it is, but your word processor may be too smart to understand this if it sees the .htm extension.)
- Open the file. If you can't see the file in the "Open File" dialog box, set the software to "display all files".

Note that this approach leaves the original downloaded HTML file as your backup, so you won't have to create a separate backup copy before you begin editing. You can also use that HTML file to guide your substantive editing; that is, you can open it in your Web browser to see what it looks like, test the links, and so on.

Save the file in your word processor's native file format

The problem with text files is that they can't contain all the fancy formatting that your word processor is capable of, including the formatting code that it uses to support its revision tracking features. The solution, of course, is to save the text file in your word processor's native file format. To do so, open the File menu, select Save As, and in the field labeled "Save as type", select the appropriate file type. For a Word document, that's the .doc format.

Edit the file's contents, *not* its tags

When you open this third version of the file, you'll see both the text that you're going to edit and all the tags that the authoring software created to describe how that text should appear in a Web browser. These tags pose two significant problems:

- If you inadvertently delete or modify an HTML tag during editing, you'll change how the page displays once it's published on the Web. Some of these deletions or modifications are harmless, but others can have disastrous effects on the page's appearance and contents, and they may be difficult for the author to detect and correct.
- The actual content you're trying to edit will be hidden amidst a thicket of tags, making it hard to see, let alone edit. That's particularly true of documents originally created in Web authoring software that defines pages as nested groups of tables, such as NetObjects Fusion (as a rule) or Dreamweaver (if the author used tables to design the layout).

The solution is fairly simple: color the tags in such a way that they are less visually prominent than the content you'll be editing, but without making them vanish so much that you risk damaging them inadvertently. For example, change them to a color such as green that clearly differs from the surrounding black text. I find that kind of color pattern difficult to work with because the colors distract me, and prefer to use a lighter color such as pale grey, but many others prefer a bolder approach.) Since you'll be doing this kind of change frequently if you edit many HTML files, and since the change takes several steps, record a macro to do the work for you the first time you go through this process. (If you need help, see Chapter 11 for details on recording macros.)

Here's how you'd accomplish this color change in Word:

- Open the Tools menu and select Macro, then Record New Macro.
- Name the macro (for example, "HideTags"), and assign a keystroke to it if you want to run the macro from the keyboard rather than from the Macro menu.
- Open the Edit menu and select Replace.
- Click the More button or the arrow used to expand the dialog box, and select the option "Use wildcards". (For more information on using wildcards in searches, see Chapter 8.)
- In the "Find what" field, type [<]*[>]. The square brackets mean "look for anything in the set of characters enclosed within the brackets"; the first set of square brackets thus searches for the opening angle bracket of an HTML tag. The asterisk means "any group of characters", and thus refers to the text contained inside the HTML tag. Last but not least, the second set of square brackets searches for the closing angle bracket of the HTML tag. The square brackets are necessary because the angle brackets have special meanings in a wildcard search, and you don't want their special meanings; you just want the brackets themselves.
- In the "Replace with" field, type ^& (on most keyboards, this is the caret character above the number 6, followed by the ampersand character). In Word, this code means "insert the search term itself here"; we're not going to delete or otherwise damage the tags, so we want to replace them with themselves.
- With the cursor still in this field, click the Format button and select Font.
- Under the heading "Font color", select a color that will leave the tags visible, but not so prominent that they keep you from concentrating on the text. A light grey color tends to work best for me; if you prefer something brighter, such as green or red, choose that color instead. You can also choose "hidden text" as a font format, then

set Word to display only text that isn't hidden. I don't recommend this approach because it's too easy to inadvertently delete tags that you can't see.

- Click the "Replace all" button.

As soon as the macro finishes its work, the file will resemble the text shown here (with a simple edit to show a typical tracked change):

<html>

<head>

<title>Example of grey tags</title>

</head>

<body>

<p>This sample text shows the effects of **coloring** ~~**("ghosting")**~~ of the HTML tags so that they are separate from the text that will be edited.</p>

</body>

</html>

In this example, I've chosen ghostly grey for the HTML tags, but with the text to be edited appearing in the usual black color. Of course, if you'll be editing the tags themselves as part of the job, you won't want them ghosted out. In that case, either don't bother changing their color, or change it so that the tags are visually distinct from the surrounding text without being difficult to read.

Edit the content

Because the file is now a word processor document, you can turn on revision tracking and edit the file in the usual way. You'll need to know a bit about how HTML formatting works if you've been asked to review the tags too, and if you're not sure how HTML tags work, it's safer to insert a comment recommending that the author make the change rather than making the change yourself and potentially damaging the structure of the tags (and thus, changing how the page will display). There are two main cautions to keep in mind:

- If you will be moving or deleting larger blocks of text, be sure to move *both members* of paired tags together with the text they surround. For example, text contained in tables falls between the <table> and </table> tags, and each row of a table falls between the <tr> and </tr> tags. You can't move a table to a new position or change the order of rows within the table unless you move the correspond-

ing tags to the new location. Similarly, if a top-level heading loses its surrounding <h1> and </h1> tags, it will become a simple paragraph. If it loses only the closing </h1> tag, a huge chunk of text is likely to end up formatted as a heading (all the way to the next </h1> tag in the document).
- Be particularly careful with search and replace. It's easy to damage key HTML tags if they contain the text that you're searching for, particularly in the case of keywords that have been typed in the Head section of an HTML document or named styles or classes in a document formatted using CSS (cascading style sheets). Rather than trying a global search and replace, it's safer to replace instances of the search term one at a time.

Make the tags reappear

Unless you need to examine (and perhaps edit) the HTML tags too, it may not be necessary to remove the formatting that you've applied to them. As I noted in my overview of the editing process earlier in this chapter (*Many file types, one approach*), the author's final step after reviewing your edits will be to save the document in text format once again, and doing so will eliminate all formatting, including the font color you applied before you began editing. But if you must restore the tags to full visibility so you can edit them, or if you want to avoid confusing the author who will review your edits and will wonder what happened to the tags, here's how to restore the original text color:

- Turn off revision tracking. (This step is optional if your software does not track color changes as an edit.)
- Select all the text (Control + A in Windows, Command + A on the Macintosh).
- Open the Format menu, and select Font.
- Under the heading "Font color", choose either "Automatic" (i.e., the color defined by the paragraph style) or "Black", depending on the original color that was used.
- Turn on revision tracking again.

Review and reimport the file

The author can now review your edits and accept or reject them just as though they were contained in any other type of file. If any of your comments or edits relate to the HTML tags, the author can either edit the tags immediately, or remember to make the necessary changes once they reopen the final file in their Web authoring software. Once they have addressed all your edits, someone (ideally you) should review the file one final time to ensure that no edits have been missed, and particularly that no comments have been left in the file. (Any comments created using the word processor's commenting feature may simply be deleted in the course of later format conversions, since they have no HTML equivalent, but they may instead be added to the end of the file or inserted at their current position as paragraphs of unformatted text.)

If no additional edits must be addressed, save the document twice: first as a word processor file containing all your comments and tracked revisions (your backup copy), and save a second copy as a text file. Saving it as text will eliminate all your word processor's custom formatting, including any colors you applied to text. Here's how to do this:

- Open the File menu and select Save As or Export, depending on the software you're using.
- Specify "Text only" as the file type. You'll be warned that certain formatting attributes cannot be saved in the text file, and asked to confirm that you really want to proceed. Since your goal is to *remove* all that unnecessary formatting, that's fine: Click OK, and you're almost done.
- Change the filename extension (usually .txt) to the correct HTML extension (.htm or .html, whichever was used in the file the author originally sent you). Even though the underlying format (text) is correct, most Web browsers won't recognize a file as HTML until you add the correct filename extension.

The middle step is the one most likely to cause problems, since there are usually several options for text format. To find out which option

Don't *export* HTML: Although it might seem logical to save or export the file in HTML format, don't do it! In most cases, the best you can hope for is that the word processor will add a bunch of useless tags. These may not cause any harm, but they do bloat the file, and a conscientious Web designer will have to remove them again to reduce the file size and prevent future problems. At worst, some software will actually rewrite many of the tags (Word is notorious for this) and cause the Web designer serious grief.

will work best for your software, test each one by opening the resulting HTML file (the one with the .htm or .html extension) in your Web browser. If the file doesn't display correctly, try a different option. This test will also give you a chance to spot any errors you introduced by incorrectly editing a tag.

More complex markup languages: XML and SGML

HTML is a markup language for the masses, and is a wonderful tool for what it does: present information that is largely unstructured and that reflects the free-form nature of the typical Web page. However, because HTML is designed to make creation of Web pages easy rather than to enforce rigorous structuring or markup, it fails for more demanding applications. For example, HTML allows considerable sloppiness in coding a Web page, and that sloppiness often has undesirable consequences, particularly in terms of how different Web browsers display a page. To address these problems and impose a bit more consistency, a more structured version of HTML called XHTML was developed. From our editorial perspective, XHTML documents are essentially identical to regular HTML, and can be edited in precisely the same way I described in the previous section.

However, XHTML also fails to address some key needs of more demanding applications, because it does not inherently control the content of a file. Consider, for example, an online magazine in which each article must start with a title, followed by the author's name and contact information, followed by a short abstract or summary of the article, and so on. As the editor, you can certainly impose such content requirements through your edits, but the magazine publisher can't impose them *automatically* during the writing process. In some cases, documents are sufficiently complex that controlling the contents and their sequence is essential, and requiring human writers and editors to exert this control is burdensome and error-prone. To address the need for more control, a powerful and complex markup language called SGML (the "Standardized General Markup Language") was developed: The *general* part of that name indicates that the language was designed to be general-purpose, allowing document creators to define their own markup—making SGML effectively a kit for constructing custom markup languages that can meet any set of requirements, such as those of the magazine I just described. The *standard* part of the name refers to the fact that SGML makes it possible to enforce these requirements and thereby produce a standard document that differs from other similar documents only in the words it contains, not in its structure. These requirements are enforced by means of something called a "document type definition" (DTD) or "schema", which specifies all the required and optional sections, and the hierarchy of these sections (e.g., that the author's name must always follow the title). In fact, HTML is based on SGML, and differs from SGML primarily in the fact that it lacks a strongly enforced DTD. XML, a more recent innovation, is an intermediate approach: it represents a specific implementation of SGML that combines all of the rigor of SGML with much of the simplicity of HTML.

SGML and XML projects tend to be managed by large organizations such as airplane manufacturers that produce hundreds of thousands of pages of documentation for each airplane, or large financial institutions that have large teams of writers, complex single-sourcing requirements (such as the need to create online help and a printed manual from the same source file), and often a great many subcontractors providing documents for their own employer's subcomponents of a larger overall system. Fortunately, despite their greater complexity, SGML and XML documents can still be saved as text files (possibly after extracting the information from a database or other central repository), and as a result, you can edit them using exactly the same approach you would use with HTML Web pages.

Nonetheless, because the DTDs that govern the structure of XML and SGML documents can be quite complex, the documents can be proportionally more complex to review than Web pages. In addition to the cautions I presented for HTML files in the previous section, there are a few key points to keep in mind to prevent problems:

- Always save the document in text format when you're done. Although it may be tempting to use the "Save as" or "Export" function to save the file in HTML, XML, or (more rarely) SGML format, doing so guarantees problems because most word processors add their own tags and may damage a carefully designed document structure. This is particularly true if you will be using Word 2007, which uses a proprietary version of XML (.docx) as its native file format. This format is unlikely to be compatible with XML or

SGML authoring software, so using it is likely to cause significant problems for your client.

- XML and SGML documents tend to be more complicated than HTML documents. Even if you don't bother changing the color of tags in HTML documents, you should seriously consider doing so in XML and SGML documents.
- Unless you really know what you're doing, and have a deep understanding of the DTD, you should never move text around or edit the tags; doing so could render the document noncompliant with its DTD, thereby making it unusable by the author without considerable extra work to repair what you have done. If you're not an XML or SGML expert, always *suggest* (by inserting a comment) that the author move chunks of text rather than moving the text yourself.

With careful management, this approach should scale up particularly well to situations that involve a large number of subcontractors, each of whom may use a different product to generate the XML or SGML files that will be integrated into the larger project. Rather than requiring each editor or reviewer to own a copy of each subcontractor's authoring software, you can instead edit the files in a word processor. Word is available on most computers sold today, and the ones that don't come with Word pre-installed usually have WordPerfect or OpenOffice installed in its place. All three programs are highly suitable tools for onscreen editing, and can be purchased for far less money (for no

SGML requires more caution: Here's an important disclaimer: I have not personally tested this approach with SGML files, nor with XML files other than in the limited case of XHTML files. The suggestions in this section have been vetted by a colleague who does extensive work in an SGML environment for a major aerospace company, so I'm confident that the *theory* I'm presented here is sound. The implementation of that theory, however, is left as an exercise for the reader. If you're interested in testing out that theory, see Chapter 18 for a detailed discussion of how to implement onscreen editing. The process of implementation described there provides a good way to analyze, plan, and implement onscreen editing in an SGML or XML environment.

money, in the case of OpenOffice) than any of the primary XML or SGML authoring software that is currently available. If you follow the approach outlined earlier in this chapter and avoid the problems I've mentioned, you can simply reimport the final text files into the original authoring software once all the editing has been approved.

If it's not possible to review the XML or SGML documents in your word processor, it may sometimes be possible to edit the files in the original authoring software without tracking the changes. This is a reasonable option when you can use a utility or built-in feature to automatically compare the original and edited files. For example, FrameMaker includes a document comparison feature that will highlight the differences between any two FrameMaker documents, and has recently added the equivalent of Word's "track changes" feature. Similarly, Microsoft offers a utility called XMLDiff (http://msdn2.microsoft.com/en-us/library/aa302294.aspx); given any two XML files, XMLDiff will create a third file showing all the differences between them, marked up using XML tags. The effect is similar to Word's track chang-

XMetal Reviewer: Designers of sophisticated modern software are increasingly recognizing the need to collaborate on documents, and some promising software such as XMetal Reviewer, by JustSystems (www.xmetal.com/index.x), shows what will soon be possible. XMetal Reviewer lets authors, peer reviewers, and editors collaborate on a single document over the Internet or an intranet using tools that closely resemble Word's revision tracking tools. Unfortunately, this software is currently expensive, proprietary, and only runs in Internet Explorer using ActiveX controls; the latter point alone makes it unsuitable for many users, since this combination of software represents a potentially serious security problem. For these reasons, I don't consider XMetal Reviewer to be a broadly useful solution. To be truly useful, the software should also be designed to work on Web pages (HTML), in any browser (particularly more secure browsers such as Firefox), and on any platform (Macintosh, Windows, and Unix), and it should be implemented using a technology such as Java that offers more acceptable security. If you agree, write to JustSystems and tell them!

es markup. However, using such a comparison feature has several drawbacks:

- It requires careful file management, since you end up with at least three files at each stage of the review (the original file, the edited file, and a file containing the highlighted differences) rather than a single file containing tracked revisions.
- Such utilities often miss or misrepresent complex changes, particularly when multiple authors review a single document and make contradictory changes.
- Such tools are generally less efficient than highly evolved revision tracking features such as the ones provided by Word.

Nonetheless, a document comparison approach may work just fine for you if revision tracking isn't available or permitted by your employer or client. In addition, it tends to integrate well with the version-control software used by the types of companies that work primarily with XML or SGML documents.

Editing desktop publishing files

Recent versions of most desktop publishing software provide an interesting option that greatly facilitates the task of editing a manuscript created in a word processor but that has already been imported into the desktop publishing software for layout. This is usually implemented by "linking" the layout to the word processor file when importing it, instead of "embedding" the file. The details of linking and embedding vary somewhat among programs, but in general, most software observes the following distinction: If you embed the file in the desktop publishing document, all its connections with the original word processor document are severed; in contrast, if you link the desktop publishing document to the word processor file, the desktop publishing software monitors that file to see whether it has been modified since you began working on the layout, and if it has been modified, offers you the option to update its copy of the text. Linking thus allows you to edit the file in your word processor using standard revision tracking tools, review and implement the changes in the word processor, then automatically update the layout of the document without having to manually reimport the word processor file.

Of course, nothing is ever that simple. Here's how the process works in Adobe's InDesign, one of the most popular of the current crop of desktop publishing programs. InDesign automatically links to graphics files when they are imported, but to link to a word processor file instead of embedding it, you must modify one of the program's settings before you import the file. To do this, open the Preferences (Macintosh) or Options (Windows) dialog box, select the Type settings, and select the checkbox for "Create Links When Placing Text and Spreadsheet Files". (Deselecting this checkbox will cause the program to embed imported word processor and spreadsheet files.) Each time you open the layout file, InDesign will check to see whether any linked files have changed. (If you're working on the word processor document simultaneously, InDesign may not be able to update the layout until you close the word processor file.) If any files have changed, InDesign offers you the option of updating the links automatically or updating them manually using the "Links" dialog box (under the Window menu). Updating the links will ensure that the layout file contains the most recent version of the text.

The good news is that this procedure generally works quite well. For example, if you delete a paragraph in the word processor file or move a sentence to a new location in the file, these changes will be reflected in the InDesign layout as soon as you open the InDesign file and update the link. The bad news is that some of the work you've done in InDesign will be preserved, and some will be lost; which is the case will depend on which version of InDesign you're using and the nature of the changes. For example, if you've flowed the imported text into two columns or broken it across two pages in InDesign, these changes will be retained when you update the link; in contrast, if you have applied new paragraph styles to each paragraph in InDesign (thereby replacing the paragraph styles used in the word processor document), this information will be lost when you update the link and you'll have to reapply the new style names. It may take some experimentation to discover the best way of resolving certain problems. For example, if you use the same paragraph style names in your word processor document that you use in InDesign, you won't have to manually apply paragraph styles when you import the file into InDesign; InDesign will replace the word processor's paragraph styles with its own paragraph styles of the same name. Simi-

> **Garbage in, garbage out:** As I noted at the beginning of this chapter, it's almost always easier to develop a production process in which the heaviest editing occurs in a word processor before the files are sent for layout. The procedure described in the remainder of this section is acceptable in the absence of such a process, but it's still a difficult, demanding, and less efficient way to edit a manuscript.

larly, if you used character styles to apply formatting, the formatting information should also be preserved. Subsequently, when you update the linked file, you won't have to reapply these styles in InDesign.

The linking and updating process may not work to your satisfaction in every desktop publishing program, and may not work at all if you're using a program that doesn't support linking and updating or if your program cannot perform this updating with the specific file formats used by your word processor. However, if the desktop publishing software allows you to export "tagged" text, you can instead try using an editing process similar to the one described for HTML files earlier in this chapter. Adobe's PageMaker (now discontinued, but still being used by many people) and InDesign (Adobe's replacement for PageMaker) both allow you to export tagged text. A tagged file exported from these programs will resemble a Web page created in HTML; that is, you'll see chunks of text surrounded by tags that define how the desktop publishing software sees the information, and that the software will use to reestablish the formatting when you reimport the edited file. In the best possible situation, this approach allows us to "round-trip" the information: the process of exporting the file for editing and reimporting it for layout works nearly flawlessly, generally requiring only minor tweaks to restore the original layout.

In reality, the process is rarely this simple. A typical export process produces a number of files—typically one per "story". (In the parlance of desktop publishing, *stories* are separate and independent blocks of text, each usually representing a separate word processor file that has been imported and placed independently into the layout.) For example, many desktop publishers lay out a publication by creating separate word processor files for each discrete chunk of text, such as chapters, sidebars, captions, and running headers and footers. In that case, each of these files becomes a separate story, and exporting the publication will generate a separate file for each story. It can be challenging to manage all these files and reimport them successfully into their original locations within the desktop publishing file. If the editing has been heavy, with many insertions or deletions, the text probably won't fit properly into its original locations, and considerable revision of the layout will inevitably be required.

How to export the tagged text varies among programs, and rather than repeating the relevant sections of the user manual for several different programs, I'll present a more general overview of the process. Clearly, this overview will be too general to serve as your only roadmap for developing a review process; you'll have to research the details of exporting and reimporting tagged text in your software's online help, and experiment with a few trial layouts that contain only a few stories until you thoroughly understand how the process works and the kind of problems you'll encounter. Only once you've gained some experience in how the process works should you attempt to use it in a production environment, particularly under deadline pressure.

Here's an overview of a typical process based on the procedures used in PageMaker and InDesign:

- Open the File menu and select Export, then select "Tagged text". If this option is not available, look for another option, such as HTML or XML, that generates a file containing a standard set of tags. Alternatively, select a file format your word processor can recognize and work with. Rich text format (RTF) typically works well.
- If you're offered the option of choosing a text encoding format, choose one that is supported by your word processor. Unicode (the modern system for defining the characters in fonts) is a good choice because most modern word processors provide good support for Unicode fonts. There are exceptions, so it may be necessary to experiment with the various available formats until you find one that works well for your specific combination of desktop publishing program and word processor.
- If you're offered a choice between short (concise) and long (verbose) tags, carefully consider which will serve you better. In principle, there is little practical difference between the two; in practice, shorter tags produce less visual clutter but longer tags will be easier

to see in your word processor and are thus less vulnerable to being accidentally changed.

- Resist the temptation to "fix" the formatting in your word processor unless you deeply and fully understand the tagging language and can make the changes by editing the tags. Such changes may conflict with the formatting tags created by the desktop publishing program. If you're confident that a change is necessary, insert a comment to explain that change to the author, and make sure that the comment is removed before the file is reimported into the desktop publishing software.
- If the text appears difficult to read in your word processor, it may be possible to change the font used to display it. It's safe to do this if you can see the font information contained in the tags, which may be the case for files exported in text format. Don't try this in files exported as RTF, since the RTF format stores the new formatting information in a way that is likely to conflict with the formatting defined by the tags; instead, use the software's Zoom feature (usually found under the View or Window menu) to enlarge the text so that it's more easily read.
- Test what will happen to special typesetting features such as ligatures (where two characters are merged into a single ligated character, such as æ), small caps, and alternative characters in an "expert" version of the font that only the desktop publisher may own. If the word processor and desktop publishing program do not define such characters in the same way, you may need to replace these characters with placeholders. These placeholders could be simple codes such as &ae for the æ ligature; when you restore the file to the desk-

Markup languages pose a different challenge: If you're editing a manuscript on the HTML language or any other tagging language likely to be recognized by the desktop publishing software, you've got a problem: the software may interpret text that describes the tagging language (and that thus contains examples of the tags) as formatting instructions. Disaster! In that case, you'll have to experiment with different export and import formats to find a combination that works.

top publishing software, you can search for these placeholders and replace them with the correct characters.

- Edit the file and return it to the author for review.
- After reviewing the edits, reimport the file into the desktop publishing software. In general, you'll have to create a new desktop publishing file to hold the revised text. If the software allows you to import the file into an existing layout, replacing existing stories that have the same name, you'll be offered the option to replace those stories.
- You can generally import the file by reversing how you exported it (i.e., open the File menu, select Import, and choose the same file format and the same encoding you used to export the file if you are given this option). If you see an import option that says something like "Read Tags", choose that option to ensure that the software will interpret the tags as formatting instructions rather than as part of the text.

Databases and spreadsheets

The modern world runs on data every bit as much as it runs on oil. The quantities of information created and stored each day are mind-boggling, and it would be impossible to make any sense of this sea of information without assistance from the computer. Two main tools are used to manage the chaos:

- *Databases* are programs designed to store large quantities of textual and numerical data and to retrieve and manipulate (sort, combine, and publish) the data. They may also be used to store more complex pieces of information such as graphics and sound files; in case you're feeling jargon-deprived, these are often referred to as "binary large objects" (BLOBs).
- *Spreadsheets* are programs primarily designed to store numerical data, and are optimized to perform calculations on subsets of the data and publish the results as tables or graphs.

It's no accident that the "store" parts of these two definitions sound similar, as the two categories of software have increasingly overlapped: modern spreadsheets provide moderately powerful database tools, and databases often provide sophisticated calculation tools. And both define the information they contain as "data". For the sake of simplicity,

I'll treat the two as if they were essentially distinct and non-overlapping entities. But because they overlap, certain problematic characteristics of the software may appear in either (although they are more common in spreadsheets), and you must pay careful attention to them:

- The designer of a database or spreadsheet may define formulas that perform calculations on the data or that obtain data from another file or elsewhere within the same file.

  These formulas are often intermingled with the data on which the formulas operate. Because these formulas will disappear when you convert the file into text format for editing in your word processor, you must carefully plan how to preserve them: either design the spreadsheet or database (or convince its creator to design it) so that the formulas are stored separately from the information that you'll be editing, or plan to recreate the formulas manually if you can't reimport the edited data without loss of the formulas.
- The original application must be able to reimport the edited file.

  Oddly, programs can sometimes export files into a format that they cannot reimport without losing information. Always test the export and import processes before you use them in a production environment to ensure that you can successfully reimport the edited data without damaging the original file. If not, the author will have to transfer the edits manually into that file. Even if the reimportation appears to be successful, someone must take responsibility for performing quality control on the final database or spreadsheet to ensure that no problems have been introduced.
- Where possible, formulas and formatting instructions should be separated from the data.

  The designer of the spreadsheet or database should try to define the format of each category of data separately from the data. Because manually applied formatting disappears if you export the information as a text file for editing, files that do not separate the data from the instructions for formatting the data will require their creators to reapply the formats manually after reimporting an edited text file. In contrast, formatting that is defined for an entire spreadsheet row or column rather than for each individual item in that column may be preserved and may not need to be reapplied, especially if the formatting is stored in a special "report" file or a template that obtains unformatted data from a separate file; in that case, the instructions in that file apply the formatting to that data. (In this approach, the original data is not affected by this formatting and remains available for use in creating additional reports—only the copy of that data that has been imported into the report file is affected.) The RTF format preserves many formatting details, and may sometimes be a good alternative to the text (ASCII) format.

As in all the other special situations I've described in this chapter, it's always easier and more efficient to edit information *before* you place it in any software that lacks strong revision-tracking tools—such as database or spreadsheet software. The procedures described in the rest of this section are acceptable workarounds when the information has already been imported into the database or spreadsheet, but are no substitute for a rigorous workflow that controls the quality of the information before it is imported into these programs. In the rest of this section, I'll describe various options for editing databases and spreadsheets.

As I've noted previously, one very useful option is to export data from the software in a format that we can edit using revision tracking in our word processor, using an approach similar to the one I described previously for HTML files. Unfortunately, this approach may be impractical or inefficient for complex spreadsheets and databases that are full of equations and links or where the data is inextricably wrapped up in those equations and links. In particular, the multiple translations between programs (from spreadsheet to our word processor to the author's word processor and back into the spreadsheet) will almost certainly create problems. When we have access to the same software the author used to create the database or spreadsheet, a better alternative is to work directly in that software, inserting our edits in empty rows of the file or even creating wholly new files (e.g., database tables, spreadsheet worksheets) to hold our edits.

When neither approach is possible, perhaps because the software we have available to us doesn't overlap or cooperate well with that used by our authors, it may be necessary to resort to the universal file format understood by pretty much any software: text (ASCII) format. Chapter 13 (*Coping when revision tracking isn't available*) describes a variety of tips and tricks for working effectively with text files. This approach is clearly more work for both us and the author, since it requires more manual labor and permits less of the automation that makes computers so darned useful, but sometimes desperate situations call for desperate solutions—possibly even editing a printout of the files if all else fails.

Editing databases

When editing databases, we're likely to encounter two types of database: *flat-file* databases and *relational* databases. In both flat-file and relational databases, each set of related information within a single file (for example, my address information rather than yours) is referred to as a *record*. Simple databases are often flat-file databases, which usually store all their information in a single file, with recurring items (such as a city name) repeated for each record in the file (such as a person and their address in a mailing list database). More complex databases are usually relational, and consist of a linked series of *tables*, each of which is a single entity (often an independent file) that represents a subset of the larger database. For example, an extremely simple relational database you could use to keep in touch with your North American friends might consist of four files: one file that lists the names, street addresses, and postal or zip codes of all of your friends (i.e., information that is usually unique to each friend), plus pointers to information in three additional files that list information likely to be shared by at least some of your friends (cities, provinces or states, and countries). When you generate a list of mailing labels so you can send out announcements of the release of your new book on onscreen editing, the database creates a new temporary file that pulls in the required information for each record (i.e., each address label) from the separate files. The advantage of this approach is that any particular recurring item of data, such as the

Garbage in, garbage out (take II): There's a famous saying in the computer business: "garbage in, garbage out". This means that if you don't control the quality of the information used to support an analysis, you can seriously compromise the quality of the results of that analysis. In many cases, we can significantly increase the value of information through developmental and substantive editing, thus helping database and spreadsheet designers to control the quality of the inputs. One way is to develop validity-checking tools that prevent the introduction of incorrect information. I'll provide more details on this later in this chapter.

name of a city, need be stored only once (here, in the file of city names) rather than stored individually for each friend living in that city. This is both an efficient way to reduce the space required to store data and a tremendous aid to consistency, since you only have to correct typos in a city name once rather than once for each friend in that city, as would be the case in a flat-file database. (Better flat-file databases now give users at least a limited ability to link files, thereby mimicking true relational capabilities.)

Editing by exporting and reimporting the data

Both flat-file and relational databases can generally export their data in a *delimited* format, in which each record is exported as a single line of text, with each item of data for that record separated ("delimited") from the ones listed before and after it by special characters such as tabs or commas. There is generally no significant difference between comma-delimited and tab-delimited listings, though you may find the tabbed format easier to read because it separates the items in each record more obviously. The only case where you should unequivocally avoid comma-delimited files is when some of the data may itself contain commas; this might be the case in a database containing sentences, for instance.

From our editorial perspective, the main implication of working with a flat-file database is that all the information is likely to be contained in a single file. That's more convenient than working with several files, but because a record may contain dozens of pieces of data, the exported data can form very long lines in which the corresponding information for each record (e.g., the city name) no longer lines up in neat columns as it did in the original database file—in an address database, for instance, the person's name, street address, city, province or state, country, and postal code may be long enough that they wrap onto several lines once we've exported them into a word processor. In this particular example, that's not a problem because the meaning of each chunk of information will be reasonably clear, but in more complex databases, it's harder to understand what each chunk of information means. Since we must understand the meaning before we can edit that chunk, our task becomes more difficult. In addition, we may need to make the same change dozens of times; for example, a complicated foreign city name such as Tenochtitlan might be spelled half a dozen different ways. This means we'll need to use the search tool carefully, perhaps supplemented by a style sheet, to find and fix each problem.

In contrast, the main implication of working with a relational database is that we may need to edit several files (one per table) rather than a single file. This also means that we will only need to make certain corrections once, because information shared by several records will be stored once in a single table rather than being repeated in multiple records or tables. (Of course, the downside of this is that if we make a mistake once, that mistake will appear in every record that uses that information. This means we must be particularly careful in our edits.) Because most operations that will be performed on the data are defined using a reporting function that draws data from one or more tables, formulas are not usually stored in individual tables, and that makes it easy to export data from each table, edit it, and reimport it back into the database. In a well-designed relational database, the nature of the contents of each table is also usually clear from the title of the table; for example, "City names" is unequivocal. This means that we understand the context in which we'll be editing the data. Poorly designed or very complex databases may have tables with names that are much more difficult to understand, making the task of editing according to the intended meaning more difficult.

Editing directly in the database

When we can't rely on exporting data for editing, then reimporting the edited data, it makes good sense to edit directly in the database software. (Most of the suggestions described in this section will also work in any spreadsheet software, with appropriate modifications.) The key is to find a way to separate the editorial comments from the contents of the database that are being edited. Doing so accomplishes one of the same goals as using revision tracking in a word processor: it makes our edits easy to see because they stand out from the original material.

In a flat-file database, all the information is typically stored in a single file. In this case, we can simply add a new column or row to hold our comments, and remind the author to delete this column or row after they have addressed all our comments. Flat-file databases let us add a seemingly infinite number of blank columns to the right of existing columns, or rows below existing rows. This makes it easy to type long comments in a field of the database to the right of the editable information, on the same line as the problem we're describing. (In some cases, the comments may fit better in a row below the rows of data. That works too!) By placing these comments in a consistent location, outside the main information-containing area of the database, we group our edits together in a single place where they're harder to miss and where they won't overlap any of the actual content. This greatly reduces the risk that the author will miss a comment or that editing will damage existing information or formulas. Yet at the same time, the comments are in the same row or column as the information they describe, so they're reasonably closely tied to that information. This eliminates much of the need for us to describe the location of the problem, which means less typing for us and an easier task for the author when it comes time to figure out what we mean. The main quality-control concern will be to ensure that the column or row containing our comments is removed from the database file after all edits have been implemented.

In a relational database, the software is designed to manage multiple tables simultaneously. This means that in addition to adding rows or columns, as I've just described for a flat-file database, we can add an additional table that includes only our edits. (This approach may also be possible in flat-file databases that offer at least basic relational capabilities.) For example, if we're editing a database table named *City names*, we can create a matching table named *City names--edited*. Each record in this new table will be linked to a corresponding entry in one of the tables that contains data: the first position in the table of city names corresponds to the first position in the table of edited city names, the second positions correspond, and so on to the end of the file. When we edit the 253rd city name in the file, our edit goes into the 253rd row in the table of edits. Needless to say, this means we must be careful to type our edits in the correct position. This is easier to do if we display the two tables side by side on our screen, with the rows lined up so that it's easier to see where to type our edits. A typical table of editorial comments would include up to three columns: the first column (which is not editable by the user) represents the position in the file (the record number), and specifies the location of the problem in the file being edited; the second is optional, and quotes the problem text or data; and the third describes the problem and provides suggestions on how to fix it. The second and third columns can also be combined. This approach clearly identifies the location of the problem, its nature, and the solution.

An advantage of this approach over simply adding new columns or rows to an existing table is that even if the author doesn't delete the new table, the information it contains is unlikely to ever become visible to users of the database: for this to happen, they would have to specifically include the table of edits in a report. Another benefit is that once the author has finished reviewing our edits and correcting the data in the original table, they can simply delete our table, with no risk of harming the tables that contain the corrected data.

Editing databases by means of validity checks

It's still easiest to edit material *before* it's incorporated into a database, but that's unrealistic in many cases because many databases allow users to enter data themselves, without supervision from an editor or anyone else. Thus, an important editorial role may be to identify certain recurring types of error and figure out ways to prevent those errors from ever entering the database in the first place. Getting the users to enter information correctly will always be more efficient than trying to spot and fix errors after they've been entered. For this reason, we should try to work with the developer of the database to prevent errors during data entry. Our goal should be to help implement *validity checks* that constrain what can be entered in each field in the database. Here are some examples of typical data for which validity checks can be created:

A limited range of choices (such as country names): List all acceptable choices, and require users to choose an option from this list, perhaps through a dropdown menu, instead of typing something themselves. With no typing, there are no typos! (However, it's still possible to select the wrong option from the list, so there should be some way to check this. One common way is to require the user to confirm the information before committing to entering it into the database.) If it's not possible to anticipate every possible choice, there should be a way for users to propose new options for inclusion in the database and a way for the database to report this new information to us so we can check it.

Only certain classes of data (e.g., numbers or words): Most databases can be programmed to validate input *as it's being entered* and display an error message if the data doesn't match the pattern for that field. For example, the programmers can define a pattern such as *nnn-nnn-nnnn* for telephone numbers (where *n* represents a single digit) and identify when the typed information does not match this pattern. Of course, this validation process must be carefully designed so that it does not forbid the entry of correct data. For example, many U.S.-

based Web sites won't accept Canadian postal codes, even if the company ships its product to Canada, because the designer only designed the database to accept U.S. zip codes.

Specific patterns of information that are not easy to constrain: Where it's not possible to easily define constraints on the data, you can often propose *affordances* (hints or explanations about the nature of the required data) in data-input screens to guide users during data entry. For example, "Enter the date as YYYY/MM/DD. Type the / character, and add a zero to the beginning of 1-digit months or days (e.g., 02, not 2)." That's a bit long for a typical dialog box, but I've chosen it to illustrate the kind of details that an affordance can provide.

There are several key cautions to keep in mind when editing databases:

- If you're editing tab- or comma-delimited files in your word processor, never delete the tabs or commas, since these characters define how the database organizes the data into rows and columns. The database software cannot correctly reimport the edited file (and may be unable to import it at all) if the columns of data in the text file no longer match the organization of the database.
- Never change the position of information without confirming with the designer that this is acceptable; if you move information to a new position, it may end up in the wrong row or column when it is reimported into the database.
- Rather than deleting an item of data from a record, always propose the deletion using a comment. Simply deleting an item leaves an unfilled hole in the database that may cause significant problems in the future.
- Confirm that no edits remain in the file before you reimport it into the database. Different programs handle these remnant edits differently; for example, comments may erroneously be added as new records in the database.
- If the database includes formulas, test what happens when you export and reimport the data. See the next section (*Editing spreadsheets*) for more details on testing formulas.

In some database projects, such as bibliographies of published reports, the data is updated only occasionally, usually to add new records. In such cases, you may be able to persuade the developer to submit all additions to the database to you in a word processor file so you can concentrate on editing the new information rather than having to review the entire database, including parts you've already edited, in a difficult and time-consuming search for errors. Once the new information has been edited and verified, it can be added to the database. This approach is essential for large, growing databases, since the time required to scan an entire database grows as fast as the database itself. (For a large database, the phrase "needle in a haystack" doesn't do justice to the problem.) Alternatively, a database developer can periodically use the database's reporting tools to create a file that contains all records that have been added or changed since the last time you edited the database. (Most databases can be configured to record the date when a change was made.) You can then review only those changes.

I've used both approaches successfully in the past, but the first approach is preferable if the data will be published as soon as it enters the database. In this case, incorrect data may be available to users of the database for some time before we have a chance to spot and fix the problem. If the consequences of such errors are serious, designers should accept a slight delay in publishing new data in exchange for the reduced risk of publishing serious errors.

Editing spreadsheets

Spreadsheets resemble databases in many important ways: the data in a spreadsheet are also stored in rows and columns, although these grids of information are referred to as *worksheets* rather than *tables*. (Each worksheet may appear as an individual page or tab in the spreadsheet file, depending on the user interface.) Thus, most of the recommendations that I made for editing the contents of databases in the previous section of this chapter will also apply to spreadsheets. That's particularly true where the spreadsheet primarily contains text or numbers, with relatively few formulas or other complications. But unlike databases, which emphasize the management (sorting, grouping, and compiling) of large volumes of data, spreadsheets emphasize the ability to perform *calculations* on their data. It's the equations and formulas that perform these calculations that cause us the biggest problem.

Editing by exporting and reimporting the data

Most spreadsheets define their calculations in a proprietary format that does not translate into text or RTF formats. Although you can often *embed* a spreadsheet in a compatible word processor document, you can't necessarily edit the spreadsheet in the word processor. When you click on the embedded spreadsheet to edit it, you are actually opening the spreadsheet software; if you watch closely, you'll see the menus at the top of the screen change to those of the spreadsheet software. That means you no longer have access to the word processor's revision tracking tools. And although some spreadsheets, such as Excel, offer their own revision tracking tools, the ones that I've worked with are so primitive that I don't consider them worth using for large or complicated edits. Similarly, some spreadsheets allow us to insert comments, but the comments can be so hard to see and work with that we might as well not bother. For example, the next page shows what the tiny comment markers look like in Excel and what the messages look like if you remember to configure the software to display them:

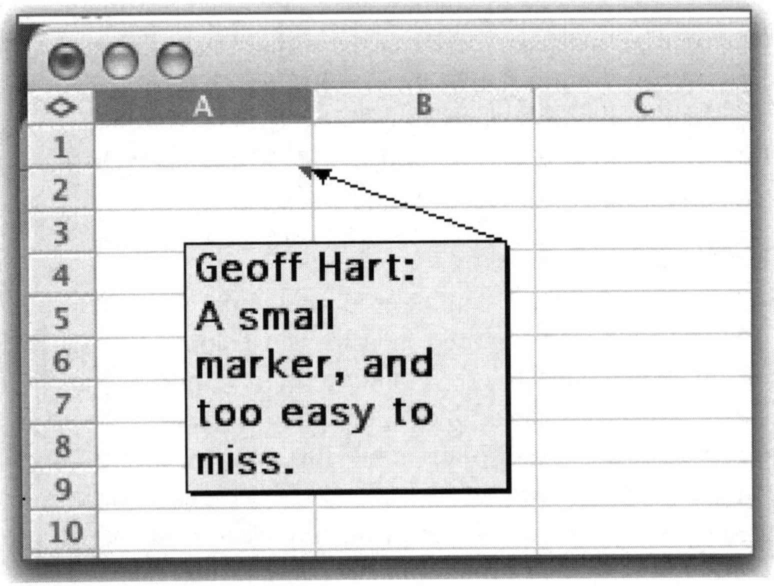

This means that we'll still want to do any significant editing in our word processor. Unfortunately, exporting and reimporting a spreadsheet is likely to lose the formulas embedded in the spreadsheet during the export or import operation. Each combination of word processor and spreadsheet software will require some testing to learn what happens when files are passed from one to the other and back again, and how to deal with any problems. For example, I use an Excel spreadsheet to maintain a running total of my income and expenses and to estimate my taxes for the year. Simple formulas sum the columns and rows, and calculate my provincial and federal sales tax liability by multiplying the base invoice value by the relevant tax rate. Exporting this file as tab-delimited text eliminates all these formulas and replaces them with the results of the calculations. Were I to reimport that file, I'd have to remember to delete the results of these calculations and recreate the formulas manually. If I failed to do this, these numbers would remain unchanged no matter what new expenses and income I added to the spreadsheet, leading to a nasty surprise at tax time.

If a spreadsheet separates the editable information (headings and other labels, plus the data associated with them) from the formulas, it's possible to copy only the cells that contain data and paste them into a word processor file, leaving the formulas safely in place. This works best if the cells containing editable data form a tidy, rectangular block instead of being scattered all over the screen, intermingled with the formulas that will perform calculations using the data. After reviewing our edits, the author can then copy the edited data and paste it right back into the spreadsheet; selecting the range of rows and columns where it should go before pasting will ensure that the original data is replaced by the edited data. As long as the author selects exactly the right cells, this process works reasonably well. If the spreadsheet software offers the ability to "protect" one or more cells (i.e., prevent their contents from being altered), this offers additional protection against inadvertently pasting data into cells that contain a formula.

In this approach, both the editor and the author must pay close attention to what they're doing to ensure that the edited data is returned to the correct cells; if the person responsible for this step misses the target by even so much as a single column or row, all the formulas that refer to the contents of specific cells will perform their calculations on the wrong data. In the best case, those calculations will simply fail, and the formulas will have to be relinked to the new cells. In the worst case, the calculations will proceed using the wrong data, leading to serious errors. Thus, someone must check the results of reimporting the data to ensure that no errors were introduced. Doing so requires careful testing, and for more complex spreadsheets, that testing may prove prohibitively time-consuming and difficult. Although it's possible to design a spreadsheet to facilitate this process, my experience has shown that many spreadsheet designers are not professional designers, are no better at spreadsheet design than they are at writing, and (despite the clear benefits of doing so) are unwilling to request or listen to our advice. This group of spreadsheet designers tends to perceive creation of the spreadsheet as more important than editing its contents, and thus they place little emphasis on designing the spreadsheet to facilitate editing.

Editing directly in the spreadsheet

If we have a client who regularly produces spreadsheets that must be edited, it's worthwhile attempting to work with them to make the review and revision process more efficient. One way to do so is to help them to develop a design that lets us edit directly in the spreadsheet in much the same manner that I described for editing in a database. For example, spreadsheets let us easily add a column of editorial comments to the right of the actual contents of a worksheet, and we can add comments in the same row as the problem we're reporting. Because even the least-organized designer will naturally place the contents of a worksheet relatively close to its top and left edges, this leaves us free to add our comments to the right of and below this area.

However, because modern spreadsheets permit the use of multiple worksheets (each equivalent to a separate page in the spreadsheet), it's easier to add an entirely separate worksheet that contains our edits (as shown on the next page). Because spreadsheets excel (no pun intended) at cross-referencing the contents of two or more cells at different locations, we could create a worksheet named "Edits" that contains three columns: the first column contains a reference to the location of the problem (i.e., the worksheet name and the cell name or number), the second repeats the problem text or numbers or formulas, and the third column holds our comments. The first column tells the author exactly where to go to solve the problem; in Excel, for instance, a typical reference to a cell in another worksheet might look like *Calculator:C12*, where *Calculator* is the name of the worksheet and *C12* is the specific cell in that worksheet. The second and third columns present the problem and our proposed solution side by side so the author can compare the two and see what we've done:

Cell	Contents	Problem (edit)
B2	300	Didn't we sell 200 units?
B6	Mean monthly sales	Could we add historical data from last year?

As was the case in editing relational databases by typing our comments in a separate table, the great advantage of editing in a separate worksheet is that the author can simply delete the entire worksheet once they have addressed all our comments. There's no risk of our comments remaining in the same screen as the author's information—though users of the spreadsheet can still see our comments if the author forgets to delete the worksheet that contains them.

If we already have a good relationship with the client because they appreciate our editing of their manuscripts, we can often extend that relationship into the realm of spreadsheet design once we establish our credibility in this area. Demonstrating the time savings (thus, the cost savings) during editing that result from working with a well-designed spreadsheet is a particularly good way to attain that credibility. A few simple design strategies can make it much easier to export or copy only the relevant data in a spreadsheet. As noted above, the trick is to design the spreadsheet so that, as much as possible, the data is stored separately from the formulas that operate on that data. There are several ways to accomplish this:

- Store the data that will be used in calculations on one page, and the formulas that will perform the calculations on that data on a separate calculation page. Because the editable information is completely separate from the noneditable information, it's easy to extract the data for editing with no fear of inadvertently damaging a formula. Note that in the following highly simplified example, data is clearly separated from formulas. Anything in columns A and B is editable, but the formulas in column C are not:

<>	A	B	C
1	**Month**	**Sales (units)**	
2	January	200	
3	February	300	
4	March	400	
5		First quarter total	=sum(b2:b4)
6		Mean monthly sales	=c5/3

- Format the calculation page so that any editable parts of that page can be easily extracted. For example, place column titles only across the top of the spreadsheet and row titles only down the left edge of the spreadsheet, rather than scattering them among the calculation formulas. If you carry this approach to its logical extreme, the calculation page could contain no editable text whatsoever: even the row and column labels could be drawn from a separate worksheet that contains only this text. This is very similar to the approach used in a relational database.
- In any single page (worksheet) that requires both editable data and non-editable formulas, separate the two categories of information as clearly as possible; for example, place the formulas and their text labels (e.g., headings) at the top and left sides of the page, and the data below and to the right of these areas. This approach makes it easier to avoid copying or modifying things that should not be edited.

These design strategies let us more easily copy a large range of cells—possibly even an entire worksheet—and paste it into our word processor without going through the import and export process. Better still, they let us use the same approaches that I described for editing directly in the database software.

Substantive editing of databases and spreadsheets

The tabular nature of the data that appears in databases and spreadsheets (i.e., the fact that information is arranged into rows and columns) also introduces the possibility of substantive problems that must be fixed in addition to the usual typos and formatting problems. For example, two columns of data that should lie side by side to facilitate comparisons by users of the software may have been separated by other columns during the design phase, when authors are often still deciding what information belongs in a table or worksheet and aren't yet sure how it all fits together. (Some authors never progress beyond this point, relying instead on various kludges to present the information effectively.) We can point out these kinds of problems and leave it to the author to solve them, but it may be more effective to actually make the change and show the author what we mean. To do so, we can save a copy of the file that we're editing and use the software's tools to rearrange the columns or rows into a more effective layout. We can then submit that sample file along with our edits so the author can see what we've done and imitate the aspects of our solution that they agree with.

In addition to simple problems with the layout of the data, there are more subtle and serious problems related to the underlying logic. It's been said that the computer is a tool for helping us to make more numerous and more significant mistakes in less time than was ever previously possible. That's a *bit* cynical, but only a bit. It's certainly true that it's far easier than it should be to make significant errors with our computers. As editors, our goal has traditionally been to protect our authors from their human weaknesses when it came to writing. But if we're expanding our editorial repertoire to encompass databases and spreadsheets, we should also start thinking about how we can protect our authors from substantive errors in this new medium. An example for databases and another for spreadsheets will illustrate the potential problems.

Data in a database is often stored with little indication of its proper context; for example, it may be clear that the data in one table of a relational database are the names of cities, but it may not be clear where those city names will be used elsewhere in the database. Although we cannot always determine whether data are appropriate until we know their context, examining the results of using that data provides an opportunity to do so. For example, in database publishing, software may assemble a Web page, a product manual, or even a newsletter on the fly using information drawn from a database. Someone must confirm that the results of such operations are correct and usable, and that they reflect well upon the author. An editor, of course, is well qualified to do this. For example, I once owned a GM station wagon whose manual had clearly been created using database publishing. An error in the selection of which records should be extracted from the database and included in the manual caused several chunks of information that would have been relevant to the station wagon to be replaced with information that was clearly intended for an entirely different model of car. Similarly, I've seen many catalogues published that contained wildly erroneous data or even missing data. One clue to the latter is the appearance of text such as *$XXX.XX*—a typical formatting instruction for how to display a price—in place of the product's price. This kind of error is likely to become increasingly common as technical writers move to "single sourcing", in which documents are assembled from chunks of standard text that can be reused in many different contexts.

Spreadsheets are subject to similar errors, but also to more significant errors of logic (i.e., incorrect calculations). Although we don't always have the expertise to review an author's logic, we can sometimes perform a reality check on the results of that logic. Years ago, I read of a study in which researchers provided young students with defective calculators that had been intentionally designed to produce wildly inaccurate answers. The researchers were disturbed to discover that very few students had enough of a sense of numbers to doubt the results produced by the defective calculators. More recently, an important client updated the spreadsheet they used to store the work I did for them and calculate payments, but incorrectly defined a formula for calculating totals. I routinely check my statements for such problems by calculating an approximate total, and comparing that with the calculated total to confirm that they are similar; doing so alerted me that their use of the new spreadsheet had led to underpaying me by several hundred dollars. This kind of problem is particularly severe for spreadsheets, since the numbers may have greater significance than the results of a student's math test—for example, in the calculation of a monthly mortgage payment that will be paid over a period of decades, or the budgeting for an important government program. Many people trust computer calculations blindly; we editors should not be among them.

As editors, we can provide a necessary reality check. In proofreading a car manual produced by database publishing, we can note both obvious errors such as information for the wrong model of car and more subtle errors. In examining the results of a mortgage calculation, we could call a few banks and ask what a typical monthly payment would be for a mortgage of a given size and term, and compare those answers with the results produced by the spreadsheet. In analyzing an invoice or a budget calculation, we can add up the numbers approximately (for example, just count the thousands and ignore the rest of the number) to provide a result that tells us whether the budget totals are in the right ballpark. So long as the results are reasonably close, we can have some confidence that the spreadsheet is functioning correctly, but if the numbers are off by any significant amount, we should inform the author that there appears to be a calculation error. Authors should, of course, carefully test their formulas to ensure that they're correct and bug-free, but some don't, and the ones who do often don't do a particularly good job. In some cases, the problem is not that the author isn't conscientious, but rather that the formulas are too complex to be easily validated.

In databases and spreadsheets, both the user interface created by the developer to help users enter data and the format of the reports or summaries generated by the software must make sense. Just as we can critique a page layout or the structure of a document during substantive editing, we can provide similar criticism to the designers of spreadsheets and databases and can offer advice on how to improve both the interface and the outputs produced using that interface. In fact, *we should do so at every opportunity*. In our role as reader's advocate, we must never forget that successful communication involves bridging the gap between author and reader. The only way we can do this for databases and spreadsheets is to actually use the software and report any problems to the author. This isn't what many designers see as our role (i.e., it goes far beyond simply checking for typos), but just as we help make authors look better through our substantive editing, we can help database and spreadsheet designers look better by advocating on behalf of the users of their designs.

When we perform substantive editing, much of the work we do will involve describing problems and how to fix them. If we have access to the same software the author used to create the file, and if that software includes a comments feature, we should at least consider using it, since it will be familiar to the author and we thus avoid having to export and reimport anything. In Excel, for instance, we can insert comments in much the same way we would do this in Word: open the Insert menu and select Comment. We can now type our comments directly into the spreadsheet. However, this approach can be risky because many authors who distribute spreadsheets to their colleagues use the software's comment feature to provide instructions on how to use the spreadsheet, instructions on what values are permitted in a certain field, and other hints or tips. As a result, we may be unable to insert a comment in a specific field because one is already present, and even if we can insert our own comments, someone must ensure that the author eventually removes them from the file—*without* removing any of their own comments. In addition, the comment markers are sometimes small and easy to miss, as I illustrated previously in this chapter in the screenshot of an Excel comment marker.

If the software offers a graphical design mode, you can instead create text boxes of various sorts that float above the rest of the screen, and these work very well as an onscreen equivalent to sticky notes: simply create a text box, type your suggestions in it, and position the box beside the onscreen information that they refer to. You can even use the software's drawing tools to link these comments to the text with an arrow. If you can give that box a yellow (or other) background color so that it resembles a standard sticky note, it's much harder to miss, thereby reducing the risk of leaving unaddressed comments in the file.

Spreadsheet (in)compatibility: Although it may be possible to use different spreadsheet software than the author—to use Quattro Pro or Lotus 1-2-3 to edit Excel files, for instance—you'll likely encounter the same compatibility problems that bedevil the interaction of spreadsheets and word processor files. That's not to say you shouldn't test out this option, but you'll need to test carefully and ensure adequate quality control after reviewing and incorporating the edits.

Font problems: dealing with special characters

Wherever possible, authors will use the core fonts that are installed with their operating system simply because this is easier than going to all the trouble of purchasing and installing funky new fonts. This is a good thing, because the standard fonts are then available to pretty much anyone with a computer. For example, modern Unicode versions of fonts such as Times New Roman and Arial are available for both Macintosh and Windows, and are installed by default along with the operating system. Unfortunately, many software developers throw in a set of bonus fonts that are installed when we install the software. Adobe, for example, installs a bunch of cool fonts for both the Macintosh and Windows versions of their software, and these fonts won't be available to those who haven't installed this software; similarly, there is no current version of WordPerfect for the Macintosh, so WordPerfect fonts from a Windows computer can sometimes pose problems for Macintosh-based editors. The core fonts may be boringly conventional choices, but using them maximizes the compatibility between operating systems and word processors. Until recently, font compatibility posed additional problems, since older software did not always fully support Unicode fonts even when the operating system did. Using pre-Unicode fonts can result in frequent and serious mismatches between many of the special characters in the fonts—those that do not appear on the keyboard. You'll need to use some of the tricks described later in this section for these more serious kinds of font mismatch.

Because we have no control over what software and operating system versions our authors use, special characters such as mathematical symbols and accented and non-Roman characters (such as those used in Japanese and Chinese) occasionally pose significant problems, particularly when transferring files between Windows and Macintosh computers or between different language families, such as Asian and North American versions of an operating system or word processor. When we need to work with clients who use a different operating system, word processor, or language, it's necessary to do a bit of testing to identify any problems and resolve them. If you're familiar with the subject area in which you'll be editing, you can create a test file that contains the special characters you expect to encounter, entered neatly beside their names. Send the file to your author so they can review this list and report any problems.

On my Web site, I've provided two PDF files that list the special characters that most often pose problems in my work (primarily scientific editing):

- Windows characters: www.geoff-hart.com/resources/accents-windows.pdf
- Macintosh characters: www.geoff-hart.com/resources/accents-mac.pdf

Neither of these lists includes all the diacritical marks (haceks and the like) that are uncommon in English but common in central European alphabets, and neither includes any non-Roman alphabets other than Greek. If you're working with authors who use these other alphabets, you'll need to test more extensively to identify and prevent any problems.

For characters that don't transfer correctly, the simplest solution is to throw up your hands in despair and simply flag each mystery character with a politely exasperated comment: "I can't see this character on my computer" or "the Greek letter beta that belongs here displays as a bullet on my computer". Of course, the simplest solution isn't necessarily the best. If you're confident that you're familiar with the main special characters and how they translate between fonts and computers (something you gradually learn through experience), you can simply replace the problem characters and insert a note to explain what you've done to remind the author to confirm that your solution worked. (If not, they can simply reject the change.) A more conservative approach, particularly if your author is a skilled computer user, would be to replace the problem characters with simple words or codes that are guaranteed to transfer successfully between computers. For example, you could replace *é* with *e-acute* if that particular character is causing problems. (It's very unlikely to, but I chose it to ensure that no matter what computer you're using to read this, you should be able to see the character.) The author could then do a search and replace to change all instances of *e-acute* back to *é* before publication. This can be a fair bit of work if there are more than a few special characters that must be replaced, in which case it becomes more efficient to write or record a macro that will automate the process. It's time-consuming the first time, but thereafter, it's a snap to run the macro and update it as required to include new characters. Needless to say, if the author is using the same software you use, it's a kindness to offer the author a macro that encodes the special characters in this manner and another one that reverses the process.

Of course, you'll have to think carefully about how to encode special characters to be sure you can do this safely. Don't use words or codes that might legitimately appear in the document, such as *bullet* in an article on typography or forensics or *acute* in a document on appendicitis. If you're not sure what codes might be safe or don't want to develop your own codes, try using the codes that an international community of experts has already developed and tested. For this purpose, there's no better solution than the character codes used in the HTML standard to identify what are known as *entities*—words or (in more recent versions of the standard, numerical codes) that use the & character as a prefix. Most HTML reference books list the codes used to define such special characters, but you can find up-to-date information that you can also copy and paste at the official site of the World Wide Web consortium (www.w3.org/MarkUp/html3/latin1.html). If that link breaks at some future point, search the main Web site (www.w3.org) for the page entitled "Character Entity Set(s)". (Of course, you shouldn't use these codes if you're editing a document that uses them itself, perhaps in discussing HTML coding.)

Another font-related problem arises from how your software displays fonts. Some of my freelance clients use the Japanese or Chinese version of Microsoft Word, and they often send me documents that are nearly impossible for me to read on the screen. Even though the authors used standard fonts, the English characters that appear on the screen are offset from their actual positions. For example, if I double-click a word to select it, the word to the right of where I clicked is likely to be selected instead. Similarly, if I use a keyboard shortcut to move the cursor to the start of a word, the screen display may still show the cursor midway through the word. As you can imagine, this makes editing next to impossible.

The solution was to install support for Asian language fonts and documents. This support may exist at the level of the operating system, or may be installed as an option when you install programs such as Word. Not all software supports the operating system's tools for working with Asian languages, forcing us to learn where the necessary support tools have been hidden for each combination of operating system and program. For some languages, such as Japanese and Chinese, Word offers authors the option of using grid-based formatting, in which characters are aligned on an invisible grid. Unfortunately, English versions of Word don't have the faintest idea how to handle documents formatted with these grids until you install the necessary tools. How to do so varies among versions of Word, so consult the online help for details. Look for help topics such as "Asian language support" and "Enable editing of Japanese text". Typically, you'll need to run a utility called the Microsoft Language Register that can be found on your installation CD. Once that installation is complete, you can then open the Format menu, select Document, select Document Grid, and disable this feature for the problem document.

If you prefer not to risk mucking up your copy of Word by installing this scary-sounding software, or if you're using software that doesn't provide a solution to this problem, there are other ways to save your sanity. With the author's permission, you can often solve the problem by converting the document into a Western rather than Asian format. (Since the document is in English, and will be read by English readers, there's no good reason to retain the grid-based formatting.) Because copying and pasting text often fails to solve the problem, more drastic measures may be required. Here's how to do this in Word:

- Open a new document based on your Normal.dot template.
- Turn off revision tracking.

> **Seeing invisible things in Word X:** Word X for the Macintosh isn't Unicode-compliant, so many perfectly legitimate characters that will display correctly in other Macintosh programs (including Word 2004 for the Macintosh) will appear as boxes or underscores (_) in this version. Fortunately, you can still see what these characters are without ever leaving Word: simply select the character, copy it, then open the Insert menu and select Comment. Paste the copied character into the comment, then close the comment pane. If you hold the mouse cursor over the comment, the small yellow popup window will display the character correctly.

- Open the Insert menu, and select File. If you are reviewing a manuscript that has already been partially edited using revision tracking, this also preserves the original reviewer's edits.
- Select the file that is causing the spacing problems, and click the "OK" button.
- When the insertion process is complete, turn on revision tracking again.
- Save the file under an appropriate name (e.g., Hart-e.doc, where the -e suffix indicates "edited").
- Because your Normal.dot template automatically defines you as the creator of any new file based on that template (i.e., it inserts the name and company information that you entered when you installed the software), you should correct this problem by restoring the author's name. To do so, open the File menu, select Properties, then select the Summary tab. Enter the correct creator information there.

This typically fixes the spacing problems and permits business as usual. Because this approach does not change any of the font information in the file, and only deals with the grid-based formatting problem, it appears to be safe. (Thus far, none of the authors who received my edited versions of these "problem" manuscripts have reported any problems.) The original font information used by the author remains intact, so when you return the file to the author, they will see the text

Copying creator information in Word: To copy the creator information between files in Word, open the original file, then open the File menu and select Properties. Click the Summary tab, and copy any information listed in this tab into the corresponding location in the Properties of the file that you'll be editing. Since you have to close this dialog box and reopen it in the new document for each field of information that you'll be copying, this can take a great many steps. To minimize the number of steps, copy each line of information in this tab into the field named "Comments", and press Return between lines. You can now copy all this information to the Properties dialog of the new file in a single step, and paste it into the "Comments" field. Then copy each line of the information, one line at a time, into the correct field.

using the fonts they originally chose. Moreover, since English text doesn't rely on a fixed grid, this won't affect what the author sees on their computer.

Calling Dr. Adobe! Even this approach sometimes fails, for reasons known only to Word. There are two desperation measures that may save you. First, if you have a copy of InDesign, try importing the document into that software (using the "Place" command). Oddly enough, InDesign often does a much better job of dealing with problematic Word files than Word itself, and you can now copy the text into a clean new Word file. Second, save the file as HTML or "text" to strip out problem formatting, including the grid alignment. This also preserves most of the style information from the original document. (I've tried saving the problem file as RTF, but that rarely solves the problem; apparently, Word's version of RTF generally retains the grid information.) Then reopen the document, save it as a Word document, and reapply any missing formatting.

Chapter 13. Coping when revision tracking isn't available

"Wisdom is one of the few things that look bigger the further away it is."
—Terry Pratchett

I've chosen to focus on Microsoft Word in this book for two main reasons: First, that's the software I use most often, and I don't want to persuade you to try any approaches that I haven't survived and proven to be effective in my own work—or in a few cases, that I haven't tried myself but have heard recommended by other experts. Second, more than a decade of participation in various writing-related communities, including the copyediting-L discussion group (www.copyediting-L.info) and the techwr-L discussion group (www.techwr-L.com), has convinced me that Word is the software most commonly used by writers in general and by editors in particular. I have no specific or general objection to any other software; it's just that I prefer to teach what I know well and what will be of use to the greatest number of editors.

However, not everyone uses Word, and whatever word processor we may use, we sometimes face the problem of having to work with authors who have chosen to use something else. WordPerfect (www.corel.com), for example, remains very popular among home users, in law offices, and in some branches of government, and FrameMaker (www.adobe.com) is popular among technical writers responsible for long, complex manuals. The open-source software movement has given us OpenOffice (www.openoffice.org), a suite of tools that is still a generation or so behind these programs but catching up fast. OpenOffice has attracted a loyal audience and has begun to pose an increasingly credible challenge to Microsoft's domination of the text-creation market. Last but not least, programmers, some Web designers, and other power users prefer powerful text editors such as BBEdit for the Macintosh (www.barebones.com) or one of the versions of emacs that are available for most operating systems. (Search the Web using the keywords *emacs* and *download*, followed by the name of your operating system, to find a range of options.)

Why is this diversity of software a problem? Because the mere notion of a computer *standard* is an oxymoron: there are few standards for file formats, and where such standards nominally exist, they are more dishonored than honored. As a result, whenever we're using software different from what our authors are using, there's no guarantee we'll be able to successfully exchange edited files. The ideal solution is to use the same software that our authors are using, in which case we can use the same efficiency tricks I've described for Word, *mutatis mutandis*. For example, all word processing software offers a search function that can help us impose consistency better than we could if we had to do all the work manually using nothing more than paper printouts. Unfortunately, we can't always use the same software as our authors.

With a little creativity, we can often apply the kinds of solutions that I've described in Chapter 12 (*Editing in special situations*) to a wide range of situations where we can't work directly with the files produced by an author. In general, if we can convert the author's information into a form that will be recognized by our word processor, we can edit it using that word processor's revision tracking tools. If the author can then review our edits and save the results in a format that their software can recognize, so much the better. If not, the ability to use the many tricks I've described in this book will at least allow us to edit efficiently (quickly and accurately) in our word processor and clearly communicate our edits to the author; if necessary, we can always print out a copy of the file with our revisions displayed or create a PDF that shows the edits.

When none of the options I've previously discussed are easily available, we may need to resort to desperate measures. Sometimes we can ask for a PDF file and use its search tools to help us impose consistency, then record our comments in our own word processor and trans-

Building a software library: Accumulating a large software collection isn't completely out of the question. Often, developers offer "competitive upgrade" pricing, in which they hope to seduce you into switching to their software. So long as you own a copy of competing software, they'll sell you their software for a large discount—sometimes for little more than the version-upgrade price. If you're a teacher or full-time student, you can also obtain educational versions of most programs for similarly low prices. (The disadvantage: you may be unable to upgrade educational versions to a full version. Check the license conditions carefully before you buy!)

mit them to the author as an e-mail message. We can even annotate the PDF file itself using a variety of free or commercial tools. *In extremis*, we can always ask for a printout and edit it the old-fashioned way. But that would be admitting defeat, and it's a rare situation that calls for this.

In this chapter, I'll discuss several last-resort strategies you can try when all else fails. As you'll see, these strategies are complicated and awkward compared with the use of modern revision-tracking tools. Before resorting to these desperation measures, have another look at Chapter 12 and ponder how you might use the techniques I've discussed in that chapter to facilitate your editing. But if you're still stuck, try some of the tricks in the present chapter. After briefly discussing the most common incompatibilities, and some ways of solving them, I'll conclude the chapter with two sections on last-ditch solutions: one on editing text, and the other on editing graphics.

Incompatibilities everywhere

The biggest technological barriers to onscreen editing when I was writing this book were due to incompatibilities between programs: at present, there appears to be no universal method for safely exchanging files between programs while preserving formatting and tracked revisions. HTML probably comes closest to a standard format, particularly now that the importance of the Web has made it essential for all software developers to address the creation of HTML files by their software; as a result, you can increasingly often exchange files between otherwise incompatible programs by saving the information in HTML format. Unfortunately, there is no standard way to track revisions in an HTML file, and the HTML format does not support all the features offered by a typical word processor (e.g., footnotes). Moreover, even though HTML is an international standard, the manner in which it's been implemented is anything but standard because every group of programmers seems to have their own opinions about how the format should be interpreted. Nonetheless, HTML is sufficiently close to a functional standard for most purposes, and if we can figure out how to track changes in that format, we can consider using HTML as our means of exchanging files with any author. HTML's younger sibling XML shows even more promise as a standard because of the tight control that the use of document type definitions (DTDs) provides over the content and structure of XML documents, but Microsoft's adoption of its own variant XML standard (for Microsoft Office 2007) will continue the long tradition of incompatibility. Nonetheless, if you and your author can create and exchange files in either HTML or XML format, then the advice in Chapter 12 may let you use revision tracking successfully.

Although you'd think that semi-proprietary (thus, somewhat controlled) formats such as Microsoft's .doc (Word) and .rtf (rich text format) would be useful for exchanging files with our authors, that's more a fond wish than a reality. When I was first researching this chapter, I sent two experienced editors a file that I'd edited in Word and asked them to edit the file in WordPerfect and return the resulting file; I also asked them to send me a wholly new WordPerfect file containing comparable kinds of edits so I could review their edits in Word. My goals were to confirm which of my edits would transfer successfully to WordPerfect, and to see which WordPerfect edits could transfer successfully to Word. Because Word is the most commonly used word processor in the world, I expected that most other programs would generally read Word's .doc file format well, and that WordPerfect in particular would do so, given that it's Word's main competitor. I tried the same test with Word and WordPerfect files saved in .rtf format (rather than in .doc format), expecting equally good results; after all, .rtf format is commonly used to exchange files between programs.

Of course, I didn't expect all the specialized formatting details to be preserved, but even so, the results of this small test surprised me. The incompatibilities were dramatic: Some edits made in one program were clear and easy to see in the other program. Other edits disappeared (deleted text was especially likely to do so), were present but difficult to recognize as changes, or were no longer tracked as changes (inserted text was likely to stop being tracked as a change). Comments were handled with varying degrees of grace, but not with complete reliability. These problems occurred whether the file was transferred in only one direction (from Word to WordPerfect or vice versa) or was transferred in two directions (i.e., made a round trip from one program to the other, then back again). The problems appeared to be equally severe whether the file began in .doc or .rtf format. I'm told that OpenOffice does a good job of exchanging files with Word, but haven't tested that (nor have I tried exchanging files between OpenOffice and WordPerfect), but given the results of the testing I did do, I'd frankly be amazed if similar surprises aren't awaiting the unwary. (Indeed, I've heard a few stories from colleagues that suggest the existence of similar kinds of problems.)

As if that's not bad enough, both colleagues who participated in my tests warned me that in their experience, *garbage* (the technical computer term for "bad things that we don't understand") tends to accumulate in files that make repeated round trips between Word and WordPerfect, sometimes leading to irreversible damage to the files. I do have other colleagues who routinely use RTF to transfer files between computers and who strongly recommend this format, but I'm uncomfortable recommending processes whose problems cannot be accurately predicted.

What's the bottom line? As a rule, it's still wiser to work in the same software our authors use whenever possible. If we plan to do a lot of work for a particular author, we may simply have to resign ourselves to purchasing a copy of their preferred software. Sometimes a client (especially a large corporation) will have purchased a software license for more copies than they have employees, and we may be able to "borrow" a copy to use while we're working on their projects. So long as we don't keep the software or use it for other clients, this is likely to be both legal and effective, but ask the client to confirm whether their license covers such use.

Unfortunately, these options aren't always available. Among other things, it's simply not economically feasible for most of us to purchase or borrow a copy of every program our authors might use. Even if we could, few of us have the time to learn to use so many programs efficiently. As a result, we must sometimes work in different word processors than those used by our authors, and must devote significant effort to discovering how well our edits transfer and developing workarounds for any problems. We must also be unusually rigorous in our backup procedures to ensure that if a file becomes corrupted by repeated transfers between programs, we can revert to a previous version and try to solve the problem. (For helpful advice, see Appendix I, *Developing a sound backup strategy*.) As a rule, we'll be happier if we do the editing long before the major formatting and layout have been done, since the file structures used by word processing and text editing programs are simpler and less likely to confuse our word processor than are those of powerful layout programs.

Last but not least, we'll need to learn a few survival strategies for how to proceed if our authors aren't using word processors at all. This may become the equivalent of communicating using clay tablets and cuneiform: the communication still happens, but not easily or elegantly. But at least wet clay beats paper in some ways. With that discouraging notion in mind, let's look at some of the solutions available to us.

Editing text when revision tracking isn't available

In addition to ensuring that the meaning of our revisions is clear, we must also ensure that they are easy to see. (Ideally, we also want to make them easy to review and to accept or delete, but the indispensable minimum is that we make the edits themselves clear.) If our software lacks a revision tracking tool, or if the incompatibilities between our software and the author's mean that revision tracking cannot be preserved as files are passed back and forth, the obvious solution is to use some form of highlighting that their software and ours both understand. However, not all forms of highlighting are equally effective.

Standard text formatting, such as boldface and underlining, transfers well between any two word processors. That being the case, the most obvious solution to software incompatibilities would be to identify our edits using these text properties. For example, immediately before typing new text, we can press the keyboard shortcut for boldfacing (in most programs, Control + B in Windows and Command + B on the Macintosh), then type the insertion, which will be boldfaced. Conversely, for text that must be deleted, we could simply select the text (using any of the selection techniques described in Chapter 5) and press the keyboard shortcut for underlining (in most programs, Control + U in Windows and Command + U on the Macintosh). Not only do these two formats stand out reasonably clearly on the screen and in print, the keyboard shortcuts, toolbar buttons, and menu choices that apply these formats are easy for authors to learn and easy to use when it's time to remove this formatting from the text after they have reviewed our edits: all they need do is select the highlighted text and press the same keyboard shortcut we used to apply the formatting (or use a toolbar or menu equivalent). For deletions, they'll only have to do this the few times they disagree with a proposed deletion: the remaining times, they simply delete the text, and the format disappears along with it.

However, both formats use the same color as the rest of the text, so they're not as easy to see as they could be. Moreover, in documents that already contain a large amount of boldfaced or underlined text, it can be difficult to clearly distinguish our formatting from standard uses of these two formats. In that case, it may make more sense to use the same two formats (boldfaced and underlined), but to enhance them by applying a color to the text so the changes stand out more clearly. Unfortunately, that approach can require repeated trips to the software's menus or toolbars, or multiple keystrokes. This becomes slightly less painful if we record a macro that applies the desired changes in a single step, then define a keyboard shortcut or add a button invoking this macro to a custom editing toolbar so we can select text to be inserted or deleted and quickly apply the necessary format. (See Chapter 11 for details on recording such macros.) The main downside of this approach is that it makes the author's life more difficult: removing the formatting after reviewing our edits can be difficult if their software doesn't offer an easy way to remove our manually applied formatting. Since this chapter assumes that we're using incompatible software, we don't have the option of sending them a macro to do the work for them. As a result, we must instead teach the authors how to cope with what we've done: for example, we can provide instructions in our cover letter to the author.

For a slightly more sophisticated approach, we could create custom character styles (see Chapter 4), such as *Inserted text* and *Deleted text*. The

Beware the highlighter marker! Some editors like to use Word's highlighter marker tool (found in the Reviewing toolbar), but even if that formatting transfers successfully between programs, it's not a good choice unless you're prepared to teach authors how to use the equivalent feature in their own program. Even if you're both using Word, this tool may be a poor choice: unless authors have stumbled across it in the reviewing toolbar, they'll never know it exists and won't know how to use it to apply or remove highlighting. (None of the usual shortcuts for removing formatting or applying a font change work. Poor design choice, Microsoft!) Again, you'll need to explain how to use the tool.

definitions for these styles can apply any kind of formatting permitted by the software, including a combination of boldfacing or underlining with a color. Because style names generally transfer successfully between programs, this approach generally works quite well. Better still, we can bind these styles to a keyboard shortcut so we can apply them efficiently during editing. But again, we must teach the author how to remove these styles after reviewing our edits. The most efficient solution is to teach the author how to select the styled text and use the keystroke that removes formatting (in Word, Control + Spacebar in Windows and Command + Shift + Z for the Macintosh) to restore the surrounding paragraph style: this is most efficient because it's a single keystroke, and thus easy to learn and use. The alternative is to teach the author to select the text and reapply the correct paragraph style from the list of available styles. However, in my experience, few authors ever master the use of styles; thus I expect most authors will have difficulty with this approach.

Could we use revision tracking to make our lives easier even if the author's software won't recognize this formatting? More importantly, could we do this without making the author miserable? Possibly! The answer depends on whether we can figure out what kinds of formatting *will* transfer successfully between our software and the author's software. Here's how this might work:

- First, use the standard revision-tracking tools to edit the manuscript as usual.
- Second, use a macro to accept each edit and convert it into appropriately formatted text in a single step. Here, "appropriate" means a format that the author's software can reliably recognize.
- Third, save the document in a format such as rich text format (RTF) that the author's software can read correctly.

Such a macro isn't easy to write, but fortunately, Jack Lyons of *The Editorium* has provided one that does the job nicely if you're using Word (http://lists.topica.com/lists/editorium/read/message.html?mid=1717497465). If that link has broken since I wrote this book, look for the 8 September 2004 issue of *Editorium Update* on his site. Jack's macro turns all revisions created using Word's revision tracking into colored insertions and deletions that will be easily visible in Word-

Perfect. The same macro, modified as a result of testing, should work equally well for transferring edits from Word to other programs.

If your software and the author's software can understand each other's note codes (the ones used to indicate footnotes or endnotes), these codes offer another communication option. Typing comments and editorial suggestions into notes separates them from the text, so that you don't create puzzle sentences made from an uncomfortable mixture of the original text and edits, but ties the comments to the correct sentence so authors don't have to hunt for the location of each change. Authors can generally set their software to display the notes in a separate window or in a separate pane of the document window. This lets them simultaneously see both the original text and the comment that relates to that text, and they can resize and reposition the two windows or panes to suit their preferences. Moreover, if notes are deleted as the difficulties they discuss are resolved, it's easy to ensure that no comments are missed: opening the notes window will reveal any undeleted notes. However, this approach won't work if the manuscript already contains a significant number of footnotes because it may become prohibitively difficult for authors to separate your comments from the real footnotes. There's also a serious risk that actual footnotes will be deleted by mistake or that some of your notes will be missed and will remain behind in the final publication, causing much embarrassment for all concerned. That being the case, if you adopt this approach, someone must take responsibility for confirming that all editorial notes have been removed and that none of the author's notes have disappeared. This poses a particularly serious challenge in footnote-heavy academic texts; fortunately, it's rare that academic authors will be using such nonstandard software that you won't be able to use revision tracking.

What about if none of these techniques will work? Nowadays, this should be a rare situation, but it may nonetheless occur. For example, many programmers and some Web designers only work in text editors that permit no formatting other than by using markup tags such as those used in HTML. (Such clients are often militant in their refusal to use Word, and may also eschew other word processors, though usually less vociferously.) In that case, we have to encode our edits so that they're both easy to see and easy to understand. In the next several sections, I'll provide some reasonably painless ways to accomplish this.

Inserting and deleting text

When we're unable to transfer any formatting information between our word processor and the author's software, the challenge becomes how to identify our edits without relying on formatting. The typical case is a text-only (ASCII) file in which no formatting information at all is permitted and we can only use characters that appear on the keyboard. Though text-only files are growing rarer by the day, the text format is still the final lingua franca that pretty much any program can produce and read. We most often encounter such files when (for example) our clients create their information using text editors (programs designed to produce and organize text, not to format it or lay it out). Text editors are often used by Web developers who prefer to code their own HTML without the benefit of tools such as Dreamweaver, people who are using UNIX shell accounts, and programmers who want us to edit text used in a program's user interface and comments that they've inserted amidst programming code to explain the code; such text is usually created with special text editors optimized for working with this kind of code.

Chapter 12 describes how to edit such files (and particularly Web pages) using revision tracking, but that approach assumes the author has access to a copy of the same word processor we're using so they can review our changes using its revision-tracking tools. If that assumption is incorrect, we can't use the approaches described in that chapter. We can still edit the file in our word processor to take advantage of the many tools it provides, so long as we save the file in text (ASCII) format when we're done. To do so, we have to replace revision tracking and the formats discussed in the previous section with another form of highlighting.

In this situation, we instead identify our edits using only the keys available on the keyboard. The low-tech approach relies on using a standard set of character pairs, such as [and] or ## and ##, to bracket our edits, thereby making them easy to find using the software's search function. (Fortunately, despite their other drawbacks, text editors offer unusually powerful search tools.) The only "gotcha" you need to be aware of is that text editors often use keyboard characters such as single quotation marks, slashes (/ or \) and the like to serve special purposes. This is particularly true for the text editors used by programmers to develop software.

With only a little extra effort, we can use such encoding schemes to simulate the effects of using revision tracking. For example:

Before:	`This best of onscreen editing will depend on the author.`
After:	`[Delete: This] [Replace with "The"] best [Is the word "method" missing here?] of onscreen editing [Delete: will] depend[s] on the author.`
Result:	`The best method of onscreen editing depends on the author.`

Note that in this example, I have mostly replaced entire words rather than making individual corrections. As I noted earlier, this is easier to read and work with both for us and for the author. However, it's still something of a puzzle sentence because the author has to pick through four changes and a comment before they can assemble the sentence labeled "Result"; in such a case, adding the final sentence in addition to the edits is a kindness to the author because it spares them the effort of having to figure out what that result will be. However, it's considerably more work for us.

If several people will review the same document, it's helpful to identify each reviewer so the author will know who to contact if they have any questions about a revision or comment. To provide this information, we should add our name or initials inside the markers. For example:

```
[Change A to B.--Geoff]
```

If at all possible, we should identify our edits using characters that don't appear in the types of files the author is creating; this avoids confusion about which of these characters indicate our comments and which ones properly belong in the file. What characters these should be depends on what task the author is performing; for example, we should certainly not use angle brackets (< >) in HTML files because these characters are used to mark the start and end of HTML tags. If the author is writing with programming software that uses special characters to indicate comments, a good option would be to use these special characters to insert our edits. For example, the sample Word macros that I presented in Chapter 11 use a single quotation mark (') at the start of a line to indicate that the line is a comment. In such a macro, the sample edits listed above could be entered as follows:

```
' In the next line, delete "this" and replace
it with "The". Is the word "method" missing
after "best"? Delete "will", then change
"depend" to "depends".
```

This is a lot more typing, but because we can copy and paste the original sentence, we won't have to retype any of the words that we're retaining in our comment. Another advantage of this approach is that if the author misses any of our edits, they will remain safely in the file as comments, where they can do little or no harm. Since it's still necessary to ensure that all comments have been satisfactorily addressed, it's helpful to tag all such comments by adding our initials or some other word such as *Query* that the author can search for using the software's search tools. For example:

```
' Geoff query: Don't forget to delete this
comment when you're done.
```

This approach may be suitable for light edits, where we will mostly be inserting an occasional comment rather than heavily modifying the text. But even with help from macros or autocorrection tools (see Chapter 11 for details), it can become unacceptably time-consuming to use this approach. Worse yet, as the previous example shows, the approach may create puzzle sentences that are difficult for authors to decipher. Instead, it may be worthwhile placing the original text on one line and the revised version plus any necessary comments on the following line. For example:

```
This best of onscreen editing will depend on
the author.
' The best method of onscreen editing depends
on the author.

' Is "method of..." correct?--Geoff
```

This is an improvement over the previous example because the results of the edit and any comments or questions are much clearer; in particular, placing the revised version immediately below the original makes it easier to directly compare the two. Moreover, if our edits are correct, the author can implement a series of changes by deleting one line (the original) and removing the comment marker from another line (the replacement text), using only a few keystrokes, rather than having to move the cursor to several smaller edits and fix each one individually. Also note that I've taken my own advice in Chapter 7 and provided both the solution (the replacement wording) and an explanation of what the author should pay particular attention to. This approach slightly increases the burden on the author, since they must figure out what changes I made by comparing the two sentences, but the burden is much smaller than if the text appeared at first glance to be a long series of randomly inserted brackets.

This approach has another advantage—though it may seem like a disadvantage at first. By breaking the text into a series of lines separated by comments and revisions, we force the author to eventually delete the extra carriage returns everywhere that we inserted a comment or revision. This is extra work, but we can make it much easier if we also insert an extra blank line between paragraphs. This lets the author see the paragraph endings more easily: wherever they see only a single line break, they know that they must delete the carriage return (¶) to restore the original paragraph. Separating the edits and comments from the original text in this manner also greatly reduces the risk that authors will inadvertently delete both our inserted text and some of the surrounding text when they respond to our edits. Best of all, the author can conclude their review of our edits by doing a global search and replace that replaces each of the single carriage returns with a space (so that the sentences don't run together) and each of the double carriage returns with a single carriage return (to restore the original paragraphs). This operation takes only three easy steps:

- Globally replace the double carriage returns with a temporary placeholder such as ***.
- Globally replace the single carriage returns with a space typed using the spacebar.
- Globally replace the temporary placeholder (***) with a single carriage return. (It may also be necessary to globally replace all instances of two or more spaces with a single space, since stray spaces often get introduced into thc file when using this approach.)

Despite these advantages, the approach remains less efficient than using revision tracking, and forces us to address certain problems:

- Many text editors use characters such as [and] as pattern-matching tools in the search and replace function. As a result, you may need the author's help to learn what special characters are safe to use. Before you begin your edit, explain your proposed approach and ask the author whether it will be suitable. Then send them a small test file to confirm that your choice of tagging characters won't make it difficult for them to find text inserted between these characters.

- Again, if at all possible, use characters that do not otherwise appear in the file to delimit your edits.
- Edits entered in this way are easy to miss because there is no tool other than the search function for finding and reviewing them, and authors are notorious for missing things using the search function. (The most common reason is that they hit the Enter or Return key or click the mouse too quickly and skip an edit.) At the end of the production process, someone must ensure that no unaddressed comments or edits remain in the file for readers to discover.

It's certainly possible to group all comments related to a paragraph in a single long comment at the end of the paragraph. This solves several of the problems created by the methods I've described thus far, but demands a non-trivial tradeoff for this increase in efficiency: the comments are no longer tied directly to the text they describe, forcing us to describe the location of each revision suggested in the comment, and the author takes longer to find each of these locations, and must then read back and forth between the text and the comment before they can decide what to do about the comment. As a result, this approach requires much more typing by us (to describe the location) and much more mental effort by the author (to understand the description and find that location).

Another way to make this process more efficient would be to obtain the author's permission beforehand to make certain types of changes silently, without marking them. For example, most authors will let you correct obvious typos without marking them, provided that you're aware of any unique spelling conventions in the author's genre of writing and won't introduce errors because you didn't understand those conventions. As always, ask the author for permission before making any change with potentially broad repercussions, and if you have any doubts, insert a comment that draws the author's attention to the proposed change and asks them to confirm that you made the right choice.

Because each of the approaches I've described in this section has both advantages and drawbacks, I don't recommend that you use any one approach exclusively. Different situations may call for different approaches, or perhaps even a combination of two or more approaches. In the next section, I'll present yet another alternative that may be the best overall solution for inserting lengthy comments in a text. If you adopt this new approach for lengthy comments, and supplement it with the approaches described in the present section for smaller edits that require no explanation, you end up with something that resembles the type of revision tracking permitted by most word processors.

Inserting comments

When you're not using revision tracking, it's important to use comments as a tool to focus the author's attention on any proposed changes (such as minor word insertions) that might otherwise escape their notice. In addition, some comments explain why we are proposing a certain change, and others propose multiple options to help the author choose a more satisfactory wording. (I discuss the basics of commenting in more detail in Chapter 7.) In the previous section, I described a few variants on a simple method of inserting comments directly in the text. However, if inserted directly in the text, long substantive comments would occupy considerable space and would make the edited text hard to read: in some cases, the comments would be longer than the sentence being commented on. In the kind of substantive editing that I do, I commonly insert dozens of such comments even into relatively short documents, and if I had to place these comments directly in the text, most authors would find the result an impenetrable mess. That being the case, it's important to find a solution that works well and that is efficient for both editor and author.

One simple solution adapts the familiar convention used for footnotes and endnotes. While edits that require no explanation can be made directly in the text, as described above, longer notes are compiled in a separate document but associated with numbers inserted in the text at the appropriate location. The process is as follows:

- In the text being edited, indicate the location of your comment within the current sentence by inserting a number bracketed by special characters, carefully chosen following the guidelines presented earlier in this chapter. The result might look something like this: [1].
- Type the comment number into a separate document, then type your comment after that number. That separate document can be in any format, including your word processor's proprietary for-

mat, so long as you can ultimately save it in a form the author can read. *Never* use the software's automatic numbering feature to number your comments, since deleting or inserting comments anywhere in your list will renumber all subsequent comments, and the numbers will no longer match the comment numbers in the edited document.

- To save time, copy longer chunks of the original text that will form part of the comment and paste them into the comments you're writing, so you don't have to retype that text (e.g., when you're rewording a sentence). Make the necessary modifications with the goal of producing a result that the author can simply copy and paste into the original document to replace the problem text.
- When you're finished reviewing the document, save both it and the document containing your comments in a format the author can use (e.g., text).
- Explain how the author can manually copy your corrections into the original document and make any required changes. Make this explanation part of your cover letter that accompanies the edited manuscript, but repeat these instructions at the top of the comments document in case the author deletes your e-mail.

Again, someone must ensure that no comment markers get left behind. If you skip this step, the worst embarrassment that you or the author will suffer is the occasional mysterious appearance of a bracketed number in the text—but that's a considerable improvement over leaving a lengthy and perhaps critical comment embedded in the text for all to see.

When all else fails...

The solutions described in this section represent more or less painful kludges that let you work around the problems that arise when you must edit a document that was created in a program that does not offer good revision tracking tools. Depending on the types of editing you do, you'll encounter various other problems that require their own solutions, many of which will be equally inelegant. Indeed, if you edit regularly for someone, it really makes sense to purchase a copy of the software they use, so you can use whatever revision tracking tools it may offer, however clumsy, and thus at least minimize the difficulties introduced by format conversions. Given the cost of your time and that of the author, this may represent the most economical investment, particularly if you plan to establish a long-term relationship with the author and can repay this investment over time.

And despite the fact that my goal in this book is to encourage you to explore the many ways you can use onscreen editing, never forget that editing on paper is still available when nothing else works. It's a proven technique, and we shouldn't shun it when it's the most appropriate solution.

Editing graphics

The most obvious problem that arises in tracking revisions is what to do when we're not working with words or numbers—that is, when cruel fate seemingly robs us of the chance to use our cherished word processor and our hard-earned word-processing skills to edit something. Much of my work involves editing the graphics that accompany an author's manuscript. In such cases, a word processor won't provide much assistance, other than as a repository for descriptive comments such as "change the line two inches down from the top right corner and one inch to the left of the right margin from blue to red and make it about twice its current thickness". Clearly, that's much less efficient than the old on-paper approach of circling the problem in red ink and writing an explanation. In the rest of this chapter, I'll provide a few suggestions on how to work efficiently with graphics—an extreme example of things your word processor really can't deal with well.

Graphics pose a very different kind of editing challenge because (unless we are using desktop publishing software such as InDesign) we can rarely edit them directly: images are not words, and the word-based tools we have mastered translate poorly to images. We face three main problems when we must edit graphics:

- To ensure that the author knows exactly what part of an image we're talking about, we must "point" at the problem rather than trying to describe its location. Descriptions work, but they're too indirect and too inobvious to be an efficient way to communicate.
- Even if we have a good grasp of graphics terminology, it may be difficult to describe certain problems in words. If we lack that vocabulary, it can be even more difficult to explain the problem. *Showing* the problem is more effective.

- Unless the graphics were created using the graphics tools of the word processor we are using to write our comments, it can be difficult to integrate our comments with the graphic.

Fortunately, there are reasonably effective general solutions for each of these problems.

Most often, authors or their graphic artist colleagues create graphics using special-purpose graphics software that accomplishes the task faster and better than the primitive tools provided by most word processors could do. This approach also produces graphics files that are more suitable for commercial printing or display on the Web. If we have a copy of the same software the author used to create the graphic, we can insert our edits and comments directly within the graphics file; this is the most efficient solution. (If we don't have a copy of the software, workarounds are necessary; I'll present some later in this section.) None of the graphics programs I'm familiar with provides formal tools for tracking revisions and inserting comments, but fortunately they all provide other options that can be equally effective.

In any graphics program, the basic approach is the same:

- Specify the location of the problem using pointers, such as lines and arrows that can be drawn with the tools provided by the software. This ties our comments directly to the problem, eliminating the need to describe the location in words.
- Copy, paste, and manipulate individual elements of the graphic to *show* what we mean rather than trying to describe a proposed change. This lets us use a precise visual image to communicate visual information; moreover, because the properties of that image can be displayed by the graphics software, the author or their graphic artist colleague can precisely copy those properties instead of guessing what they are.
- Rather than separating our comments and proposed solutions from the graphic, we can integrate the two in a single screen.

The problems that arise when we work directly on an image are the same ones that arise in editing spreadsheets and databases, as I discussed in Chapter 12: we risk inadvertently modifying part of the image when we insert our proposed corrections, the author may inadvertently delete part of the image when they delete our comments, and some comments may be left behind in the graphic. There are two effective solutions.

First, some graphics software, such as Photoshop, provides a *layer* function. Layers are the software equivalent of transparent acetate sheets laid over the image. Just as we can annotate a printed graphic without harming the underlying image by writing on the acetate, we can annotate a graphics file by adding a new editing layer to contain our comments. We can also copy problematic elements of the underlying graphic and paste them into the editing layer so we can modify them without affecting the actual graphic. This approach lets us clearly explain those aspects of the problem that can be explained with words using the software's text-entry tools, show the visual aspects of the problem and its solution using the software's graphics tools, and relate both parts of the explanation to the problematic part of the graphic using an arrow that precisely identifies its location. For example, see the following image:

Graphics software typically lets us create a text box or frame that will hold our comment, and lets us reposition that container the same way we would move a paper sticky note around a printed page. For the non-verbal aspects of the problem, copying the problematic element of the graphic into the layer that contains our comments lets us experiment with the properties of that element until we produce what we consider to be a satisfactory solution. The last step is then to connect our comment and the revised graphic to the original image using a pointer arrow (sometimes referred to as a *callout arrow*). If the problem involves a change in position, we can use two arrows: one to point at the element that must be moved, and a second arrow that indicates where to move it. Because our annotations are contained in a separate layer, we don't risk damaging the underlying image, and the author can simply delete the entire comments layer after they make the necessary changes, thereby ensuring that no comments remain in the final graphics file. Better still, if the software lets us define "nonprinting layers", we can choose that option; the software then ignores these layers whenever it produces a printable version of the image or an onscreen version such as the .gif or .png files used for Web graphics. This approach offers the additional reassurance that even if the artist forgets to delete the comments layer, our comments won't appear in the final graphic. Of course, the comments will still remain in the original file, and if they're likely to embarrass anyone, someone should take responsibility for removing them from the file once all the corrections are complete.

Second, if the graphics software does not offer a layer feature, we can use the same approach I proposed for spreadsheets and databases in Chapter 12: ensure that all comments lie well outside the image area so they cannot affect the image, and so the author can select and delete them without affecting the main image. For example:

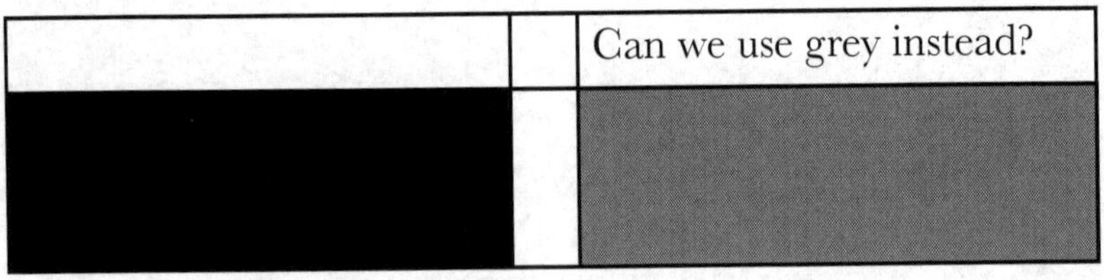

Many programs allow users to select the image area, then use an "invert selection" command to select everything outside that area. (In Photoshop CS, for instance, open the Select menu and select Inverse.) Once all comments have been addressed, the author can select the im-

Where possible, use the same software: As is the case in all other aspects of file exchange, the most effective solution is to edit using the same software the author used to create the graphics. Even nominally compatible programs are never 100% compatible, and using the same one as the author eliminates most problems. However, if we can't use the same software, we can still use compatible software to solve the problem of describing the location of a problem and visually communicating the necessary change. The author can then make those changes in their own copy of the graphic.

age itself, invert the selection, and press the Delete key, thereby eliminating all the comments in a single step without harming the image.

We can modify these approaches in a range of ways to make them more closely resemble traditional on-paper editing. For example, we can change the text color of our comments to the red traditionally used for text edits, or to any other color that is clearly different from the colors used in the graphic. Similarly, we can change the background color of text boxes or frames to sticky-note yellow so they stand out from the background of the graphic. Both techniques clearly distinguish our work from that of the creator of the graphic. Some graphics software

Editing multimedia and video: What about multimedia files such as Flash-based multimedia or actual video movies? I'm not aware of any good solution to these problems other than the one I proposed in Chapter 12 (under the heading *Edit twice, publish once*): adopt a traditional workflow in which the heavy editing is done before the movie is created. Most producers of such movies start by developing *storyboards*, whether on paper or on the screen. A storyboard is a series of graphics and associated text that let the designers visualize the sequence of images and narration that will appear in the final product. If the storyboards are produced on paper, they can be scanned into PDF format and you can use standard PDF annotation tools to provide comments. If they are created using a word processor, in a table that presents the image in one column and the accompanying text in the other column, you can use the word processor's revision tracking tools to edit the text, and the techniques described in this section to edit the graphics.

even lets us automate the process of making our edits distinct by offering named styles similar to those used in a word processor or the ability to record a series of actions much as word processors let us record macros. Using a style or a macro would let us format our comments with a single click rather than having to manually change each of several visual aspects of each comment.

If we don't own the necessary graphics software, Adobe Acrobat and other comparable tools for working with PDF files let us achieve an effect similar to that of layers. Because most software used to create graphics can easily generate a PDF version of the graphics, we can use PDF-annotation tools to add comments over the top of the image. (However, depending on the software used to create the PDF file, the creator may need to explicitly allow commenting and annotation when they generate the PDF file.) Annotating a PDF file allows us to point directly at the part of the graphic that must be changed, but may not allow us to create a solution; we may be stuck describing it in words.

Unfortunately, some authors use the tools provided by their word processor to create their graphics. This is generally a poor choice because most publishers won't accept such graphics, but that doesn't stop these authors from doing it. Often, the graphic will be created entirely in a special "drawing layer" provided by the word processor as a way to separate graphics from the text. In that case, we can use the word processor's own graphics tools in the same way I described above: type a comment into a text box in the drawing layer, move the text box to an appropriate position near the problematic part of the graphic, then connect the comment to the problem by drawing an arrow using the software's drawing tools.

Similarly, if we need to describe a visual change, we can copy the problematic part of the graphic, then use the word processor's tools to make the desired changes in the copy. If the graphic was created using graphics software and inserted into the word processor's drawing layer, we generally can't copy individual parts of the graphic, but we can still use the word processor's drawing tools to create something that looks sufficiently similar to the problem element that we can give a good impression of what we're hoping to achieve. The resemblance doesn't need to be exact; it only needs to be sufficiently good that the author can *see* what we're trying to say.

If the graphics are finalized in graphics software and embedded in the word processor document, which is most commonly the case, we won't be able to edit them directly, and it may be cumbersome to attempt to use the graphic layer to hold our comments. The easiest, but least effective and least satisfying option, is to simply type our comments in the manuscript next to the graphic. This is ineffective because we must describe the nature and location of the problem and its solution in words, which may be poorly suited to the task: consider, for example, a description such as "the symbol that looks sort of like a squashed bug—one with six arms, not eight arms—roughly two inches down from the top left corner, and half an inch inward from the left margin, should be half an inch higher and slightly to the left, and in the same slightly lighter grey you used for the squashed bug with eight arms, not six arms"). A better solution would be to simulate the effects of using a drawing layer by creating a table that will hold both the graphic and our comments. After inserting a table using the word processor's table tool, we can paste a copy of the graphic (often at a smaller size) into a cell in the table—a central cell if there are problems on all sides of the graphic, or one of the side cells if the problems only lie on one side. The result might look something like this:

<table>
<tr><td colspan="2">Comment for top left corner</td><td>Comment for the top</td><td colspan="2">Comment for top right corner</td></tr>
<tr><td rowspan="3">Comment for the left side</td><td>\</td><td>|</td><td>/</td><td rowspan="3">Comment for the right side</td></tr>
<tr><td>—</td><td>*</td><td>—</td></tr>
<tr><td>/</td><td>|</td><td>\</td></tr>
<tr><td colspan="2">Comment for the bottom left corner</td><td>Comment for the bottom</td><td colspan="2">Comment for the bottom right corner</td></tr>
</table>

Note my use of simple keyboard characters such as forward and backward slashes, horizontal lines created using em dashes, and vertical lines created using the "pipe" character (located above the Enter or Return key on most keyboards) to serve as pointers towards the areas of the graphic that contain problems. These characters can be centered, as I've done in this illustration, or aligned top, bottom, right, or left, within a cell so that they point more directly at the problem. If none of the table cells precisely aligns with the problem we're trying to point at, it's easy to split existing cells that lie near the problem until one of the new cells aligns more closely with it. Of course, this works best for problems that lie near the edges of an image. Problems that lie closer to the center of the image are more challenging. Fortunately, most word processors that let authors insert graphics also let us *crop* the graphics (select only the relevant parts) until the problem lies at an edge or corner of the graphic adjacent to one of the table cells. For each such problem, we can repeat this process to create a simpler table that contains only a cropped copy of the graphic and a table cell beside the problem. Of course, when we crop a graphic, we should always retain enough of the surrounding visual context that the author can easily see which part of the overall graphic we're describing. For example:

<table>
<tr><td>Add a lobe?</td><td colspan="2">Make this lobe bigger?</td></tr>
<tr><td>|</td><td>/</td><td rowspan="3">Should we add a lobe on the left?</td></tr>
<tr><td></td><td>—</td></tr>
<tr><td>|</td><td>\</td></tr>
<tr><td>Perfect!</td><td colspan="2">Make this lobe smaller?</td></tr>
</table>

For really complex graphical editing, it helps to have some basic skill with graphics software. Personally, I can barely draw a straight line even using the straight-line tool provided by graphics software, but that doesn't stop me from doing the kind of basic editing that I've described in this section. If editing graphics is an important part of your own work, I encourage you to become as efficient with graphics tools as you are with your word processor. The fact that we editors are primarily seen as word geeks doesn't mean we should restrict ourselves to words when it's time to edit nonverbal aspects of a manuscript.

Graphics created in spreadsheets or databases: What if the graphic was created using the graphics tools in spreadsheet or database software? If so, the solutions I described in Chapter 12 for editing text in these types of program can be applied—provided that you have access to the same software the author used. If not, try the other solutions described in the present section.

Chapter 14. Using the Internet to improve your editing

"Knowledge is of two kinds: we know a subject ourselves, or we know where we can find information upon it."—Samuel Johnson

In this chapter, I'll depart slightly from my practice thus far and focus on some of the things we can do on the screen that don't actually involve editing—but that clearly support onscreen editing by answering some of the questions that inevitably arise while we're plugged into a document. If we're already working on the screen and using tools such as onscreen style guides and style sheets, it's not much of a stretch to extend those tools to include the greatest editing resource of all: the Internet. Don't forget that when I use the word "Internet", I'm also including the communities of experts and knowledgeable amateurs who create the Internet and participate in its discussion groups; in many cases, we humans prove to be the greatest resource of all.

Having spent the past several years plugged into a high-speed connection, with my Web browser constantly ready to respond to queries, I can't imagine ever going back to paper-only research—and I say that as someone with more than more than 20 dictionaries living within 10 feet of me, and two complete bookshelves of textbooks and other refer-

Switch to high speed: If you're still using a dial-up connection, switch to a high-speed connection if one is available in your neighborhood. Currently, the two main options are a DSL line, available from your phone company, and a cable connection, available from your cable company. (Of the two, cable connections tend to be faster and more reliable, but this also varies among service providers.) In remote areas, satellite Internet is also available, but may be prohibitively expensive. If you already spend enough time online to need a second phone line, you may find the cost of a high-speed line easy to justify. When my wife and I began sharing an office, we found it easier and less expensive to install a cable modem and share that connection than it was to pay for two phone lines or use a single line and have to frequently disconnect in case someone was trying to reach us.

ence materials in my office. Using the Internet as a research tool greatly improves the quality of my editing, and in this chapter I'll tell you how it can do the same for you.

A word on credibility

Not all Internet resources are created equal, and if your research is at all important to you, don't accept the first plausible-seeming answer that you come across. The great thing about the Internet is that millions of people freely contribute their knowledge; that's also the bad thing about the Internet, since not all these people are qualified to pronounce upon the subjects in which they claim expertise.

As a general rule, give precedence to sites with clear and rigorous editorial policies for controlling the quality of their data. Dictionary and encyclopedia publishers are not perfect, but they try harder than most. Peer-reviewed journals are another good source of information if you can gain access to their content; most require some form of payment. Government Web sites are also a generally credible source, since most of these sites have full-time editorial staffs and (for the science and medical sites) a peer-review process for additional safety. Standards organizations are similarly reliable, since the material they publish has been subjected to careful scrutiny over a long period of time. For product information, the manufacturer's Web site is generally your best bet, but there are also many online discussion groups that may provide an unofficial story that the manufacturer hasn't been willing to admit publicly.

The second tier of quality includes university Web sites and the sites of professional associations. University researchers tend to be well-informed in their area of expertise, and careful about what they say because they know that their colleagues are keeping an eye on them; nonetheless, since most universities exert surprisingly little control over what their staff publish, it never hurts to confirm a professor's opinion using other sources, just in case you've stumbled across someone with an overt agenda or an unacknowledged bias. (University researchers are humans too, and not immune to these sins.) Speaking of biases, professional associations are a great source for current knowledge in their area of expertise, but they also tend to be biased in favor of their profession, and are often strongly influenced by internal and external politics. Again, a reality check never hurts. Similarly, respected authorities in a

> **Look for the bias:** We humans are not the most logical and objective beings, and anything we communicate is affected to a greater or lesser degree by our hopes, fears, and conscious and unconscious biases. Keep this in mind whenever you assess the quality of information, and always ask yourself: "What agenda or bias might this source have?" Biased information in support of an agenda is not necessarily useless, but you must be aware of that bias or agenda so you can consider how it might affect the information you find.

field (such as Alan Cooper in the field of software design) often maintain Web sites, and these sites can be a great source of knowledge. However, experts are also humans, and have the same weaknesses as university researchers. Experts outside academia and university professors are also both vulnerable to another problem: most really interesting fields develop certain schools of thought, and the combat between rival philosophies can be intense. Being aware that the conflict exists lets us seek a middle ground between the schools.

The third and lowest level of quality includes Web sites published by individuals with unknown or dubious credentials and the discussion groups that these and other people participate in. You can obtain an enormous amount of high-quality information from these people, since not all experts are festooned with credentials and diplomas—but you'll have to sift carefully through the information to identify the good stuff amidst all the background noise. For all such information sources, be sure to seek confirmation and apply a skeptical eye, and don't rely solely on majority opinion; as many elections have shown, the minority often sees the truth more clearly than the majority.

These three levels of quality are somewhat general, often overlap, and have numerous exceptions. Communally developed Web resources such as Wikipedia (www.wikipedia.org) are a case in point. Though some articles in this free online encyclopedia have been produced by the world's foremost experts in a subject, and have had their content continually refined by criticism and feedback from equally knowledgeable peers, other articles are of considerably more dubious provenance. In consequence, the best advice I can give you about using the Web as a source of knowledge is to do so with a large dose of skepticism, and never blindly accept the opinion of any single authority, no matter how credible, as the final word on a subject if that opinion seems illogical or contradicts your own experience. (That's doubly true for topics likely to have become politicized, such as religion and history.) For important searches, finding two or more concurring opinions from credible sources will always give you more confidence than a single opinion from a single plausible source.

With these cautionary notes in mind, how can we use the Internet to improve our editing? In several ways. For example:

- to investigate word usage
- to understand a subject before we query the author
- to consult online reference material
- to consult online style guides

In short: to browse the world's biggest and most eclectic library!

Investigate word usage

"A language is never in a state of fixation, but is always changing; we are not looking at a lantern-slide but at a moving picture."—Andrew Lloyd James, linguist

Dictionaries are a beloved source of inspiration and knowledge for any editor; I wasn't kidding when I mentioned the 20+ dictionaries that I keep close at hand, and an open unabridged dictionary always sits beside my keyboard while I'm working—though often buried beneath piles of other things. But printed dictionaries are somewhat limited in that they are always a few years out of date by the time they make it into print, and no printed dictionary is ever truly comprehensive. Moreover, how could any word geek (i.e., any editor) settle for a mere 20 dictionaries when online resources are so much richer? For example:

- OneLook (www.onelook.com) claimed to have incorporated nearly 1000 dictionaries at the time I was writing this book.
- The Merriam-Webster unabridged and collegiate dictionaries are available online (www.m-w.com).
- The 4th edition of the American Heritage dictionary, a respected authority, is available from Project Bartleby (www.bartleby.com/61).
- The "free online dictionary of computing" (http://foldoc.org) provides access to a growing repository of computer terminology.
- The Acronym Finder (www.acronymfinder.com) provides a large and growing list of definitions of common and obscure acronyms.

- The United States Patent and Trademark Office (www.uspto.gov) provides a large, searchable database of registered trademarks and trademark applications currently pending.

Google (www.google.com) goes one step further by offering a special definition search that scans its entire Web database, including dictionaries, to find any reference to a word or phrase that appears to be a definition. To take advantage of that resource, type *define:keyword* (with the actual search term replacing *keyword*) into the Google search field and see what turns up. One particularly nice feature of the Google definition search is that it provides multiple definitions at once, allowing you to scan them for differences and common threads. If a definition search comes up empty, delete the *define* prefix and add new search terms such as *example*, *explanation*, *glossary*, *dictionary*, *example*, or *usage*. If you happen to know synonyms or related words, try searching for those words too; many relevant sources will compare and contrast closely related words. You can also try going directly to a subject-specific source, such as the hundreds of glossaries you can access via the Glossarist site (www.glossarist.com).

If you're seeking guidance about a phrase or quotation with two or more variants or a word with multiple spellings, searching the Web for this text can provide strong clues about trends in modern usage. Google is a great place to start, and offers a great many helpful tools. For example, you can click the Images link above the search field and automatically constrain your search to pages that contain visual information on a search term—a great way to find a visual explanation for something that isn't clear in words alone. There's also a helpful automatic correction feature that suggests close cousins of a word or phrase if you're not certain about the spelling; for example, searching for "even is you have money" prompts Google to ask "Did you mean 'even *if* you have money'?" Google's suggestions sometimes turn up profitable leads, particularly if you found nothing in your original search because the phrase was spelled wrong, but you didn't know that and therefore couldn't try alternatives. The automatic correction feature compares what you typed with the results of many previous searches and suggests similar words that other searchers, possibly better informed than you were, have used. For example, it has helped me find the correct spellings of many of the obscure Latin species binomials used by my scientist clients.

The problem with any good search engine is that it may turn up far more hits than you can possibly check out. The solution is to progressively refine your search. Each search engine provides different options for doing this, so it pays to spend some time consulting the online help for your favorite site; for example, Google provides a comprehensive list (www.google.com/support/?hl=en) of all of the categories of information it can search. You can further refine your search by taking advantage of a few tricks supported by most major search engines:

- Add quotation marks around a phrase to search for the entire phrase rather than the individual words.
- If the site offers a "search within" button, it will perform your next search within the results produced by the first search. If not, you can sometimes search manually within the results displayed for your initial search using the Find tool provided by your browser and a new word that will appear only in the most relevant results. Most often, this is accessed by pressing Control + F (Windows) or Command + F (Macintosh), or by opening the Edit menu and looking for the option Find or Search. Most browsers also let you repeat the search without opening the menu by pressing a keyboard shortcut; open the Edit menu to see if a keyboard shortcut is listed for repeating a search.
- *Add* keywords or phrases, one or two at a time, to progressively narrow down the results.
- *Exclude* keywords if your original search turned up too many irrelevant results. You can accomplish this in Google by typing a hyphen in front of each word (or quoted phrase) that you want to exclude. (Memory aid: "Show me the results *minus* results containing this term.")
- Include a country name in your search terms to narrow your results to pages that mention that country.
- Add a date to constrain your search to pages that include that date.

There are many more alternatives for conducting powerful and effective searches. Tara Calishain's Research Buzz site (www.researchbuzz.org) is a cool place to learn about the latest and greatest sources of information on the Web, but she's also written a few books you'll want to check out if searching becomes an important part of your editing work. I've listed some good choices in my bibliography.

In contrast to carefully refined searches, unconstrained Web searches that use only your search term are a great way to get an idea of how a word or phrase is being generally used. For example, you can search for two variants of a phrase to see which one produces the greatest numbers of results, and thus appears to be the most commonly used version. Of course, the majority isn't always right, and you shouldn't accept such search results uncritically. The less-common phrase may actually be the better bet in certain contexts (e.g., a specific field of research) even if it's not correct in general use. On the other hand, resources such as newsgroup archives may be useful if you're interested in exploring how common usage has diverged from expert usage. Look carefully at the search results to determine whether spelling or usage is affected by regional differences, such as the differences between British and American English.

If you edit in more than one genre (e.g., sciences and humanities), you'll find that different fields often use similar words in different ways, and you'll need to screen your results carefully to ensure that you're examining usage in the correct field. You can constrain an overly productive search by including additional keywords that are likely to occur in one genre, such as the name of a field (e.g., microbiology) or the name of an author (e.g., Darwin). You can also narrow the search by excluding words that are only used in other genres. For example, searching for *Darwin* will return one large group of results related to evolution and another group on the Darwin Information Typing Architecture (DITA); adding *-DITA* (note the hyphen!) to your list of search terms in Google would remove the latter group from your research results, whereas adding *-creationism* would remove results related to creationism.

Understand before you query the author

When the facts or logic of a manuscript seem wrong, but you don't understand the subject well enough to pin down the problem, researching the subject may provide the knowledge you need to identify or even solve the problem. When that research doesn't reveal the solution, it at least allows you to frame an intelligent query to the author, one that neither insults the author nor demonstrates your own ignorance. Difficult terms or concepts that are missing from your dictionary are often explained online by governments, encyclopedias, and other expert sources, not to mention in journal papers and other published material produced by experts. The tips I provided in the previous section will help you quickly home in on useful sources.

The key in searching is to pick enough keywords relevant to your topic that you'll turn up mostly relevant results, without making your query so specific that you exclude relevant resources or find nothing. That's particularly important early in a search, when it's not always clear what keywords will prove most useful. When a search produces thousands of initial results, this often means that your search terms were insufficiently precise. For example, search on *Geoff Hart* and you'll find my messages to various discussion groups and many publications on my Web site, but also information contributed by a British Geoff Hart who seems quite voluble on the topic of computing; excluding a few of my namesake's commonly used words from a search will eliminate most of his contributions and help you find more of my writing. Similarly, if you're seeking information on male deer (an older meaning for *hart*), neither Geoff has much to say on the subject. Excluding keywords that *must not appear* on the Web page narrows the number of possible results that you'll have to pick through (in this case, adding *-geoff* to the search text would probably do the trick).

In the remaining results, look for specific categories of information. For example, if you need the most technical discussion possible of a topic, look for search results that include manuscripts produced in peer-reviewed academic journals; studying the words that appear in the first few lines of a search result will reveal commonly used technical terms you can include in your research. Conversely, if you're seeking a layman's explanation, exclude these technical terms to find less-complex Web pages. Often, the words used in the manuscript you're editing will be good choices; adding those words to your search terms will find manuscripts similar to the one you're editing and will exclude information less closely related to your topic.

Encyclopedias are another wonderful reference, and many classics such as the Encyclopedia Britannica (www.britannica.com) are available in free or subscriber-supported formats. Indeed, Wikipedia (www.wikipedia.org) provides a great place to start a search for reference material. Use it to find basic information, then use keywords from the Wikipedia articles to do a focused Web search that will turn up sources to confirm (or correct) what you've read there.

If necessary, consult several of these resources. Some will be too technical or advanced for your current state of knowledge; others will be too basic. But with a bit of patience, you'll almost always find something at the right level of expertise, or find something basic that provides just enough information that you can understand something more technical.

Don't neglect the possibility of joining relevant e-mail discussion groups that turn up in your search. Much though I love the cornucopia of information provided by the Web, I still find many situations when human experts are my best source of information. If you can afford to wait a few minutes or a few hours for a reply, a quick question posted in a relevant online forum will gain you answers tailored to your level of expertise, along with useful links to obscure but important Web sites that only an expert would know about. Netiquette suggests that rather than blindly doing a commando raid on a group, getting what you need and never showing your face again, you should spend some time observing how that group functions before asking your question, so you can attempt to fit in. If you'll be asking many questions of that group, you should consider joining it and offering the benefits of your own expertise. One rule of thumb that applies to most online communities is that you'll be received more kindly if you attempt to answer your own question—perhaps by searching that group's archives as well as trying other resources—before you abandon that responsibility and ask someone to do the work for you. This effort will also help you to phrase a focused question that is most likely to provide the answer you need. Some groups are far more tolerant of dumb or poorly focused questions than others.

Consult online reference material

Even the best printed references rapidly become outdated, but their online versions are often updated more frequently—both because updating online information is far less expensive than reprinting a thick book and because the pressure to keep information current is stronger on the Web. There's no shortage of options. For example, if you're searching for words, a Google search for the phrase *online dictionary* yielded nearly 2 million hits (up from 1.5 million a year earlier when I first drafted this chapter). I provide these numbers purely to give you an idea of the magnitude of the resource and how fast that resource is increasing; the number itself is meaningless because I made no attempt to narrow down the search and because many results point to the same locations from different perspectives. Other resources such as encyclopedias are similarly abundant; a quick Google search for *online encyclopedia* turned up nearly 1 million results. Again, use this number only as an indicator of the magnitude of the resource.

Resources abound for just about any kind of reference material you might be seeking. Consider the following examples:

- For science editors, the BIOSIS list of organism names (www.organismnames.com/about.htm) is a great place to find out the officially and internationally accepted names.
- The U.S. National Institute for Standards and Technology (http://physics.nist.gov/cuu/Units/index.html) provides an excellent guide to the units of measurement used in the International System of Units (more formally, SI, the *Système Internationale*).
- The *Index Academicus* (www.akademisyen.com/author) provides quick access to a huge list of guidelines to authors—for more than 15 000 journals at last count.
- Federal, state or provincial, and municipal government Web sites provide legislative, statistical, and other useful information.
- National, state, and provincial archives include all kinds of historical information.
- Newspapers and other news organizations often maintain substantial online archives.

There are many more such sites, but I haven't made any attempt to list them; too many that interest me will bore you to tears. In addition, URLs change too fast for any such list to remain useful, and new sites are always being added, some of which are better than older ones. It's often easier to find such sites through a Web search than it is to add them to your list of bookmarks and be constantly forced to update that list; I used to maintain a long list of key sites, but now I find that it's faster to type the resource name in Google than it is to sort through hundreds of bookmarks. If you prefer not to search, general reference sites such as Refdesk (www.refdesk.com) provide myriad links to useful references. If you work in a specialized field, search for the names of preeminent organizations in your field and visit their Web sites to see what reference material they offer.

A little thought about the nature of the information you're researching goes a long way towards helping you find that information. Another, slightly more specialized, example illustrates the general principle: Consider, for example, the task of checking literature citations in a manuscript that provides numerous references to an existing body of knowledge. In such a case, you may need to find accurate publication data—either to confirm every last detail of a literature citation, or simply to confirm your suspicions about an odd-seeming reference. In my experience, it's a rare author who produces a clean manuscript in which all citations in the text match the details in the bibliography; names and dates mismatch so often that making the citations consistent becomes a major chore. When you can't simply say "something looks wrong here, so please fix it", the work of helping the author fix the problem is much easier if you use online resources such as the following:

- Large general library databases, such as the U.S. Library of Congress online card catalogue (www.loc.gov) and WorldCat (www.worldcat.org), and more specialized databases such as the National Library of Medicine (www.nlm.nih.gov).
- Major universities often provide full or limited access to their research library or online catalogue. Some even offer the most valuable resource of all: an "ask the librarian" link in which a human expert in literature searches can help you find what you're looking for. (Librarians aren't appreciated nearly as much as they deserve to be.)
- ERIC, the Education Resources Information Center (www.eric.ed.gov), is a favorite resource for researchers. I've also had considerable luck using the Ingenta service (www.ingentaconnect.com); though you have to pay for access to the full text of articles, searching for titles and bibliographic information is free.
- For the latest books and upcoming releases that you can't yet find in the library, head over to Amazon (www.amazon.com), Barnes and Noble (www.barnesandnoble.com), or their Canadian equivalent, Chapters-Indigo (www.chapters.indigo.ca). If you live outside North America, your own country undoubtedly has its own superstores that can help.

- Google and Amazon both offer specialized book search tools. Google's book search (http://books.google.com/) provides a scanned version of the cover (a great way to confirm the title), and lets you search within some books to locate a snippet of text or jump directly to a specific page to confirm the words in a quotation. Amazon's "search inside the book" feature is a bit more difficult to access. To use this feature, first use Amazon to search for the book in question, and navigate to the page that displays full information on the book. Scroll down to the heading "Inside this book". For instructions on how to use this feature, click the "learn more" link beside this heading.
- Microsoft's book search (http://search.live.com/results.aspx?q=&scope=books) is much like Google's book search, except that you must register with the site to gain full access to its features. (Like many Microsoft sites, this one doesn't work properly in Apple's Safari browser. If you don't have access to Internet Explorer, try the Firefox browser instead.)
- The Internet Archive (www.archive.org/index.php) provides access to an eclectic collection of documents, including old Web pages that have disappeared, in a range of formats such as PDF and HTML. The site also provides a special file format (DJVu) that provides smaller files than PDF, but requires a free plug-in for your Web browser. You can download a version of the DJVu plug-in from LizardTech (www.lizardtech.com/) for Macintosh, Windows, and Linux computers.
- For out-of-print and antiquarian books, try online groups of booksellers such as Alibris (www.alibris.com) and ABEbooks (www.abebooks.com).
- If you need more help finding something obscure, try the Antiquarian Booksellers' Association of America (http://abaa.org), which provides links to experts at finding information in very specific areas. Since these people earn their living selling their services, don't expect a free ride; at a minimum, be upfront about the fact that you're not intending to buy anything from them so that they can gracefully decline the opportunity to help.
- Consider contacting a publisher directly. Many are willing to help you find accurate information on anything they've published, usual-

ly at no cost; after all, providing accurate information on their publications can only increase the number of readers interested in buying their publications.

Some of these resources also offer attractive additional information, such as scanned book covers and even excerpts of the content. Amazon and Google have both made strong efforts to provide this kind of information via their Web sites. This is a great way to check that authors have accurately quoted a text.

When these resources fail to turn up the necessary information, try entering details of the reference you're trying to confirm, such as its title, in any search engine. Obscure references sometimes turn up when you enter the author's name and a few words from the title. Even if the author is long dead, the odds are good that somewhere, some fanatically devoted disciple has published information on that author's works. Searching for titles is particularly helpful for current journal and symposium articles, since many authors now maintain their full list of publications online and sometimes even provide downloadable copies (whether preprints or final versions) of their published papers. (Note, however, that the bibliographic and other details in these copies may be incorrect, particularly in preprints.) If you can't find the specific publication, try hunting for the author instead. Many authors now have their own Web sites or can be contacted by e-mail, and most are happy to confirm bibliographic details.

Don't forget to verify your search results; any online resource may contain typographical errors introduced during data entry, and as I've noted earlier, not every source is equally credible. For example, library collections generally have tighter quality control than personal Web pages, though this is sometimes more true of large university libraries than of small local collections. If you still can't find specific details, the results of your searching can at least confirm your suspicions that something is wrong and let you send the author a well-researched query. "I could not find any information about this reference in any library card catalog or in a Google search" is a much more compelling statement than "please check this reference".

Consult online style guides

"It is often forgotten that [dictionaries] are artificial repositories, put together well after the languages they define. The roots of language are irrational and of a magical nature."—Jorge Luis Borges, writer (1899–1986)

After dictionaries, what could be dearer to an editor's heart than online grammar and style resources? The Bartleby Project offers, among a great many other interesting resources, an online version of William Strunk's classic *The Elements of Style* (www.bartleby.com/141) and the *American Heritage Guide to English usage* (www.bartleby.com/64). The style guide of *The Economist* is now available online (www.economist.com/research/styleGuide/), and other news sources may provide similar resources.

If you're looking for advice on grammar, Charles Darling's home page at Capital Community College (http://grammar.ccc.commnet.edu/grammar) is one of many university resources that offer online grammar advice. Purdue University's online writing lab (http://owl.english.purdue.edu/) offers a great list of online resources for grammar, including basic grammar lessons and summaries of the APA and MLA style guides. A little research at university Web sites should turn up comparable tools.

If you're doing academic or scientific editing, the home pages of key research journals in your field can also provide excellent resources. You can find the journal by searching for its name, perhaps adding keywords such as *author guidelines*, *instructions to authors*, or *manuscript preparation.* All the large journal and monograph publishers provide online guidelines for authors interested in sending manuscripts to their journals. For example, "the big three" scientific publishers all have their own Web sites:

- Blackwell Publishing (www.blackwellpublishing.com)
- Elsevier (www.elsevier.com)
- Springer-Verlag plus the former Kluwer Academic Publishers (www.springerlink.com)

Many journals and magazines also provide downloadable sample articles that can help you reconstruct their preferred style when the style guide itself is insufficiently precise. (As these style guides are more often written by academics and scientists than by editors, that happens more often than you'd think.)

The world's biggest library

The Internet is the world's biggest library— or perhaps the biggest flea market, given the dubious quality of much of what you'll find surrounding occasional real treasures. The tips in this chapter are only a shallow sampling of the many resources you'll find with a little thinking about what to look for. As a result, I encourage you to invest some time looking for similar tools that relate to your specific type of work. Once you've found a key resource, commit the keywords you used to find it to memory—or record the address somewhere safe, such as your Web browser's bookmarks list or a personal Web site—to be sure that you can find it easily again in the future. If you edit in a wide range of genres, you may not have the time to regularly update your list of resources, and in that case, recording the list of search terms that brought you quickly to that site may help.

Despite the wonders of the Web, I personally consider the greatest resource on the Internet to be the communities of experts that it gathers together via Web sites, Web logs (blogs), chat rooms, and e-mail. The copyediting-L (www.copyediting-L.info) and techwr-L (www.techwr-L.com) discussion groups are great resources for editors and technical writers, respectively. Comparable groups that focus on most professions now exist, and though no list of groups is ever complete, many Web search sites provide a listing of major groups and related resources; see, for example, Yahoo's well-organized Web directory (http://dir.yahoo.com).

And never neglect a traditional and usually underappreciated resource: your local librarian. Not everything meaningful is available online, and sometimes it helps to have an older librarian who still re-

Google a specific site: Sure that a certain Web site contains key information, but can't find it through that site's own navigation or search tools? Try Google instead. If you add the keyword *site:sitename.com* (where *sitename.com* is the actual name of the site you want to search), you can access Google's index of that site. This often provides better results than the Web site's own table of contents or search tools, and is a particularly good resource for searching huge sites such as Microsoft's.

members the value of printed matter help you with your research; for example, enormous quantities of information available on microfiche (e.g., newspaper archives) are not available online, and may never be. If you don't have a local librarian, consider contacting the American Library Association (www.ala.org), its Canadian equivalent (www.cla.ca), or the equivalent elsewhere in the world for assistance. Or try an online version: the British Ask-a-Librarian service (www.ask-a-librarian.org.uk), the U.S. equivalent (www.loc.gov/rr/askalib), or a volunteer effort offered by the Internet Public Library (www.ipl.org/div/askus).

Needless to say, since these are people rather than Web sites, try to solve a problem yourself before you take advantage of their services, and if you do ask them for help, treat them with the respect and gratitude that they deserve.

III. Identifying and overcoming barriers

Chapter 15. Developing safeguards

"The most likely way for the world to be destroyed, most experts agree, is by accident. That's where we come in; we're computer professionals. We cause accidents."
—Nathaniel Borenstein

Murphy's many laws: If anything can go wrong, it will. If there is a possibility of several things going wrong, the one that will cause the most damage will be the first one to go wrong. If anything simply cannot go wrong, it will anyway. If you perceive that there are four possible ways in which something can go wrong, and circumvent these, then a fifth way, unprepared for, will promptly develop. If everything seems to be going well, you have obviously overlooked something.

O'Toole's commentary on Murphy's laws: Murphy was an optimist.

In onscreen editing as in on-paper editing, we must safeguard our work. We may no longer need to worry about the dog eating our homework, but the cat may still knock our coffee cup over, flooding our expensive new laptop and instantly electrocuting our hard drive. Toddlers may not be able to insert slices of processed cheese into the CD or DVD drive, but they can still knock the whole computer onto the floor, and pet hair can accumulate inside the ventilation system of computers until the fan grinds to a halt, the computer overheats, and we end up with an expensive doorstop.

The hazards that are most obvious to anyone who uses a computer are the many ingenious ways software has developed to ruin our day. Indeed, what with computer viruses and commercial software that itself often seems just one step above a virus, it's not surprising that working on the computer seems much more fraught with risk than working on paper. It's easy to forget that *any* editing process contains numerous opportunities for disaster. For example, I've experienced, seen, or heard of many problems even with traditional "safe as banks" on-paper editing. Manuscripts have been:

- stolen in a burglary.
- damaged during an unscheduled visit by teenage vandals, not to mention scheduled visits by friends of our children.
- destroyed by a fire or a malfunctioning sprinkler system.
- drowned under a spilled mug of coffee (or worse yet, beer).
- eaten by the dog!

- thrown out by the janitor or a malevolent colleague. (More likely it was accidentally thrown out by the editor, but that's not how the story is told.)
- misfiled by the editor's boss or a secretary (or just possibly by the editor).
- forgotten in a coffee shop, library, or commuter train.
- stolen along with the editor's briefcase.

Each of these catastrophes has a clear counterpart in onscreen editing, and you should take appropriate precautions: keep a copy of your files somewhere you can easily recover them if the originals are stolen or damaged, keep liquids far from valuable electronics, keep pets out of your office (or, more realistically for those of us who are domestic servants to our pets, keep them off the computer), and pay attention to what you're doing.

But computers pose their own special risks as well, and you need to develop an editorial routine that protects you from the disasters occasionally inflicted on us by modern technology. In this chapter, I discuss several important steps that can protect us from the worst computer disasters.

Never work on the original file

Always retain the original file somewhere safe and work on a copy. If worse comes to worst, you haven't been making good backups, and your work file is damaged or lost, you can always start over from the beginning. If you're working on a long project such as a book, where loss of or damage to the file would require you to repeat a prohibitive amount of work, make copies of your work at the end of each day or even each time you take a break for lunch, and continue working on the most recent copy. That way, if file corruption arises, you can revert to a previous version of the file, minimizing the amount of work you must redo.

Here's a simple approach that protects you against both loss and damage:

- Open the original file.
- Immediately save the file under a new name. If it's a small job, simply add *--edited* to the end of the file name.

- When you take a break, save the file to preserve all your work up to that point. If it's a big job, consider saving another copy of the current version under a new and informative name, such as *--edited August 12 at noon.* (Most operating systems record the date time a file was last modified, but do not create a separate new version of the file. Thus, you need to create your own dated copies.)
- Continue working in the *--edited* version of the file.
- At the end of the day, save the file once more to protect your work, then make another copy under a new name, such as *--edited August 12 at midnight.*
- Store these timestamped copies separate from your computer—on a CD, flash drive, or private directory on your Web site. You can even send yourself a copy by e-mail.

If this strikes you as too much effort—and it won't after you've lost your first file—at least turn on some of the automatic protections afforded by your software. I've described a batch of these in Chapter 4.

Back up your work

None of these timestamped copies does you any good whatsoever if your computer is stolen, destroyed in a fire, or wiped clean by a particularly nasty virus—or if your computer goes the way of all flesh and shuffles off to meet its maker. To be safe, you need to make ongoing backups of the data and keep them somewhere safe. At some point, Murphy's law will do something unfortunate to a file or to your entire hard disk, even if you've followed my advice in the previous section. Appendix I provides a detailed discussion of how to protect yourself by developing a sound backup strategy. If you don't have time to read the full appendix, here are the key points:

- Make a new backup each time you finish your work. At a minimum, make a backup copy once per day. More frequent is better.
- Don't erase old backups until the author has received and approved your final job; you may occasionally need to return to an intermediate version. Consider archiving them for at least a year afterwards, and longer if you have the space; clients occasionally lose their copy of a file (whether because they accidentally deleted it or because a virus did the job for them) and ask you for a copy.

- Copy your work to a device (a flash drive a CD or Zip disk, a directory on your Web site, or your Google Mail account) that is not physically attached to your computer and that you can store somewhere safe if it's a physical device such as a CD.
- Store physical devices somewhere far enough from your computer that it's difficult to lose both simultaneously. Ideally, store it in a different building, but at a minimum, store it a good distance away in a relatively secure location.

Obtain a backup computer

Speaking of disaster planning, what would you do if aliens abducted your computer two days before an urgent deadline? If you can't answer that question to your satisfaction, it's time to develop a backup plan. What's *my* plan? Glad you asked. I own a Windows PC that is mostly used by the kids, but in an emergency, I can take over the computer and move my work there. Better than that (since I work on a Macintosh), I can generally borrow my wife's iBook until I can order a replacement.

Most of us who work as freelancers immediately discard our old computer hardware whenever we purchase a new model, or sell it for next to nothing, but that can be a false economy. Older computers are usually not worth selling because we simply can't earn enough on the transaction to make it worth our time. The $100 or $200 you can ask for a typical 3-year-old computer often isn't enough to justify the sale, particularly if you consider the time it takes to advertise the computer and handle the details of the sale, such as scrubbing the hard drive to remove our confidential information. If you're an employee, you may not have the option of defining your old computer's fate, but then you probably also have additional resources, such as a spare computer or a computer department, that can help you in a crunch. If not, you may also want to look into obtaining a backup computer.

Consider the advantages of keeping your old computer after you move to a shiny new one:

- You have a stable, proven system that you know you can use to work productively. It may not be as fast as your new system, but it's fast enough.

- You can switch to that system in the time it takes to haul it out of the closet and plug in the power.
- There's no need to go out in the depths of the Canadian winter to visit the nearest computer store, and no need to max out your credit card.

If your old computer simply isn't capable of meeting your needs, consider purchasing a backup computer that someone else is discarding or selling at a loss. Over the years, I've purchased many capable computers for my kids for less than $200, including the one I'm currently using as my backup. A particularly good time to look for a backup computer is after Christmas, when many families have upgraded to a new model and no longer have room for their old computer. Another good time is at the end of the school year, when many university students from foreign countries are preparing to return home by air, and have no economical way to bring their school computer. For many, it's simpler to sell the computer, even at a loss.

If you're the one who has to pay for the backup computer, and its cost (or the cost of forgoing the income you could receive if you sold it) strikes you as too high, remember that you're a working professional, and that you're operating a business. Any expenses you incur to protect that business are tax deductions you can write off against your earned income.

Update your software, but not too frequently

It's easy to get into the *status quo* mindset: your current software works just fine, so why risk destabilizing it with an update? The answer requires us to distinguish between *necessary* and merely useful updates. For example, if our software is unstable and prone to crashing, an update that fixes the instability is essential. In contrast, if our software works just fine and the update only adds a few features of questionable value or fixes bugs we haven't yet encountered in features we never use, it's probably not worthwhile installing that update. Check the developer's literature carefully to see what problems the update solves before you decide to install it. Then research the update on the developer's Web site, on the Web in general, and in your favorite online discussion groups to ensure that it works as advertised and that there have been no major adverse consequences for those who upgraded. If you get a bad feeling about the safety or utility of the update, wait a while until the developer has had a chance to work out any bugs.

With the exception of critical updates, such as the seemingly endless stream of critical security updates for Microsoft Windows, it's generally safe to wait a while before you install an update. Some companies have a reputation for releasing updates that create more problems than they solve, but even for these companies you can avoid the worst problems by waiting a week or two after an update has been released before you install it yourself. If any problems arise, some of the early adopters of the update will encounter them and report them to the developer. They will also complain loudly and in detail in various online communities. Such communities are great sources of information on software updates. If discussion indicates that an update is likely to be more trouble than it's worth, hold off on installing it and watch for an announcement (from community members or the software company itself) that the bugs have been ironed out. If you must install a problematic update anyway—perhaps it enables crucial features or plugs a drastic security hole—members of the community are likely to be able to help you ameliorate the problems that result. There are many communities like this; see the list of resources in the bibliography for some suggestions. A discussion group for professional editors or writers may be particularly useful, since its members will be using the same kinds of software and facing the same kinds of problems as you are, and such a group may well be a friendly collegial space in other ways as well.

If at all possible, try to keep your existing copy of the software when you update. For example, most versions of Microsoft Office let you upgrade to a new version without erasing the old version from your hard disk, and that's a wise choice. It may not be an *easy* choice, since you'll have to carefully read through the installation instructions to see wheth-

Avoid the "bleeding edge": Those of us who are veterans of the early days of the computer revolution have learned a hard lesson: never be the first to update your software, and never install version 1.0 of any update. The gruesome but precise phrase "on the bleeding edge" was developed specifically to describe those brave souls who feel obliged to always be the first to install new software.

er and how this is possible, but it's a worthwhile option if you can manage it. Where you can't, consider installing the old version on a backup computer if you have one.

The key exceptions to the "wait a bit" advice concerns your antivirus and anti-spyware programs. If you don't have such software and you're running Windows, stop reading and buy some right now—or download good free software such as GriSoft's AVG antivirus and Lavasoft's AdAware antispyware software. (They do different things, and you need both. I've listed these and several other useful programs in the software list at the end of this book.) You should also have a software firewall. Then learn how to set all these defenses to update themselves automatically if you aren't sure you'll remember to update them yourself. The modern computing environment has simply grown too dangerous for working professionals to operate without appropriate protections. Macintosh users should also beware: Conventional wisdom has held that Macintoshes are inherently safer than Windows computers, and this certainly used to be true. It's still true to some extent; for example, when I wrote this chapter, there were no confirmed cases of spyware that affected a Macintosh. But as the number of Macintoshes grows, they become a more tempting target for malefactors, and if you run Windows on your Macintosh (increasingly common now that Apple computers use the same Intel chips as Windows computers), you're vulnerable to all the problems that afflict Windows computers.

Keep confidential information confidential

Though most of us work on documents that are only truly important to the author, some of the information we may see is confidential and some special projects may require a high degree of security. In these cases, it behooves us to ensure that nobody inappropriate has a chance to see the information. This is true, for instance, of legal or medical documents, proposals written to secure funding, descriptions of trade secrets, marketing plans, and sometimes even the results of scientific or technical research. If this is the case, the author is likely to be fully aware of the problem and will provide specific instructions on how we should handle the manuscript. But oddly enough, some authors are extremely naïve about the risk posed by theft of their manuscripts.

Pay attention to what you're editing, and if you feel that the release of this information to someone other than the author (e.g., to a business competitor) could damage your client, take appropriate precautions.

What precautions are appropriate? You'll need to protect the information both while it's on your computer and while it's in transit back to the author. For relatively basic security that will keep out even moderately determined snoopers, you can sometimes just restrict access to the document. Recent versions of the three main operating systems (Windows, Macintosh, and Linux) let you create user accounts on your computer and protect them with passwords. A snooper would have to log into the correct account, using its password, just to see that a particular document exists. Of course, this system is only safe if you choose a strong password and don't tape a reminder to your computer.

Of course, if you leave your computer running full-time, then nobody will ever have to know your password: they only need physical access to your computer. In such cases, you can provide weak but possibly acceptable protection by requiring the computer user to re-enter the password if the computer has been left idle for more than a specified period of time. This is usually done through the screensaver control panel, which defines how long to wait before blanking the screen and whether a password is necessary to start using the computer again after the screensaver kicks in. For stronger protection, shut down your word processor and log out of your user account if you'll be leaving your computer unattended for any significant amount of time (e.g., to have lunch with a client).

For even stronger protection, you need to be able to encrypt your data. Encryption works in a variety of ways, and is too complex a topic to discuss here in any detail. Simplistically, you encrypt a document by using specialized software to turn it into an unreadable format; you choose a password (also called a key) when you encrypt the document, and that password must be provided before the software will undo the encryption and make the file readable again. Most file compression software, such as the many "zip" utilities (available as downloads for Windows and built into the Macintosh operating system) and the program StuffIt (available for both the Macintosh and Windows), allows you to encrypt a file when you compress it. For stronger protection, look into software such as the solutions provided by RSA Security Systems (www.

rsasecurity.com). Without the appropriate password or key, nobody can open the file—including you, so be sure to store the password somewhere safe. Encryption that will stop your government's top spies from reading your confidential information will also stop *you* from reading it if you lose the password. You can also encrypt entire sections of a hard disk, but if a disk problem develops, it may be impossible to recover the encrypted files.

If you retain your confidential files on backup devices (such as CDs or USB memory keys), you need to both protect these devices against theft and protect them against snooping if they are stolen. But there are subtler traps to be aware of, such as the loss or interception of files in e-mail. See my discussion of these issues in Chapter 3.

Protect yourself too

Thus far, there's little compelling evidence that computer use causes serious physical damage to computer users, with a few key caveats:

- We must be in good health to begin with, since prolonged computer use can exacerbate existing problems. Most of us are far too sedentary, and as we age, we may develop various health problems that computer use can only make worse.

Picking a strong password

What constitutes a strong password? First, it should be at least eight characters long, should not be a word found in a dictionary, and should contain both letters and numbers (or symbols, if your operating system allows this). Some authorities have recently recommended using a short and easily remembered phrase such as "my password sure is inscrutable"; the individual words are easy to guess, but if you use several words, the password becomes long enough that it's unlikely anyone will ever figure out what combination of words you used. Moreover, because the password is so long, it will take a prohibitively long time for even modern password-cracking software to guess it. Second, the password should not be stored anywhere near your computer. The strongest password in the world is completely useless if a thief needs only three seconds to find it taped to the bottom of your desk.

- We must learn how to set up a computer and work environment so as to minimize the risk of injury.
- We must learn to take periodic breaks from our work, even when we're facing a tight deadline. Particularly then, in fact, since stress makes us more vulnerable to injury.

Appendix II provides a detailed description of some of the main steps you should take to protect yourself while you use your computer.

Chapter 16. Solving the proofreading problem

"A life spent making mistakes is not only more honorable, but more useful than a life spent doing nothing."—George Bernard Shaw

"Quis emendet ipsos editores?" (Who shall edit the editors?)—Geoff Hart, with thanks to Christine Shuttleworth for Latin assistance

Many editors are asked to perform what clients call proofreading—*proofing* for short. In the classical definition of proofreading, a laid-out document is read through one last time to ensure that no errors slipped through the previous stages of production—stages that included, at least in theory, a detailed and intensive edit before the manuscript reached the layout stage. For this task, we can use all the techniques I've discussed in this book, with the exception that the work should be easier because scrupulous reviewers and editors should have already caught and fixed all the significant problems beforehand.

If a client requests proofreading when the document actually requires moderate or heavy editing, we find ourselves in an unpleasant situation: the client often isn't prepared to pay for that time-consuming and expensive service or may be too close to an immovable deadline to be able to wait, yet as ethical professionals, we don't want to do shoddy work simply because there's no time or budget to do the job right. When we face an unedited or poorly edited manuscript that contains so many problems that proofreading or even a light copyedit can't possibly fix them all, it's our responsibility to report the problem to the client as soon as possible and request instructions on how to proceed. If the client is unwilling or unable to provide time or money for an adequate edit, we must then decide whether we're willing to grit our

Clients don't always "get it": Of course, some clients really don't understand the publishing process, and wait until the last possible instant to do any editing at all—and then call this emergency quality control proofreading. This is another example of why it's so important to discuss editorial work with the client until we clearly understand what is being asked of us and can define any tradeoffs implicit in this understanding.

teeth and fix only the most egregious problems—and politely but firmly insist that the client not publicly acknowledge our work—or should gracefully turn down the job. (In this sense, "graceful" means that we refer the client to someone else who may be willing to do the work. Never leave a client in the lurch if you can avoid doing so!) This won't be a manuscript to include in our portfolio. Sometimes explaining the situation can earn us an opportunity to fix the most serious problems, since "urgent" deadlines are often more flexible than they seem. The only way to know is to ask.

To avoid this problem in the future, we must educate the client about the value of editing before a document goes to layout and about the importance of providing us with enough time to do the work that's required. Sometimes it only takes one nightmare experience of rushed last-minute editorial corrections to persuade a client of the value of getting the work done well before the text is sent for layout. Other times, clients never seem to get the message, and our only recourse is to clearly define what we can and cannot do for the manuscript under these conditions—and again, to insist that we not be acknowledged or identified as editors of material that, through no fault of our own, is of an unacceptably low standard. If the quality of the manuscripts is consistently and painfully low, it may even be necessary to fire the client; few of us enjoy doing work that we would be ashamed to include in our portfolio, and life's too short to waste what remains on work we don't enjoy. Moreover, agreeing to do such work may cost us future work if another client finds out we were responsible for a shoddy edit; this can happen when a clueless client "helpfully" introduces us to a potential new client by giving them an example of the work we did under unreasonable conditions.

It's important to note that if a manuscript hasn't yet been laid out, calling the work proofreading is inaccurate. We have no idea what may still happen to the manuscript during layout and production; thus, we have no real proof that these tasks will be performed properly or that their results will be competently checked. If the manuscript is not in proof—its final version, as it is intended to be published—it cannot be truly proofread. In the remainder of this chapter, I'm going to assume that we're in the happy situation of actually doing proofreading rather than a full edit.

A bit about production processes

To understand what proofing is about and how it relates to editing and the processes used to produce either a printed document or one that will be used exclusively on the computer screen, it helps to understand the production process well enough that the word *proof* becomes meaningful. The origin of the word *proofreading* is in the phrase *reading [printer's] proofs*. Printer's proofs were traditionally produced by gathering ("setting") lead type into blocks called *galleys*, inking the lead type, then pressing it onto paper. Because the printed result was produced from a galley of type and was used to prove (in the word's original meaning of "test") what the reader would see when the manuscript was actually printed, it was called a *galley proof*. Even though production processes have changed dramatically, and lead type is no longer used, you'll still often hear proofreading described as checking the galley proofs (or *galleys*).

In modern printing, manuscripts are produced on computers, and setting type (*typesetting*) means the process of arranging text into its final layout in a word processor, desktop publishing program, or more sophisticated software. To obtain proof of what will eventually be printed, printers use the files created with this software to produce photographic film negatives on a machine called an *imagesetter* (less commonly, a *typesetter*), which is something like a laser printer with extremely high resolution that prints on film. In turn, the negatives are used to produce flexible metal (or sometimes paper or plastic) printing plates that will be used to transfer ink (via a few intermediate steps) onto paper. Because film is much cheaper than printing plates and printing presses are expensive to operate, printers save us money by using the film as our proof. However, because film negatives are fragile, printers use the negatives to produce "positives" by exposing a special photographic paper on which the resulting text appears blue; the result is called, logically enough, a *blueline proof* (or just *blues*). To ensure that the publication will be assembled properly, the blues are folded and gathered together into a model of the final publication.

Because blues represent a photographically exact copy of what will appear on the printing plate, and because the plate represents an equally exact copy of what will eventually appear on the paper, blues are an economical way to find out what will eventually come off the printing press. If the plates are subsequently used to print an actual paper copy, this copy is called a *press proof* because it's our proof (or test) of what will come off the printing press. In some production processes, blueline proofs have been replaced by laser printer proofs because the imagesetters used to produce the films use the same computer software as the laser printers, and paper is even cheaper than film; in practice, what you see on the laser printer is what you'll get on the film. Because PDF files contain the same printing instructions that are used by laser printers and imagesetters, it's increasingly common for printers to print from PDF files instead of from the files produced by desktop publishing and graphics software. Indeed, sometimes the PDF files themselves are treated as the only proof that's required; because PDF proofs are not hard (physical) copies, they're often referred to as *soft proofs*.

More interesting documents also include graphics, whether line art (images formed from solid lines of ink) or halftones (photographs, which are printed using patterns of dots). For simple one-color printing, blues or black and white laser printouts are adequate for most needs because all we're looking for is accurate positioning of the lines and dots that make up the letters and images. Things become much more complicated in color printing, because we also need to confirm that the colors are correct. Depending on the printing process and our budget, we may be asked to check color laser printer, color-key, inkjet, matchprint, or chromalin proofs, among other kinds.

This is a vastly simplified description of the printing process, but it captures the essential details from the editorial perspective: our goal in proofreading is to look for errors in the computer files by examining laser printer, blueline, or other proofs, thereby providing a chance to fix the problems before the printer manufactures expensive printing plates or performs the even more expensive step of printing the final product on a printing press. How does this process (examining what is effectively a printed copy of the manuscript) relate to the subject of this book, which is *onscreen* editing? The answer is twofold:

First, almost all typeset material is now produced on computers, and transmitted to the printer as desktop publishing or PDF files. This means that we have the option of performing onscreen proofreading by examining these files instead of checking laser printer proofs or blues. Second, even if we must ultimately work with paper proofs or blues, we still have an opportunity to spot major problems before the publisher wastes money producing those more traditional proofs. These two answers explain why the tools offered by onscreen editing are relevant in proofreading, and in the rest of this chapter, I'll concentrate on how to apply those tools.

Of course, anyone who uses a computer understands that information no longer lives solely on paper. In fact, the explosive growth of the Internet means that it's increasingly likely that documents created on a computer are destined to be used exclusively on a computer rather than being printed; the most obvious examples are the online help files that ostensibly teach us how to use our complicated modern software and the Web pages we consult when the online help fails us. The proofreading we will do of these documents is quite different from what we do for printed materials: we still want to eliminate the same kinds of typos and other errors we look for on paper, but in addition, we must ensure that the final result will display and behave correctly on the computer screen.

One big difference in what we must look for arises from how onscreen documents are created. In some cases, the author works in a WYSIWYG environment, and what they see while they're writing is what readers receive when the files are distributed. In that case, production problems are likely to be fewer and less severe, because authors and editors will generally see them as we're writing and revising the document. Other production systems use software called a compiler to convert what the author has created into a different file format; this is the case for PDF files, Flash movies, Windows online help files (in both the older WinHelp format and the newer HTMLHelp format), and Web design tools (such as the text editors described in Chapter 12) that don't offer a WYSIWYG view. In this case, the file that goes into the compiler may look nothing like the file that comes out, and the compilation process can cause significant errors if the input file wasn't prepared correctly or if the compiler contains its own bugs.

Despite these differences, proofreading of onscreen documents is more similar to than different from proofreading documents that will be printed: in both cases, the goal is to ensure that users of the information we're publishing will see exactly what we intend them to see.

From this description, it's clear that proofreading includes all the editorial tasks we usually perform, but we'll be performing these tasks at the end of a long production process that should have eliminated almost all of the errors before we begin proofreading. In addition, we'll be looking for a different set of problems, many of them created by the processes used to produce the information. In the rest of this chapter, I'll discuss how the techniques you've learned for working on the screen can make you a more effective proofreader, whatever the final format of the manuscript. In keeping with the overall theme of this book, I've assumed that you already know the rudiments of proofreading, and thus, I haven't attempted to teach you everything you need to know to be a successful proofreader. Instead, I've chosen a few important examples to illustrate how you can apply your knowledge of traditional proofing to onscreen proofreading. For an introduction to proofreading basics, consult standard editorial references such as *The Chicago Manual of Style*.

When proofreading resembles light copyediting

If a proper job of editing has been done before creation of the proofs, our task should involve primarily light proofreading: all the significant errors should have been fixed in previous stages. However, we must look for new problems that can arise from how the production process works.

The proofs we're given to check may be traditional blueline proofs or more modern laser proofs, but in both cases, the source of these proofs was a computer file. Because most desktop publishing and graphics software can now generate PDF files, and because most printing is now done from PDF files, this means that we can generally ask our client to provide us with a PDF file even if they can't send us paper proofs or the original desktop publishing files. Less commonly, we may own the same desktop publishing software used by the client, in which case we can request the desktop publishing file. Our goal is to treat both kinds of file the same way we'd treat old-fashioned galley proofs: to look for the kinds of problems that inevitably arise when humans are involved. The advantage of using the PDF or desktop publishing file in place of or in addition to a physical proof is that we can use all the onscreen techniques described in this book to improve our effectiveness. Because revision tracking will only be available to us if the client is producing final files in a word processor, we may need to use some of the techniques I described in Chapters 12 and 13 to communicate our changes to the client.

If the document will be printed rather than used on the computer screen, it's appropriate to do at least some of our proofreading on a paper printout. (I'll discuss documents that will only be used on the computer screen separately at the end of this chapter.) To truly have proof that the printed publication will be correct, we need to inspect it in its final form—in this case, on paper. (See the section *Replacing printer's proofs* later in this chapter for an explanation of why this is so.) Still, although it's helpful and sometimes even necessary to proofread using a printout of the manuscript, this doesn't mean that we must wholly abandon onscreen editing. For example, if a PDF file of a manuscript is available, the annotation and commenting tools provided by the Acrobat and Adobe Reader software are available to us. These tools are inefficient and more difficult to use than true revision tracking, but they work well enough for the small changes that are typically made at the proofreading stage. For a good discussion of using traditional proofreading markup in PDF files, see John Clifford's 2004 article *Traditional Proofreading in PDF* at the PlanetPDF Web site (www.planetpdf.com/creative/article.asp?contentid=6667&ra).

We must look for the same things we look for in traditional on-paper proofreading: infelicities such as bad line breaks, awkward hyphenation, and inconsistencies such as headings that were accidentally formatted as body text. The key to performing these checks *on the screen* is that each of the traditional kinds of problems we'll be looking for can be found automatically. For example:

- We can perform a spelling check to spot typos faster and probably more accurately than would be possible on paper. Each of us has certain blind spots (typos we're likely to miss), and we're at risk of missing the same error repeatedly; spellcheckers have different blind spots that complement ours, and combining our talents with theirs improves the result. As I noted in Chapter 10, a spellcheck should always be the last step in any edit, but it doesn't always work out that way.
- In some software, we can search for hyphens at the ends of lines to see whether a manually inserted line break is good, bad, or indifferent. (In most software, automatically generated hyphens, al-

More than just light editing in Acrobat: At a recent conference, I learned that version 8 of Acrobat Professional may have finally become a useful tool for heavy substantive editing. If you install this software and let it add a "create PDF" toolbar button in Word, Adobe claims you can then export files to PDF, edit them using Acrobat's editing tools, and review those edits to Word using revision tracking. If this works as advertised, it eliminates my biggest objection to editing in Acrobat: the difficulty of incorporating your edits in the file used to create the PDF without having to retype each correction. Unfortunately, I didn't have time to test this before I release the revised edition of the book, but if you've already got Acrobat 8, why not test whether this will work for you?

though visible, aren't actually present in the file, so we can't search for them.)

- To help with consistency checks, we can use the search tools to find each heading. For example, we can search for each heading style, to confirm that each heading in that style is correctly capitalized. To find manually numbered headings, we can search for the end-of-paragraph marker followed by the code for a number (e.g., ^p^# in Word). By finding each heading in turn, we can check that its number is in the correct sequence.
- We can search for recurring patterns such as "Figure", "Fig.", and "Table" followed by a space to check both the numbering sequence (to find gaps or repetitions) and to ensure that the format is correct; for example, we may want to use *Figure* in text, but *Fig.* inside brackets.
- We can check bibliographic citations in the text to ensure that they match those in the bibliography, with no missing references and no references that have not been cited in the text. These kinds of problems should already have been pointed out during previous stages of editing, but sometimes the author makes mistakes in implementing those edits, and this is our last chance to spot and fix the problem.
- We can sometimes look for unacceptably large patches of white space visually by zooming out (shrinking the size of the page) until white space stands out against the background. Some software

even has automated tools for finding and highlighting excess white space.

And so on. In short, most things we can do on paper, we can also do on the screen, using search tools to help us find all instances of a potential problem. When we do spot a problem in a proof, it's possible that a similar problem occurs elsewhere, and if we were working exclusively on paper, we'd have to reread the entire manuscript to spot any instances of that problem we missed. The search tool provided by Adobe Reader is particularly helpful because it generates a list of all locations in a document where a particular search term occurs, letting us quickly go to each location by clicking on the corresponding search result. (Below, I've shown the same feature in Apple's Preview software.) For PDF files, we also have the option of copying the text into our favorite word processor and using all the tools and skills we've developed using that software for onscreen editing; for example, we can use the spellchecker, use the search tool to look for inconsistent capitalization or formatting, and so on. It may still be necessary to annotate the printed copy or the PDF file to indicate the necessary changes, but we at least

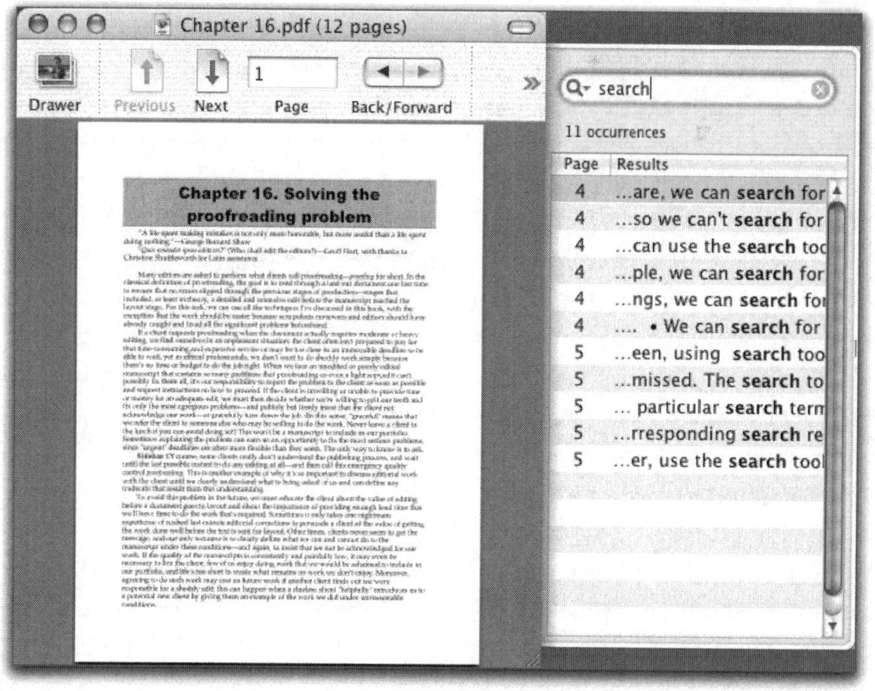

Extracting text from PDF files: To extract text from a PDF file, open the File menu and select Save As to save the contents in a format such as RTF that is supported by your word processor. It's also possible to select a chunk of text using the selection tool and copy it into a word processor.

have recourse to tools that can make the task of determining what those changes should be faster and more accurate.

However we work on a file submitted to us for proofing, it's crucial to remind our clients that someone must still check that our corrections have been implemented correctly. Ideally, we should be the ones who perform this check, since we're the ones who proposed the corrections and are thus the ones best suited to confirm that the corrections have been implemented correctly. Moreover, we have the skills required to do the work right, and authors may not. But where this isn't possible, someone must still take responsibility for the final check.

Comparing the laid-out document with the last edited version

"Reading against copy" (also referred to as "reading to proof") is an increasingly rare activity these days. In the old days, when everything was typed and retyped manually, errors were common: typists often missed words, sentences, paragraphs, or even entire pages (when two pages became stuck together), particularly when they weren't given time to check their own work, and someone had to check every last bit of ink on the final, approved typescript to ensure that it had been transferred successfully into the layout. To accomplish this, the proofreader compared that original typescript with the final layout by reading both, side by side, to ensure that both were identical. The two names for this process result from how this proofreading used to be done: the proofreader would place the original beside the proofs, and "read the manuscript against (placed beside) the original copy" while seeking differences. Sometimes a second person was pressganged into reading the typescript aloud ("reading to the proofs") so the editor could concentrate on matching the proofs to what the reader was saying. Such proofreading teams developed an entire verbal repertoire for identifying punctuation marks, accents, and so on, and it could be quite entertaining to hear someone reading "periods comma commas comma semicolons comma and exclamation points exclamation point". (Yes, that *does* make sense. Read it again as if you were reading the punctuation too.)

Because most production work is now done entirely on the computer, the risk of lost or misplaced text is believed to be lower, and in consequence, this kind of proofreading has become increasingly rare. That's particularly true in high-pressure publishing environments, where tight time constraints often limit us to reading the final text without reference to the original and assuming (or praying!) that nothing has disappeared, been repeated, or been replaced with something of mysterious provenance. It's the proofreader's responsibility to spot any accidental insertions by the fact that they make no sense in context, and to spot deletions by the logical holes they leave in the text; although such insertions are usually obvious, holes resulting from deletions may be harder to spot. If we're not given access to a copy of the document that was sent for layout, it's important to clearly inform our client that we can't accept responsibility for fixing all omissions. Nonetheless, it's still our responsibility to read with sharp eyes and alert minds to ensure that we spot as many errors of omission or commission as we can.

A broken promise: Fully electronic workflows offer the promise that no information will ever be lost, from the initial creation, through review and revision, to final production. Alas, these workflows are liars: they cheerfully ignore the possibility of human error, such as accidentally deleting a chunk of text or mistakenly pasting a chunk of copied text at the wrong location. Moreover, the imperfect software we're forced to deal with can't always live up to the workflow's promise. In the early days of PDF, it was not uncommon to receive a PDF file in which a single letter was mysteriously missing throughout the file; ironically, I once encountered this problem in a document produced by Adobe. That problem has supposedly been solved long ago, but occasional software glitches still bedevil us. A 2006 issue of *The Magazine of Fantasy and Science Fiction* contained not a single period anywhere in the text! This so-called "antiperiodical" is now being sold as a collector's item—but for editors, it's a cautionary note about the importance of proofreading.

An interesting new group of potential problems has resulted from the way that desktop publishing software works. Adobe's InDesign, which inherited some of these procedural quirks from its predecessor (PageMaker), provides a good example of the new kinds of things that can go wrong in modern layout software. The problem begins with the manner in which text (and other content such as graphics) is imported into the software. In InDesign, this is done by means of the Place command: when you select a file to be imported, InDesign changes the cursor into an icon that resembles a paragraph of text:  Clicking the cursor at the margin of an area that has been defined as a column of text drops the text into that area, where it flows to fill the area; alternatively, you can drag the cursor to define a text area, and as soon as you release the mouse button, the text flows to fill that area.

The first way this can go wrong happens if something on the page is selected before you place the new material: in that case, the new text replaces the old, just as it would if you pasted text into your word processor.

The second way involves the settings for the Place command. A word processor automatically expands the available space, as needed, to make room for whatever new text you type or paste. In contrast, most desktop publishing software requires you to define layout areas that will hold text; these containers may be called *text areas*, *text boxes*, or *frames*, depending on the software. If you haven't specified that text should automatically flow from the current container into the next available container (usually by changing one or more of the program's preference settings or by holding down a special modifier key on the keyboard) or that a new container should be created if more space is needed, the inflow of new text stops at the end of the current container. To help you remember that there's some text that has not yet been placed, the software displays some form of visual clue. In InDesign, for instance, that clue is a small [+] at the end of the text frame that reminds you that you still need to find a home for that text:

But if you don't happen to notice that there's unplaced text (the [+] icon is small and easy to miss), it's easy to forget about it and never add it to the layout. Moreover, if you add new text by typing in the middle of a chunk of placed text and there's insufficient room for that text in the current container, the text at the end that can't fit will disappear from the screen and need to be placed somewhere. Again, it's easy to miss this. Of course, if another container is linked to the current one, the text will flow into it automatically, but if that container fills up, the problem recurs. Worse yet, since it occurs on another page than the one you're looking at while you type, it's even easier to miss.

Importing graphics can cause similar problems: if the text wraps automatically around the imported graphic, then some of the pre-existing text is likely to be pushed off the current page, possibly ending up in limbo. Conversely, if your software is not configured to automatically wrap text around graphics, the text will print on top of ("overprint") the graphic. Thus, whenever you place a new graphic in a document, you must watch for both problems. Other problems may occur in how pages are handled. In your word processor, new pages are automatically added as the length of the text increases, but in most desktop publishing software, you must manually add new pages. If you add too many pages, blank pages will be left within the document. In contrast, if you spot those blank pages and choose to delete them, it's easy to select the wrong page icon and delete pages containing text and graphics. (In many cases, the text itself isn't actually deleted; it remains in the file as unplaced text, and only needs to be placed again.)

Similarly, most desktop publishing programs control page layouts using templates called "master pages". Because these must be selected from a menu or from a palette of small page icons, it's easy to apply the wrong master page in documents that use a different master for each chapter or for each type of page. Thus, you must not only confirm that the running headings and other standard features are consistent within a chapter—you must also confirm that they're the correct ones for that chapter.

Cross-references are another problem: if they were generated (manually or automatically) in a word processor, they may need to be recreated in the desktop publishing software. If the links will have "behaviors" such as launching the reader's Web browser and taking them to a certain site (a common design goal when we produce PDF files such as the PDF version of this book), the behavior must be correctly specified. The "continued on page Y" and "continued from page X" lines that are commonly used when stories are broken across several pages are another possible source of trouble: the continuation line will point to the wrong page, or perhaps to no page at all. In InDesign, for instance, the blocks of text used to define these links are created manually (not automatically) and must be physically adjacent to their parent text block (the text before a "continued on page Y" line or the text after a "continued from page X" line). If the two text containers don't touch, the link points to the wrong place or to no place.

We can read against copy on the screen to ensure that nothing has gone missing and nothing weird has been added: all we need to do is open the original document in the word processor (or other program) that created it, open the layout in the desktop publishing software or display a PDF created from that software, then juggle windows so the original and the layout are visible simultaneously. (The same approach works equally well for Web pages and online help.) However, this requires a large monitor or possibly even two monitors side by side so we can display enough information to reduce the amount of scrolling required to an acceptable level. Some editors (myself included) find this uncomfortable and unproductive, and prefer working on paper. That's okay: never forget that my goal in promoting onscreen editing is to make your editing faster and more accurate, not to teach you blind allegiance to your computer. If on-paper work makes us more productive or effective, we should never hesitate to include it in our editing repertoire.

If you're willing to adopt a more technological approach, your computer can facilitate the task of reading to proof by reading the document aloud while you follow along in a printout and mark omissions

Talk to me: In OS X, the speech utility can be found under the menu that has the name of the software (e.g., "Word"). Open that menu, select Services, select Speech, then select Start or Stop from the submenu. To choose the voice that will be used to read the manuscript and control its characteristics (such as speed), open the "Text to Speech" tab of the Speech preferences panel. Similar options are available for Windows.

or discrepancies. This "text to speech" capability has been built into the Macintosh operating system for many years, and with most Macintoshes, no additional hardware is required because the built-in speakers are adequate for the job. A comparable feature has recently become part of Windows (www.microsoft.com/enable/training/windowsxp/adjspeech.aspx), though you may have to add a sound card and external speakers to a budget PC before you can use this feature effectively. (And, of course, it will not explicitly read out punctuation, as a human proofreading partner would do.)

More sophisticated screen-reader software has been developed for blind and visually impaired computer users. Examples include JAWS (www.freedomscientific.com/fs_products/software_jaws.asp) and IBM's Home Page Reader (http://www-03.ibm.com/able/solution_offerings/hpr3upgrade.html) for Windows, and Apple's Voiceover software for Macintosh (www.apple.com/accessibility/voiceover). The AccessAbility special interest group of the Society for Technical Communication (www.stcsig.org/sn/visual.shtml) is a good place to turn for more information on such tools, but local societies for the blind will also be a good source of information on this technology.

Replacing printer's proofs

If you still produce printed materials, you need some kind of assurance that what you sent to the printer is what you'll get when the printed materials arrive, hot off the press. Except for the problems I discussed earlier in this chapter, which are easy enough to detect once you know that they exist and start looking for them, it's generally safe to

> **Before you take off:** "Preflight" software, so named because it resembles the preflight checklist used by airline pilots before they ever leave the gate, is designed to find a wide range of problems, including many of those described in this section. However, the basic preflight tools provided with most desktop publishing software are not always capable of finding subtle problems, and won't find *any* problems if you forget to use those tools because you're rushing to meet a deadline. If you're going to be using soft proofs, make sure to use whatever preflight software you have available, and if you don't have any, ask your printer to use their own software.

assume that the information you see in a desktop publishing file or PDF file won't be lost in any modern production system. Nonetheless, many unfortunate things can happen to that information between your computer and your printer's imagesetter: font substitutions can occur if the printer doesn't have the same fonts on their computer that you have on yours, special characters may disappear for similar reasons, incorrect software settings can produce unexpected results, and a variety of other problems can still trap the unwary and the unfortunate.

Many proponents of fully onscreen production claim that soft proofs (onscreen images) are an acceptable alternative to laser or inkjet printer proofs or blueline proofs, but I remain skeptical. It's true that if everyone involved in the production chain does their job properly, the odds of success are strongly in our favor, and soft proofs are a great way to spot overt problems, such as font substitutions, missing graphics, or incorrect colors. But as I noted earlier in this chapter in my anecdote about the "antiperiodical", subtler problems are easy to miss. Having done on-paper and onscreen editing for nearly 20 years, I'm increasingly convinced that real proofing can only be done accurately in the actual medium that will be used for the final product. (This may eventually change, but we're not there yet.) I have no rigorous statistical data to support this opinion, but a list of only some of the many problems I've encountered with soft proofs over the years may convince you:

Lack of gestalt

Even the largest monitors can't display tabloid-size two-page spreads at full magnification, and we can't even display single pages at full size on the typical monitors most of us use unless we're working with small page sizes. This prevents us from seeing the full effect of a layout (the *gestalt* of a two-page spread) the way that the reader will actually see it, and makes it difficult to review layouts without prohibitive amounts of squinting or scrolling.

Low legibility

It's difficult to distinguish between similar characters such as commas and periods on most monitors, particularly at small type sizes and with relatively light typefaces such as Palatino. We must either zoom in on the display repeatedly whenever something looks suspect, which is inefficient, or do a separate pass on paper, in which case we might as well just accept the fact that we're not exclusively doing onscreen proofing.

Inaccurate screen display

Even the best displays top out at fewer than 100 pixels per inch—not much better than early dot matrix printers. In addition to the aforementioned legibility problems, the mismatch between the display resolution (typically from 72 to 100 pixels per inch) and the actual output resolution (600 to several thousand dots per inch) inevitably leads to what are commonly known as "display artifacts"—errors in what you see on the screen. For example, PageMaker displays line breaks correctly at 100% magnification, but does a poor job of displaying word and letter spacing within those lines at magnifications less than 200%. To spot significant spacing problems, you sometimes have to zoom in.

Incorrect color

If you're also responsible for verifying colors, you can't do it onscreen—though you can come close. Even expensive color-calibrated monitors have *color gamuts* (ranges of colors that it's physically possible for the monitor to display) that don't overlap completely with the gamut provided by paper; in some cases, what you see on screen won't come close to matching what you see on paper, particularly if you change the ambient lighting. Moreover, even seemingly identical monitors vary greatly in how well they display colors, and the problem is exacerbated if you move between operating systems (e.g., from Windows to Macintosh), so even proofing Web colors can be challenging. Color calibration hardware and software can take you very close, but won't solve the problem completely unless you're aware of gamut problems so you can tell when you're "in gamut" and when you're not. Another common problem arises when the graphic artist responsible for a design forgets to choose the correct display mode: onscreen color is defined using the RGB (red, green, and blue) color system, and is the default system for what we see on the screen, but printed color is defined using the CMYK (cyan, magenta, yellow, and black) color system. The two gamuts don't overlap in many areas, so sending graphics in RGB format to the printer won't produce the results you expect on paper, even though the colors will look just fine on the screen.

Low ease of use

It's currently difficult to annotate PDF files and other onscreen media as easily as writing with a pen or pencil on paper. The inefficiency of having to transfer on-paper edits into a computer file after proofreading is sometimes compensated for by the tremendously greater efficiency of writing on paper. Investing in hardware such as a graphics tablet or even using a tablet computer (both of which let you use a pen to draw on the screen) will let you annotate PDFs and other files as easily as if you were writing on paper, but given that these annotations must still be manually transferred into the computer file used to generate the PDF, it's not clear that this approach offers any real advantage. (As I noted in a previous sidebar, this problem may have been solved by the latest release of Acrobat.)

Errors in subsequent production steps

The first time I printed my own business cards, I carefully set the PDF options the way the printer instructed me to do—only to receive cards with unacceptably low text resolution because the production staff chose the wrong settings on their imagesetter. Because I'd followed the printer's instructions to the letter, they reprinted the cards at their own expense, but sometimes the responsibility for an error is less clear. Printed (paper) or film proofs are the only sure way to spot such problems and fix them before it's necessary to redo an entire print run.

Font substitutions

Most modern desktop publishing software lets you either embed all your fonts in your document files or ship them to the printer along with the files. Of course, you have to remember to do this, and the fonts must be compatible with your printer's systems. If you use older fonts or homemade fonts you found somewhere on the Web, they may not be processed properly by the printer's imagesetter, leading to problems with the output.

Missing graphics

Most desktop publishing software checks for broken links to graphics as part of the preflight process, and provides some kind of "bundle for the printer" function to help ensure that we send all linked files to the printer. But again, we have to remember to use these features.

In many publishing programs, other components such as spreadsheets and animations are separate files that are linked to the publication instead of being embedded within it. Preflight software will check to ensure that all these files are present when you ship the files to the printer, but not all publishing software includes such tools and not everyone remembers to use them. As a result, a link that works fine on your computer will be broken (e.g., the content won't be visible) on the publisher's computer. If nobody checks the proofs, the missing information will be missing in the printed publication.

Not yet a perfect solution

As these examples illustrate, onscreen proofing remains a challenge. None of these problems mean that you should abandon soft proofs entirely. Soft proofs remain very useful for spotting obvious problems, and (as I've described in previous sections), using them appropriately can improve our proofreading effectiveness and efficiency and spare us from costly problems in creating film or publishing the manuscript. My point in listing these problems is to convince you that for important jobs, soft proofs should be a first step in proofreading, not the only step. If you'll be producing your information on paper, these problems suggest that you should still use a paper copy for your final proof.

Still not convinced?

Another reason why "soft proofs" should not be your only means of proofing a publication is that many other problems can occur at the printer. For example, the 20 November 2007 issue of the Washington Post ("Printing Goof Nullifies U.S. Reading Exam") reported that the company responsible for producing a test booklet for the Program for International Student Assessment missed a serious error that occurred at the printer. The original publication design called for text to be printed on the inside cover of the test booklet, but when the color on the outside cover bled through onto this page during printing, the printer shifted that text onto the following page. As a result, references to text "on the opposite page" in one part of the test no longer made any sense.

Although the printer is clearly at fault for changing the layout without consulting with the client, a traditional printing process would have included blueline proofs or some other form of printout that the client would be asked to approve before proceeding with the print job. The designer responsible for approving those paper proofs would have had a chance to spot the problem, particularly if all the pages were paginated (because even-numbered pages would then incorrectly appear on the right-hand page of the spreads) and insist that the printer fix it. Verifying the page sequence is one of the first things you learn to do when checking paper or blueline proofs, and even though you can do this with soft proofs, these proofs are sufficiently different from paper that it's easy to miss such problems.

Proofing online information

Of course, if your documents will appear exclusively on the screen, then you must proofread those documents on the screen—and confirm that no drastic problems arise when they are viewed on different computers or when using different operating systems. In this section, I'll discuss some things to keep in mind when you're proofing documents that will be used exclusively on the screen.

Most of the things we look for in printed proofs have onscreen equivalents, and we must include all of these things in our checklist for onscreen proofreading too. For example, if the software used to create the document requires authors to manually place text (e.g., into a complicated Web page template) or manually select which contents should and should not be included in the final product (for things like Windows online help files that must be run through a compiler to produce the final result), there's always the possibility that something will go missing or that the wrong thing will be included. The solution to some of these problems can be found in the section *Comparing the laid-out document with the last edited version of the file* earlier in this chapter.

But when we proofread a document that will only be used on the screen, we must remember that the creation process has certain idiosyncrasies related to the nature of the online medium that can affect the results. As a result, we must check many aspects of the document that have no equivalent on paper:

Hyperlinks

One of the great advantages of online information is that it can let us jump directly to cross-referenced topics. However, just as we check "see page X" and "see Chapter Y" references in print, we must check their onscreen equivalents. Whether these links are created manually or automatically (by compiler software), there's always a risk of error. Thus, every link must be tested carefully. Some may have broken (become nonfunctional), and others may take us to the wrong location.

Button behavior

Most onscreen documents have two main kinds of buttons:

- Standard buttons such as the "Forward" and "Back" buttons in a Web browser must be tested to ensure that they do what they're supposed to. In online help files, the author may have defined a "browse sequence" (the order in which readers should move from topic to topic); that sequence must also be tested. If the buttons are created correctly in a template, they should behave correctly in all screens based on that template, but some authors create them individually because they don't understand how to use templates.
- Custom buttons that produce special behaviors, such as the controls that play a movie or sound file, must also be tested to ensure that they produce the correct behaviors.

Consistency of the content

Just as chapters in a book may have different running headers and footers but the same style of page numbering, onscreen documents will have different and similar recurring items. For example, every Web page should have a title that appears in the title bar, but because not all Web authoring tools require authors to provide a title when they create a new page, Web pages sometimes end up with the inspiring title "Document 1"—or with the same title as a different page if the author simply copied that page. Similarly, every graphic on a Web page should be given a textual description (defined using the HTML "alt" tag) so that the image will be meaningful to visually impaired readers using screen-reader software. Although some authoring tools (e.g., Dreamweaver) can be set to require this information, the designer must choose this setting, and some don't.

Visual consistency

In addition to ensuring that formatting is correct (e.g., that no headings have accidentally been defined as body text), we must ensure that pages of the same type look similar. If the designer has used CSS (cascading style sheets) to control the appearance of an HTML document, it's our job to ensure that the correct style sheet was used for each group of pages with similar roles. Similarly, if the interface interacts with the user by (for example) changing the color of a button when the mouse cursor passes over it, or if a pressed button looks different from one that has not been pressed, all parts of the interface must be tested to ensure that they behave as they were designed to do.

Correctness

Just as printed documents must be checked to ensure that chapter titles match the running headers and footers and that the page sequence is correct, so too must we check the correctness of such elements in on-screen documents. For example, indexes of PDF files sometimes count page numbers from the start of the PDF file, rather than using the page numbers that appear on the pages when they are printed (the page numbered 1 is often not the first page; it may be preceded by unpaginated material).

Graphics

Graphics must be carefully checked to confirm that they are clear and legible on the screen. Screenshots are a particular problem, since users may choose widely different resolution settings when viewing the document; what works well on one monitor may be problematic on another. Similarly, if the author compressed the graphics file to save space, it's important to confirm that the resolution of the image has not degraded to an unacceptable level. Color shifts between different computers can also be a problem. If you're aware of this problem, you can test the graphics on two or more computers to ensure that these color shifts don't prevent the graphic from communicating successfully.

Navigation aids

Every screen of an onscreen document must contain the same navigation aids, unless there is a good reason for one screen to differ from the others. Such good reasons do exist, of course. For example, the opening "welcome" screen of a presentation may not include any buttons other than "start presentation", whereas the following screen may present a table of contents in which each entry is linked to the corresponding chapter; for the chapters themselves, navigation aids may refer to the previous and subsequent chapters by name rather than just "previous" and "next". But each page in each chapter should offer the same options in the same way: these include navigation to the next and previous pages, navigation to the next and previous chapters, and a link back to the table of contents.

Fonts

We must also ensure that nothing was lost during compilation. Doing so requires testing the files on at least two computers: ours and the author's. Ideally, we should also test across a range of operating systems to ensure that Windows, Macintosh, and Unix or Linux users all see the same thing.

Demand proof!

Proofreading will remain important as long as humans are fallible and computers remain malevolently contrary. That being the case, it behooves us to remind clients of the need for proofreading and to keep an eye on the technology available to help us proofread. In some types of proofreading, the computer can be a valuable ally; in others, it'll be some time yet before we can fully apply its power to this task. Use the guidance I've provided in this chapter to choose your own balance between the on-paper and onscreen approaches to proofreading.

Chapter 17. Overcoming resistance to onscreen editing: coping with the human factor

"In order to understand what another person is saying, you must assume it is true and try to imagine what it could be true of."—George Miller, psychologist (interviewed in *Psychology Today*, January 1980)

"Every man is a damned fool for at least five minutes every day. Wisdom consists in not exceeding the limit."—Elbert Hubbard, author, editor, printer (1856–1915)

We humans are a stubborn, recalcitrant, annoying bunch, and each of us is stubborn, recalcitrant, and annoying in our own unique way. The author–editor relationship brings this observation into particularly sharp focus, and I've repeatedly emphasized the human aspects of this relationship in this book because you'll never succeed as an editor without accounting for the human angle. Authors and editors each bring their own idiosyncrasies to the relationship, and this makes each interaction a new challenge in negotiation and consensus-building. George Miller's keen insight provides the key to success: none of the solutions I'll discuss in this chapter can work if you don't invest the time required to understand the other person's viewpoint.

The reasons why people resist onscreen editing can be loosely classified into three main categories: fears, unfamiliarity with the tools at their disposal, and a combination of prejudices and a desire to protect the status quo. Since you've stuck with me thus far, you're not likely to be someone who's resisting onscreen editing. Instead, you're likely dealing with colleagues, co-workers, or clients who are hesitant to take the leap. In this chapter, I'll deal with each of these potential obstacles in turn to help you understand where their reluctance comes from and how to deal with it.

Fears

As you might expect, there are several fears someone may have to overcome when you're trying to encourage them to adopt onscreen editing:

- Fear of change and of failure

- Fear of transgressing the rules
- Fear for job or income security

Fear of change and of failure

The fear of change is probably one of the most common fears we face on the job. Sometimes the rapid pace of technological change creates anxiety that we've reached the limit of our ability to cope, and that we'll reveal our incompetence by proving unable to master yet another new technology. This particular fear is compounded by the fear of failure, particularly when our continued employment and financial well-being are at risk. This book is one small tool to help overcome these fears, since I've lived through the hard work involved in learning how the technology works and have used that experience to write this book: my goal is to explain how you and your colleagues and clients can adopt the technology safely and in so doing, make your life easier. When authors are afraid, sharing what you've learned from this book and helping them work through the problems they face is a powerful start to easing their fears. It's important that they *know* in their hearts, as well as in their minds, that they'll never be alone in trying to master the technology.

As a general rule, people won't embrace change unless they have a strong reason to believe that the change will improve the quality of their lives. Moreover, they must be confident either that they won't fail if they embrace that change or that they won't be penalized if they do fail. This is the old "carrot and stick" situation, but with an important difference: you must provide a particularly tasty carrot and, to the extent that it's possible, throw away the stick. Your goal must be to motivate people

> **If it works...** There's another familiar cliché to beware: "if it works, don't fix it". Colleagues and clients may well ask you to justify why you want to change a system that has worked well since the first cuneiform manuscript was muddily rejected by the publisher with a request that the author hire a good potter. The old on-paper system does work well—but onscreen editing works better still. See Chapter 2 for a discussion of how onscreen editing can improve the process. See the rest of the book for suggestions about how to minimize the risks and take maximum advantage of the new technology.

to try the new technology, not give them a reason to fear changes to the status quo. The incentives capable of achieving this vary greatly among individuals, and what motivates one person may not interest someone else at all. Sometimes simple self-interest is enough to persuade someone: for example, show them how they can save an hour per day by editing on the screen, and most will eagerly embrace this approach. Other people prefer more tangible rewards, such as a cash bonus or time away from work, and those too are legitimate motivators.

At the same time, you must reduce the risk of failure and eliminate penalties should failure nonetheless occur; we're all human, and even under the best of circumstances, we sometimes screw up. Allowing time for people to fail, and to learn from their failures and move on, removes the most intimidating stick. Knowledge (this section of the book, for instance) is a powerful tool for reducing both the risk of failure and the fear that this risk creates. Providing reassurances that you don't expect anyone to succeed perfectly the first time they try, and that you'll provide all the resources (time and support) necessary to master the new technology, reduces the risk of failure and robs the occasional failure of much of its sting.

Making time to try: Office workers often find themselves in an ironic situation: a good manager truly believes that they're intelligent, capable individuals, and thus decides they don't need training because they've proven they can figure things out themselves. (Of course, some managers only provide empty flattery in the hope that employees won't notice the absence of a training budget.) No matter how smart, most employees already have a full day's work and face the pressures of completing that work well and on time. If managers don't remove this pressure, how can they hope to find time to study anything as new and complex as onscreen editing? If you're managing such people, provide training, whether formal classroom training or informal coaching during scheduled breaks from the daily grind, so that they have time to learn without sacrificing their other responsibilities. Building some wiggle room into those responsibilities can free up the necessary time.

Fear of transgressing the rules

Even the simplest and most efficient workplace has many formal, written rules that dictate how people must work. More intimidating still, many informal or unspoken rules exist simply because everyone agrees that "this is how things are done"—or perhaps because some powerful and vindictive individual has made their preferences widely known. Penalties for breaking a written rule may be clearly spelled out in a policies and procedures manual, but the penalties for breaking the unwritten rules tend to be more nebulous, and that makes them considerably scarier. Collectively, these rules pose significant barriers to change, since it's natural to want to go with the flow and accept existing practices rather than making waves by trying to change them.

To overcome these fears, start with a clear understanding of what the formal rules allow, and of whether the informal rules shape how the formal rules are applied and create new complexities. You must understand whether and how your proposed change (adopting onscreen editing) will conform to or contradict these rules. If it does contradict them, determine who can authorize you to break the existing rules. For example, if a writing group has always worked with printouts, most editors will continue to edit that group's manuscripts on paper rather than risking the ire of temperamental authors or departmental managers by suggesting a change in this approach. It doesn't matter that no formal written policy forbids the new approach. Getting the manager's encouragement to proceed removes the author's fear of earning that manager's disapproval, and may even provide an incentive to try something new.

There's an old saying that it's easier to get forgiveness than permission, and though this is sometimes true, it's an unwise strategy to follow if you don't have an unusually forgiving manager. (I've used this approach successfully several times in my career, but only when I knew my manager well enough to be confident they wouldn't penalize me.) More importantly, such a strategy ignores the very real fear many people experience when they're asked to bend the rules—let alone break them. Giving the impression that you're trivializing someone's fears by insisting that they break rules is guaranteed to make them resent you, and resentment undermines the sense of cooperation that is necessary for change to occur. Thus, the wiser approach is to recognize that breaking the rules can have serious consequences, and that people may be right to fear doing so. To eliminate this fear, work with those who enforce the rules to eliminate any adverse consequences. That's harder than simply proceeding and asking forgiveness later, but arguably far more effective.

In addition, where you want to change the status quo but an author or editor is reluctant, seek a compromise that gives both of you what you want. For example, if an author insists on receiving your edits on paper but you want to edit on the screen, the obvious compromise is to do your editing as you prefer, then teach the author how to print out your edits so they can see what you've done. (Chapter 4 discusses how to customize revision tracking so you can print edits legibly and review them on paper.) Willingness to compromise preserves or strengthens your relationship with an author, and may open the door to more daring experiments in the future, such as reviewing your edits on the screen.

Fear for job or income security

If onscreen editing is anywhere near as efficient as I've claimed, then it's logical to wonder whether we might work ourselves out of a job or reduce our income if we become too efficient. For example, if a department currently employs 10 editors and onscreen editing reduces the time required to complete the work by 10%, a keen-eyed manager under heavy budgetary pressure might seize the opportunity to lay off one of the editors. In this modern age, with short-term budgeting having replaced critical thinking, that's not an idle fear. Similarly, if you're an editor who can still charge your clients by the hour rather than quoting a fixed price per job, it seems reasonable that working faster will reduce your billable hours, and thus reduce your income. Let's look at each of these concerns in turn.

The first concern is certainly valid if you're working in an overstaffed department where most of the editors have too much free time on their hands and are desperately seeking ways to look busy. In that case, your job security is probably already at risk, and adopting onscreen editing won't pose any additional dangers. But onscreen editing can turn this perceived risk into an opportunity to preserve an endangered job: it may offer the opportunity to seek out new clients within the company and offer them your services. For example, even though I was originally hired by one employer as a technical editor primarily responsible for editing scientific manuscripts, I expanded my work to cover business letters, funding proposals, annual reports, and PowerPoint presentations, among many other types of editing. By using onscreen editing to greatly increase the efficiency of my work, I was able to accomplish more work in the same time period; more importantly, I demonstrated my value to many more people than I could have reached if I'd continued editing only scientific reports. That increased comprehension of my value actually *increased* my job security because I eventually became valuable to so many people that laying me off would have significantly disrupted the work of the company. (It also made my work much more interesting and diverse, which is not a trivial consideration for most editors.)

Far more often, the editors at a company are overworked to the point that it's a desperate scramble to get everything done without tons of overtime, and even then, the quality of the work suffers because of the need for haste and the cumulative fatigue that results from unrelenting deadlines. Editors in these situations must often resort to editorial triage, fixing only the most serious problems and letting many lesser problems slip past because there's simply no time to fix them. Such an environment guarantees editorial errors, since the faster we must work, the less time we have to think carefully about what we're doing and do the job right. Increasing our efficiency makes it easier to meet deadlines without working faster or longer hours than is safe, and thereby offers an opportunity to increase the quality of our work. That increased quality is often clear to managers, and will be rewarded. Even where it's not clear to managers, authors appreciate it, and that brings different rewards.

The second concern is that income might decrease. For those of us who freelance, the ability to get work done faster can indeed decrease our income if we bill by the hour. (If you're a wage slave, keep reading; there's useful information for you too later in this section.) If you're an established editor and earning a good living, this may not be a problem, because you may find (as many of us do) that time is a more precious resource than money, and anything you can do to free up some time from your busy work life is a priceless benefit. Even if you're struggling to earn a good living, getting work done faster can be a lifesaver when, as commonly happens, all your clients simultaneously drop urgent work with tight deadlines on your desk. In such cases, it's sometimes a wise investment to sacrifice a bit of income to ensure that you get all the jobs done on time. Meeting tight deadlines without sacrificing quality is a guarantee of future work, and freeing up enough time to maintain the quality of your work lets you accomplish this.

But none of this addresses the legitimate point that you'll still earn less money if you bill for fewer hours. The answer, of course, is to stop working on an hourly basis and start charging a fixed price per job. Peter Kent, a well-respected author, explains clearly how making this change can dramatically increase your income, particularly since clients usually prefer to be quoted fixed prices so they can budget more confidently for their editing costs. (For details, see his book, listed in the bibliography.) Here's a summary of how this works:

- Estimating a fixed cost by multiplying your hourly rate by the time you estimate the job will take makes it more likely that you will earn your desired hourly rate—if you estimate your productivity accurately.
- Getting the job done faster than estimated (perhaps because on-screen editing makes you more efficient) but still being paid that fixed amount increases your effective hourly rate.
- Increasing your effective hourly rate lets you work fewer hours to earn the same income, or more hours to increase your income.

To successfully adopt this approach, you must spend enough time tracking your editing productivity that you develop a good understanding of how fast you can work under various situations. Although there are many published figures on average editing speeds, these figures are useless and probably dangerous when it comes time to estimate the time a particular job will take. Why?

- These figures are averages for many different editors, and don't reflect your unique skills and how intensively you edit. If you edit heavily and with minute attention to detail, you may work far slower than these averages.
- These figures are averages for a wide range of authors, and don't reflect the actual authors you'll be working with. If your authors are significantly more difficult to edit, you'll take much longer to complete your work than the averages would suggest.
- These figures are averages for a wide range of subject matter, and thus don't reflect the difficulty of the actual subjects you'll be editing.

If your work is unusually difficult or demanding, you'll take much longer to do the job right.

In each case, you can lose significant sums of money if you base the cost of a job on "industry-average" estimates that ignore the specifics of your style and skill, the authors you work with, and the subjects you work on. The solution is to track your own productivity with a range of authors and types of work, and use this data to guide your estimates. If you have a scientific personality, you can come up with enormously complex methods of tracking your productivity, such as developing mathematical indices of document complexity and formulas for calculating the influence on your productivity of that complexity, the time of day, and the weather outside. In many cases, this offers a false sense of precision, and far simpler measures work just fine. For example, I maintain separate lists of completed jobs and the times they took in the following broad categories:

- The English and French authors based at a former employer who are ongoing clients and whose work is intimately familiar to me.
- The Japanese authors who are currently my main clients.
- The Chinese authors who are becoming an increasingly large proportion of my clients.

Each of these groups is sufficiently different from the other groups that it makes sense for me to record my productivity separately for each group. Similarly, when I work repeatedly for a particular author, I track their work separately so I can better understand my productivity for that author alone; where I don't do enough repeated work for a given author to make this level of detail valuable, I can instead use averages for all clients in a similar category. (If an author is a particular problem, I note this so I can inflate my estimates accordingly.) Over a period of nearly 10 years, I've collected enough data to provide reliable estimates of my likely productivity for each kind of client, as well as best- and worst-case scenarios. This data lets me estimate with surprising accuracy how long a job will take:

- For a specific author who is a regular client, I can use my average productivity for that author.
- For a new author who belongs to a particular category, I can use my average productivity for all such authors (or, if our preliminary interactions indicate significant writing problems, my lowest productivity for that category).

- If I won't have a chance to see the job before bidding on it, I can use my lowest productivity in case the current job is a worst-case scenario, and (to sweeten the deal) tell the author that I will reduce the price if I can get the job done quicker.

When you're just getting started, or are working with a new client in a new subject area, you won't have such data yet, but you can still come up with something useful. To estimate your initial productivity:

- Obtain a copy of the full manuscript, and skim through it quickly, looking for the most difficult parts.
- Edit a few of these parts (at least a few hundred words each) and record how long the work takes you. Calculate your productivity for that work in words per hour. (If you select a block of text before you use Word's word count feature, you'll get a total for just the selected text.)
- Count the number of words in the manuscript.
- Divide the total word count by your productivity to estimate how many hours the job will take. If the manuscript quality is highly variable, use the lowest of your productivity values for this estimate.
- Multiply this total time by your desired hourly rate. Add a fudge factor of at least 10% (many editors recommend much higher values) to account for any unpleasant surprises.

You can and should make these estimates even if you're a wage slave, but then the goal is different: knowing your productivity lets you budget time and other resources more effectively. This can be a real

Tracking productivity: I track my own productivity about as simply as you can imagine—using a simple table in Word for infrequent clients and a simple Excel spreadsheet for repeat offenders. Before I start work, I use Word's Word Count feature (under the Tools menu). I note when I start and stop work, and use that information to calculate how long I spent on a manuscript. The number of words, divided by that time, tells me my productivity in words per hour, and that's what I record. If you prefer something a bit more formal, there are many programs available to automate the process. I've listed a few useful utility programs in the *Helpful Internet Resources* section at the end of the book, under the category of "time tracking" programs.

sanity saver when you know a huge editing project is coming, and need hard data to persuade your manager to hire a contractor who can help you through the coming time crunch.

Unfamiliarity with the available tools

Unfamiliarity with the available tools arises from three main sources:

- Not understanding what the software can do
- Ignorance of the ability to customize the software
- Lack of practice with the software

Not understanding what the software can do

Many editors feel that current software doesn't meet their needs, but this is often based on long-ago experience with a much earlier version. A shameful confession: I once fell into this trap too. When I first had the opportunity to begin editing in Word, I had already been doing onscreen editing in other software for some time, and was comfortable using that software; moreover, Word had acquired a reputation for difficulty and unreliability. Naturally, I vigorously resisted my employer's proposal that we adopt Word. But when the change was forced upon me, I resolved to make the situation as painless as possible, and set out to explore the software until I fully understood its power and limitations. I call this my "if life hands you Microsoft Word, make lemonade" experience, because I soon discovered the enormous payoffs from getting past my prejudices and finding out the truth for myself. That took some work, but another lesson I've learned is that investing some effort in making my life easier quickly repays that investment in time savings and reduced frustration. Plus, using Word has earned me enough mon-

Word (mis)counting words: Word's word count feature isn't 100% accurate, but it's good enough that you can rely on it. Just be aware that you have to specifically tell it to include footnotes and endnotes; to do so, select the checkbox for "Include footnotes and endnotes" in the "Word Count" dialog box. Word also doesn't include text boxes in the word count. You'll have to open each one and count its words individually.

ey over the years that I've stopped making my own lemonade and now simply buy it.

Before anyone can use software productively, they must make a conscious decision that doing so is a worthy goal. Next, having made that decision, they must spend some time finding out what the software can and cannot do for them. Talking to other colleagues will reveal what they like and dislike about the software, as well as their tips and tricks for dealing with the problems. If you're in the position of talking someone through this process, remind them not to take someone else's griping as fact without first making time to explore the software themselves to see how bad the situation really is. (It's human nature to remember problems more strongly than the good things, and one person's problem is another person's opportunity.) The book you're reading right now resulted from this kind of journey, and now you're benefiting from the souvenirs and scars I accumulated along the way. If you want to fully comprehend just how much power a modern word processor can offer you, you'll have to actually try out my advice, because there's no better way to learn than actually doing the work and no easier way to appreciate what I'm talking about than by experiencing its benefits firsthand. Then share your knowledge with someone else who's unconvinced to give them an idea of the software's potential. The advice that I've provided in this book applies broadly to any word processor, not just Word, and should provide many examples of the benefits of onscreen editing—but you'll have to do a bit more research to see how other software implements a particular beneficial feature and how you can take advantage of that feature.

Ignorance of the ability to customize the software

Close behind complaints about the unreliability of modern computer technology is the complaint that the tools don't work the way we want them to and force us to work in bizarre and often counterintuitive ways. Shouldn't computers adapt to us rather than vice versa? Indeed they should, and many of the complaints about how software works arise from simple ignorance of just how extensively we can customize most software. This widespread ignorance is why I devoted an entire chapter in this book (Chapter 4) to learning how to make a word processor work the way we want it to work. Given how heavily we can customize software, it's only a slight exaggeration to describe something as flexible as Word as a kit for building our own word processor. That's doubly true if you discover that you enjoy working with your word processor's macro language; macro experts can redefine just about any aspect of how a program works.

The key to making software fit comfortably with the way we work is to spend some time playing with its settings. If some aspect of how the software works annoys us, the odds are excellent that somewhere, buried deep in the interface, there's a switch that lets us turn off that function or an option that lets us modify how the function behaves. Skim through Chapter 4 looking for functions of your software that make you think, "that sure annoys me and I wish I could change it". Then use the information in that chapter to make the necessary changes. If you're working with an author or editor who has similar complaints, spend a few minutes showing *them* how to make the necessary changes and encouraging them to explore other possibilities. This not only removes one or more of their objections to adopting the technology; it also builds a relationship in which you're seen as a helper rather than just one more obstacle on the road to publication.

Word processors are much like a new pair of shoes: They look good and seem exciting, but they chafe our feet and cause considerable pain at first. Customizing a word processor is like walking a dozen miles in a new pair of shoes: once we break them in so that they conform to the shape of our feet, they stop chafing and we can start enjoying the walk. (Of course, we'll also develop an occasional painful blister along the way until we adjust the fit properly, and will develop calluses from years of friction. The end result is the same: comfort.)

Lack of practice with the software

Even when someone understands the potential of onscreen editing, they may think there's no time to learn how to use the tools effectively. The busier they are, the more likely they are to feel this way, and the greater the payback they'll experience from making time to try new things and practice them until they get good at each new trick. Unfamiliar tools always appear more difficult than they really are, and the familiarity gained through experience with these tools makes them seem increasingly easy.

Efficiency alone isn't enough: Never forget that what works for me may not work particularly well for you or for someone else you're trying to train: if the shoe doesn't fit, don't wear it! Pay careful attention to your own work or the work of someone you're training to spot signs of discomfort so you can take appropriate action. In particular, you'll sometimes find a better way to do something than what I offered—with the caveat that *better* is not defined solely in terms of raw efficiency; a better solution is also *comfortable*. If a solution isn't comfortable, you simply won't use it, and you won't be able to force anyone else to use it either.

The trick is to get past that initial hurdle of choosing to invest time now to save considerable time later. If someone is at all skeptical about this, convince them to start slowly and focus on the things with the biggest payoffs. For example, if they must write the same comment in a manuscript dozens of times, teach them how to use the software's autocorrect feature (Chapter 11) to type the comment for them, or show them how to store such comments in a file of standard comments so they can copy and paste them into each new manuscript. Encourage them to use the time they save by not having to rewrite the same comment dozens of times to learn one more feature of their word processor, and use that feature to save even more time. If they find it difficult to impose consistency on a manuscript, and are frequently correcting things they missed during a first or second pass, show them how to use the search tools (Chapter 8) to find each instance of a term that must be made consistent and try out the tricks I provided to make replacing problem text quick and efficient. In the time they save using search and replace, encourage them to learn another feature that will save still more time. And so on. Each thing they learn frees up time to learn something new. At some point, they'll find the pressure from deadlines beginning to ease because of their newly improved productivity, and you can both relax and think about formally scheduling time each day to practice new tools and develop proficiency. There's no substitute for uninterrupted practice and exploration when it's necessary to improve proficiency in a hurry.

If you're a full-time editor, you will obviously become far more proficient with the tools than someone who uses the tools only occasionally.

Keep this in mind when you deal with your authors; those who don't have writing as their primary job may only use the tools once or twice per year, rather than daily, and thus won't be particularly skillful with them. Be patient, and help them remember. If someone does well with written instructions, write down a few notes to help them remember the procedures more quickly. You can download a primer (in PDF format) on using Word's revision tracking tools from my Web site (www.geoff-hart.com/resources/Using-revision-tracking.pdf) and print a copy for your authors, or modify this information to meet your own needs. For my own sake, I created a file that lists all the shortcuts I created in Word so I can periodically remind myself of all those cool shortcuts I created but keep forgetting to use. (I can also use this list to quickly rebuild my customizations should disaster strike and require me to reinstall Word from scratch when I don't have access to my backups.) Create your own list of shortcuts, and share it with your colleagues!

What similar tools could you develop to remind yourself of how to proceed or to help your authors? Anything you can do to answer questions and remove the fear caused by uncertainty will make it easier to begin working with the software.

Prejudices and the status quo

Each of us has a range of preconceptions, only some of which we're aware of, that prejudice our way of thinking. Some of these derive from attachment to the status quo, in what I call the "we've always done it this way" syndrome. Although it's not always possible to identify these prejudices without a lavish budget for psychological counseling, you can achieve surprisingly effective changes in the way you think simply by asking yourself a few questions:

- Why am I reluctant to try a new thing?
- Why is a procedure being done in the current way?
- Is that the only way to accomplish this goal?
- Is this goal truly useful, or would another goal be more appropriate?
- What can I do to overcome my reluctance in order to accomplish the same goal more effectively, or to accomplish a more important goal?

If you're a manager or mentor, substitute someone else's name for the *I* in those questions. The answers may have something to do with fear, and I've discussed how to deal with fears earlier in this chapter. But they may also reveal prejudices—beliefs that lead us to think in a particular way without questioning whether this way is appropriate. Once you've identified the real problem, you can work on solving it.

Organizational prejudices

An organization's *culture* can be defined as the collection of formal and informal practices that have become established over the years and that constrain how people are permitted to work. In many cases, these practices do little harm, but when they become overly ritualized, they change from being useful into rote responses that have long since lost their reason for being. When that's the case, it's time to question the prejudice and see whether you can change it into something more useful for the workers and more effective for the organization.

Inertia—the tendency to continue doing what you were already doing—is a powerful human force. Without a strong reason to change, people tend to keep doing what they're doing. (This is the human equivalent of Newton's first law of motion: objects in motion or at rest will stay in that state until acted upon by an external force. If you're trying to implement onscreen editing, *you* are that external force.) For example, if you've always worked with printed manuscripts provided by your authors, it's natural to want to keep working with those printouts. Requesting the word processor file used to generate that printout requires you not only to make the leap of faith necessary to try onscreen editing, but also to justify that choice to the author. Doing so may be particularly difficult if you lack a friendly or professional working relationship with the author, in which case it's natural for them to fear that you'll somehow destroy the original file or make changes without giving them the chance to approve what you've done. To allay those fears, you must make a clear case for the change, and reassure the author that there are no hidden drawbacks. I was able to persuade one author to try onscreen editing because we both agreed that my handwriting was appalling, and that he would have a much easier time reading my typed comments. Once I'd demonstrated the truth of this, the author embraced onscreen editing with no reluctance.

Some organizations separate their authors from their editors, often for patently ridiculous reasons such as the desire to protect the authors from being disturbed. Such a policy clearly undermines the chance to build the kind of mutually respectful relationship that leads to effective author–editor collaborations. The solution is to attack the problem (disruptions) in such a way as to make the rule irrelevant. Even the most toxic corporate cultures, which formally discourage and actively interfere with this dialogue during working hours, are unable to completely prevent dialogue during the lunch hour, while waiting to catch the bus home, during intramural sports, and so on. Each of these opportunities for contact is an opportunity to develop a relationship that leads to cooperation. Once that relationship exists, it's possible to negotiate ways and times to communicate that will not be disruptive to either the author or the editor. Once you've come to this understanding, the "no disturbance" rule becomes irrelevant because you're no longer disturbing the author, and managers can often be persuaded to look the other way. Better still, if you've adopted some of the techniques I've recommended to save the author time, the interaction with the author miraculously changes from a disturbance into a time-saver, and an alert manager who recognizes this may even eliminate the rule.

Other organizations go to an even more ridiculous extreme by explicitly giving authors the authority to overrule edits without discussion. We editors are not always right, and authors should certainly have some say about whether an edit is wrong; it's the attitude that there should be no dialogue that creates problems. An author who respects our expertise and sees the advantages of paying attention to our opinions will learn to ask why we made a change that they didn't understand. In any author–editor relationship, it pays to be very clear that your edits are all *suggestions*, and that you're eager to work with the author to find more palatable solutions that resolve your objection to an original wording while still giving the author considerable control over their own manuscript. One author I worked with early in my career had developed a reflexive dislike for editors and editing based on some bad experiences he'd had with a previous editor who didn't understand his work. The first time I worked with him, he coldly announced that he had no intention of paying much attention to my edits because I clearly had no understanding of his writing. Rather than letting that statement go unchallenged, I proceeded to demonstrate just how well I did understand his work, and followed up with several examples of problems with the way he'd tried to communicate his findings. The author, now reassured that I was changing his words for valid reasons, was able to overcome his prejudices enough to begin working with me. Eventually, he even learned to call me with questions before he submitted a manuscript for editing, thereby saving both of us time.

Another good example of a traditional practice whose original justification is generally no longer valid is the requirement for a *paper trail.* Some organizations have invested heavily in paper-based workflows, particularly where legal or practical requirements require that they keep copies of all versions of a manuscript. One common goal is to let managers return to earlier versions of a document so they can discover when and by whom errors were introduced; good managers then use this information to ensure that the error doesn't happen again, and bad managers may use it to punish, on the principle that "beatings will continue until morale improves". Another goal may be to provide legal protection, for example by having signed releases from technical reviewers on file to confirm that the manuscript and any changes resulting from the review process were thoroughly reviewed and approved by people with expertise and authority to do so. Such organizations often resist the change to onscreen editing because (self-evidently) "there's no paper trail". But given an understanding of the goal, it becomes clear that you can easily create an onscreen paper trail that works every bit as well as a true paper-based solution: retain copies of each version of the document, and if you don't have digital signature technology to establish proof of the reviewer's identity, print out file copies showing the revisions so reviewers and authors can sign the copies and confirm that they approved each version of the manuscript. The goal of the paper trail is to provide a record of the process, not to prevent you from editing on the screen; printing copies that were edited on the screen combines the efficiency of onscreen editing with the required paper trail—one of those proverbial win–win solutions.

Personal prejudices

Personal prejudices also arise from accepting the status quo. One of the more common misperceptions about onscreen editing is that the relatively low resolution of the computer screen compared with paper inevitably leads editors to miss more errors when we edit on the screen. This may well have been true early on, when computer displays had low resolutions and computer typography was relatively primitive, but increasingly, the screen itself is no longer a limitation on our ability to edit. That's doubly true with a modern high-resolution monitor with a flicker-free display that has been fine-tuned following my recommendations in Chapter 4 on how to customize that display. Most of my colleagues now insist that their editing accuracy has significantly improved since they adopted onscreen editing, and also report increased client satisfaction. I can emphatically confirm that this is true for me, especially with respect to improved consistency, which was always one of my editorial weaknesses.

Most claims of lower accuracy are likely to result from a lack of familiarity with onscreen editing, combined with a lack of understanding of how to customize the editing environment. When you're doing something for the first time, it's unlikely that you'll be as good at it as you are with something you've been doing well for years, so it's unreasonable to expect immediate proficiency and perfect accuracy when you first move to onscreen editing. It takes time to get good at anything, and onscreen editing is no exception. This is particularly true if you're an inexperienced editor, and must simultaneously master both the software tools and the intellectual tools you require as an editor.

The solution is simple: combine onscreen and on-paper edits. Editing is never an either–or solution: you can always take advantage of the different things that work best for you in onscreen edits and in on-paper edits. It's been argued that working on paper defeats the purpose of onscreen editing, but that's a spurious objection. There are two common objections to combining onscreen and on-paper editing, and simple reasons why these objections make no sense:

- The approach requires two passes (one on the screen, and one on paper) to do the same job: In point of fact, most editors make a minimum of two passes through a document anyway (once for major issues and a second time to spot anything they missed during the first pass), so why not do one of those two passes on the screen?
- The approach takes longer: This misperception is based on the assumption that two steps will always take longer than a single step. In fact, onscreen editing generally saves enough time (by fixing the majority of the problems quickly) that the second pass (editing a printout of the revised manuscript on paper) is much faster than it would otherwise be.

Why not combine the two approaches (on the screen and on paper) to use each for the problems it solves best? If you're new to onscreen editing, it makes good sense to print a copy of an edited manuscript to show the results of your edits. (You can do this by creating a temporary copy of the file in which you've accepted all edits; in Word, you can instead print a copy of the edited file with the tracked changes concealed.) This gives you a chance to examine the document in a second medium (paper) to spot things you may have missed while working in the first medium (on the screen). If you discover that you're routinely missing a particular type of problem, you can make a special effort to watch for that problem the next time you edit on the screen. Sometimes you can even use the software's tools to help you. For example, I have great difficulty spotting the difference between a lower-case L (l) and the number one (1) in many fonts, and some authors early in my editing career didn't understand the difference well enough to press the correct keys on the keyboard. (They're dear people, and ensure that I won't have to seek an honest living elsewhere, but sometimes you have to wonder what they're thinking.) Using the search tool lets me find all the cases where a lower-case L has been used in place of a 1 in the text, or vice versa.

Another common myth, fed by the media, is that working with a computer will cripple us with repetitive-stress injuries (commonly referred to as *RSIs*), such as carpal-tunnel syndrome. Ironically, writers and editors who once suffered from debilitating writer's cramp and painfully bleary eyes after a day spent manually annotating low-quality photocopies are often most vocal in this regard. In fact, evidence for an increased frequency of RSIs among computer users is weak. Editors who complain of eyestrain and cite the greater ease of reading printouts ignore the current optometric consensus that working with properly configured high-quality monitors causes few visual problems—certainly no more than the eyestrain caused by staring intently at printouts all day. Whether you work on the screen or on paper, editing (or any other kind of repetitive work, for that matter) is likely to exacerbate some kinds of pre-existing medical conditions. In contrast, maintaining good health and adequate levels of physical fitness protects against both computer-induced injury and other types of injury and illness. Better still, using a computer permits many forms of automation that can actually reduce the amount of repetition, and thus reduce the risk of RSI.

In researching an article on RSI, which I've summarized for you in Appendix II, I found no recent studies that supported the widespread perception that onscreen work increases the risk of injury. The solution is the same in both onscreen and on-paper editing: take periodic breaks in your work, make sure you've got an acceptably ergonomic setup, and watch for signs of trouble so you can correct a developing problem before it becomes serious.

Facilitating the dialogue

This chapter has a recurring thread you may not have noticed, and that is therefore worth making explicit: It's not sufficient to offer criticism once you detect a problem; you should also offer a solution. Finding the correct solution depends on understanding the other person's viewpoint, because all that's necessary for a problem to truly exist is for the other person to believe in the problem. Understanding that belief lets you seek a solution that will make that problem, real or illusory, go away.

You can't understand the other person's perception if you can't talk to them about it. This is why dialogue is such an essential part of any author–editor relationship. At some happy point, you may reach the kind of understanding with an author in which they trust your judgment implicitly and know when to ask you for clarification. Ideally, authors should learn to ask us about anything they disagree with rather than rejecting an edit out of hand. Sometimes it only takes a simple statement to establish this relationship: "If I misunderstood the sentence, someone else will too. So even if the current wording is technically correct, we can work together to make that correctness more apparent."

If you work in the same building as an author, this dialogue can be conducted face to face, thereby reinforcing the human aspects of the dialogue. But many editors, and particularly freelancers with an international clientele, may work through an entire career without ever meeting their authors. In that case, the dialogue occurs through the impersonal medium of correspondence. Even a telephone call to the author is somewhat impersonal, though it at least permits the give and take of human interaction that is so essential in a relationship. Suzette Elgin, author of *The Gentle Art of Verbal Self Defence*, reported studies of human communication that indicated somewhere between 50 and 90% of the information being conveyed in a conversation was nonverbal. Irrespective of the accuracy of these numbers, their meaning is clear: if you're not talking with an author face to face, you're working at a great disadvantage, and need to make a particularly strong effort to ensure that the author gets the right message.

Chapter 18: Putting the theory to work: a four-step implementation process

Hofstadter's Law—"The time and effort required to complete a project are always more than you expect, even when you take into account Hofstadter's Law."

The human and technical barriers to implementing onscreen editing that I've discussed throughout this book can be formidable, and you can't successfully implement onscreen editing until you solve each of the problems I've identified. But because the journey of a thousand keystrokes is halted by a single stet, the first step is to make a conscious decision that you want things to change. Whether you're a manager tasked with the job of managing the implementation for your department, an editor or author working in that department, or a freelance editor trying to work with clients living on the opposite side of the world, the steps in a successful implementation remain the same:

- Obtain permission to explore the proposed change. In a hierarchical relationship, that permission should come from the manager who will suffer the consequences if the change fails or produces undesirable side-effects.
- Propose a test case to demonstrate the benefits of the change. Change is easier to accept once you know that it will work.
- Explain how you'll solve anticipated problems. Hiding problems or pretending they don't exist immediately undermines trust in a proposal; in contrast, showing an awareness of problems and of their potential solutions reinforces that trust.
- Propose how you'll detect and resolve unanticipated problems. Because it's never possible to know everything about a situation, there will always be surprises. Admitting this, and explaining how you plan to deal with those surprises, also builds confidence that you're competent to do what you propose.

Stet? The word *stet* comes from the Latin "let it stand". In editing, it means "don't make this change". Far too many organizations have made stet the basis for their organizational cultures.

This chapter provides an overview of each of these steps. My focus will be on the manager who must implement the process with one or more editors and authors, but the same process works equally well, *mutatis mutandis*, if you're a freelance editor who wants to adopt onscreen editing with a client or an author who is tired of on-paper editing and willing to try something that would be more efficient for both you and your editor. The steps are identical; all that differs is the context, and it should be obvious how to modify the steps to account for that context.

Step 1. Get permission to try

"Any simple problem can be rendered unsolvable if enough meetings are held to discuss it."—Bill Smith, writing in the Elroy (WI) *Tribune Keystone*

There's a truism that it's easier to simply go ahead and do something, then ask for forgiveness later if someone objects, than it is to ask for permission in the first place. Indeed, as I mentioned previously, I've actually done this several times during an occasionally checkered career and have escaped with my skin largely intact. But I can't in good faith recommend this approach for everyone. Making a change without the permission of the manager who will be affected by the change can be a recipe for bad blood (at best) and could be career suicide if things go wrong. That's particularly true if you haven't tried something before and thus can't guarantee that you'll succeed. Some managers really do understand the need to take risks and as a result, are willing to encourage risk-taking behavior, but they often seem to be in the minority. If you're not confident your manager is one of this enlightened minority, it's wiser to take the more difficult step of requesting permission.

A general approach that works well in almost any situation is to propose the change to the manager or managers who will be affected by the consequences of that change. In some organizations, you may need to present a formal business case for the proposal. In others, a reasonable summary of the proposal will suffice. In both cases, the goal is to make your proposal seem as reasonable as possible: you must explain the benefits and drawbacks, list what you already know and what you don't know but plan to find out, and describe how you plan to overcome any problems. The two biggest barriers to making a change are the very human fear of undesirable consequences, and the lack of understanding of why you want to change something that seems to work. To succeed in your proposal, you must address both barriers: you must provide reassurance that the undesirable consequences will be either prevented or limited, and must demonstrate benefits so tasty (without exaggerating or over-promising) that the manager can hardly resist trying—particularly if you're the one who will bear the responsibility for any failures, thereby relieving the manager of this responsibility. I described the main benefits of onscreen editing in Chapter 2, and describing those benefits in the context of your actual situation should be your first step. Chapter 17 describes the most common fears and proposes how you can address those fears, although again, you'll have to modify the approach to account for the idiosyncrasies of your situation. The rest of the present chapter will walk you through the process of creating a compelling proposal for change.

Demonstrate the benefits

The first step in proposing any change is to give everyone a reason to keep reading your proposal: answer the question "what's in it for me, my staff, and the organization?" This means that any proposal to implement onscreen editing should start with a discussion of its benefits, possibly in the context of a problem the organization is facing that should be solved. Chapter 2 summarizes the benefits of onscreen editing, and it's worth spending a moment or two explaining these benefits to everyone involved in the process. In summary, here's what everyone can expect once the process is up and running:

- increased editing accuracy, thus improved document quality
- decreased editing and revision times, thus fewer missed deadlines and faster times to publication
- decreased repetitive manual labor and duplication of effort
- improved relationships between authors and editors

That's *my* claim, and though I've found each of these to be true in my own editing work, that anecdotal evidence won't persuade anyone. Your goal at this stage is to convince someone to give you an opportunity to demonstrate that these claims are true in your own specific context. How can you come up with reliable estimates (of saved time and effort, and of increased quality) that your manager will accept, and that you can live up to? Develop the kind of test case that I'll describe later in this chapter.

One important point to keep in mind: Avoid extravagant promises at this point. Adopting any new process takes time, and the results won't initially be as dramatic as they may become over time as you tailor your approach to the unique characteristics of your workplace and the individual personalities involved. Moreover, allowing yourself some leeway gives you some breathing room in case things don't go as well as you expect. (That's a particularly important caution if you've just adopted a new version of some software and are still figuring out the bugs introduced by that new version.) Another benefit of estimating the benefits conservatively is that people are generally more impressed when you deliver more than expected. (This is the source of the common business advice to "underpromise and overdeliver".) Don't work harder than you expect to work in the future just to make the results seem spectacular, because doing so will set a standard you won't be able to meet in the long term because the level of effort required will prove unsustainable.

Eliminate or minimize bad consequences

The second step is to carefully identify the needs of everyone who will be affected by the proposed onscreen editing process. For each need, you must propose a solution that seems likely to meet that need and that provides a means of detecting and solving any problems. Here's an example of how this might look:

Person affected	**Needs and solution**
Employer (manager)	**No serious problems arise:** The subsequent sections in this chapter explain how to detect and resolve problems. In the next section, you'll develop a test case that lets you demonstrate the absence of problems or reveal and solve any problems that do arise.
	A paper trail is kept: Describe how you will retain backup copies of each file, and create paper printouts if these are needed.

Person affected	Needs and solution
Employer (manager)	**Work gets done at least as quickly and accurately as before:** Onscreen editing can be faster for both the author and the editor, thereby reducing total time. But large time savings are less likely (and delays are even possible) while you and the author are still learning the technology, so your proposal should be scheduled for implementation at a time when any delays won't be critical. Thus, propose that the test occur *after* a deadline or busy period, not before. In addition, you'll want to collect statistics that demonstrate improvements in speed or accuracy.
	Accountability is maintained: Describe how the new process can provide all the same accountability as the traditional on-paper process: for example, changes can be tracked by date and by the name of the person who made the changes, and you can save ongoing copies of the file to let anyone return to a previous version and investigate what each person did.
	Staffing needs remain constant: Demonstrating the efficiencies of the process ensures that the manager will not need to request additional staff, but if you're too efficient, there may be a fear that some staff will need to be laid off, thereby diminishing the manager's "empire". The solution is to make it clear that you are aiming to give the current staff more time to do the job right, particularly under deadline pressure, or to take on more work and thereby eliminate the need to hire contractors during busy periods.

Person affected	Needs and solution
Employer (manager)	**Any adverse changes in work quality are quickly detected and fixed:** By performing your second pass on paper, you can quickly determine whether you're missing anything by working on the screen, and can correct anything you did miss. Once you stop finding problems in the paper copy, you can eliminate this step and do your second pass exclusively on the screen.
	No damage is done to the human relationships in the department: Emphasize that working onscreen will not mean you never again see the authors in person. Instead, make it clear that you will use the new approach to preserve and even improve existing relationships.
Author	**The technology is easy to understand:** I've provided a "primer" on my Web site (www.geoff-hart.com/resources/Using-revision-tracking.pdf) that you can give to your authors to help them learn how to use Word's version of revision tracking. But rather than just dropping off a printout and leaving them to their own resources, reassure them that you'll be happy to work directly with them to help them use the technology effectively. Then ensure that you actually *do* work with them; make that willingness more than empty promises.
	The author can still review your edits: Teach the authors how to review your edits both with the changes displayed and with the changes concealed. If necessary, teach them how to print a copy that shows your changes so they can do the review on paper.

Person affected	Needs and solution
Author	**Author and editor continue to collaborate:** Emphasize that the editing process will still be collaborative, and that no edits will be made without the author's approval. The easiest way to sabotage this trust is to make a change "invisibly" without the author's permission and get caught.
	The author can review and implement edits as least as quickly as before: Work with the author to demonstrate how much easier it is to read typed comments than hand-written ones, and how to incorporate your changes automatically using the revision-tracking tools. Also demonstrate the efficiency of copying and pasting typed comments (compared with having to retype them from scratch.)
Editor	**Accuracy is maintained or improved:** This should never be a problem, since the procedures described throughout this book are designed to make you a better editor. But the reassurance of being able to edit on paper to spot anything you're missing until you're confident that you're improving your effectiveness often provides the necessary confidence to proceed.
	The work is done at least as quickly: Again, one of the primary goals of onscreen editing is to improve efficiency, which means both accuracy and speed. Collecting statistics on your on-paper and onscreen editing rates will convincingly demonstrate the time savings. In particular, be sure to collect data that will show an ongoing improvement as you become more expert in using the technology.

Person affected	Needs and solution
Editor	**Relationships with authors do not suffer:** If you think of yourself as working *with the author* rather than with the file, your relationships with authors should never be adversely affected. On the contrary, once the authors begin to see the advantages of the new approach, your relationships can improve. (Authors are people too, and appreciate the efforts of people like you who save them time and effort.)
	Managers appreciate the work: If you spend some time understanding the needs of the managers affected by the process, you can go a long way towards solving problems they may never have complained about previously. Ask them what specific problems they have with the current process, then emphasize how your proposal will help solve those problems. (Managers are people too, and appreciate people like you who solve their problems without introducing new ones.)
Other staff (e.g., secretaries, desktop publishers	**Other people's work is not disrupted:** If you itemize and address the needs of everyone in the entire publishing process, from the person who formerly typed handwritten edits into the word processing file (often a secretary) to the person who must lay out that information (whether for on-paper or onscreen publishing) at the end of the process, you can detect any adverse consequences your actions might have for their work. This knowledge lets you avoid the problem or take steps to mitigate it.

Person affected	Needs and solution
Other staff (e.g., secretaries, desktop publishers	**No one is laid off:** In the modern workplace, it's rare for a worker to have so little work that further reducing their work will jeopardize their job. Emphasize that the goal is to free up enough time that everyone can do a better job of their existing work or perhaps add to their responsibilities.

Note that I have called this table *an example*. Although it covers the main points, you should interview each of the people listed in the table to find out what points *they* consider important. Some of those points will clearly be serious and significant. Others may seem trivial and irrelevant, but have enormous practical significance to the people who raise those concerns. Addressing their concerns convinces these people that you're really on their side, and removes much of the fear that comes from a belief that their concerns are not being taken seriously. (Sometimes the process of consultation is every bit as important as the results of that consultation.) If the concerns truly are trivial and irrelevant, then they'll be easy to address. But every so often, those concerns prove to be more serious than you thought, and you'll be glad you identified and tried to solve them.

Step 2. Develop a test case

"In seeking wisdom, the first step is silence, the second listening, the third remembering, the fourth practicing, the fifth—teaching others."—Ibn Gabirol, poet and philosopher (ca. 1022–1058)

Good managers thrive on numbers and other objective data, not just opinions. This is also true of scientists, engineers, accountants, and anyone else who makes a living working with numbers. The only way to convince such people that the hypothetical benefits of onscreen editing are real will be to collect enough productivity statistics that you can demonstrate the improvements. To do so, you'll have to perform at least one test that generates the numbers you'll need to make your case, and the results of that test will have to be compared with similar numbers collected before you made the switch. (That is, you need to collect some baseline productivity data if you haven't already done so.) You'll need to find an author–editor pair willing to work together in this test case, and willing to record what they're doing for the benefit of those who will be monitoring the test case and of those will follow in their footsteps. Next, you'll need to pick an appropriate project. Last but not least, you'll need to help this pair work through the project in a satisfactory way.

Obtain good numbers

It's difficult to predict what numbers a given person will find persuasive, since despite our occasional pretensions of objectivity, each of us uses very subjective criteria for assessing a situation. That being the case, the only way to develop persuasive statistics is to ask the person you're trying to persuade what numbers they want to see. This should be obvious, but from my experience working with editors and technical writers, it's clear that many in this community believe that quality or improvement can be measured objectively. (These people evidently never heard Mark Twain's enumeration of the three kinds of lies: "lies, *damned* lies, and statistics.") The two main types of statistics you can use are completion times and error rates, but as the following examples show, there's great variation in how you can collect this information:

Simple productivity tracking: I track my own productivity about as simply as you can imagine—using a simple table in Word. When I start and stop work, I jot down the times and use that information to calculate how long I've spent on a manuscript. If you need something a bit more formal, there are many programs available to automate the process. Have a look at my list of utility programs in the References section, under the category of "time tracking" software.

Type of statistic	**Details**
Completion times	It's easy enough to calculate how much time you spent on a particular job, but how can you translate this into a value you can use for prediction? You can count the number of words in a manuscript and calculate how long it takes you to process (say) 1000 words, and that's enough to satisfy some people. Others will demand to know how much work you accomplished (e.g., how many keystrokes you typed) while you read and edited those thousand words. Others will want you to calculate separate times for work in different genres (e.g., technical reports vs. staff newsletters), for different authors, or even for different levels of difficulty (e.g., rocket science vs. cafeteria menus).
Error rates	Errors are very subjective things. Spelling errors are hard to argue with, but what about grammatical problems and subtle logical problems in the original manuscript? The subtle problems are arguably far more important than the typos, since most readers will eventually figure out spelling errors and won't be led far astray by them. Moreover, without having absolute, 100% knowledge of every conceivable error that existed in the unedited manuscript, how can you possibly determine the number that you missed? How do you account for differences between manuscripts? (Some may be particularly difficult, and others particularly easy, so the expected error rates—both those in the original manuscript and those made by the editor—will clearly differ.) If the person you're trying to persuade is willing to accept a final on-paper edit as a way of determining what you missed in editing onscreen, sometimes that's the simplest thing to propose.

Since you'll need to demonstrate improvements, you'll also need a benchmark against which to compare the new process. If you're proposing to replace on-paper editing with onscreen editing, you'll need to collect matching statistics for the on-paper edits that you're currently doing. Resist the temptation to inflate your estimates of on-paper editing times and error rates. Apart from the ethics of lying to your manager, you don't want to give the impression that you're not doing a good job already.

How do you come up with numbers that are defensible and reasonable? One of the simplest and most persuasive ways is to pool all your data for on-paper editing. If you don't already have this data, monitor your editing times over a period of a month or two. (You can do this simultaneously with your test case for onscreen editing, but it takes a bit more organization to track two different classes of statistics at the same time.) What you're looking for in this benchmark is a long-term mean productivity: the number of words per hour you can edit for all your work combined. If you do enough work to "stratify" your statistics (e.g., to distinguish between demanding technical documents and undemanding documents such as the staff newsletter, or between different projects or authors for whom you do significant work), calculate a mean value separately for each client or type of work, because you'll develop a more realistic mean value for those specific jobs. Also calculate some measure of the magnitude of the variation around that mean: the range from lowest to highest productivity is useful to know, but if you're collecting enough data (at least half a dozen edits, and preferably more), consider using statistics such as the standard deviation. (Your favorite spreadsheet can probably calculate these statistics for you.)

Next, calculate your work times for onscreen editing. Don't start this data collection until the participants in your test case have been trained to use the software and the revision tools, and have had a chance to read this book (or your summary thereof) and practice with some of the tools that they'll be using. The information you collect should reflect the re-

> **The metric system:** In case you need to use business jargon to persuade someone, feel free to call your statistics *metrics*. The meaning is essentially the same, but now you're using the same language as your audience.

sults of applying the tools, not the time lost while they learn those tools. (It can be helpful to track this learning time separately so you can include it in your final proposal: this data lets managers know how much training time to budget for.) Ideally, gather data for several edits so that you get a better idea of the range of variation and even have a chance of demonstrating speed improvements. Any single result is not broadly representative, so you want a sufficiently good sample size that your results will cover the typical range of productivities.

Your goal is to compare the numbers for on-paper editing (your baseline) and onscreen editing (the improved process). If the types of edits you did to collect the baseline and onscreen data were very similar, you'll see a clear difference, with a clearly larger mean productivity for the onscreen editing but some overlap of the two ranges. The ideal situation, of course, would be no overlap at all in the ranges, with the onscreen editing productivity clearly higher, but that's not likely to occur for some time, if ever. If you keep tracking your productivities for long enough, you'll see mean productivity continue to increase for onscreen editing.

You can use a similar approach to measure the accuracy of your work. One useful way of doing so is to assume that one form of editing, whether on paper or on the screen, produces a final manuscript that can be used as your standard for comparison. You can then count and categorize any subsequent corrections to that edited manuscript, each of which represents an editing error. These corrections may be made by several people at various stages of the publishing process:

- the author, when they first review your edits
- yourself, if you get to edit a manuscript a second time and catch your own omissions
- peer or technical reviewers who examine the manuscript after editing and revision
- proofreaders who will have the final look at the manuscript before it is presented to its audience

By counting instances of each class of error that was missed (e.g., typo, inconsistency, grammatical error, unclear wording), you can develop statistics on how often each type of error may be missed in that form of editing. Each stakeholder in the process, whether author, editor, manager, reviewer, or someone else, may propose specific types of editing error that they want you to track; for example, if a desktop publisher must spend considerable time correcting formatting errors that are missed during editing, this is yet another category of error that should be tracked.

Although hard numerical data are persuasive, don't neglect to collect more qualitative, subjective data from the participants. Gathering this information shows that you actually care what the participants think, and that's never a bad thing. But subjective impressions of the process also reveal good things that you should emphasize when you report the results of your test case to your manager and other people who you want to participate. More importantly, they sometimes reveal subtle or dramatic problems that need to be solved but that won't be obvious from purely numerical data such as error rates. As I've noted previously, a process that is super-efficient but that nobody wants to use will be difficult to implement.

Statistics 101: If you're a number geek, you can actually use statistics software to test the statistical significance of any differences you observe. (Statisticians? Stop reading now! You know how to do this right, and won't be impressed by the advice that follows.) If you're *not* a statistician, and you're not willing to crack a statistics text to learn how to design an experiment correctly, think simple: You can perform a statistical test with as few as half a dozen data points if you want, but you'll get more credible results with more points for each alternative (on the screen vs. on paper). A dozen or so data points will let you perform a credible "comparison of means" test such as the *t*-test. Don't have statistics software? UCLA offers the *t*-test on their Web site (http://calculators.stat.ucla.edu/twosamp/). If the link changes, use Google to search for "two-sample test" and "online calculator"; you'll find several options. In UCLA's version of this test, use the default selections. In this test, larger *P* values mean it's more likely your results differ significantly; values larger than 0.95 are good. Other tests work differently: the lower the *P* value, the less likely a difference occurred by chance, and *P* values less than 0.05 are significant. Read the test description carefully to find out which form of *P* value it uses.

Pick at least one suitable author–editor pair

As I've mentioned repeatedly, the human aspect of the author–editor relationship is probably the most important factor in achieving success. Thus, you can only expect your test case to succeed if you can identify an author and editor who are willing to work together to test out the new process. An ideal author–editor pair has the following characteristics:

- a history of working well together, so as to minimize the risks posed by the human factor
- a willingness to try something new, so that they won't resent or resist the new process
- above-average proficiency with the word processor you'll use, so that basic competency with the software won't be a limiting factor (at a minimum, both must be skilled typists)
- sufficient competence to work quickly and accurately, so that delays will merely slow them, not bring them to a grinding halt

Your goal will be to work with these individuals to develop a simple, efficient process that satisfies their needs and identifies any problems that arise so you can resolve them. Because your workplace situation will be different from every other workplace situation to a greater or lesser degree, it's important to emphasize the need to adapt the various generic solutions I've proposed in this book to create a custom solution that fits your workplace perfectly. Moreover, it's human nature to more eagerly embrace a solution that you helped to create and that you proved to be workable than a solution imposed on you from above, with no reality check to confirm that it's appropriate.

Once you develop a process that works, you'll find it much easier to sell the process to others in the organization. Even inherently recalcitrant authors and editors lose their reluctance to try something new once their colleagues begin to enthusiastically evangelize on behalf of the new process—or at least report that it has merit, isn't as bad as they had feared, and has been debugged. Because you will have already solved most of the problems that the resisters would face by the time your test case is complete, you remove another barrier to implementation: resisters will encounter fewer problems, and you'll be able to solve those problems faster than might otherwise be the case because of your increased experience with the process.

One final note: I've concentrated on the author and editor because these are the two most obvious participants in the new process. But if the manager and other staff will also be involved, you must ensure that there are as few personal incompatibilities as possible. If the manager dislikes the author, and the desktop publisher dislikes the editor, you've added two complications that you don't want to have to resolve. In such cases, it may be beneficial to pick an author or an editor who doesn't meet all the criteria listed above, but who interacts sufficiently well with all the other staff members to compensate for any deficiencies.

Pick appropriate projects

The next step is to pick an appropriate manuscript for your test case. A good choice has the following characteristics:

- It is representative of the *typical* range of editing challenges that your editors will face. This helps ensure that you have an opportunity to encounter and solve all or most of the kinds of problems that will occur in every manuscript that you subsequently edit.
- It is *not* representative of the worst challenges that your editors will face. If you start with something that is likely to be more difficult than average, you're more likely to run into problems that you can't easily solve. You'll still have to confront such manuscripts eventually, but try to do so only after you've acquired some skill and confidence in the new procedure. (In short, learn to walk first; try to fly later.)
- It must have a reasonable deadline, with room for slippage. This is so that if you encounter unexpected problems that take some time to resolve, the resulting delays don't cause serious consequences for the author, the editor, or the organization. Adverse consequences can poison people's minds against the new process.
- It must be sufficiently important to justify editing it in the first place, but not so critical that any failures in your initial test will have serious consequences for the author or the organization. A manuscript that will undergo peer review after your editing is an excellent choice, since the peer reviewers will have an opportunity to catch any problems and actually expect to catch these problems as part of their job. A manuscript that will go directly into print or onto your Web site is a poor choice because it offers a chance to display your errors to a large audience, most of whom expect perfection.

- It must clearly demonstrate the potential payback. Small, simple manuscripts fail this test because the time savings may be unimpressive and the possibilities for identifying and resolving errors may be too small for the exercise to prove useful. For example, a manuscript must be sufficiently long that even small speed improvements produce significant savings: a 10% time saving produces negligible savings in a 20-minute edit (only 2 minutes saved), but impressive ones in a 10-hour edit (1 hour saved). Similarly, a manuscript in which many terms appear dozens of times provides obvious opportunities to improve consistency; a manuscript in which most terms appear only once provides no such opportunity.
- Despite that advice, it may be worthwhile working on a small document purely for the sake of learning how to use the tools before you inflict them on someone else. Just don't expect to gather truly useful statistics from such a document.

You may not find a single project or a series of small projects that meets all these criteria. So long as you understand why each criterion is important, you can make the necessary allowances, such as extending a deadline or combining the times for several small edits to simulate the time needed for one longer edit.

Support the author and editor

The goal of the test case is more than just to demonstrate that you can save time and improve accuracy. These are certainly good things to achieve, but there's a less obviously important goal to keep in mind: you want to develop a process that works well enough that others will want to adopt it. Thus, your test case must support the development of a simple process that meets everyone's needs. Because the author and editor may have reservations, and may fear failure—after all, they're the ones in the spotlight—your goal must be to reassure them and provide any support that they feel is necessary to succeed. Spend some time thinking about how you can overcome their fears and motivate them to remain interested in the process:

- Emphasize that the test case is primarily intended to detect and solve problems, that you expect problems, and that they won't be evaluated poorly if problems arise. It's the *process* that is being evaluated, not them.

- Provide a safety net by making it clear that failures will have minimal consequences. If you've chosen the test cases appropriately, as described in the previous section, both the risk of failure and its consequences should be small. If the consequences will be larger, take the necessary measures to protect the participants.
- Offer incentives for all participants to try the new approach. For some, the intangible and (at this early stage, hypothetical) benefits of a reduced time investment, increased ease of creating and reviewing edits, and increased accuracy will be sufficient. But some will want some tangible benefits right away to keep them interested in the process. Those benefits may be recognition in their next performance evaluation, the chance to leave work early on Friday, or even a financial reward if your situation permits such bonuses.

Since editing is all about human relationships, make an extra effort to protect those relationships and promote their development throughout this process. Be prepared to spend a bit more time asking for feedback on how things are going and listening to complaints about the process. Your willingness to listen to and work with the participants should establish a precedent and standard for future interactions. That's particularly true if your workplace hasn't already established a culture of cooperation and teamwork. Implementing this process may help you to begin building such a culture.

Provide adequate time

How long will the test case take? There's no way to be sure. In an ideal situation, mastering and applying the techniques I've presented in this book should increase editing efficiency sufficiently to compensate for any initial awkwardness as participants learn to use the technology. Of course, that assumes you can give the participants time to learn those techniques before you actually assess how well they've learned. Once they understand what they will be doing and how they will be doing it, the statistics you collect will measure the actual work rather than the learning process. At that point, the onscreen editing process should take no longer than it would take on paper, and if you know how long the on-paper edit would take, you can use that to predict how long the onscreen edit will take.

Unfortunately, the real world is not so ideal. It's highly unlikely that you will be able to completely separate an author and editor from their daily work until the test case is completed. Thus, you'll have to budget enough time to allow them to cope with their real job—producing edited manuscripts, not testing a new process. Moreover, you'll have to add some time for designing the new process, discussing alternatives, testing the alternatives, revising your process accordingly, recording all the data you need to make your case, and analyzing that data. You'll also lose some time to solving problems, teaching the participants those solutions, and documenting the solutions for future reference. If you have to sell your proposal to managers before you can begin, you'll need to allocate time for these negotiations too. These small annoyances can add up to a considerable amount of time, and you can't neglect them or they'll come back to haunt you.

Moreover, if you're working with more than a single author–editor pair, you'll need to carefully consider how to implement the new process across an entire workgroup or even an entire company once you've proven that it works. You'll need to include time for training, and possibly even time and money for computer and software upgrades so everyone can benefit from the new process. Although it's tempting to extrapolate from the learning curve in your test case to the organization as a whole, it's rarely safe to do so. Since you've chosen an ideal test situation (the best people and the most suitable manuscripts), reality is likely to hold several unpleasant surprises for you. That being the case, you'll need to plan to phase in the new approach over a period of time. How long that period will be depends on the personalities and competence of your colleagues, on the nature of your workplace, on the time you have available to train your colleagues, and on many other unquantifiable factors.

You'll also have to devote some time to detecting and solving problems, which are the topics of the next two sections of this chapter.

Step 3. Solve anticipated problems

"By three methods we may learn wisdom: First, by reflection, which is noblest; second, by imitation, which is easiest; and third, by experience, which is bitterest." —Confucius (ca. 551-478 B.C.)

I've discussed the various problems you're likely to encounter throughout this book, and provided solutions or coping strategies for each one. In this section, I'll summarize the main things you'll need to plan for, and suggest how to deal with the problems. (I'll discuss the less predictable problems in Step 4.) The predictable problems fall into three main categories:

- organizational and bureaucratic
- human
- technological

Organizational and bureaucratic problems represent the first class of issues you'll need to address. The main organizational problem you'll face is the resistance to change, as discussed previously in this chapter and in Chapter 17. Once companies reach a certain size or have been doing something in a certain way for a long enough time, it can be very difficult to get them to try something new. In really bad cases, the change can't occur at all without direct intervention from someone powerful enough to impose it. In most cases, though, you can accomplish surprisingly powerful things if you understand one trick: it's easier to harness the energy of an existing process for your own purposes than it is to stop the process in its tracks and try to replace it with something new and different.

Expressed a bit more directly, this means that you must determine how to accomplish the same goal as the current process by following that process—only with the relevant changes made, such as substituting onscreen edits for on-paper edits. Given that the goal is to implement a new process, this seems a bit nonsensical at first until you see how it can be accomplished. Consider, for example, an organization that requires a paper trail for reasons ranging from the practical (legal accountability) to the nonsensical ("that's the way we've always done it"). The problem with onscreen editing, of course, is that there's not necessarily any paper, and the manager who requires a paper trail will quite properly raise this as an objection. The solution? Rather than trying to persuade the manager to abandon a paper trail, print a copy of each version of the manuscript with all edits visible, add a date stamp, have the person responsible for that version sign their name beside the date stamp, then add the printout to the filing cabinet. (And, of course, make careful electronic backups of each version of the project files, as described in Appendix I.) The end result is that you'll satisfy the manager's need for a paper trail even though most of the work is occurring on the screen.

In short, you've used the established practice to provide the source of energy for your new process, rather than fighting those who are invested in the old process over what in the end proves to be an insignificant point.

The organizational and bureaucratic problems you'll encounter fall mainly into several distinct categories:

Category of problem	**Description and solution**
Record-keeping	This usually takes the form of a paper trail, whether literal (paper copies) or virtual (electronic backups of each version). Printouts provide the former; a sound backup strategy provides the latter. If your organization tracks time expenditures on different types of project, make sure to record the necessary data as you begin to use the new process. The data may be unnecessary in an objective sense, but as I noted earlier, it's wiser to follow existing processes where possible rather than fighting against them. Moreover, this data adds to your body of statistics, and can often be used to support some of your assertions.
Accountability	This involves keeping careful records of who was responsible for making each change, and who was responsible for accepting or rejecting the change. Teach everyone how to stamp their names on a document, whether literally (with a pen or a rubber stamp on printouts) or virtually (by typing their user name in the "Preferences" or "Options" dialog box before they begin using revision tracking).

Category of problem	Description and solution
Location of work	Most editors work at a desk in their own office, but others must be able to work in the same room as an author while discussing a manuscript, in a different building while comparing a manuscript against some product that it describes, in a library while doing research, and so on. Paper provides the ultimate in portability, and easily lets the editor change locations when required. As you might expect, a printout of the document serves the same purpose, but now that lightweight laptop computers have become less expensive than desktop computers used to be, there's no reason why editors can't carry their computer wherever they go. Tablet computers, which can be carried like clipboards, are even more portable. Bringing the computer to the work location lets you keep your editing on the screen rather than on paper.
Hours of work	Some managers require editors to track their time in different projects so that they can bill other managers for the editor's time and use the data for scheduling future projects or justifying current staffing levels. Such managers will be relieved to know that there are many programs available to help editors track their time on projects; these programs offer the additional benefit of providing data electronically, without the need for retyping. (I've provided a list of sample programs in the references section at the end of the book.)

In each case, the solution to bureaucratic resistance is not to fight it, but rather to adopt the existing process, modified so as to take advantage of onscreen technology. This is not to say that you won't occasionally encounter an unusually recalcitrant manager who resists change purely because doing so is their way of demonstrating their power. But most times, understanding the manager's goal in following a particular process reveals a reason for insisting on that process that goes beyond the mere exercise of power. If you can understand that reason and the goal it is intended to support, you can often propose a solution that the manager will accept.

Human nature represents the second group of problems, and as I mentioned earlier, we humans can be the most difficult obstacle in any implementation process. This means you must anticipate the most common objections people will raise so you can plan answers to these objections right from the start. The following strategies can help you respond to the most common objections in a way that will reduce or possibly even eliminate resistance to the new process:

- Provide at least basic training so people have the intellectual tools to do their work. For those who will be called upon to master the software (the editors), provide more advanced training and encourage them to use the tools at every opportunity so they can develop proficiency.
- Teach everyone how to customize the way the software works so that it better fits their preferences. The more closely the software fits those preferences, the less irritating it will be to use, and the less resistance it will raise. Customization also means not insisting that everyone perform every function on the screen or in the same way; particularly in the beginning, let each person use the aspects of computerization that provide clear benefits and make the most sense to them, but let them use older methods (e.g., working on printouts) for functions that they find easier or more effective on paper. Over time, you may be able to persuade them to move more of their work onto the screen, but if not, at least you've succeeded in persuading them to adopt tools that will make them more productive.
- Ensure that there is enough time for authors and editors to practice using their new tools. You may sometimes have to insist that they use the tools for a certain minimum number of hours per day to ensure that they obtain enough practice to become comfortable with the tools. Initially, the work will be unfamiliar and uncomfortable and slow. But as the work becomes familiar, their level of comfort will increase and productivity will improve.
- Recognize that authors for whom writing is only an occasional job will typically use the tools much less frequently than the editors, and will thus require periodic retraining; without ongoing practice, it's

easy to forget once-learned skills. Editors should thus budget time to help authors remember how to use the editing and review tools. Use this time as an opportunity to strengthen the relationship between author and editor rather than considering it as unproductive, lost time. In particular, remember not to grow frustrated with authors who "just don't get it"; some of them will never do the work sufficiently frequently to acquire real expertise.

- It's possible that people will initially make more errors while editing on the screen than they would make while editing on paper. Combining onscreen edits with a final on-paper edit will reassure them that any errors they might miss in one medium will be caught in the other medium. If you see a pattern of consistent errors, think about how you might fix the problem; my discussion of exclusion dictionaries in Chapter 10 provides one example of how you can help authors or editors spot problem words that they seem to be missing on the screen. Similarly, the discussions of search tools in Chapter 8 and of automation tools in Chapter 11 provide a range of suggestions on how you can develop tools that help people overcome many of their blind spots. Of course, tools alone are not enough; users must be trained to use the tools productively. Again, use this as an opportunity to improve relationships between authors and editors.
- In some workplaces, there's an imbalance in the relative power of authors and editors; for example, authors may have the right to overrule editors without discussion. In other places, there are physical (geography) or organizational (office politics) barriers that prevent authors from discussing changes with the editors. The solution in both cases is to nurture cooperative relationships that slip around or gradually undermine these barriers. Authors must learn that if an editor misunderstood something and felt obliged to change it, then other readers will too; thus, the author should consult the editor to learn the cause of the misunderstanding. Where that dialogue cannot take place in person, use technology to provide other alternatives: e-mail works well to exchange questions and answers at the convenience of the correspondents, whereas a phone call or some form of instant messaging permits interactive, immediate dialogue.

- Because much editing work is very repetitive, editors may fear that the computerized approach will take longer than long-practiced paper-based methods. The solution is to help them develop shortcuts such as the macros described in Chapter 11, and to provide a bit more slack in the schedule until they come up to speed.
- Many people believe that computers greatly increase the risk of repetitive stress injuries (RSIs) such as carpal tunnel syndrome. This is largely a myth, provided there are no pre-existing injuries or medical conditions that will be exacerbated by computer use, and provided that you take certain measures to provide a safe working environment. Encourage people to have regular medical checkups (including of their vision) to spot any developing problems before they become serious. Provide good lighting, a comfortable chair, and a high-quality monitor and keyboard. And of course, as in any other repetitive activity, people should remember to take regular breaks. I've provided more information on protecting yourself and your colleagues from RSIs in Appendix II.

Note that these are only the most common problems. It's wise to ask your colleagues what *they* are worried about, particularly once they have actually begun using the new process. In addition to establishing a precedent for dialogue and ongoing consultation right from the start, and making it clear that you do care what your colleagues think, this approach allows you to identify problems you might not otherwise discover. It's always more effective to learn about these problems early and deal with them than to leave them to fester and create bad feelings that will be difficult to resolve later.

The third and final class of issues relates to technological problems. If you've spent any length of time grappling with your computer, it may not seem plausible that the technological problems are the *easy* ones to solve, but that's actually the case. It's particularly reassuring that if you've experienced a problem, someone else has probably encountered it, brainstormed or researched a solution, and reported that solution somewhere. Many such solutions are included in this book. The vast majority of other problems are described, along with their solutions, in the world's most comprehensive reference work—the Web. You can find solutions to just about any software problem on the Internet with a little searching. Chapter 14 tells you how.

But what about the really obscure problems that may require interactive troubleshooting and possibly some virtual hand-holding? For those, you'll learn to depend on a few key discussion groups; the copyediting-L group for editors (www.copyediting-L.info) and other large communities of experienced computer users are usually happy to help. (I've included several of these groups in the bibliography.)

I'll conclude this section of the chapter with a discussion of the technological problems that you can expect to encounter at some point and what you can do about them.

Incompatibilities

Modern word processors remain surprisingly incompatible (i.e., there is no universal file-exchange format), so as a general rule, using the same software minimizes incompatibilities. This is occasionally even true of different versions of the same word processor; Microsoft, for instance, has been somewhat notorious for releasing new versions of Word that are not fully compatible with older versions, and with the release of Office 2007 (and the new .docx file format), the company has once more demonstrated that it hasn't learned from its own history. There have also been occasional significant incompatibilities between the Macintosh and Windows versions of Word and between the Asian and English-language versions. To minimize such problems, try to ensure that everyone uses the same software and the same version of that software. Some editors with a wide range of clients retain installations of several different versions of their main word processor on their computer, and sometimes even install several different word processors, to ensure that they always have a version compatible with what their clients are using.

In most cases, this is overkill. In my experience, the version of a word processor immediately before the most recent release is usually highly compatible across a product line, although you may need to download and install a patch from the software developer's Web site for full compatibility with newer versions. The older version of the software is generally also the most stable version, since it's been around for some time and has been patched and repaired both frequently and well. The newest version is usually not worth installing until the developer has issued at least one major "service release" to fix all the bugs discovered by users. If you must upgrade to the newer version for compatibility with your clients, investigate whether you can retain your older versions in case of future need. Some software installers provide an option to retain the old version of your software, and that's the easiest solution if it's available to you. If not, you can usually solve the problem by creating a new user account on your computer. Each account can have different software installed, and setting up a new test account to hold the new software may let you install it without affecting your current configuration.

Workflow

Using the same software as everyone else is the ideal situation, but because it's ideal, it doesn't often exist in the real world. For example, many publishers of printed materials produce those materials in specialized desktop publishing software such as Ventura Publisher, FrameMaker, Quark Express, or InDesign. Such software offers many key features that are lacking in a word processor, particularly the ability to publish color information that a commercial printer can accept. (Most word processors only understand the RGB color scheme of the computer screen, which bears little relation to the CMYK color scheme used to print colors on paper.)

This leads to obvious problems with onscreen editing, since word processors are generally unable to read desktop publishing files directly, and this prevents you from taking full advantage of onscreen editing once manuscripts reach the layout stage. The same problem arises in publishing other kinds of texts, whether Web pages or spreadsheets. (I've discussed some workarounds in Chapters 12 and 13, but these

Beware the upgrade! Rule 1 of software upgrades is that they often fail. Always have a contingency plan in case they do. If the worst-case scenario is that you have to dust off your 3-year-old installation disks for the previous version, that's not a bad solution. If you're using an "electronic-only" version (typical for software downloaded from the Web), make sure you burn a backup CD containing a copy of the installer before upgrading to the new version. It always pays to have Plan B ready to implement. As Colonel Jack O'Neill wondered in the television show *Stargate SG-1*: "Since when does Plan A ever work?"

are still ways to patch a bad situation rather than examples of a truly efficient editorial workflow.) The best solution is to design a workflow that lets you edit the contents of a publication *before* layout. Content creators (writers!) use word processors to create the material that designers will subsequently lay out, so it makes considerable sense to keep the text in a word processor for as long as possible. Significant changes at the layout stage are generally more expensive than comparable changes during the writing stage because even a relatively simple layout can require considerable rework if the text must be revised extensively (all that formatting work may have to be undone and redone). Moreover, layout often occurs very close to a deadline, when there's little time to implement changes and review the results to ensure that no new errors have been introduced. Last but not least, desktop publishing software, as a class, lacks effective revision-tracking features, thereby making it far more difficult to communicate and implement changes. (There are solutions, such as the InCopy software for use with Adobe's InDesign desktop publishing software, but the comments I've seen from professional editors suggest that the software is not quite ready for prime time.) These observations provide a powerful argument for doing the editing early and in a word processor.

An obvious exception arises when, as is often the case in technical publishing, everyone uses the same software and all layout is done by the writer using that same software. This is most often true in companies that use FrameMaker, but some companies use Word to both create and publish their information. The advantage of this situation is that everyone is using the same software, so incompatibilities largely disappear and there is no need to export text for editing, then reimport it back into the desktop publishing software. In this situation, all of the revision tracking tools offered by the software can be used. If these tools are absent or inadequate, then many workarounds exist, including those I've discussed in chapters 12 and 13.

Text must often be exported and reimported during the creation and editing of Web pages as well, with the additional complication that the ease of publishing Web pages (no commercial printer to delay the publication and no cost to republish) and the perceived impatience of the Web audience greatly increase the temptation to publish too soon. This increases the risk of publishing something that will embarrass the publisher before a large audience. Again, editing early and heavily minimizes the changes that must be made in the Web authoring software and the amount of exporting and importing, with the attendant problems, that must be done.

There are, of course, many workarounds. For example, Chapter 12 explains how you can edit spreadsheets, databases, desktop publishing files, Web pages (HTML), and advanced markup languages such as XML or SGML almost as efficiently as you can edit word processor files. Where such relatively efficient approaches aren't available, there are more general solutions. For example, you can either export the text in a format capable of being reimported (as discussed in chapters 12 and 13) or copy text out of just about any program and paste it into a word processor for editing. The edited text can then be pasted back into the originating program, or the changes can be manually retyped in that program. Alternatively, the final resort is to create a PDF of the information and do onscreen proofing, as discussed in Chapter 16. But it's clear that doing the majority of the heavy work before moving the information to another program for layout is still best. This is how most major publishers work, and they work that way because they've proven it to be efficient, not because of corporate inertia or tradition for its own sake.

Fonts and special characters

In an increasingly international world, you may find yourself working with colleagues from distant lands, whether a team of software developers in India or a Chinese scientist hoping to publish in a North American science journal. In this situation, pernicious font incompatibilities can cause you considerable grief. If you're like most freelancers, you and your clients are caught amidst a remarkable number of permutations of semi-compatible operating systems (Macintosh, Windows, and sometimes Linux, with various localized versions of each), mostly compatible word processors (I count nearly 10 versions of Word alone in current use, ranging from Word 6 to 2004 on the Macintosh and Word 95 though 2003 under Windows), and often incompatible font technologies (ranging from PostScript to TrueType to OpenType). Even if you're an employee working for a single employer, the odds are reasonably good that you'll have different authors using slightly or radically different versions of your core word processor and operating system, and thus, slightly or radically different sets of fonts. You can imagine the font incompatibilities this leads to. None of these incompatibilities are fatal, but all of them need to be dealt with in your planning.

Most word processors do an adequate job of resolving these difficulties, but until everyone is using fully Unicode-compliant word processors and operating systems, special characters (here, defined as anything you don't see on your keyboard) will continue to pose problems. As a general rule, none of these problems are more than inconveniences, and most of the ones you'll encounter involve the special characters used in the Windows and Macintosh operating systems. Because special characters don't appear on your keyboard, they're handled less gracefully than they could be. The problem originated back at the dawn of modern computing, when Apple and Microsoft chose to define different standard encodings for many of these characters; as a result, when the encodings don't match, the software displays the wrong character or a blank space with a box, an underscore, or even no visible character at all. The underlying data that define which character to display are not affected; only how that character displays. Fortunately, this means that the problem is not data loss, but rather a problem of how to see what the author wanted you to see. It's worth noting that this particular problem is gradually disappearing, as most software now supports the Unicode standard for fonts and most operating systems come with Unicode-compliant fonts. However, you still see occasional problems, such as software that is only partially Unicode-compliant (e.g., Word X on the Macintosh).

Where we have no control over the fonts that have been installed by our colleagues—as is most commonly the case—we need to plan how to cope. In Chapter 12, the section *Font problems: dealing with special characters* provides more details on the nature of the problem and some typical coping strategies. In long-term collaborations, such as the kind of implementation of onscreen editing that I'm describing in the present chapter, the best solution is to standardize on a common set of fonts that you know will work. (You'll discover such fonts by testing them using all the special characters that commonly appear in your work to ensure that they're as compatible as you thought.) Where you can't standardize on the same fonts, you can sometimes achieve a comparable result by researching whether your software provides any font-substitution options. Most software offers the option of using a font that you do have on your computer whenever it encounters a font that your colleague specified but that isn't installed on your computer; better software, including most desktop publishing software, lets you specify substitutions for any font, even if you do have the author's fonts installed on your computer. Font substitution is most often temporary and confined to your own computer; this means that the substitute font is only used to *display* information while the file is on your computer, and that none of the original font information is deleted. That's the best solution, since whichever substitute font you choose, your colleague sees their original font when you return the file.

Font substitution works particularly well when you must work on files created in an operating system configured to use a different language. For example, Japanese and Chinese versions of the Macintosh and Windows operating systems provide English fonts that authors can use when they need to exchange files with their English colleagues. However, if the underlying styles in the word processor have been defined to use Asian fonts, and the author has manually changed the fonts rather than changing the style definition, display problems may result. This is particularly true if the document has been configured to use the grid-based font display that is commonly used in Asia. I've discussed a solution for this in Chapter 12; in summary, you must either install support for Asian languages in your word processor or operating system and properly configure the grid options or other aspects of font display, or banish the document grid for that document.

To avoid problems, examine a sample of typical documents that you'll be producing and list all the special characters used in these documents. Create a file containing the names of these characters followed by the characters themselves, then send the file to all your colleagues so they can review the file and look for any font display problems. Where they encounter a problem, they can insert their own version of the problem character and send that to you to confirm whether it's visible. If it is, then you know that you can both safely use the author's version of the character. After incorporating all these preferred characters in the file, test the file one more time, just to be safe. Eventually, you'll accumulate a list of characters that everyone can see, and at that point, you can request that authors copy and paste the appropriate characters from that file rather than creating the characters in their own idiosyncratic way; when you encounter characters that you can't see, but know what they must be, you can then replace them with the preferred characters, confident that everyone will be able to see them.

If there are characters that not everyone can see, no matter what font you use for them, you may need to adopt a more draconian solution, such as replacing problem characters with temporary placeholders such as the HTML entities I discussed in Chapter 12. Where inserting and using these placeholders will be awkward, consider creating macros that insert them automatically and parallel macros that reverse the process and reinsert the special characters (in whatever font is appropriate for the next step of production). Clearly, this whole process takes a bit of work, but that work only needs to be done once, at the beginning of the implementation process.

Ergonomics

If you've worked for any length of time with computers and computer software, you can be forgiven for wondering whether both were deliberately designed to inflict pain and suffering. Conspiracy theories notwithstanding, the end result is that computers and computer software can lead to both short- and long-term problems if you don't take appropriate precautions. Although there's no particularly good evidence that a properly configured computer is inherently dangerous to healthy individuals, most people pay inadequate attention to the ergonomics of their computer setup and are far too sedentary, fatigued, or poorly nourished for good health. Moreover, as we age, we tend to accumulate damage to our bodies that can render us more vulnerable to injury. If you'll be spending many hours per day working on a computer, there are inevitable consequences for your health.

Given this problem, you should apply the kind of thinking that lies behind most workplace safety regulations: avoid the problem in the first place rather than trying to fix a problem after it has occurred. The potential for serious injury is clear if you're working with toxic chemicals or heavy construction equipment, but because the injuries office workers are most vulnerable to are far less dramatic, they're easier to ignore. Ignoring them is a bad choice. Back problems, eye fatigue, and carpal tunnel syndrome aren't sufficiently graphic and disturbing to make the evening news, but they're no less disabling to those who suffer from them. That being the case, and in the absence of workplace legislation to protect you, take responsibility for your own safety and—if you're a manager—that of your employees.

Appendix II provides a detailed discussion of the usual types of problems and what you can do to prevent them. Here, I'll provide only a summary of the basic principles. The three words in the phrase "repetitive stress injury" each reveal a key part of the problem and hint strongly at its solution:

- If it's the *repetitive action* that will lead to the health problem, develop shortcuts (see, for example, the discussion of macros in Chapter 11) or other automated solutions that minimize the amount of repetition. You can't develop a repetitive stress injury in the absence of repetition. Don't forget to take breaks; they interrupt the repetition long enough for your body to begin healing.
- If the problem arises from *stress*, eliminate or minimize that stress. For example, purchase a comfortable chair and an ergonomic keyboard—both should support the position your body will naturally take without forcing you into contortions. If you relieve a stress sufficiently, a healthy body will cope well with whatever stress remains. In this sense, *healthy* means well-nourished, well-rested, and in good physical condition as a result of regular exercise.
- If the problem results in an actual *injury*, learn to pay close attention to the signals your body is sending you. Apart from obvious exceptions such as falling asleep at the keyboard and striking your head on the monitor, most computer-related problems develop gradually. Pain, and sometimes its cousin, numbness, are warning signs that precede almost every computer-related injury; fatigue may be an early warning sign that precedes actual pain, as in the case of eye strain. The solution is as simple as these observations suggest: if you find yourself experiencing fatigue, pain, or numbness by the end of the work day, this is a strong warning that you need to diagnose the cause and fix it before your body's warnings are replaced by actual injuries.

Step 4. Watch for unanticipated problems

Brasington's Ninth Law: "A carelessly planned project takes three times longer to complete than expected; a carefully planned one will take only twice as long."

Murphy's law ("if anything can go wrong, it will") applies to computers to a greater extent than to most other areas of life. If you're planning to implement onscreen editing and your only experience with the approach is reading this book, plan to encounter an occasional unexpected problem; experience is the best teacher, and until you've studied long and hard under that cruel schoolmaster, you're still an apprentice and subject to surprises. Even once you're a master, and have progressed to teaching your own apprentices, you can still expect the unexpected every now and then—particularly if you've gone long enough between problems to have grown overconfident. As all teachers know, this is also true if you'll be teaching students who aren't smart enough yet to realize that you've already discovered and fixed every problem and that they're not allowed to discover new ones. It's doubly true if you'll be teaching students who *are* smart enough to explore on their own and encounter problems you never imagined.

The key to controlling chaos is to recognize that it exists, and plan accordingly. This means that you should both take measures to minimize the frequency and severity of surprises, and have a plan for how to respond when those measures aren't enough. Here's a simple procedure for doing so:

- Take steps to minimize incompatibilities.
- Adopt an effective workflow.

Word(im)Perfect: One well-known problem affects files created in older versions of WordPerfect. For reasons that date back to the pre-Windows era of computer fonts, the developers of WordPerfect used alternative fonts to display things such as the typographic (curly) quotes that are now standard in most modern fonts. These special characters display as strange characters or codes in Word (e.g., = for a quotation mark), and the only solution is to replace them with their equivalents in a more modern font.

- Phase in the new process gradually.
- Create paper trails to spot problems.
- Provide ongoing support.
- Ensure that communication happens.
- Relax a little!

Needless to say, this simple procedure suffers from the same flaw as all elegant theories: reality doesn't like conforming to our simplistic expectations. But at least following this procedure gives you some confidence that the inevitable surprises will be rarer and more easily survivable than they might otherwise be.

Take steps to minimize incompatibilities

Most editors work in one of two kinds of situation, each with different implications. If you're working for the same employer as your colleagues, you may have a computer support staff who can help you or impede your efforts; if you're working alone or in a company too small to have a support staff, you may be entirely on your own in solving problems.

If everyone uses the same version of the software on the same version of the operating system, this will clearly minimize the risk of incompatibilities. Unfortunately, this is typically only possible when you're working exclusively within a single company that has a strong policy on software compatibility. Even then, you'll need support from your computer staff when you attempt to implement onscreen editing, since it takes significant effort and expertise to ensure that everyone's system is updated to the same state. If any employees have the right to purchase

There's no substitute: Sometimes you can specify a permanent font substitution, which means that the underlying data is changed. Although this may be acceptable when you will be the last person to handle the file, it's not a good solution if you will return the file to the author and you're not certain that they have a font compatible with yours. The main exception is when you are acting as the intermediary between an author and a publisher, and the publisher specifies which fonts must be used. In that case, changing the text to use those fonts and solving any of the problems that result may be very helpful to the author.

> **Standard character codes:** For a list of the standard keyboard shortcuts for inserting special characters in the Macintosh or Windows operating systems, download the corresponding PDF files from my Web site: Macintosh character codes (www.geoff-hart.com/resources/accents-mac.pdf) or Windows character codes (www.geoff-hart.com/resources/accents-windows.pdf). The advantage of these keyboard shortcuts is that they should work in all standard fonts within a given operating system, and many will work in both Macintosh and Windows (with certain tweaks; e.g., the command key on a Macintosh is usually the equivalent of the control key in Windows).

and install their own software or fonts, systems gradually drift out of full compatibility. Some companies adopt the draconian solution of locking down all computers so that only computer staff can make any changes. Though this can effectively ensure ongoing compatibility, it's generally bad for morale, and if the computer staff is (as is usually the case) overworked and under-trained, they may be unable to make important changes (such as installing bug fixes or modifying document templates) that would immediately improve productivity.

The solution is simple—at least compared with quantum mechanics—if you can develop a professional, mutually respectful relationship with the computer staff. (Computer staff are often too busy and stressed to give you a chance to develop such a relationship, and some of them really do have the kind of personalities that make them nearly impossible for you to befriend.) One common solution is to give each computer user the authority to customize their own computer, and the responsibility for taking the blame if they screw something up. You can largely eliminate any reason to blame someone for such accidents by learning how to create a *disk image* of a stable computer configuration for their computer; if someone messes up their computer, you can restore its original, stable state by copying the disk image back onto the hard disk. (This can take as little as half an hour on a fast modern computer.) Another solution is to obtain a clear commitment from each computer user that they will discuss all upgrades with the support staff; that way, the support staff can investigate the proposed upgrade and warn the user of any likely problems, and if a problem does develop, they will know what to do about it.

When you're on your own, you can try similar solutions. For example, if you work with authors who use a wide range of hardware and software, it may make sense to purchase compatible hardware and software yourself. Indeed, some freelancers purchase both a Windows computer and a Macintosh so they can work on whichever gives them the fewest problems for a given client. I work almost exclusively on a Macintosh, but both as a backup in case of disaster and to maximize compatibility, I also purchased an inexpensive used Windows computer and full versions of Microsoft Office and WordPerfect for Windows. My spare computer mostly just gathers dust when my kids aren't using it, but if serious problems ever develop with my Macintosh or if I need to use WordPerfect (which is no longer available for the Macintosh), I've got a backup computer that will let me continue working uninterrupted.

Similarly, it's worthwhile keeping older versions of your word processor available so that you can use the most compatible version. There's no simple way to describe how to do this, since different programs and operating systems have different ways of allowing (or, sadly, disallowing) the installation of a newer version while still retaining the older one. The one solution that does work well for most modern operating systems is to create several different user accounts, each with its own custom software installation, then log in to the appropriate account for a given job. Keeping current backups, and particularly current disk images, is an important part of this process.

Adopt an effective workflow

I've discussed the key aspects of an effective workflow in Chapter 3 (*A standard process*), and such a workflow works particularly well when you're using fully or mostly compatible software. Where significant software incompatibilities exist, you'll need to modify the workflow to account for known problems and minimize or avoid surprises. This will most often be necessary when you're part of a publication workflow in which writing is done in one program (such as Word or WordPerfect) and design or publishing is done in another program (such as InDesign or FrameMaker).

No current desktop publishing, Web design, or other authoring software offers revision tracking features as effective as those available in word processors such as Word and WordPerfect. (FrameMaker has recently added this feature, but I have not tested it and cannot report how well it works.) This suggests a large part of the solution: develop a workflow in which you perform all writing and review using your preferred word processor, then move the near-final manuscripts to the layout or design stage only once editing and expert or management review is complete. Where significant incompatibilities exist and workflows can't be changed to solve these problems, you can develop workarounds. For example, you can create simplified markup schemes that will help you communicate your changes to authors and designers, such as those discussed in chapters 12 and 13. Sometimes you can suggest alternatives, such as opening HTML files in your word processor and saving them temporarily in that program's native format so that you can take advantage of powerful revision tracking features. Where possible, you can then reimport those files into the original program; if not, you can at least communicate your edits clearly to the author or designer. When none of these options are possible, some of the suggestions in Chapter 16 (*Solving the proofreading problem*) may help.

Phase in the new process gradually

The easiest way to ensure that onscreen editing will fail is to impose the system without consultation, without training, without enthusiastic support ("buy-in"), and without testing—in short, to rush through the process without taking the necessary time to understand what you're doing and grow comfortable with it. Unfortunately, identifying all the problems you may encounter requires careful testing, and there are no easy shortcuts. A basic approach resembles the following:

- Ask all of the authors and editors who will be adopting the new process, or at least a representative sample of these workers, to define their needs and the problems they typically face. Meeting those needs and solving those problems should become your priority; among other things, this provides faster and more satisfying results than does wasting your time on trivial problems. If you're a manager rather than one of the people who will be most strongly affected by the change, you'll have an incomplete picture of the realities they face until you ask them; even if you do much the same work, you're only one person, and diverse viewpoints provide a more complete picture.
- Provide formal training, and time for students to practice what they learned. Even skilled computer users who are enthusiastic about

Backups 101: I've long since mastered the art of sounding sympathetic to friends who lost a file to a computer crash and who had no backup copy. The universal principle of poetic justice dictates that some day I'll inevitably be hoist on my own petard and have to listen to the same well-intentioned sympathetic noises. In case you want to avoid finding yourself in that situation, I've provided full details on developing a sound backup strategy in Appendix I.

learning new tools often lack sufficient time in their busy schedules to make the necessary effort. You may need to plan long in advance to create an opening in the schedule when you can isolate your colleagues from the stress of the daily workload and provide time for study and practice.

- If your colleagues aren't eager (or are only cautiously willing) to adopt the new approach, some may try to sabotage your efforts so as to restore the comfortable status quo, and others may merely plod along without making any significant effort to help you succeed. Making a clear effort to support them and meet their needs throughout the implementation, and proving that you value their opinions by accepting some even when you think you might know a better way, is one way to obtain this support. If you really do know a better way, your task is then to convince them to try your solution; one way to do so is to promise that you'll try their way if your way doesn't work, or even to run parallel trials in which both solutions are tested.
- Compile a list of problems encountered during the implementation, explanations of how to avoid them, and solutions for when you can't avoid them. If you gradually phase in the process by testing it with a few authors and editors, you'll quickly spot the most common or serious problems and have time to develop solutions or find ways to avoid them. Each problem solved is one less problem that future adopters must face, and that means these latecomers to the process will be able to adopt a proven, smoothly functioning system rather than going through the same learning curve. The fewer problems they encounter, the less reason they'll have to oppose the implementation and the more reason they'll have to embrace it.

Create paper trails to spot problems

If you're currently working on paper and planning to move towards onscreen editing, it clearly makes sense to use your existing paper-based process as a reality check: you should already know where this approach works and where it breaks down. This knowledge provides a clear standard for comparison and lets you confirm that the new approach works at least as well as the old one. If you've been working onscreen for some time and are trying to persuade someone else to adopt onscreen editing, the same suggestion applies: combine onscreen and on-paper edits. In both cases, the goal is to use a familiar approach (editing on paper) to spot anything you're missing in the onscreen approach or, if you're not missing anything, to demonstrate that the new approach works at least as well as the old one.

This means that you'll be doing the editing twice (once in each medium), and this may seem inefficient at first glance. In reality, this isn't an inefficiency at all. As I noted earlier, most professional editors try to make at least two passes through a manuscript irrespective of their preferred editing medium: once to do the major work, and once to catch anything they missed or any errors that they introduced. Moreover, if you design the first pass to accomplish the heaviest editing onscreen, the on-paper edit of a printout that incorporates all your changes will require relatively little additional work because most of the work has already been done on the screen. As a result, the on-paper follow-up should find relatively few things to correct. Keeping track of the kinds of edits that you're missing on the screen adds some overhead to the process, but it also identifies targets for improvement (things you need to learn to spot on the screen) and lets you spot unanticipated problems (e.g., font substitutions) so you can develop solutions. Paying careful attention to these problems may also provide advance warning about whether they may recur in future edits.

To develop a supportive and cooperative atmosphere, use these paper trails to identify and solve problems, *not* to assign blame. If the process becomes adversarial, you raise the level of tension and increase resistance among your colleagues; moreover, tense authors and editors are likely to make more mistakes, not fewer. In contrast, treating the testing process as a means of helping everyone work faster and more effectively, with less stress, can smooth an otherwise bumpy implementation. If, as several colleagues have reported, you find that few errors slip through the onscreen editing process, you may be able to dispense entirely with on-paper editing faster than you expected.

Provide ongoing support

One of the truisms of editing is the observation that, as an editor, you'll be using the editing tools far more often and for longer periods than your authors. That's particularly true if you're working with people for whom writing is only a secondary aspect of their work; for example, scientists primarily do research, engineers develop products, and academics do research and teach students. All of them write as part of their work, but it's not their primary role; for some, it may not even be an important role. This fact has several consequences, most notably that these authors will tend to forget how to use the editing tools or will not learn how to use them particularly well. It's not that they're stupid or forgetful, but rather that they have less incentive than we do to practice and acquire proficiency; they may have many more important priorities.

This means that you'll have to provide ongoing coaching to help authors use the tools productively. Although this may seem to be wasted time, that clearly isn't the case if you consider the benefits of developing productive and perhaps even friendly working relationships with authors. Time invested in nurturing those relationships—in this case, by helping authors do their job faster and more effectively—is time well spent. It encourages dialogue and cooperation, both of which lower their resistance to being edited and multiply opportunities to work together to develop the best possible solutions for communication problems.

Unfortunately, some authors never do learn to use the tools, despite repeated, long-term coaching and hand-holding. It's not that they're stupid, though it's tempting to leap to that conclusion; things we have learned so well that we no longer think about them seem easy, even if they're inherently difficult. Most often, the problem is a simple lack of motivation, since writing isn't the author's main job. Motivation isn't something we can provide unless we also manage the authors. Because we don't always have time to coach them, it's helpful to provide tools that can help authors help themselves when we're unavailable to provide coaching. One such tool is the "primer" I developed to summarize the key things authors need to know to use revision tracking effectively (www.geoff-hart.com/resources/Using-revision-tracking.pdf). Feel free to distribute this primer or to modify it to better meet your specific needs.

Ensure that communication happens

As I've repeatedly noted in this book, the synergy between author and editor only happens if you encourage an ongoing dialogue. This dialogue can occur face to face, in the form of e-mailed questions and comments, or in the form of a telephone call or an instant messaging chat while the document being edited is simultaneously displayed on both your computers so both of you can see what you're talking about and discuss alternatives. If you're working with a wiki or other modern tool for collaboration, you may even be able to update the information dynamically as you discuss solutions.

Never forget that the technology only supports and encourages communication; it is not, in itself, communication. Whether you're a solitary editor implementing onscreen editing with a host of clients, or a manager implementing this process for a department of writers and editors, your goal must be the same: to keep a watchful eye on the author–editor interactions to ensure that people are communicating effectively. Check periodically to confirm that everyone is satisfied that their voice is being heard, and if you spot a problem, intervene to solve it before it destroys the dialogue.

Relax a little!

In this chapter, I've somewhat exaggerated the difficulty of implementing onscreen editing in the workplace by attempting to comprehensively discuss all the possible problems. In many cases, you'll encounter few significant problems and can move quickly and painlessly through the implementation process. Follow this four-step approach honestly, demonstrating clear concern for the needs of your editors and writers, and it can be surprisingly easy to implement onscreen editing. If you're working in a high-pressure environment, that pressure can make you feel that implementation must occur immediately and must produce instantaneous, dramatic payback.

Resist that feeling.

To the extent that this is possible, let everyone ease into the process gradually, ideally after going through the preliminary testing that I've described in this chapter so you can adopt a proven process that addresses all the unique aspects of your specific situation. Expect the full payback to take some time to become apparent, but also make sure that everyone knows what is working well and why that success is important.

I've had good success following the approach described in this chapter at two workplaces (a federal government research center and a non-profit research institute), and have successfully implemented onscreen editing with several hundred individual clients from every continent but Antarctica and from many different cultures. You can succeed too!

Customized seminars and consulting

If you're interested in learning more about onscreen editing, or in learning how to implement the process in your own workplace, please contact me at the following address:

Geoff Hart
c/o 112 Chestnut Ave.
Pointe-Claire, Quebec
H9R 3B1 Canada
ghart@videotron.ca / geoffhart@mac.com

I'm happy to develop customized seminars to teach you, your employees, or a group of colleagues how to use the techniques described in this book in your own work and in your own workplace.

IV. Appendices and miscellaneous resources

Appendix I. Developing a sound backup strategy

Brasington's laws of backups: "You will never use the backup copy you just made. The only backup copy you will ever need is either the one you didn't have time to make, or the one you did make but cannot read. There is no danger in x-raying a disk or tape, but a Boy Scout's magnet can destroy the only copy of a file at 50 yards."

It's often been said that there are only two types of computer user: those who have already lost important data to a crash or other mishap, and those who soon will. Although this is a slight exaggeration, it also bears an unfortunate grain of truth. Viruses, worms, spyware, power failures, computer crashes, malfunctioning sprinkler systems, hurricanes, earthquakes, and miscellaneous other disasters can all cause you to lose data. If you're an editor working on a tight deadline, you can't afford that loss, and this means you must develop a simple, robust, reliable backup strategy for your data. In this Appendix, I've boiled down one of my published articles to focus on the essential elements of a successful backup strategy. For more details, have a look at the article itself (www.geoff-hart.com/resources/2001/backups.htm).

Elements of a backup strategy

Any successful backup strategy must meet four important needs. It must:

- let you recover the most recent version of your work
- let you recover earlier versions, in case the current version somehow becomes damaged
- offer protection against viruses and other malware
- protect against losses due to theft, fire, or natural disaster

In each case, the goal is to let you recover as much of your work as possible. Whether you purchase specialized backup software or archive your files manually, you must pay careful attention to all four points. You must make copies of all working files on your hard disk and possibly of your operating system and other software too (*full* backups) and copies of only the files that have changed since the last full backup (*incremental* or *differential* backups).

Full backups are easiest to work with, since they contain the full contents of your hard disk and all the most recent version of each file.

However, full backups can take considerable time to create, particularly as the total size of the files grows beyond the capacity of a floppy disk, Zip disk, USB flash drive, CD, and potentially even tape or DVD (all of which are referred to as *backup media*). Incremental or differential backups are faster and take less space, since you only copy the few files you have updated since the last full backup, but without specialized backup software, it can be difficult to find all recently modified files and to reconstruct an entire hard disk from a series of incremental backups. Here's a compromise solution that works well for many computer users:

- As soon as you finish work on a file, immediately make a backup copy. Use a single backup medium (e.g., a fresh floppy disk) for each day of the week, so if that medium fails, is damaged, or is stolen, you lose no more than a day's work.
- At the end of the week, make a backup of all the files you worked on that week (i.e., an incremental backup).
- At the end of the month, make a full backup of all files on your computer. If you're willing to devote the necessary time, you can make full backups each week. (That's my strategy, because it simplifies my backup process by eliminating the incremental backups.)

To minimize the risk of losing data to electrical problems, I've also purchased an affordable uninterruptible power supply (UPS) for my computer. This is much like a surge suppressor, but offers two important advantages: it offers better protection against power fluctuations (including overvoltage that can damage your computer and "sags" that can cause it to shut down), and it provides enough battery power for me to save any open files and shut down the computer if the power fails. Highly recommended.

The remainder of this appendix describes how to create a successful backup strategy that meets each of the four key goals.

Recovering the current version of your work

The simplest and most common problem occurs when your computer or word processor crashes and you lose the currently open files. These crashes can result from software bugs, hardware problems, or even unpleasant facts of life such as power failures. When the crash occurs, you lose any data that hasn't yet been saved to your hard disk, and in extreme cases, the files that were open at the time of the crash may be hopelessly corrupted. To let you recover as much as possible of your work, you should make interim backups over the course of the work day. Here's how to do this:

Automated backups

Most software lets you create ongoing automatic backups of your work (see Chapter 4 for details). If your software allows you to create a backup copy each time you open a file, it's useful to enable that feature. If your software can be configured to automatically save an open file at regular intervals, enable that option whether or not you use the automatic backup feature. Then remember to periodically save the open file yourself; no automated system is ever 100% foolproof.

These precautions assume that the crash is sufficiently minor that you can reboot your computer. For those situations when that's not the case, create manual backups.

Manual backups

All the automatic backups in the world won't help you if the cat spills your coffee into your computer, and the resulting short-circuit destroys the computer and the ensuing fire destroys most of your office. (I admit this isn't very likely, but it does dramatize the problem.) Use some form of removable backup media (e.g., a floppy disk) so you can save copies of the file that are physically separate from your computer. When I write, I always keep one of those nifty USB flash drives plugged in, and I periodically copy the current version of my file to that device. When I'm feeling truly paranoid or when I'm working on something crucial, I alternate between flash drives so that if the computer crashes while the file is being copied to the device, I still have a recent copy

Buy effective backup software: Although you can certainly perform your backups manually, it's easy to miss one or more key files, particularly if you're tired or in a hurry. It's generally wiser to invest in specialized software that will do the hard work for you. There are many alternatives, and I've listed several of them in the references at the end of the book.

on the previous flash drive. E-mailing yourself a copy of the file also works.

Recovering previous versions of your work

Recovering the most recently saved version of your work is well and good, but sometimes that version isn't enough. Files can be infected by viruses or slowly corrupted by bugs in the software that created them. Moreover, everyone will at some time make extensive changes to a manuscript only to discover later—perhaps much later—that these changes were wrong. In that case, the easiest and fastest way to undo these changes may be to return to a version of the file that predates those changes and start over. Also, material deleted from an earlier version of the file sometimes turns out to be valuable after all, and the only way to recover that information quickly will be to find an earlier version that contains it. In such situations, you're in trouble if you don't have a sufficiently early version saved.

The automatic backups that I described earlier in this Appendix only retain the previous and current (working) versions of a file, and thus can't solve these kinds of problems. The solution is to retain incremental copies of all files. I always retain the following copies of every file that I'm working on:

- The original file that the author sent me. Although you can recreate this file simply by rejecting all tracked changes and saving a new copy, that won't work if the most current copies are damaged.
- Today's version of the file on today's backup medium, and yesterday's version of the file on yesterday's backup medium. A more complete strategy would be to use a separate backup for each day of the week, which is how most businesses protect their crucial data. In my case, two copies generally suffice because I usually return files to the author the day after I begin working on them. When more time is required, I alternate between three flash drives, so I always have at least the three most recent versions of the file available.
- Complete weekly backups of all word processor files on my hard disk for the past 4 weeks. I use rewritable CD-RW disks to reduce costs. I use one disk per week, and rotate to the next disk each week.

- A monthly backup to CD-R that contains all data on my hard disk. These disks are more stable and last longer than rewritable CDs, but you can't reuse them the way you can reuse a CD-RW. (If your disk drive or software offers a "multi-session" feature, you can copy as many days of backup data onto the disk as the disk will hold. However, doing so means that you're placing all your eggs in one basket. Given that 12 months of monthly CD-R backups costs about US$3 at current disk prices, using new disks is a small price to pay for the extra security.)

By the end of a 4-week cycle, I have daily, weekly, and monthly copies of all the files I have worked on in that time, and although it's rare for any problem to go back farther than that, my CD-R copies stretch back much farther, letting me recover older files that I haven't worked on in months or even years.

Protecting yourself against viruses and other malware

Malware is the general term used to describe the wide range of programs that are designed to damage or steal your data; some may even take control of your computer and turn it into a "zombie" that can be used to send out spam or viruses. These programs are sometimes relatively innocuous; they may simply display advertising messages on your computer or redirect your Web browser to a particular site. But some are quite nasty, and will modify, corrupt, or even entirely destroy your data files. (One recent program encrypted data files, and only allowed recovery of the data if the owner paid a bribe to the creator of the malware.) If you're running updated antivirus software, have a good spyware blocker installed, and have a strong firewall properly configured, you're largely safe from these problems. (If you don't, stop reading now

Beware hot and cold temperatures! Although modern recording media are quite robust compared with floppy disks, they have their limits. Don't leave your backups in a car in the hottest part of the summer or in the coldest part of the winter; temperature extremes can damage the recorded information, making it unrecoverable.

and buy and install this software. Really. I've provided some simple, effective recommendations in the software list at the end of the book.) The backup strategies described thus far will help you recover from sudden major problems because these problems become evident quickly and can be solved equally quickly once the vendor of your antivirus or anti-spyware software releases updates that solve the new problems.

The real danger is when the problem isn't sufficiently acute or dramatic to alert you. Some malware is quite slow and subtle, and does its damage progressively over long periods of time, only revealing its presence after some time has passed and you discover that some of your old files are no longer usable. Indeed, malware is growing increasingly subtle, and it's likely that we'll soon see programs that do their work largely undetected, slowly and surely damaging files to the point that they're unrecoverable. If you're victimized by such software, the only good defense is the long backup history I described in the previous section. If you've got archives dating back several months, you can fix the problem by installing the latest release of your protection software, using it to eliminate the problem, then using that software to search back through your archives until you find an undamaged version of the most important files.

If you update your protection software infrequently, your backups should stretch back at least as far as the last time you updated the software. This way, a new problem that your outdated software didn't detect won't stop you from recovering at least some of your old data; simply update your protection software, remove the malware from your hard disk, use your updated protection software to find a clean version in your archives, then copy that version to your hard disk. A CD-R backup is particularly useful because viruses can't erase or change any data once it has been safely stored on the disk.

Since some viruses attack your computer settings or other hidden files that your computer uses to determine how your software should function, you must learn where these files are stored so you can include them in your backup strategy:

- In Windows, include the Registry file in your backup. The online help provides details on how to do this for your specific version of Windows. On the Macintosh, all you need to do is copy the Preferences folder. In OS 9 and earlier, you'll find this in the System folder; in OS X and later, look in the Library folder stored under your user name.

- In both operating systems, learn where your e-mail software, address books, calendars, personal information manager, and other key programs store their data. Make sure you include these in your ongoing backups.
- Some software stores its settings at obscure locations on the hard disk. If you can't find these locations, try this trick: Change one or more of the software settings, then search the hard disk to find files that changed within the past few minutes. (Most operating systems let you search based on a file's "modification date", but you may need to specify that the search should include "invisible" files too.) One or more of these files are likely to be the files that you should include in your backup.

Protecting yourself against theft and damage

The best backups in the world do you no good whatsoever if a thief steals them along with your computer, if the family dog uses your backup disks as a chew toy, or if a house fire destroys them. That being the case, it's important to always store backups away from the computer you used to create that data. When I was a wage slave, I rotated my backup disks between home and work; that way, if I was robbed at home, my

Scan your backups before copying files to your hard disk: Though it's tempting to copy the most recent backup to your hard disk, then run the protection software to clean up those files, this isn't always the best strategy. Some malware is particularly difficult to eradicate, and leaves parts of itself on your computer that can reestablish an infection from contaminated files. If you want to copy the most recent, potentially infected backups onto your hard disk, scan them first to determine whether they contain problems. If they do, contact the developer of your protection software to determine whether it's safe to copy them to your hard disk and disinfect them there, and how to do it safely, or whether the risks outweigh the benefits of using your most recent backup.

copies at work (protected by an alarm system, security guard, and fire suppression equipment) were likely to be safe. On the other hand, if the copies at work were lost or damaged, I could replace them immediately from my home computer as soon as I discovered the loss. A bank safety-deposit box makes a good alternative if you're working from home, but it may also be possible to swap backup disks with a nearby friend or neighbor. Provided that they have a safe location for the disks, this can be much simpler (and certainly less expensive) than other options.

For truly critical data, it sometimes pays to obtain additional peace of mind by making multiple backup copies, and storing them in different places. Sometimes you can store the data online and rely on someone else to safeguard it; for example, Apple's Mac.com service currently provides 1000 Megabytes of online storage. Of course, if the data is confidential, you'll need to find a means of encrypting it to protect it from prying eyes. If the data is stolen, the thief will still have to decrypt it before they can use it. I discuss a few encryption options in Chapter 3.

A final word of wisdom: Always *test* your backups to ensure that they were successful. (For example, if you've copied your files to a CD, open two or three recent files from the CD.) Modern computer hardware is generally quite reliable, but when it starts to fail, it often provides little warning. A damaged backup device may give all the usual indications that it has recorded your backup data correctly, but if the backup failed and you don't discover this immediately, you won't discover it until you need the backup in an emergency—when it's too late. Better to test now than to discover several weeks later that you've lost all your files to a hardware malfunction and have no backup! If the test fails, immediately take other steps to protect your key data (e.g., e-mail it to a friend) while you repair or replace the backup device.

Bank deposit box too small? You may find that the standard safety-deposit boxes will be too small for you: many are too narrow to hold a CD. If that's the case, investigate the possibility of using a portable hard drive. Mine is about half the width of a CD, and cost less than US$100. (Some lower-capacity drives are available for as little as US$50.)

Make a new, clean backup: Don't forget to make a new backup, free of the infection, and discard any infected copies. It makes little sense to go to all this trouble to clean up your system, only to reinfect yourself by inadvertently copying a single infected file from an old backup.

Appendix II: Protecting yourself from injury while using the computer

"Any sufficiently advanced technology is indistinguishable from a personality, and an obnoxious one at that." —Kim Roper

The more you use your computer, the greater the risk that you'll eventually encounter a repetitive-stress injury (RSI) such as carpal tunnel syndrome. That's not because computers are inherently any harder on your body than (say) jogging, but rather because we tend to pay less attention to the subtler kinds of problems that develop from computer use. Simplistically, any kind of RSI results from overuse of a body part without giving it time to recover. In fact, "overuse injury" is probably a more immediately obvious term for this problem, and given how much time many of us spend using computers, overuse is indeed a risk. The most common problems fall into three categories:

- Aches and pains
- Hand and arm problems
- Eye strain

This appendix provides the basic information you'll need to understand each of these categories of problem and take the necessary steps to protect yourself. A longer version, complete with many useful references, is available online; I've included it in my bibliography.

Aches and pains

It's not natural to sit still for hours at a time, and if you become a computer potato, you can expect your body to suffer. If you have to contort your body into awkward positions to compensate for a deficient

> **Always seek professional medical advice:** Although the article that formed the basis for this appendix was reviewed by medical and ergonomics professionals, *it is not a substitute for professional advice.* If you're currently experiencing a problem, or worried that one may be developing, seek medical advice *now*. Don't wait for the problem to become serious. It's always much easier and less painful to stop an injury from becoming serious in the first place than it is to treat it once it becomes serious.

workspace, this exacerbates the problem. The solution is surprisingly simple: get up and stretch every so often, exercise regularly enough that your body stays in good shape, and create an ergonomic workspace that will minimize the stress on your body caused by working at the computer.

The seat of the problem

Sitting still for hours compresses the tissues of your buttocks and upper thighs, thereby reducing blood flow to your legs. Improperly positioned backs and seats on chairs encourage a slumped posture that misaligns your spine and places additional stress on muscles, bones, and connective tissues (ligaments and tendons). Given that you'll be spending many hours in your chair each day, buy a good one. A good chair has the following properties:

- All cushions comfortably distribute and support your weight, thereby minimizing the pressure on any one part of your body.
- The back rest must be adjustable so it can cradle and support your back, and the seat height must be adjustable; the height should be sufficiently low that your legs don't dangle but sufficiently high that your weight doesn't come to rest solely on your buttocks.
- If the chair has armrests, they must be sufficiently adjustable that they support your arms without creating painful pressure points.

Don't skip the "test drive": the only way to tell whether you'll like a chair is to sit in it long enough to ensure that it fits *your* body comfortably. Test the chair in the store by adjusting it to your body, then spend at least half an hour sitting, and at the end of that time, ask a friend to confirm that the chair appears to be encouraging good posture while you're sitting in it. Bring a book to help you pass the time!

> **Take frequent breaks:** Remember to occasionally take breaks, even when you're facing a tight deadline, so your body's own self-repair mechanisms have time to work. If you need help remembering, consider using software to remind you. Any alarm program will do, but special-purpose software may work better. Colleagues have recommended Ergocise for Windows (www.ergocise.com/download.html) or Stretchware for both the Macintosh and Windows (www.stretchware.com/sw_dl_form.html).

Some people find that a footrest elevates their feet enough to shift some weight to their lower legs and knees, thereby reducing pressure on their buttocks, hips, and thighs. When this works, it improves blood flow to the legs and reduces compression of the tissues of your legs. However, an overly high footrest can place *too much* weight on the buttocks and their underlying bones. If you buy one, make sure the height is adjustable (or that you can compensate by adjusting the height of the chair's seat) and pay close attention to whether it improves sitting comfort—or just shifts the pain elsewhere.

Layout of your work area

An ideal desk–chair combination lets your body adopt a "natural" position, as close as possible to the position your body wants to assume if left to its own devices. While seated:

- Your upper arms should hang straight down from your shoulders.
- Your forearms should be horizontal, and angled slightly inwards in front of your body.
- Your shoulders should not be hunched, and your neck and your spine should not twist.
- Only your buttocks and thigh muscles and your feet should experience any significant pressure from your weight.
- Your head should be vertical, not tilted to view the monitor.

Cornell's ergonomics Web site provides a straightforward diagram of a suitable workstation layout (http://ergo.human.cornell.edu/dea651/dea6512k/ergo12tips.html) that you can use as the basis for your own design.

Workspace problems can be subtle. During my first year of intensive onscreen editing, I began experiencing pain in my right shoulder. I discovered that the problem was my mouse: because a mouse typically lies to the right side of the keyboard, the additional width of the numeric keypad was forcing me to reach out at an awkward angle, with my forearm extended away from the center line of my body (i.e., outwards to the right). That small additional bit of stretching put too much stress on an old shoulder injury. So I moved my mouse to the left side of my keyboard and used it with my left hand, and the pain went away. The importance of this anecdote is that by paying attention to my body, I recognized the pain before it became chronic, and was able to solve the problem by eliminating the source of the pain.

Mouse alternatives

Some people find the standard computer mouse difficult or painful to use, particularly if they purchased a cheap computer that came with a cheap mouse. Fortunately, there are many alternatives, most of which you can test-drive at your local computer store to see whether they help. These include trackballs, trackpads, graphics tablets, keyboards with integrated pointers, and even keyboards that let you replace mousing with gestures.

Although I have suggested that if a given device such as a mouse is causing you pain, you should try replacing it with a different device, it's not inevitably an either/or decision: in some cases, it may actually make more sense to add a new device rather than discarding the old one, and periodically alternate between them—or use each device only for those tasks it does best or least painfully. Since the problem with RSI is the "repetitive" part, reducing repetition is part of the solution, and changing devices every few hours or every day can be enough of a change that it accomplishes the same thing as eliminating repetition. Graphics tablets are an interesting alternative because holding the plastic stylus is very different from holding any other type of pointing device.

Another solution is to remember the "repetitive" part of RSI and reduce how much you use the mouse in the first place. In Chapter 5, I listed a range of keyboard shortcuts and other tricks for moving around a document while keeping your hands on the keyboard and letting your mouse grow dusty. Chapter 11 provides tips on how to automate certain repetitive tasks so you can make the computer do some of the hard work. The sidebar on the next page provides some additional suggestions.

Hand problems

Pay close attention to your hands. Spending a whole day typing is obviously stressful, and carpal tunnel syndrome is just one of many problems that can result. These problems are often difficult to diagnose, and you may need an expert to pinpoint the true source of a problem. Your family doctor is a good place to start troubleshooting your body, but many general practitioners lack the necessary expertise to diagnose RSI problems. Ask to be referred to a specialist who can pay attention

Programmable devices: Many pointing devices (and particularly graphics tablets) come with software that lets you program their buttons to perform certain activities. If you have a device with buttons that you're not using, spend a few moments playing with its software to see whether you can bind some useful shortcuts to the device's unused buttons. If you're really ambitious, check out the X-keys programmable keypad (www.xkeys.com) and other automation tools. The manufacturer, P.I. Engineering, provides a range of devices with 16 to several dozen user-configurable buttons that you can use to replace any number of painful keyboard shortcuts with a single button, and even a set of foot pedals you can use to replace key modifiers such as the Control key. Combine this with software such as the MacroExpress automation software for Windows (http://macroexpress.com) and the QuickKeys automation software for the Macintosh or Windows (www.quickeys.com) and there's no end to the number of keystrokes you could eliminate.

to both the unique aspects of your body and how you're using your body to work.

Position your hands comfortably

Many hand problems arise from flexing your wrist too sharply outwards, with your little finger pointing further towards your elbow than it would with your arm at rest. Bending your wrists at awkward angles compresses the tissues of your wrist enough to cause pain and, eventually, nerve damage. When I first began experiencing hand pain, I helped myself enormously by switching to Microsoft's Natural Keyboard; that's the one with the split between the left and right columns of keys and a strange upward twist; the combination keeps your arms and wrists straighter while you type, eliminating much of the stress on your wrists. Logitech and Adesso offer comparable keyboards. More expensive ergonomic keyboards exist, and are worth investigating if you have or are developing serious hand problems. But try the Microsoft and Logitech keyboards first, since they're inexpensive and sufficiently common that you can find and try them at most local computer stores.

Keeping warm: Cold fingers and cold finger muscles are more vulnerable to injury, and also lead to slower circulation of the blood in your hands, slowing the removal of fatigue poisons and the delivery of oxygen. Thus, keeping your hands warm is a good way to protect your fingers. I've read good things about Handeze gloves (http://handeze.com/) in a couple places, so it's worth giving them a try. If you're not prepared to spend the money, try a pair of light cotton gloves with the fingertips removed; though less effective, they might be good enough for you. If you try such gloves, make sure they're not so tight they cut off circulation. No sense trading one problem for another! If you want a different solution, try "wristies" (www.wristies.com): these are like turtleneck sweaters for your forearms. They don't provide some of the special features of Handeze gloves, but provide good warmth to keep your arms and fingers flexible.

Reinventing the keyboard

Many keyboarding problems originate from the poor design of the standard keyboard. The straight arrangement of keys is bad enough, but even with ergonomic keyboards the order of the keys poses problems. The traditional QWERTY layout is inherently inefficient, leading to more finger travel than necessary— increasing the stress on your fingers. The newer Dvorak keyboard layout was based on careful studies of letter frequencies, and is designed to minimize finger travel. Dvorak-style keyboards can be purchased from various suppliers, but there are also ways to remap your existing keyboard to use a Dvorak layout. If you're still learning to touch-type, learning the Dvorak layout will be a particularly good idea.

If your main computer is a laptop, you've already noticed that laptop keyboards are ergonomic disasters even compared with traditional desktop keyboards. Even when the keys don't lie too close together, they generally don't travel as far when you depress them, making your fingers "strike bottom" harder and more often. If you mostly use your laptop at a desk, consider using a good external keyboard instead. Whatever keyboard you use, try to avoid jarring your fingers at the end of each keystroke; each keystroke jolts your fingers, creating vibrations that travel right up your arm, but these shocks are worst if your fingers try to travel farther than the keys permit. Enough of these shocks causes sore fingers and arms. The keys of soft-touch keyboards require relatively little pressure and may cushion the impacts, but some people find these keyboards uncomfortably mushy; if you don't, your fingers will be much less sore at the end of the day if you use one. But no matter what keyboard you choose, the best solution is to not pound on the keys in the first place.

Of course, the least stress comes if you don't strike the keys at all, and "keyless" keyboards have been invented to avoid finger impacts. Keyboards such as those that were produced by FingerWorks (now sadly out of business) let you *touch* rather than strike the keys, greatly reducing the stress on your fingers, and use finger gestures to replace mousing. Like all specialty products, they're pricey, but can prove a wise choice if you really need them, particularly if your company has a budget for ergonomic equipment and will buy one for you.

Watch out for awkward keyboard shortcuts. Many of these are designed more for ease of memorization than for ergonomics, and that's doubly true on laptop keyboards that require you to press a function key in combination with the usual hand contortions. Pay close attention to how you hold your hands, and consider customizing your software to use a less-painful keyboard shortcut or creating macros to eliminate the most painful contortions.

Rest your wrists?

Some people use cushions or other devices to support their wrists, which is certainly less painful than resting your palms and wrists on a hard surface such as a desk or the edge of a keyboard while you type. However, doing so can compress the tissues of your wrist, bruising them and reducing circulation to your hands; in fact, the cheap plastic wrist rests built into many ergonomic keyboards are no better than resting your hands on the desk. When I began experiencing hand problems, I purchased a foam-rubber rest, and found myself in more pain at the end of the day than I had been before. Sure enough, I was now placing significant pressure on my wrists in the mistaken belief that I was protecting them by resting them on the rubber. Some experts now suggest that all wrist rests are unsafe, even the softest gel pads.

Ideally, your hands should float above the keyboard rather than resting on it—assuming that this posture keeps your wrists largely unbent and doesn't create additional strain on your shoulders, arms, hands, or fingers. Occasionally resting your palms on a soft support can indeed prove helpful, but only in moderation. Wrist rests may not be unwise for everyone, but if you do try one, pay close attention to whether it really does help.

Eye strain

Human eyes work best when they move around and focus on objects at varying distances from our face, so spending a day in front of a computer monitor will clearly stress our eyes. Optometrists advise taking frequent breaks to gaze upon something more distant than your monitor so as to exercise the muscles that help your eyes focus. Taking breaks is easiest if you have a window with a nice view, but even if you work in a cubicle farm, you can still make time to walk around the building during your coffee break to encourage your eyes to focus on moving targets at varying distances. Here are a few other things to consider:

Help your eyes focus

Your monitor should generally lie at least arm's length from your body. That's far enough that you don't strain to see the whole picture, but not so far you must squint to see the text. Although no one distance works best for everyone, start with this distance and adjust it until you find a comfortable match for your eyes.

If you wear eyeglasses, ask your optometrist about computer glasses that specifically help your eyes focus at the distance of your monitor. Multifocal lenses (e.g., bifocals) help you focus comfortably at different distances by looking through different parts of the lens, but not everyone finds these glasses comfortable to use. If, like me, you rarely look away from the screen while computing, it makes more sense to get glasses specifically designed for computer use. Use a second pair of glasses for distance viewing while you're driving a car or walking around.

Crisp pixels, relaxed eyes

A high-quality monitor is a great investment in protecting your vision. Staring at fuzzy text all day seriously fatigues your eyes, which must work harder to focus. Current CRT ("TV-style") monitors provide adequate sharpness of focus, but that sharpness varies between brands and between units within a brand. That's doubly true if you work with small fonts, which are hard to draw crisply on the screen. Because your eyes are the best judge of a monitor's quality, don't buy a monitor without being able to see it in action. If you must buy from a catalog, research the brand and model first using a reputable source such as *PC Magazine* (www.pcmag.com) or *Mac World* (www.macworld.com), and choose vendors with a liberal return policy in case you purchase a substandard unit. LCD monitors are an excellent alternative, since each pixel (dot) on the screen has a fixed location, thereby creating a much sharper display. Their main drawback is that it can be difficult to use them at anything other than their native resolution (the number of pixels physically present on the screen) without creating fuzzy type; in contrast, CRTs support multiple resolutions, so you can generally find a resolution that works best for you. If your computer's operating system offers some form of font smoothing, such as Microsoft's ClearType or Apple's Quartz, experiment with that function to see whether it improves the situation.

Irrespective of which type of monitor you use, test the various available typefaces to see which ones display most crisply on your screen. The unending argument over whether sans serif typefaces such as Arial are easier to read onscreen than serif type such as Times New Roman is largely irrelevant here; typography is highly subjective, and *your* eyes should be the ones to judge which typeface works best for you. Once you've chosen a legible typeface, test different font sizes to see which ones are easiest on your eyes; for example, an 11- or 12-point font size can be much easier on your eyes than the 10-point fonts many people use. Since some fonts work best at specific sizes, no rule of thumb can tell you which size is best: experiment to find the size that works best for *you*.

If you'll be doing onscreen proofreading and the type size is fixed by the design specifications, don't assume that you're forced to examine the text at that size. Most software offers a View menu (or an "Options" or "Preferences" dialog box) that lets you zoom in on the display, thereby enlarging the text without affecting the design. Of course, this works best if you own a large monitor. Given how steeply monitor prices have declined over the past few years, it no longer makes any sense to use anything smaller than a 17-inch model, and 19-inch or larger models are increasingly affordable.

Large versus multiple monitors: Although there are distinct advantages to having two monitors hooked up to your computer, you may be able to achieve similar results by purchasing one of the new breed of wide-screen LCD monitors. These are available in 20- to 22-inch models for less than US$400 (sometimes much less) and this size of monitor is enough to display two documents side by side at a reasonable size.

Stamp out flicker

CRT monitors flicker because they create images by sweeping a beam of electrons across the screen to light up each pixel. The gradual fading of these pixels before the electron beam returns to brighten them again creates a flickering that can stress your eyes, even if the flicker is nearly unnoticeable. Most current video cards and monitors let you select a vertical refresh rate (how fast the screen is redrawn) of at least 75 Hz, a rate at which flickering is imperceptible to most users. The documentation that accompanies your monitor and video card will tell you how high you can set the refresh rate, and you should set it at or near that maximum. Cheap video cards may force you to reduce the number of colors displayed or the screen resolution to achieve higher refresh rates, whereas a high-performance video card is not likely to cost too much more, and is a good investment because it will permit the use of more colors or a higher resolution at the fastest refresh rates.

LCD monitors can ease eye strain because the liquid crystals that form the display don't have to be constantly refreshed and they occupy fixed positions on the screen; thus, they flicker far less. Unfortunately, the pixels can't change as fast as those on a CRT, so if you work frequently with video or multimedia, a CRT may still be a better choice. If you choose an LCD monitor, look for the following features:

- Good brightness: This is sufficiently subjective that you should rely on your eyes rather than on published specs.
- High contrast: To make the text stand out clearly from its background, look for a contrast ratio of at least 400:1 and preferably much higher; many newer monitors offer ratios of 800:1 or more.
- Fast pixel response: This determines how fast the pixels can change from on to off. Though the meaning of this number varies among manufacturers, aim for a pixel response of less than 25 ms to re-

duce smearing when the image changes rapidly, such as when you're watching video or scrolling quickly; the best current LCD screens offer speeds of less than 8 ms.

Arrange for suitable lighting

Monitor flicker can be greatly exacerbated by traditional fluorescent lights. These flicker slowly enough that many people can see them do it, and since the light flickers at a different frequency from the monitor, the difference can strain your eyes further. Traditional incandescent light bulbs do not flicker, but an even better solution may be compact fluorescent lights, which flicker much less noticeably than traditional fluorescents and draw considerably less power than traditional incandescents while providing comparable levels of light.

Whatever lighting you choose, arrange the lights and computer to eliminate reflections on the screen from lamps or nearby windows. Failing to do so creates glare that fatigues your eyes by forcing them to concentrate harder to see past the glare to the underlying image. Positioning a screen to face away from windows and lights or adding a special glare-reduction filter can help. Although working in a darkened room might seem to solve the problem, that's usually a bad idea; the excessively high contrast between the bright screen and the dark room can increase eye strain. Because LCD monitors often produce less glare than CRTs, they may be a good alternative in bright workplaces.

If your screen flickers despite these precautions or appears somewhat distorted, you may be encountering electromagnetic interference. Electrical junction boxes create magnetic fields that can interfere with the screen display. Moving your monitor away from the wiring can solve the problem, but where you can't move, shielding the monitor or the wiring can solve the problem. In this day of mail-order computers, it's also important to pay attention to the source of your monitor; monitors are factory-calibrated to perform well under "typical" conditions, and these conditions include the expected condition of Earth's magnetic field. As a result, workplaces in the northern and southern hemispheres generally require different models of monitor; if you've moved across the equator and suddenly find that your old monitor no longer works, this may be the source of the problem. Rotating the monitor into a new position can sometimes minimize this problem, but often the only solution is to buy a new monitor.

Computers aren't "tear jerkers"

There's considerable evidence that people blink less often while staring at computer monitors, and this probably causes the common complaint of dry eyes at the end of a day of computer use. The solution, of course, is to use nature's own lubricant for your eyes: remember to blink while using your computer, thereby moistening your eyes. Taking regular breaks will help, because you'll blink more often when you're not looking at the screen.

Working in a room with appropriate humidity levels also helps. To keep humidity at comfortable levels, grow plenty of household plants in or near your office. In unusually dry climates, consider installing a humidifier. If your eyes remain dry, consult your optometrist to confirm that there's nothing medically wrong, and ask them to recommend a good brand of eyedrops. Use a kitchen timer or your computer's reminder program to remind you to periodically moisten your eyes or take breaks.

Solutions

The good news about most overuse injuries is that you can do a lot to protect yourself. See your doctor and your optometrist at least annually so they'll have a chance to detect developing medical problems that you might miss. Between visits, pay close attention to your body so you'll know whether you're beginning to have a problem that you can solve yourself or one that requires professional help. An RSI expert will evaluate more than your symptoms; they'll also ask you about your lifestyle, your work habits and work environment, and various other factors related to the problem. But as a general rule, it's far simpler and much less painful to head off problems *before* they require treatment.

In summary, here are things you can do to protect yourself and minimize the risk of problems, or the severity of problems once they arise:

- **Invest in good tools:** Your computer equipment and workspace are the tools of your trade. Invest in high-quality tools just as any other professional would do. Set up an appropriately ergonomic workspace, invest in a good keyboard and monitor, and try alternatives to the standard mouse until you find a comfortable pointing device.

- **Improve gradually:** If the cost of building a sophisticated ergonomic workspace is making you hesitate, consider improving things in phases, concentrating first on the problems that are causing you the most grief.
- **Stay in shape:** Most of us have an overly sedentary lifestyle. Make time in your daily schedule to exercise. A balanced exercise program will also strengthen the muscles that support your neck, arms, wrists, and fingers, and will thus help ward off typical computer-related injuries. Strong muscles keep your body properly aligned. Exercise also strengthens your heart and improves circulation, thereby keeping muscles more limber and clearing away fatigue poisons more quickly.
- **Talk to your computer:** If you have intractable hand problems, try out voice recognition software such as IBM's ViaVoice or Dragon Naturally Speaking. Both provide a measure of control over your computer's operation, and let you dictate text rather than typing. I haven't discussed voice recognition software in any depth because I don't use it, and I try to avoid recommending potentially expensive solutions I haven't tried myself. But the software is certainly available, and with a bit of patience training yourself and your software, it can be a great help—particularly if it's built into the current version of your computer's operating system. If you have this software already, I encourage you to give it a try. (You may have a copy of such software and not even know it. For example, my version of Word 2003 came bundled with speech-recognition software. Does yours?) A few readers have reported considerable success using this class of software. Of course, dictation software may also cause RSI problems—for the voice. Pay close attention to ensure that you're not simply trading one problem for another.
- **Listen to your body:** Nobody knows better than you do when you're feeling pain. Listening to your body's complaints is the best way to detect problems early enough that you have a chance to fix them; if you have a hard time listening to your body, ask someone to watch you while you work to see if they can spot problems such as hunched shoulders, slumping at the keyboard, squinting, and so on.

Don't forget the "repetitive" aspect of RSI: If you spend long enough doing *anything*, you'll grow tired, and if you push past the point of fatigue, you'll greatly increase the risk of injury. Take a break from the computer and enjoy the other things that life has to offer. In moderation, of course.

Appendix III: A summary of key changes since Word 2000

"Word happens."—Anonymous

"With Linux, customers end up being in the operating systems business, managing software updates and security patches while making sure the multitude of software packages don't conflict with each other."—Microsoft spokesperson in a *News.com* article. *"And just how would that be different from Windows?"* —Adam Engst, *TidBITS*

Microsoft badly damaged the Track Changes feature when they introduced Word XP for Windows, also known as Word 2002. Their intentions were good: they wanted to make things easier for non-editors by providing more flexibility. Instead, they made things more complicated for everyone, and much more difficult for editors. Word 2003 for Windows allows you to customize the software enough that you can fix the worst of the problems created by Word XP, so the best bet is to just skip XP and go right to 2003—or upgrade as soon as feasible if you've already been afflicted with XP.

The rest of this appendix summarizes how to make the most recent versions of Word behave. Because I've focused on onscreen editing in this book, I'll discuss only the features most closely related to primary editing functions. My criticisms of the new versions of Word notwithstanding, there are some very useful new options once you learn where they're hidden.

The basics

Control + Shift + E (Command + Shift + E for the Macintosh) still lets you toggle between tracking and not tracking revisions if you don't want to do this using your mouse and the Reviewing toolbar. There appear to be no default keystrokes for accepting and rejecting changes, individually or collectively, so you'll have to define them yourself using the Customize feature (under the Tools menu). I've provided details on how to do this in the sidebar on the next page.

As in older versions, you can control revision tracking from the Reviewing toolbar. To display this toolbar, open the View menu, select Toolbars, then select Reviewing. The familiar tools from older versions

Keyboard shortcuts for accepting and rejecting: To create a keyboard shortcut for accepting tracked changes, open the Tools menu and select Customize. Click the "Keyboard" button. Under the heading "Categories", select Tools, then under the heading "Commands", scroll the list until you reach ToolsRevisionMarks-Accept. Select this command, then type a new keystroke for this command in the field "Press a new shortcut key for this command". To create a keyboard shortcut for rejecting tracked changes, scroll down a bit farther to find ToolsRevisionMarksReject and give it a new shortcut too.

are still there, letting you skip ahead to the next revision or backwards to the previous revision, then accept or reject that change. The dialog box that accomplished this in older versions is gone, but it's no longer necessary, since the toolbar accomplishes the same purpose.

The newer versions of Word now clutter your screen with panels called "panes". Think of them as "window panes" attached to the main window (i.e., the document you're editing), or as an ironic typo for *pain*, which is what they cause considerable amounts of until you figure out how to master them. I'll provide some useful tips for mastering panes in the rest of this section.

Balloons

Potentially the worst problem in new versions of Word is the use of balloons to show comments and changes. These balloons probably seemed like a logical way to build on the feature in previous versions that let you display comments by moving the mouse cursor above a comment, but in heavily edited documents the number of balloons can make the screen nearly unusable. If you find the clutter distracting, disable this feature:

- Open the "Options" (Windows) or "Preferences" (Macintosh) dialog box.
- Click the Track Changes tab.
- Under the heading "Use Balloons (Print and Web layout)", select "Never".

Don't forget that most software settings are a matter of personal taste, not one of right or wrong. Much though I dislike balloons, others

Macintosh users have to wait: Until recently, the most recent version of Word for the Macintosh is Word 2004, which is functionally equivalent to Word XP for Windows. Word 2004 offers certain advantages over previous versions, most notably the ability to display Unicode fonts correctly, and that may justify upgrading from older versions if you're struggling with font problems. The next upgrade, Office 2008, shipped in January 2008. Based on Word's history, I recommend waiting until at least the first service release is available before upgrading. Unfortunately, Microsoft announced that they will no longer support VBA, the macro language that previous versions shared with Word for Windows. If you upgrade to Word 2008 for the Macintosh, all your macros will instantly become useless. If that enrages you, tell Microsoft. It should be possible to automate much of Word using AppleScript or QuicKeys (see *Helpful Internet resources* at the end of the book for details). But to be safe, don't uninstall your older copy of Word; you can still use it to run macros, then transfer the file into Word 2008.

love them. Here are some significant advantages of using the balloons that may persuade you to give them a try:

- The display of line endings and other formatting is not altered by the presence of comment markers such as [GH1], so you can more easily see where line breaks occur. This can be particularly helpful in tables, where the markers can screw up text wrap and alignment within cells of the table.
- Balloons can also remain constantly visible, so there's no need to open a separate window just to see the comment text or before you can copy and paste text. If you like working with a split window view (see Chapter 4), you don't have to close the second pane just so you can see the comments. (In older versions, opening the comments pane would make the second pane disappear.)
- Some folks report greater stability, though this may simply be a function of the version updates, not the feature. I've never had problems with comments, but if you have, this will be important. On the negative side, I've received several comments about a dramatically increased frequency of crashes when using balloons with Word

2004 on the Macintosh, so if you're using that version, do so with caution.

- Some folks also like the ability to print the document with the comments beside the text, which is certainly more efficient than having them all appear at the end—no flipping pages!

If you do decide to use balloons because they work well for you, the Track Changes tab is where you specify when and where to use them and how they should behave when they do appear. If you want to display balloons, you must set Word to use one of two views: under the View menu, select Print Layout or Web Layout.

The text in balloons can be difficult to read using the default settings, but unlike in previous versions of Word, you can now change the size and other characteristics of the balloon text:

- Open the Format menu, then select Styles and Formatting to display a new pane at the right side of the screen that lists the available styles.
- Scroll down to the "Balloon Text" style. (If it isn't visible, select "All styles" under the heading "List:".)
- Click on this style name with the right-hand mouse button (Control-click on a Macintosh), then select Modify Style from the popup menu.
- Make the desired changes to this style (e.g., increase the font size), then click OK to close the dialog box.

If you prefer the old way of editing style definitions, you'll probably want to add this feature to the Format menu; Microsoft unhelpfully removed it in the newest versions. To add this feature:

- Open the Tools menu, select Customize, then select the Commands tab.
- Under the heading "Categories", select Format.
- Under the heading "Commands", select Modify Style.
- Hold down the mouse button and drag this command onto the Format menu. When the menu opens, move the cursor to the desired position within the list of commands and release the mouse button.

Comments and the Reviewing Pane

Selecting the Reviewing Pane option opens a new pane at the bottom of the document window that displays all the changes that have been tracked. (Selecting it again closes this pane.) The default Reviewing Pane contains so much information that it's often hard to pick your changes out of the clutter. To simplify that mess, open the Show menu (discussed later in this Appendix) and select each type of edit you want Word to display, then deselect any types of edit you want to conceal. There appears to be no default keyboard shortcut to open and close this pane, and there's no "Close" button. Thus, to banish this pane, select Reviewing Pane again from the Show menu, click the icon for the Reviewing Pane () in the Reviewing toolbar, or use the mouse to drag the top border of the Reviewing Pane downwards until the entire pane vanishes, leaving only the main editing window. Right-click on any line in the Reviewing Pane (Control-click on the Macintosh) to display a popup menu that lets you accept or reject that edit.

The old way of viewing comments is long gone: there used to be a Comments command under the View menu, but it has been removed. If you add it back using the Customize feature under the Tools menu, you'll find that opening the View menu and selecting Comments no longer lets you view comments. Instead, it switches the screen between showing and concealing the comment markers.

If the reviewer selects text before inserting a comment, that text is still highlighted in the new versions, and in Word 2003 (but not Word 2004) you can still see the initials of the editor (e.g., mine look like [GH1]), but Word now adds small, difficult-to-see brackets around the selected text. In fact, they're sufficiently difficult to see that I've faked the following illustration of what they look like instead of trying for a legible screenshot:

(This text has an attached comment)

To view the comment text, you can still hover the mouse cursor over text to which a comment is attached, and the text will display in a balloon above the position of the mouse cursor. If you want to open the comments so you can edit them, either click on the comment with the right-hand mouse button (Control-click on a Macintosh), or open the Reviewing Pane by displaying the Reviewing toolbar and clicking the Reviewing Pane icon (). If you double-click on a comment marker, the Comment pane will open. (If the Reviewing Pane is open, it will close; Word can only display two panes simultaneously in any window.)

The Display for Review menu

The Display for Review menu in the Reviewing toolbar lets you choose between two new views:

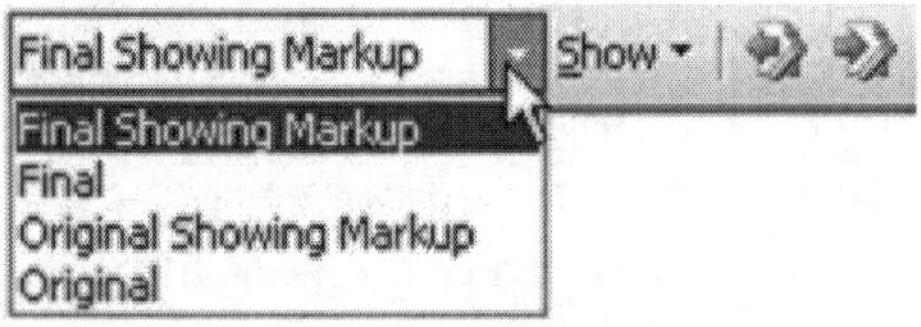

- *Final view* shows only the results of the edits, just like when you turned off the display of your edits in older versions. (This was done by opening the Tools menu, selecting Track Changes, then selecting Highlight Changes. You could then deselect "Highlight changes on screen" to conceal your edits.)
- *Original view* lets you ignore all your edits and see only the original text.

Switching back and forth between Original and Final views lets you see where you started and where you've ended up as a result of your edits. Both views offer the additional option of "Showing Markup". If you are not displaying balloons, this setting will show your changes directly in the text in both views, as in older versions of Word.

The Show menu

The Reviewing toolbar also includes a Show menu (shown below) that you can reach from the keyboard by pressing Alt + S:

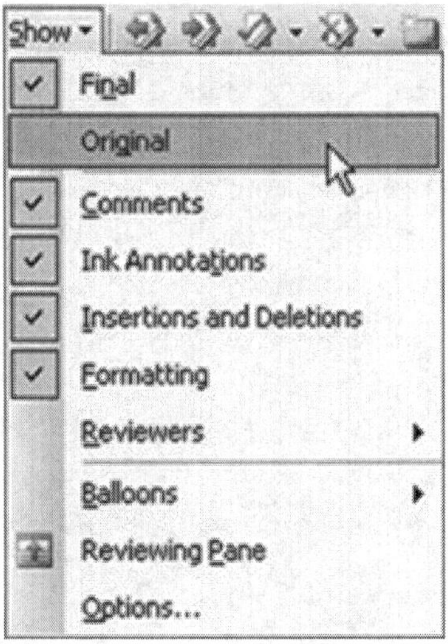

(There does not appear to be a keyboard equivalent in Word 2004.) The Show menu helps you fine-tune the screen display, regardless of whether you're working in Original or Final viewing mode. You have the following options:

Final view vs. Original view: These options show (respectively) the results of your editing and the original unedited document.

Balloons: This option lets you toggle between displaying and concealing the balloons in Print Layout and Web Layout views.

Comments: This option lets you switch between showing and concealing the comment markers. If the Reviewing Pane is displayed (see the next page), this also controls whether your comments appear in that pane. It's best to leave this turned on to ensure that you don't miss any comments.

Formatting: This option lets you choose whether to display changes in formatting, or just the results of these changes. If the Reviewing Pane is displayed, this also controls whether your format changes are displayed in that pane.

Ink Annotations: On computers that allow input and onscreen editing using a pen (i.e., tablet computers), this option lets you switch between displaying and concealing these edits.

Insertions and Deletions: This option lets you choose whether to display or conceal inserted and deleted text. (You cannot show or conceal only insertions or only deletions.) If the Reviewing Pane

Opening the Show menu from the keyboard: If the Alt + S keyboard shortcut does not open this menu in Word XP and 2003, you may have assigned this shortcut to another feature. To change this, open the Tools menu, select Customize, then select Customize Keyboard. Position the cursor in the field labeled "Press new shortcut key", then press Alt + S. If the keystroke has already been used, Word will tell you what command currently has that shortcut and give you a chance to cancel the change. Close this dialog box, then find the command that currently uses the Alt + S shortcut. Delete that shortcut by selecting it, then clicking the "Remove" button. Alt + S should once again open the Show menu. Unfortunately, I wasn't able to discover any way to accomplish a similar effect in Word 2004.

is displayed, this setting also controls whether your insertions and deletions appear in that pane. Concealing insertions and deletions is most useful if you want to display only formatting changes (see the next item) so that you can review all these changes without having to pick your way through all the inserted or deleted text.

Options: This menu choice displays the standard "Options" or "Preferences" dialog box (available under the Tools menu) that lets you choose the colors and formatting used to display insertions and deletions. Unlike in older versions of Word, selecting a color with which to display each type of change does not automatically cause Word to display your changes in color; you'll first have to tell it what style (e.g., boldface) to use for that type of change. For example, select "Color only" if you want to use the same style as the surrounding text, but with a different color. If you've chosen a color but your tracked changes do not appear in this color, make sure that "Color only" is selected.

Reviewers: This lets you display the changes made by all reviewers (as in older versions of Word), but also offers the useful new option of showing only the revisions made by a specific reviewer.

Reviewing Pane: This option lets you display and conceal the Reviewing Pane.

Upgrading to Word 2007 or Word 2008

If you're thinking of upgrading to Word 2007 (and eventually, Word 2008 if you're a Mac user), have a look at Microsoft's interactive "Word 2003 to Word 2007 command reference guide" (http://office.microsoft.

Invisible edits: If you have tracked your edits using revision tracking, and they're not visible to the author, there are various possible causes for this problem. First and foremost, make sure that you've chosen one of the "... showing markup" options, and explain to the author how they can do this. But you may find it easier to do the following instead: open the Options (Windows) or Preferences (Macintosh) dialog box, select the Security tab, and select "Make hidden markup visible when opening or saving". This should work across all versions of Word to ensure that the tracked changes will be visible until you specifically turn off this option.

com/en-us/word/HA100744321033.aspx?pid=CH100487431033). Probably the most useful feature will be the guide to where all your old favorite features have been moved, but the demos should also help bring you up to speed.

Word 2008 for the Macintosh was released in January 2008. If you purchase a copy of Office 2004 now, Microsoft will give you a copy of Office 2008 for only US$10 plus taxes (www.microsoft.com/mac/go/promotions/). I'm not a big fan of Office 2004, but if you shop around, you can save a significant amount of money by buying Office 2004 instead and then upgrading to 2008. As I noted previously, this may be a useful way to gain access to the new features of Word 2008 while still retaining the ability to run macros (using Word 2004).

Appendix IV: Word keyboard shortcuts (plus selected shortcuts at the level of the operating system)

For clarity, I have chosen to use capital letters for all keyboard shortcuts that use letters. Unless I have specifically added the word "Shift" to such a shortcut, don't hold down the Shift key.

Task	Keyboard shortcut
Accented characters	See: Type accented characters
Activate the menu bars	To navigate through a program's menus using the keyboard alone: • **Windows:** Press the Alt key, then either type the underlined letter in a menu name, or use the arrow keys to move between and within menus. • **Macintosh:** In Word 98, press the F10 key. In OS X, this key has been taken over by the Exposé software that manages open windows. Instead, use Control + F2. Then use the arrow keys to navigate between and within menus.
Boldface text	Select the text and press the following keyboard shortcut (or use this shortcut before typing new text): • **Windows:** Control + B • **Macintosh:** Command + B
Change between programs	See: Switch between open programs
Change between windows in a program	See: Switch between open windows in a program
Change font size	See: Increase or decrease font size

Task	Keyboard shortcut
Change keyboard layout (key assignments for different languages)	Because this keyboard shortcut can cause so much trouble if you forget that it exists (e.g., you may suddenly find yourself typing using the French keyboard), it may be worth your while disabling the feature. If not, the default keyboard command is: • **Windows:** Left Alt + Shift (or Control + Shift) • **Macintosh:** Command + Spacebar
Copy selected text	• **Windows:** Control + C • **Macintosh:** Command + C
Copy or cut noncontiguous text	See: Select noncontiguous text
Create a shortcut (Windows) or an alias (Macintosh) to a file	• **Windows:** Right-click on the file and select "Create Shortcut" from the popup menu • **Macintosh:** Select the file and press Command + M
Cursor movement	See: Move cursor, Chapter 5
Decrease font size	See: Increase or decrease font size

Task	Keyboard shortcut
Delete menu items or toolbar icons	Because this keyboard shortcut can cause so much trouble (e.g., you can delete several menu items before you notice what is happening), it may be worthwhile removing this keyboard shortcut. (See the description in Chapter 4 of how to customize keyboard shortcuts.) To turn off this function if you inadvertently select it, simply press the Esc key. To use this function: • **Windows:** Press Control + Alt + Hyphen to turn the cursor into a large – sign, then click on items you want to delete. • **Macintosh:** Press Command + Option + Hyphen to turn the cursor into a large – sign, then click on items you want to delete.
Delete a word	• **Windows:** Control + Delete (for the word following the cursor); Control + Backspace (for the word preceding the cursor) • **Macintosh:** Command + Delete (for the word following the cursor); Command + Backspace (for the word ahead of the cursor)
Diacritical marks, typing	See: Type accented characters
Enable revision tracking	See: Turn on revision tracking

Task	Keyboard shortcut
Extend (enlarge) a selection	• Hold down the Shift key before using the arrow keys to move the cursor to the end of the desired selection or clicking with the mouse to define the end of the selection. • Move the cursor with other keys, such as Page-Down, to extend the selection faster. See Chapter 5 for details. • To extend the selection without holding down the Shift key: position the cursor at the start of the selection, then press F8 repeatedly to select the next word, sentence, then paragraph; at the end of the selection, press Control (Windows) or Command (Macintosh) plus the period (.) key.
Find text	• **Windows:** Control + F • **Macintosh:** Command + F
Go to	The "go to" command lets you jump to bookmarks, sections, comments, and other useful locations. • **Windows:** Control + G • **Macintosh:** Command + G
Increase or decrease font size	Select the desired text, then to change the text to the next largest or smallest predefined font size: • **Windows:** Control + Shift + > to increase the size; Control + Shift + < to decrease the size • **Macintosh:** Command + Shift + > to increase the size; Command + Shift + < to decrease the size
Insert accented characters	See: Type accented characters
Insert copied text	See: Paste copied text

Task	Keyboard shortcut
Keyboard (change key assignments)	See: Change keyboard layout
Menu control from the keyboard	See: Activate the menu bars
Move cursor	• To start of line: Home • To end of line: End • To beginning of a paragraph: Control (Windows) or Command (Macintosh) plus the up arrow • To the end of a paragraph: Control (Windows) or Command (Macintosh) plus the down arrow • Up one screen: PageUp • Down one screen: PageDown • To start of document: Control + Home (Windows) or Command + Home (Macintosh). • To end of document: Control + End (Windows) or Command + End (Macintosh).
Navigate through a program's menus	See: Activate the menu bars
Open two windows on a Word document	See: Split a Word document into two panes
Paste copied text	• **Windows:** Control + V • **Macintosh:** Command + V
Programs (switching between)	See: Switch between open programs

Task	Keyboard shortcut
Remove manually applied formatting	If you have overridden the formatting instructions defined by a paragraph or character style, and want to return the text to its original, underlying formatting, select the text, then: • **Windows:** Control + Spacebar • **Macintosh:** Command + Shift + Z
Remove menu items or toolbar icons	See: Delete menu items or toolbar icons
Replace text	• **Windows:** Control + R • **Macintosh:** In OS 9, the keyboard shortcut is Command + H; in OS X, Apple reserved this command for the operating system, and the replacement is Command + Shift + H.
Return to your previous position	Either insert a bookmark (using the Bookmark feature or by typing a temporary placeholder such as *** that you can search for), or use the "go back" function: Shift + F5.
Revision tracking (enable)	See: Turn on revision tracking
Search for text	See: Find text
Select all the text in a document window	• **Windows:** Control + A • **Macintosh:** Command + A

Task	Keyboard shortcut
Select a sentence or a paragraph, then extend the selection to include additional sentences or paragraphs	• Hold down the Control key (Windows) or the Command key (Macintosh) and click to select a sentence; to select a paragraph, triple-click without holding down any keys. • Holding down *only* the Shift key and clicking again anywhere in a subsequent or preceding sentence or paragraph will extend the selection to include the entire sentence or paragraph and all intervening text.
Select noncontiguous text	You can't do this in older versions of Word, but if the goal of selecting is to copy or cut the text, you can instead use the "spike": • Select the first chunk of text. • Hold down the Control (Windows) or Command (Macintosh) key and press F3 to add the text to the spike (to "spike the text"). • Repeat these two steps (select then spike the text) for each additional selection you want to place on the spike. • When you're done, position the text cursor at the desired destination, hold down the Control (Windows) or Command (Mac) and Shift keys, then press F3 again. In Word X and 2004 on the Macintosh and Word XP and 2003 for Windows, you can select noncontiguous text. To do so, select the first block of text as usual, then for the second and subsequent blocks, hold down the Command key (Macintosh) or the Control key (Windows) before you use the mouse to make additional selections.
"Spike" text	See: Select noncontiguous text

Task	Keyboard shortcut
Split a Word document into two panes	• **Windows:** Control + Alt + S • **Macintosh:** Command + Option + S Repeat this keystroke to unsplit the document. Press F6 to move the cursor between the two panes.
Switch between open programs	• **Windows:** Alt + Tab • **Macintosh:** Command + Tab
Switch between open windows in a program	• **Windows:** Control + F6 in Microsoft Office; Alt + Tab for windows that appear in the Task Bar. • **Macintosh:** Command + F6 in Microsoft Office; Command + ` (accent grave, on the key to the left of the 1 on most keyboards) in all programs
Text size (increase or decrease)	See: Increase or decrease font size
Track revisions (edits)	See: Turn on revision tracking
Turn on revision tracking	• **Windows:** Control + Shift + E • **Macintosh:** Command + Shift + E

Task	Keyboard shortcut
Type accented characters	• **Windows:** Press Control plus the appropriate accent character (e.g., ‘, the single quotation mark, for an accent aigu), then release both keys and type the letter (for example, typing Control + ‘ followed by *e* produces *é*). • **Macintosh**: Press the Option key plus the appropriate accent (e.g., ‘, the single quotation mark, for an *accent aigu*), then release both keys and type the letter (for example, typing Option + *e* followed by *e* produces *é*). • For a list of standard keystrokes to create the most common accented letters for Windows and Macintosh, see the links on the Resources page of my Web site (www.geoff-hart.com/resources.html).
Underline text	Select the text and press the following keyboard shortcut (or use this shortcut before you start typing new text): • **Windows:** Control + U • **Macintosh:** Command + U
Undo an action	Not all actions can be undone, but many can, and there's no harm in trying. The standard keystrokes are: • **Windows:** Control + Z • **Macintosh:** Command + Z
Windows (switching between, in a program)	See: Switch between open windows in a program

Glossary

"What we call 'language' is, in fact, a formal collective of imprecise verbal signals that serve as oblique coefficients of intuitive states wedded to analytical and discursive figurations of thought, and secondarily referential to perceived experience. This is why communication is so difficult."—Sandra Boynton, *Don't let the turkeys get you down*

"When ideas fail, words come in very handy."—Goethe

"Fictionary (fik' shun air ee) n. The word reference that engineers and software developers use when they write documentation."—Kay Robart

"Vah! Denuone Latine loquebar? Me ineptum. Interdum modo elabitur. (Oh! Was I speaking Latin again? Silly me. Sometimes it just sort of slips out.)"—Henry Beard, *Latin for all occasions*

Account: In a computer that requires you to log in (enter a name and password) before you can use it, you can establish a separate identity called an *account* for each user. Each account can have a different password, different settings, and different access rights to the information stored on the computer.

Affordances: Hints or explanations about the nature of the input or response required from the user of a program. The best affordances describe the required response concisely, but in sufficient detail that the user need never consult the online help.

Antialiasing: A software technology that lets the video software on your computer simulate the existence of more pixels on the screen than the display resolution actually provides. Examples include Microsoft's ClearType and Apple's Quartz software.

Antispyware software: Software designed to prevent computer criminals from installing software on your computer that is capable of spying on your activities. Compare: *antivirus software.*

Antivirus software: Software designed to defend a computer against computer *viruses*. Compare: *antispyware software.*

Archive: Old material stored in a safe place in case we need to use it again in the future. Also, a synonym for a compressed file. (See: *compression software.*)

ASCII: The American Standard Code for Information Interchange, which was one of the original attempts to standardize how information (specifically, each character in a font) was encoded. Unfortunately, although ASCII is fairly standardized for the main characters you see on your keyboard, it was not standardized between operating systems for the special characters that aren't on the keyboard, often leading to font display problems when documents are exchanged between operating systems. The *Unicode* standard was developed to solve this problem.

Attachment: A file sent "attached" to an e-mail message.

Audit trail: A series of records used to help an auditor determine what was done to something, when it was done, and by whom. Compare: *paper trail.*

Authoring: In general, authoring is the $10 word for the $1 concept of "writing" or "creating". However, the term has become standard jargon in areas such as Web page and multimedia development and goes beyond writing to include design roles such as creating an effective structure or creating interactivity.

Backup: A copy of a file stored in a safe place so you can return to that version of the file if it becomes necessary.

Backup medium (media): Any device, from the traditional floppy disk to the currently trendy flash drive, used to store backups.

Blog: An online journal maintained by someone who has opinions on a subject and isn't afraid to state them. These blogs range from personal diaries to communities of experts gathered around a respected commentator.

Blues (blueline proofs): A common form of printed proof created by covering a piece of specialized film with the film negatives that will be used to create the metal plates used in offset printing, then exposing the underlying film. The name results from the blue color of the resulting image.

Boilerplate: Any recurring element, such as a standard copyright statement or corporate logo, that should appear in every document in a series. This material is often stored in a template for that series of documents.

Business case: A carefully thought-out proposal that explains what you intend to do, the benefits and risks of doing it, and how you intend to achieve the benefits while coping with the risks. Where money, people, or other resources must be provided, the business case should provide logical, defensible estimates of the quantities of these resources.

Button: Any *icon* (particularly one that is button-shaped) that you click to make software perform a certain task.

Callout: A way to connect a text comment to a specific part of an image, usually by means of a pointer such as a line with an arrowhead at the pointing end. "Callout" may also refer to the comment itself.

Carriage return: An etymological legacy from the days of typewriters, when the entire "carriage" that contained the paper being typed upon "returned" to the start of the next line so you could begin typing on that line. On computers, a carriage return is created by pressing the *Enter* (Windows) or *Return* (Macintosh) keys.

Cell: In a table, each cell represents an "information container" whose position is defined by a column and row number.

Change bar: A vertical line in the margin of the page that indicates which parts of the text contain editorial revisions.

Character style: A collection of formatting instructions that can be applied to chunks of text smaller than an entire paragraph or heading. Compare: *paragraph style*.

Chat: A synonym for *instant messaging*. The differences between the two terms are of interest only to true geeks.

Clipboard: The name given to the part of your computer's memory where anything that you copy or cut from a document is stored so you can paste it elsewhere in the current document or in a new document.

CMYK color: The approach used to display color in printed materials. In this approach, cyan (C), magenta (M), yellow (Y), and black (K) inks are merged to create a wide range of on-paper colors. A more modern variant of this traditional system, called *hexachrome*, adds two additional colors—orange and green—to improve color fidelity. Compare: *RGB color*.

Comma-delimited: A *delimited format* in which individual chunks of information are separated by commas. Compare: *tab-delimited*.

Command key (and ⌘): The Macintosh equivalent of the Windows Control key. On most keyboards, this key appears twice, once on each side of the spacebar.

Compression software: Software that uses special encoding techniques to reduce the size of a file without losing any data.

Concordance: A list of all words in a document, as well as (optionally) their frequency and the text surrounding each occurrence of each word. See: *keyword in context (KWIC) concordance*. Compare: *index*.

Consistency: A manuscript is consistent when important words are used identically throughout a manuscript and there are no logical or other contradictions within it (in references, cross-references, statements of fact, conclusions, etc.).

Control-click: A mouse action in which you hold down the Control key before you press the primary mouse button (usually the left-hand button). On most computers and in most programs, this will display a popup menu that allows you to choose among several actions related to the object that was clicked. Compare: *right-click, shift-click*.

Control code: The term used in Word to identify certain special characters, such as paragraph markers or field codes, in the search and replace dialog box. The "control" part of the name comes from the fact that the code controls how a feature (in this case, the search function) operates.

Control panel: Software that lets you control a specific aspect of your computer's behavior.

Copyediting: Editing that focuses on grammar, punctuation, and consistency of formatting and word use, as well as on conformity with a publisher's style guide. Thus, it focuses more on the "micro" level of sentences and the phrases that make up sentences than on larger-scale issues. Compare: *developmental editing, substantive editing.*

Corpus: A collection of works in a given language such as French, in a specific subject area such as geology, or in a specific author's body of work.

Cropping: The process of defining which parts of a graphic should be retained and which should be excluded ("cropped out").

CRT: A computer monitor resembling a traditional television (a "cathode-ray tube"). Compare: *LCD*.

Cursor: An onscreen indication of where the mouse is pointing (the *mouse* cursor) or where text will be inserted once you begin typing (the *text* cursor).

Custom dictionary: A feature that lets us add new words to the main spelling dictionary used by the software. (Also called a *personal dictionary*.) Better software allows us to create multiple custom dictionaries for special purposes.

Data: In most cases, this is the $10 word for the $1 concept of "information". However, it may also be used to mean information that will be acted on by a program, and in that case is more nearly equivalent to the input for that action, whereas the result of that action becomes the information that the program's user sees.

Database: Software designed to store large quantities of text and numerical data and to retrieve and manipulate (sort, combine, and publish) the data. A database may also be used to store more complex pieces of information such as graphics and sound files, often referred to as "binary large objects" (BLOBs). Compare: *spreadsheet.*

Database publishing: An approach in which specialized software (or a report template created within a database) assembles a Web page, a product manual, or even a newsletter using information drawn from a database according to specified criteria for what should be included and excluded in the output.

Default: An initial setting that software uses until you change that setting.

Delimited format: A file format in which each individual chunk of information is separated from the next chunk by a "delimiter" such as a tab or comma. Commonly used for exchanging information between databases, spreadsheets, word processors, and other programs.

Developmental editing: Editing that helps the author to develop the overall plan for their manuscript, often before they even begin writing. It includes both obvious tasks such as creating an effective outline and less-obvious tasks such as defining what is to be communicated, the nature of the communication's audience, and how to bridge the two to produce an effective manuscript. Compare: *copyediting, substantive editing*.

Dialog box: A window that appears on the screen so you can respond to a question from the software (i.e., "initiate a dialogue with the computer") or choose from a range of alternatives (most often, the settings that will govern an action that you asked the software to do, such as printing a document).

Dingbat: In traditional typesetting, dingbats were the ornamental characters (such as ☞, ☆, and ❤) that fell outside the usual range of type. The origin of this word is unclear.

Directory: The Windows name for what Macintosh users call a *folder*. Basically, a named location on your hard disk in which you can store files (e.g., to group related files).

Disk image: A copy of your hard disk (more specifically, of your operating system and programs) created using a special utility so that you can quickly restore your setup if you encounter a hard disk problem or are struck by a serious computer virus.

Dogsbody: See: *editor*.

Double-click: A mouse action in which you press the primary mouse button (usually the left-hand button) twice in close succession. This action selects a word or opens a program in most operating systems and most programs. Compare: *single-click*.

Double-click speed: How quickly you must click the mouse button for two consecutive clicks to be interpreted as a single command (e.g., to open a file).

DTD: A "document type definition", which specifies all the required and optional sections in an *SGML* or *XML* document, and the hierarchy of these sections. *HTML* also uses DTDs, but they are not usually enforced by most HTML *authoring* software.

Editor: The neglected, underappreciated hero of the publishing process. The author's knight in shining armor, and slayer of the dread dangling participle. See: *dogsbody*.

Encryption: Using software to encode a file or message in such a way that only someone with the correct password can decode and read (or use) the information.

Enter key: A key on a Windows keyboard pressed to "enter" information into the computer's memory. On a Macintosh keyboard, this is often labeled *Return* instead.

Entity: See: *HTML entity*.

Export: To save information from one program in a format that another program can read. Compare: *import*.

Field: In computer parlance, anywhere in a dialog box that you can type information or select a choice from a popup menu. Compare: *field code.*

Field code: A special code that allows some software (including Word) to automate certain special features, such as inserting the current date, a link to a page number, or the results of a calculation. Compare: *field.*

Filename extension: Several letters or numbers (most often three) added to the end of a file name to help you (and your computer if you use Windows) identify the type of file. For example, .doc files belong to Word, whereas .htm and .html files are Web pages you can display in your Web browser.

Firewall: A software or hardware solution that prevents criminals and other malefactors from gaining entry into your computer.

Flash drive: A small (finger-sized) storage device that contains "flash" memory that retains its contents after the power is turned off. These devices are great tools for saving an ongoing series of backups of different versions of a file, and have the additional advantage that you can slip one in your pocket and take it somewhere safe; that way, if anything happens to your computer (e.g., theft or fire damage), you still have the most recent copy of your data on the flash drive.

Flat-file database: A database in which all the information is stored in the rows and columns of a single file (or sometimes a small number of files). Compare: *relational database.*

Folder: The Macintosh name for what Windows users call a *directory*. Basically, a named location on your hard disk in which you can store files (e.g., to group related files).

Font: The shape and size information that your computer uses to determine how to display a particular typeface on the screen. Compare: *typeface.*

Font metrics: The parameters that define character size and spacing for a given font.

Font substitution: If someone sends you a file that is formatted to use a font that isn't installed on your computer, most software will offer you a chance to replace that font (temporarily or permanently) with another font that is installed on your computer. If another font is not substituted for the missing one, you may be unable to see the text typed using that missing font.

FTP software: Software designed to directly transfer files between two computers without relying on intermediate software such as your e-mail program.

Galley (proofs): Originally, a printed copy of a page produced by inking the lead type and engravings locked together in a "galley" and pressing those materials to a piece of paper to provide a "proof" (i.e., test) copy of what will be printed. With modern computer typesetting, the term "galley" is typically used for any first-draft proofs of a layout that must be proofread before finalizing the layout and proceeding with printing.

Gamut: In the context of color, the gamut represents the full range of colors that it is possible to display using a given device, whether that device is paper or a computer monitor. Computer monitors use transmitted light, whereas paper uses reflected light, so their gamuts do not fully overlap. See: *CMYK*, *RGB*.

Gestalt: The perceived "whole" that is both the sum of its parts and the result of any synergies produced by the interaction of those parts.

Global: Just as *global* refers to *anywhere in the world* in normal conversation, the computer use of this term refers to *anywhere*, though the *where* may be a single document (as in a *global search and replace* operation) or all documents on your system (as in a *global style*).

Global search and replace: A replacement operation that replaces every occurrence of a search term throughout a document. Some software can extend this operation across multiple documents.

Global style: A style that is available in all documents on your computer. In Word, for example, styles stored in Normal.dot are global styles. Compare: *local style*.

House style: The specific style preferences of a given "publishing house" (i.e., publisher).

HTML: The HyperText Markup Language, which is the system used for defining how the contents of Web pages should be displayed.

HTML entity: A character code used to identify special characters such as accented letters, mathematical symbols, and Greek letters, among many others, in documents that will be published on the

Web. Standardizing these codes greatly increased the likelihood that a given Web browser would display the correct character.

Hubris: See: *poetic justice.*

Hyperlink: A clickable cross-reference in a computer document that takes you to the location described by that link.

Icon: A small picture intended to serve as a visual reminder of the function of some button or other interface object provided by an operating system or program. Compare: *button.*

Imagesetter: A type of high-resolution laser printer used to create the film negatives that are in turn used to create the printing plates used in offset printing.

Import: To bring information into a program, whether by converting a file in a different format to the format used by that program or by inserting the information directly into an existing file. Compare: *export.*

Index: A list of the locations (page numbers in print, and hyperlinks or page numbers on the computer) of all key terms in a manuscript, including their synonyms, intended to help readers find a specific term or concept in a specific context. The key factor that defines an index is that each index entry defines how the term is being used in the location the entry refers to, so readers can determine whether the information they are seeking can be found there. Compare: *concordance.*

Insertion mode: A setting in which newly typed characters push existing text aside to make room for themselves. Compare: *overstrike mode.*

Instant messaging: Better known nowadays as "chat", this is a technology in which the author and editor establish a link between their computers ("open a session") and take turns typing questions and comments. The "instant" part of the name refers to the fact that the communication occurs with little or no perceptible delay, in contrast to e-mail, which may not receive a response for minutes to days.

Internet telephony: Using a service such as Skype to conduct a telephone conversation over the Internet (typically using a microphone attached to a computer) rather than using a traditional telephone.

ISP: Internet service provider. The companies that provide us with access to the Internet.

Keyboard delay: How long the keyboard will wait after a key is pressed and held down before beginning to repeat that keystroke. Compare: *keyboard repeat rate*.

Keyboard repeat rate: How fast the computer repeats a keystroke when a key is held down. Compare: *keyboard delay*.

Keyword in context (KWIC) concordance: A *concordance* that also provides the location of each word and the surrounding text (i.e., its context). Compare: *index*.

Kludge: An inelegant workaround used to force the software to do something it would do more elegantly if only the designers had spent five seconds thinking about your needs. Such workarounds are described as *kludgy*.

Layer: Layers are the software equivalent of a transparent acetate sheet laid over the top of a sheet of paper. Just as you can annotate a printed page without harming the paper by laying an acetate sheet over it, you can annotate a graphics file by adding a layer that contains your comments.

LCD: A computer monitor in the form of a "liquid crystal display". Sometimes referred to as a "flat screen", though this can be misleading because certain CRTs are also referred to as flat screens. Compare: *CRT*.

Lingua franca: Any shared language used as a means of communication among people—or programs—that have different linguistic backgrounds. *Text format* files, for example, are the current lingua franca for file exchange, since most programs understand this format; XML is rapidly becoming the lingua franca of the future.

Local style: A style that is available only in the currently open document. Compare: *global style*.

Macro: A small program that carries out a specified series of actions, saving us the trouble of doing them ourselves. Most often, we create a macro by recording our actions as we do them. More advanced users can learn a programming or scripting language and write their own macros. Once recorded or programmed, the macro can repeat all the specified actions at a single keystroke or mouse click.

Macro virus: A virus in the form of one or more *macros*, usually attached to a Word document. Because Word can run macros automatically when a file is opened (ordinarily a useful feature), a macro virus can infect a computer without requiring any action on the part of the user other than opening the infected document. Once activated, the virus can spread to any other document opened on the infected computer or perform a range of harmful actions.

Malware: Viruses and other nasty programs that can damage the software components of our computer, harvest e-mail addresses, record our keystrokes, and sometimes even steal documents. Suitable protection requires *antivirus software*, *anti-spyware software*, and a *firewall*—all supplemented by a large dose of caution and common sense.

Markup language: A system of codes used to "mark" text so as to identify its function or format. Common markup languages include *HTML*, *SGML*, and *XML*.

Menu bar: A horizontal bar that runs across the top of the screen and contains a program's most important menus. Compare: *pop-up menu*.

Metadata: Literally, "data about data". For example, in a boldfaced word in a word processor document, the data is the word; *metadata* is the hidden code that tells the word processor to boldface that word.

Mode: A specific manner in which the software operates. For example, in a layout mode, you may have access to special tools for formatting a document and moving text around the screen that are unavailable in the normal "typing only" mode.

Mouse: In this book, I have used the term to mean any pointing device you use to control the position of the cursor. This includes traditional mice, trackballs, trackpads, and other tools.

Mouse cursor: An onscreen indication of where the mouse is pointing. Compare: *text cursor*.

Mouse tracking speed: How fast the *mouse cursor* moves in response to movements of the mouse.

Multi-session CD: With the exception of CD-RW (rewritable) disks, CDs were originally designed to be written to only once—that is, in a single session. Modern CD drives and the software that accompanies them often allow us to write additional information to discs that have already been written to once, thus writing to them in two or more sessions.

***Mutatis mutandis*:** Latin for "the necessary changes having been made". That is, use the approach that I just described, but modify it to take into account differences between your situation and the one I described.

Native file format: The standard format used by your software to store all its formatting instructions. For Word files, this is the .doc file format or the *rich text format* (*RTF*); for Web pages, this is the *HTML* file format.

Netiquette: The formal and informal rules of politeness (etiquette) for the 'net (Internet). These rules include trying to help others rather than focusing exclusively on your own needs, and the wise advice given to world travelers: study the culture of a community before diving into it and making a fool of yourself.

Non-breaking hyphen: Most software will split a word that includes a hyphen over two lines when the word occurs sufficiently near the right margin of the text. If you don't want the word to be split in this manner, use a non-breaking hyphen instead. The code for typing this hyphen depends on the software you're using, and may not translate successfully between programs.

Non-breaking space: Most software will split an open compound (a phrase that includes a space between the two words that constitute the compound) over two lines if the words occur sufficiently near the right margin of the text. If you don't want the words to be split, use a non-breaking space instead. The code for typing this space depends on the software you're using, and may not translate successfully between programs.

Noncontiguous text: Two or more chunks of text that are not touching; that is, they are separated from each other by intervening text, graphics, or other material.

Nonprinting characters: Special characters that govern how the software will perform certain functions, such as the display of text on the screen. For example, Word uses several of these characters as visual cues for the location of such features as tab stops and end-of-paragraph markers to help you understand what you're seeing on the screen.

Object: In computer parlance, an object is more than just "something you can point at". Most often, an object is something within a document that has its own settings (e.g., the position of a graphic) or that contains programming that lets you perform actions that are not available elsewhere in the software; for example, a *spreadsheet* object is a spreadsheet file embedded in a Word document that provides access to the tools offered by the spreadsheet software.

Offset printing: A traditional form of printing in which ink is transferred from an inked printing plate onto a rubber pad or other device that then transfers the ink to the paper.

Onscreen editing: Editing using a word processor or similar tool. It's important to note that this definition makes no assumptions about the final destination of the information; that is, it does not apply only to editing materials that will be published online, such as Web pages.

Overstrike (overtype) mode: A setting in which newly typed characters replace ("type over") existing text. Compare: *insertion mode*.

Palette: A group of tools gathered into a single group (the palette) and presented as clickable *icons* (*buttons*) for ease of use. Palettes most often contain more than a single row of icons, but may be fixed in place or capable of being moved. Sometimes used as a synonym for *toolbar*.

Pane: In software that lets you split the window of a document into smaller sub-windows, each of those sub-windows is referred to as a "pane".

Paper trail: A printed copy of every version of a manuscript, usually date-stamped and signed by the person who was responsible for that version. Used as a tool for identifying problems and determining who was responsible for those problems; in a healthy organization, the goal is to find ways to avoid repeating a problem, but some organizations use a paper trail as a tool for figuring out who to punish. It is sometimes used to show compliance with government or other regulations (e.g., to prove that a particular kind of review was performed), in which case it may also be referred to as an *audit trail*. Some organizations can accept a *virtual* paper trail (versions of each word processor file); others may require a print-out with tracked changes.

Paragraph: In software parlance, a paragraph is defined as all the text between two *carriage returns*, rather than in the grammatical sense of a series of related sentences. Thus, a paragraph can be a single-word heading, a grammatically correct paragraph, or a long and rambling collection of loosely related thoughts. The key point is that the entire paragraph is treated as a single unit for purposes such as cursor movement and the application of *paragraph styles*.

Paragraph style: A collection of formatting instructions that can be applied to entire paragraphs (including headings). Compare: *character style*.

Patch: A small program that the developer of a larger program such as a word processor or operating system provides to update that larger program to solve a known problem, such as an incompatibility between two versions of the software. Compare: *service release*.

PDF: The "portable document format" (or a file in that format) created using Adobe's Acrobat software or various competing programs. PDF files are designed to ensure that the layout of the document and all the information it contains will be preserved and correctly displayed on any computer.

Personal dictionary: See: *custom dictionary*.

Pixel: A "picture element" (i.e., a dot) on the computer screen.

Poetic justice: The inevitable comeuppance of would-be pundits who become sufficiently confident in their expertise that they dare to write a book on some subject. (cf. *hubris*)

Popup menu: A menu embedded in a dialog box or toolbar (rather than in the *menu bar* at the top of the screen) that "pops up" when you click on it. Compare: *menu bar*.

Power user: Someone who takes maximum advantage of all the obvious and many of the unobvious features of their favorite software.

Preference panel: The term for a Macintosh *control panel* in OS X.

Proofing: See: *proofreading*.

Proofreading: Editing a manuscript after layout to catch any errors that escaped previous editing stages, to ensure consistency in formatting, and to ensure that the content works well in its final format. Often called *proofing* for short.

Proofs: A sample of what is expected in the final product, whether a printed book or a single screen from online help. This sample allows you to prove (in the word's original sense of "test") that whatever you submitted for production will appear as you intended (both layout and content) when the final version is published. In short: proofs are your last chance to catch any errors before your information is presented to its audience.

Reading to proof ("reading against copy"): A form of proofreading in which the proofreader reads the original material used to create a laid-out document, and compares it with the document itself to identify any omissions or other errors. Sometimes a second person reads the original material aloud so the proofreader can check it against the document without having to look back and forth between the two.

Record: A single set of related information stored in a *database*.

Refresh rate: How fast the image on the screen is "refreshed" (drawn again). Slow refresh rates can lead to visible flickering.

Relational database: A database in which information is stored in separate "tables" (often independent files), with related information linked by means of a shared index number or key. Compare: *flat-file database*.

Repetitive stress injury (RSI): Any injury that arises from repeatedly performing an action that causes stress to your body without providing time to recover from that stress; eventually, a significant injury may result.

Return key: A key used to insert a *carriage return* so that you can begin typing on the next line. In most software, this performs the same role as the *Enter key* (i.e., "entering" information into the computer's memory) and marks the end of a *paragraph*. Windows keyboards tend to use "Enter"; Macintosh keyboards tend to use "Return".

RGB color: The approach used to display color on a computer screen. In this approach, red (R), green (G), and blue (B) light are merged to create a wide range of onscreen colors. Compare: *CMYK color*.

Rich text format (RTF): A file format developed by Microsoft that is supported by many other programs, and that allows you to exchange files between Word and other programs while retaining most formatting information. A handy alternative to Word's own .doc format, particularly since RTF format cannot contain *macros* and is thus a good way to prevent the transfer of *macro viruses* between computers.

Right-click: A mouse action in which you press the secondary mouse button (usually the right-hand button). This action usually displays a popup menu that lists the available options for the object that was clicked. If your mouse only has a single button, hold down the Control key and press that button. Compare: *control-click*, *shift-click*.

Round-tripping: Exporting information from one program into another program for editing, then returning the edited information into the original program with minimal fuss. Rarely as easy as it sounds, but often possible with a bit of planning.

RSI: See: *repetitive stress injury*.

RTF: See: *rich text format*.

Ruler: A visual reference that the software provides to assist in tasks such as positioning text using *tab stops* or specifying the size of paragraph indents.

Screen resolution: The number of dots (*pixels*) that will be displayed on the screen. Screen resolution may be specified as the pixel dimensions of the entire screen, or as the number of pixels per inch.

Script: Another word for a *macro*. A scripting language is the programming language used to create or implement the script.

Search term: The specific character, word, phrase, or pattern that the software's search tool will look for.

Service release: A fairly major update to software such as a word processor or operating system, provided by the software's developer to solve one or more major problems, such as bugs and incompatibilities. Compare: *patch*.

SGML: The Standardized General Markup Language, which is a tool for constructing *markup languages* such as *HTML*, but also considerably more sophisticated ones. In particular, SGML allows publishers to require the inclusion of specific information, in a specific order, in each document of a given type. This is done by means of a *DTD*.

Shell account: A software environment in which all commands are sent to the operating system from the keyboard rather than using a mouse combined with icons and menus. Used primarily in the Unix and Linux operating systems.

Shift-click: A mouse action in which you hold down the Shift key before you press the primary mouse button (usually the left-hand button). On most computers and in most programs, this will extend the selection from the previous cursor position to the position where you clicked. The result depends on the context. For example, in a word processor document, shift-clicking will select the text between the original cursor position and the position where you clicked, whereas in a window displaying a list of files, one of which is already selected, shift-clicking will select all files between the selected file and the position where you clicked. Compare: *control-click, right-click.*

Single-click: A mouse action in which you press the primary mouse button (usually the left-hand button) only once. Single-clicking (usually called simply "clicking") positions the text cursor in a document, causes an icon or button to perform the action it was programmed to do, or selects a file, depending on the context. Compare: *double-click.*

Single-sourcing: The creation of two or more outputs (e.g., a printed user manual, a Web page, and an online help system) from the same underlying set of information. This is achieved by designing the information for ease of reuse in each of these multiple contexts, and is often implemented by means of a *database* or a specialized *markup language* such as *XML* that defines which chunks of information belong in each output.

Soft proofs (soft proofing): An alternative to printed *proofs* and on-paper proofreading, in which the person responsible for approval of the proofs examines only an onscreen set. (The "soft" part of the name comes from the fact that the proofs are software, such as a PDF file, rather than "hardware", such as paper.) Although this may be a sound strategy for spotting errors before you pay the potentially high cost of real proofs, it's no replacement for the real thing (i.e., printed proofs for materials that will be printed).

Spread: The full image you see when you open a publication and "spread out" the pages. Most commonly used to refer to a "two-page spread" that shows the opposing left-hand and right-hand pages.

Spreadsheet: Software designed to store primarily numerical data, and optimized to perform calculations on subsets of the data. Compare: *database*, *worksheet.*

Spyware: Software designed to install itself surreptitiously on your computer so it can spy on your activities. A form of *malware.*

Standard: To ensure that all computer hardware and software can work happily together, developers of these products enter into a gentleman's agreement to adhere to a common set of specifications. As soon as the ink on the agreement is dry, they promptly begin creating their own variations on the standard, thereby ensuring that no two programs or pieces of hardware cooperate properly. The word is often considered the best example of a one-word oxymoron.

Stet: From the Latin "let it stand", thus the editorial equivalent of saying "please ignore that edit" or "don't do that".

Story: A term commonly used to describe the separate blocks of text (often from separate files) that are imported by a desktop publishing program and placed independently within the layout.

Storyboard: A term used by animation, multimedia, and movie producers to describe how they visualize the sequence of images and associated text that will appear in the final animated product. Traditionally, this was done by illustrating key scenes in the story on art board (similar to cardboard), hence the name. Because it can be so expensive to produce animations, storyboards are used to permit rapid prototyping of the final product, and constitute the equivalent of a blueprint for how the final product will appear. Designers can then produce the final product with fewer errors by working from the storyboards.

Style (text): A named set of specifications for how a chunk of text should be formatted. See: *character style*, *paragraph style*, *template.*

Style (writing): The combination of an author's "voice", word choice, and any guidelines the author followed in creating the manuscript.

Style guide: A compendium of proven solutions to typical difficulties that editors face when editing a manuscript. Since no style guide can ever be fully comprehensive (none, for example, includes a complete unabridged dictionary), editors must also create *style sheets* that extend the chosen style guide. Compare: *style sheet.*

Style sheet: A list of all the decisions we have made during our efforts to impose consistency on a document. As a general rule, style sheets primarily include difficulties that are not solved in the *style guide* chosen for a given manuscript. Compare: *style guide*.

Sub-menu: Some menu choices have an arrow at the right edge of the words that indicates the availability of more options related to this menu:

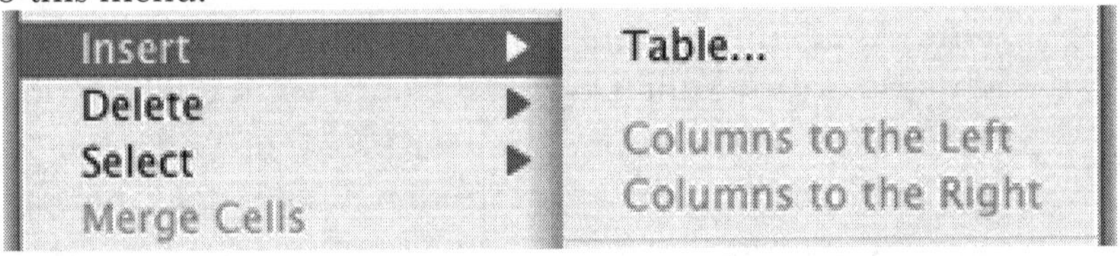

When you move the mouse cursor over the arrow, a new menu (the submenu) opens to display these options.

Substantive editing: Editing that focuses on the organization, logic, and clarity of the content. Substantive editing also verifies the internal *consistency* of a document and may verify its external consistency with the broader consensus in a field of study. In short, substantive editing focuses on the "big picture" items. Compare: *copyediting, developmental editing.*

Synergy: When two things produce a more powerful effect together than you would expect from simply adding them, the enhanced result is called a *synergy*. The collaboration of authors and editors is one example of a way to obtain synergy.

Tab (in a dialog box): Most programs now group related functions within a dialog box by dividing the dialog box into sections using "tabs" that resemble the paper or colored plastic tabs used in a three-ring binder. In a dialog box, clicking the name of the tab reveals only the functions grouped under that heading. For example, in the image at the top of the next page, Word's search functions appear on the Find tab, the replacement options appear on the Replace tab, and the Go To tab allows fast movement within a file.

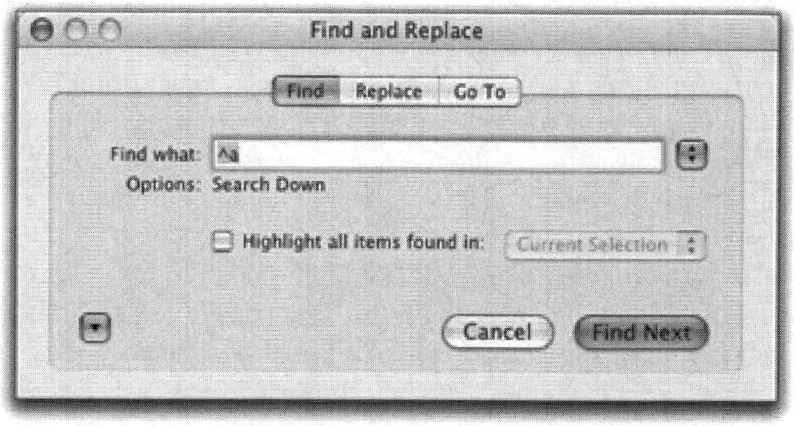

Tab (tab stop): A predefined position to which the text cursor will move whenever you press the keyboard's Tab key.

Tab-delimited: A *delimited format* in which individual chunks of information are separated by tabs (tab stops). Compare: *comma-delimited*.

Tag: A marker or pair of markers that define how a word or chunk of text should be handled by the software. For example, *HTML* uses pairs of angle brackets (< >) to identify its tags, and encloses the text to be handled in some way between a start tag and an end tag (the latter identified by a slash, /); for example, paragraphs begin with <p> and end with </p>.

Template: A collection of standard text and styles that can be used to define the initial content and formatting options available to any document. In software such as Word, templates can also store *macros* and other customizations. See: *character style, paragraph style*.

Text cursor: An onscreen indication of where text will be inserted when you begin typing. Compare: *mouse cursor*.

Text editor: A program designed specifically to manipulate text in *text format* files rather than in the proprietary formats used by most word processors. This software may be as primitive as an onscreen typewriter, or may come with bells and whistles that put your word processor to shame.

Text format: A document format that contains only *ASCII* characters and that thus cannot contain any of the special formatting features provided by the proprietary formats used by word processors. However, formatting can still be specified in a text-format file by using a *markup language*, such as *HTML*.

Toolbar: A group of tools gathered into a single group (the toolbar) and presented as clickable icons (*buttons*) for casc of use. Toolbars most often contain a single row of icons, but may be fixed in place or capable of being moved. Sometimes used as a synonym for *palette*.

Translation memory: A list of preferred translations for standard phrases. Often used to improve the consistency of translations.

Triage: From the French word for "sorting", editorial triage involves sorting the editing tasks into those that are crucial, those that are important but can wait for a second pass, and those that we can skip—though they would be nice to do if time permits. (The existence of these three categories often leads people to mistakenly assume that the word derives from the Latin *tri*, which means three.)

Triple-click: A mouse action in which you press the primary mouse button (usually the left-hand button) three times in close succession. This action selects an entire paragraph in many programs.

Typeface: The graphical design that characterizes a set of characters (letters, numbers, and other symbols) and makes them appear visually distinct from characters in another typeface. Compare: *font*.

Unicode: A more modern version of the old *ASCII* system for defining the characters that make up a given *font*. Unicode fonts are better standardized between operating systems (i.e., there are fewer differences in the character definitions in different operating systems) and provide a much larger range of characters, including those used in many foreign languages. Visit the Unicode Consortium's Web site (www.unicode.org) for more detailed information on the standard.

Uninterruptible power supply (UPS): A device that, like a surge suppressor, protects your computer from sudden spikes in electrical current (e.g., during a lightning storm), but that offers two important additional advantages: it offers better protection against electrical surges, and it provides enough battery power for you to save any open files and shut down the computer if the power fails.

Unix: A powerful operating system used as an alternative to Windows and the Macintosh operating system. Outside corporate and scientific workplaces, Unix is most familiar in its Linux flavor.

UPS: See: *uninterruptible power supply*.

Validity check: A rule or definition that defines the permissible information (what is allowed and what is not) for each field in a *database* or *spreadsheet*. Validity checks validate information before it is accepted, and ask the user to correct any errors before they become part of the stored body of information.

View mode: A specific way of displaying information on the screen; for example, Page Layout mode will provide a close approximation of what the document will look like when you print it.

Virtual: Literally, "not real". In practice, used to refer to something stored or displayed on a computer.

Virus: Software designed to invade a computer (possibly to damage its software or steal information) and spread to other computers. A form of *malware*.

Voice: The general sense of what an author "sounds like" that readers gain from reading their writing, as if the author were physically present and talking to the reader. Compare: *style*.

Web log: See: *blog*.

Wiki: A Web site or similar online resource that allows its users to add and edit content collectively. The term comes from the phrase *wiki wiki* in the Hawaiian language, meaning *rapidly*. The classic example is the Wikipedia (http://en.wikipedia.org), a free online encyclopedia created in this manner.

Wildcard: In many card games, certain special cards can be used as though they were other cards (sometimes as any other card in the deck). Borrowing from this usage, most search and replace tools offer a wildcard function that lets you use a single character (e.g., ? or *) to represent any single character or group of characters. More sophisticated software lets you use wildcards to define character types, ranges or sets of characters, and other useful patterns.

Word: Short for "Microsoft Word", word processing software that most editors have a love–hate relationship with. The origin of exasperated phrases such as "Word happens".

Workflow (workflow solution): The "flow of work" from one stage to the next, such as from writing to editing, from editing to review, from review to layout, and from layout to publication. Workflow solutions arc a form of automation that guide their users through the sequence of tasks involved in the overall publishing process.

Worksheet: One "page" in a multi-page *spreadsheet* file.

WYSIWYG: "what you see is what you get". In short, the onscreen display closely matches what will appear on paper or what viewers will see in the final onscreen document.

XHTML: A more tightly controlled version of *HTML.*

XML: A specific implementation of *SGML* that provides all of the benefits of SGML, with some of the simplicity of *HTML.*

Bibliography

"The instruction we find in books is like fire. We fetch it from our neighbours, kindle it at home, communicate it to others, and it becomes the property of all."—Voltaire, philosopher and writer (1694–1778)

"Every reader finds himself. The writer's work is merely a kind of optical instrument that makes it possible for the reader to discern what, without this book, he would perhaps never have seen in himself."—Marcel Proust, novelist (1871–1922)

"To be well informed, one must read quickly a great number of merely instructive books. To be cultivated, one must read slowly and with a lingering appreciation the comparatively few books that have been written by men who lived, thought, and felt with style."—Aldous Huxley, writer (1894–1963)

Associated Press. 2004. AP stylebook. Basic Books. 420 p.

Berkowitz, P. 2007. Moving from Microsoft Office VBA to AppleScript: MacTech's guide to making the transition. (http://www.mactech.com/vba-transition-guide/index-toc.html) [Consulted January 2008]

Calishain, T. 2004. Web search garage. Prentice-Hall. 264 p.

Clifford, J. 2004. Traditional proofreading in PDF. (www.planetpdf.com/creative/article.asp?contentid=6667&ra). [Consulted January 2008]

Council of Science Editors. 2006. Scientific style and format: the CSE manual for authors, editors and publishers. 7th ed. The Rockefeller University Press. 658 p.

Dayton, D. 2003. Electronic editing in technical communication: a survey of practices and attitudes. Technical Communication 50(2):192–205.

Dayton, D. 2004. Electronic editing in technical communication: the compelling logics of local contexts. Technical Communication 51(1):86–101.

Dayton, D. 2004. Electronic editing in technical communication: a model of user-centered technology adoption. Technical Communication 51(2):207–223.

Dornfest, R.; Calishain, T. 2004. Google hacks: tips & tools for smarter searching. O'Reilly Media Inc. 479 p.

Einsohn, A. 2000. The copyeditor's handbook: a guide for book publishing and corporate communications: with exercises and answer keys. University of California Press. 560 p.

Fricnds of OpcnDocumcnt Inc. 2007. OpenOffice.org 2.x Writer Guide. (http://www.lulu.com/content/690763) Free PDF versions of this and other books are also available at the OpenOffice site: (http://documentation.openoffice.org/manuals/oooauthors2/) [Consulted January 2008]

Gaskell, D.; Cobb, T. 2003. Can learners use concordance feedback for writing errors? Département de Linguistique et de Didactique des Langues, Université du Québec à Montréal, Montreal. (www.er.uqam.ca/nobel/r21270/cv/conc_fb.htm) [Consulted January 2008]

Gibaldi, J. 2003. MLA handbook for writers of research papers. 6th ed. Modern Language Association of America. 360 p.

Hart, G.J. 2000. The style guide is dead: long live the dynamic style guide! Intercom, March:12–17. (www.geoff-hart.com/resources/2000/dynamicstyle.htm).

Hart, G.J. 2001. "Backing up" doesn't mean retreating. (www.geoff-hart.com/resources/2001/backups.htm).

Hart, G.J. 2004. Using Microsoft Word's "track changes" feature: a guide for authors. (www.geoff-hart.com/resources/Using-revision-tracking.pdf).

Hart, G.J. 2004. Avoiding repetitive-stress injuries: a guide for the technical communicator. (www.geoff-hart.com/resources/2004/avoidrsi.htm).

Hart-Davis, G. 1997. Word 97 macro & VBA handbook. Sybex. 807 p. + CD.

Judd, K. 2001. Copyediting: a practical guide. 3rd ed. Crisp Learning. 304 p.

Kent, P. 1998. Making money in technical writing: turn your writing skills into $100,000 a year. MacMillan. 280 p.

Knopf, D. [no date] Autonumbering with RoboHelp and Microsoft Word. (www.knopf.com/tips/autonumber.html). [consulted January 2008]

Leonard, W. Woody's books: Woody and friends book recommendations. (www.wopr.com/html/books.shtml). [Consulted January 2008]

Leonard, W.; Hudspeth, L.; Lee, T.J. 1997. Word 97 annoyances. O'Reilly & Associates. 338 p.

Lyon, J.M. 2002. Advanced find and replace for Microsoft Word. 27 p. (www.editorium.com/freebies.htm). [Consulted January 2008]

Lyon, J.M. 2008 (in press). Microsoft Word for publishing professionals: power-packed tips for writers, editors, typesetters, and indexers. To be published by The Editorium (www.editorium.com).

McElhearn, K. 2005. Take control of customizing Microsoft Office. 84 p. (www.takecontrolbooks.com/office-customizing.html). [Consulted January 2008]

Microsoft. 2003. Microsoft manual of style for technical publications. 3rd ed. Microsoft Press. 608 p.

Negrino, T.; McElhearn, K.; Binder, K. 2002. Microsoft Office v. X inside out. Microsoft Press. 1008 p.

Neuberg, M. 2004. Take control of what's new in Word 2004. 73 p. (www.takecontrolbooks.com/word-1.html). [Consulted January 2008]

Neuberg, M. 2004. Take control of what's new in Word 2004: advanced editing & formatting. 78 p. (www.takecontrolbooks.com/word-2.html). [Consulted January 2008]

Powers, H. 2007. Making Word work for you: an editor's guide to the tool of the trade.Editorial Freelancers Association. (www.the-efa.org/res/booklets.html) [Consulted January 2008]

Sun Technical Publications. 2003. Read me first! A style guide for the computer industry. 2nd ed. Prentice Hall. 384 p.

University of Chicago. 2003. The Chicago manual of style. 15th ed. University of Chicago Press. 984 p.

Weber, J. 1999. Electronic editing: editing in the computer age. WeberWoman's Wrevenge. 248 p. (http://jeanweber.com/newsite/?page_id=97). [Consulted January 2008]

Weber, J. 2002. Taming Microsoft Word 2002. WeberWoman's Wrevenge. 122 p. (http://jeanweber.com/newsite/?page_id=94). [Consulted January 2008]

Weber, J. 2004. OpenOffice.org Writer: the free alternative to Microsoft Word. O'Reilly Media, Inc. 234 p.

Helpful Internet resources

All resources listed in this section were available as of January 2008. If you can't find one at the specified address, try a Web search using its name; the majority of these resources should remain available for some time, though perhaps at new locations.

Communities

See: People

Miscellaneous

- The Unicode consortium (www.unicode.org): Information on the Unicode standard for computer fonts.
- The World Wide Web consortium (www.w3.org): Information on all the primary standards that govern the Web.

Newsletters

- *Editorium Update* (www.editorium.com/euindex.htm): Jack Lyon's free newsletter for users of Word contains many sample macros, and offers answers to questions posed by readers. Also look at Jack's article *Using "found" macros* (http://lists.topica.com/lists/editorium/read/message.html?mid=1706922855) for information on how to bring useful macros into your own Word environment.
- *Intercom* (www.stc.org/intercom): A magazine of tips for technical communicators published ten times per year by the Society for Technical Communication.
- *Research Buzz* (www.researchbuzz.org/wp): Tara Calishain's free newsletter on the latest and greatest innovations in Web-based research.
- *Windows Secrets* (http://brianlivingston.com): Brian Livingston's excellent free newsletter, offering a wealth of useful information on Windows, and particularly an ongoing series on the security measures Windows users must implement.
- *Woody's Office Watch* (http://office-watch.com): Woody Leonard's free weekly newsletter on everything you need to know about Microsoft Office. One particular strength is its detailed explorations of the intricacies of upgrading Windows and installing Microsoft

patches. (From the same Web site, you can subscribe to many other free newsletters of interest to editors.)

- *WordTips* (www.vitalnews.com/wordtips): Allen Wyatt's ongoing series of delvings into the enigma that is Word, offering many solutions plus a forum in which you can seek help with Word-related problems.

People

- American Library Association (www.ala.org): A professional association for American librarians, with a range of useful library-oriented resources.
- Canadian Library Association (www.cla.ca): A professional association for Canadian librarians, with a range of useful library-oriented resources.
- Copyediting-L (www.copyediting-L.info): A helpful and welcoming community of editors from around the world, eager to provide assistance with editing problems as well as with the mysteries of on-screen and on-paper editing.
- Editorial Freelancers Association (www.the-efa.org): The largest American organization for editors, and not just freelancers.
- Editors' Association of Canada (www.editors.ca): The largest Canadian organization for editors, not just freelancers. Also offers useful French resources.
- Electric Editors (www.electriceditors.net): An Internet community for editors, proofreaders, indexers, translators and publishers, offering the *Grapevine* discussion list, plus many free Word (Macintosh and Windows) and WordPerfect (Windows) macros contributed and tested by working editors.
- McEdit: A discussion group for editors who use Macintosh computers that focuses exclusively on Macintosh-related issues. Contact the owner of the discussion group (mcedit-owner@yahoogroups.com) or visit the group's site (http://groups.yahoo.com/group/McEdit) to join.
- Microsoft's Word MVPs site (http://word.mvps.org): A community of Microsoft-acknowledged experts capable of solving most Word problems.

- Society for Technical Communication (www.stc.org): The world's largest organization of professional technical communicators, including many editors and an editing special-interest group.
- Society for Technical Communication AccessAbility special interest group (www.stcsig.org/sn/visual.shtml): A community of experts on making computers and online and other resources accessible to people with various handicaps and disabilities.
- Techwr-L (www.techwr-L.com): The Internet's largest discussion group for technical communicators from around the world.
- U.K. Ask-a-Librarian service (www.ask-a-librarian.org.uk): A service by which researchers can ask for advice from professional librarians working in the U.K.
- U.S. Ask-a-Librarian service (www.loc.gov/rr/askalib): A service by which researchers can ask for advice from American professional librarians.
- Word-PC discussion group (http://listserv.liv.ac.uk/archives/word-pc.html): A discussion group devoted specifically to Word for Windows, though many of the same solutions apply on the Macintosh. A counterpart Word-Mac group used to exist but disappeared recently; most of its members moved to McEdit.
- WordPerfect Universe (www.wpuniverse.com): An essential resource for WordPerfect users, with FAQs, tips and tricks, useful links, and a discussion group.

Reference and research

- Acronym Finder (www.acronymfinder.com): A large collection of acronyms and their meanings.
- Amazon (www.amazon.com): The biggest online bookseller, and a great resource for looking up bibliographic details. Amazon also has several international sites (e.g., www.amazon.co.uk for the U.K. and www.amazon.co.jp for Japan) that may help you find books published only in certain countries.
- American Heritage dictionary, 4th ed. (www.bartleby.com/61): A well-respected dictionary that both describes word usage and prescribes how words should be used according to the verdict of a panel of editors.

- American Heritage guide to English usage (www.bartleby.com/64): An online guide to English usage.
- Barnes and Noble (www.barnesandnoble.com): Like Amazon, a good resource for researching bibliographic details.
- BIOSIS list of organism names (www.organismnames.com/about.htm): An official list of the Latin species binomials for living organisms.
- Blackwell Publishing (www.blackwellpublishing.com): The publisher's official Web site, and a good resource for finding author guidelines for its journals.
- Chapters-Indigo (www.chapters.indigo.ca): Like Amazon, a good resource for researching bibliographic details.
- Cornell University's ergonomics Web site (http://ergo.human.cornell.edu): A site that provides copious information on ergonomics that will be relevant to anyone who must use computers for a living.
- Darling memorial (Capital Community College Foundation) guide to grammar (http://grammar.ccc.commnet.edu/grammar): A useful online grammar reference to supplement your printed references.
- Elsevier (www.elsevier.com): The publisher's official Web site, and a good resource for finding author guidelines for its journals.
- ERIC, the Educational Resources Information Center (www.eric.ed.gov): A favorite resource for researchers seeking bibliographic details on journal articles in the field of education.
- FOLDOC, the free online dictionary of computing (http://foldoc.org): A growing glossary of key computer and software terminology.
- Glossarist (www.glossarist.com): A list of hundreds of subject-specific glossaries.
- Google (www.google.com): My favorite Web search site, but there are many other options.
- ICT4LT. 2005. Information and Communications Technology (ICT) for Language Teachers Web site (www.ict4lt.org/en/en_mod2-4.htm): A list of resources for foreign language teachers interested in using concordances as a teaching tool in the classroom.
- *Index Academicus* (www.akademisyen.com/ author): A huge list of journal guidelines for authors.

- Ingenta (www.ingentaconnect.com): Access to bibliographic information and (for a fee) full texts of a large number of journal articles from a wide range of publishers.
- Internet Public Library (www.ipl.org): A volunteer effort by librarians willing to help you research information over the Web, plus a large collection of resources catalogued by this group.
- Jean Weber's Web site (www.jeanweber.com): The personal site of an experienced editor who has published several useful books on editing and using word processors.
- Justus-Liebig University (www.uni-giessen.de/~ga1007/ComputerLab/concordance.htm): A helpful Web resource if you're interesting in learning more about concordance software and the available options.
- Library of Congress card catalogue (www.loc.gov): One of the best sources of bibliographic information.
- Lifehacker (www.lifehacker.com), a site packed with tips for making your computing life easier.
- *MacWorld* (www.macworld.com): One of the premier sources for all things related to the Macintosh computer. Includes a wide range of instructional materials, product reviews, software downloads, and other resources.
- Merriam-Webster (www.m-w.com): Online versions of the unabridged and collegiate editions of the company's well-respected dictionaries.
- National Institute for Standards and Technology (http://physics.nist.gov/cuu/Units/index.html): A comprehensive and authoritative guide to the SI (système international) scientific units of measurement, sometimes called "the metric system".
- National Library of Medicine (www.nlm.nih.gov): A great source of bibliographic information for medical publications (via the PubMed database), and access to some online articles.
- OneLook multi-dictionary search (www.onelook.com): A Web site claiming to offer access to more than 7.5 million words defined in nearly 1000 online dictionaries.
- *PC Magazine* (www.pcmag.com): One of the premier sources for all things related to Windows computers. Includes a wide range of instructional materials, product reviews, software downloads, and oth-

er resources. Those who find this magazine too technical often prefer *PC World.*

- *PC World* (www.pcworld.com): An excellent alternative to *PC Magazine* for information on Windows computers.
- Refdesk (www.refdesk.com): A "portal" page that offers conveniently organized access to a wide range of online reference materials.
- Research Buzz (www.researchbuzz.org): Tara Calishain's source of news on the latest and greatest innovations in Web-based research. Sign up for her free newsletter!
- Springer-Verlag plus the former Kluwer Academic Publishers (www.springerlink.com): The publisher's official Web site, and a good resource for finding author guidelines for its journals.
- Strunk, W. The elements of style (www.bartleby.com/141): An online version of the first edition of Strunk's classic reference work.
- Unicode characters: You can find the complete official list of these codes for most known languages at the Unicode Organization's Web site (www.unicode.org/charts/), but unfortunately, the codes are provided in hexadecimal format, which Word won't recognize. To convert them into decimal format, search the Web using the keywords "hexadecimal to decimal conversion utility" (without the quotes). For example, try EasyCalculation.com's Hexadecimal to decimal converter (www.easycalculation.com/hex-converter.php).
- United States Patent and Trademark Office (www.uspto.gov): A large, searchable database of both registered trademarks and trademark applications currently pending.
- Wikipedia (www.wikipedia.org): A huge free encyclopedia that offers both highly credible and precise articles contributed by the world's foremost experts and material of more dubious provenance.
- World Time Server (www.worldtimeserver.com): A resource that lets you enter your current date and time and learn the corresponding date and time anywhere in the world.
- World Wide Web consortium (www.w3.org/MarkUp/html3/latin1.html): A list of the special characters ("entities") defined in the HTML standard; useful for exchanging files with authors when font incompatibilities prevent direct exchange of files between computers or software. The main site (www.w3.org) offers access to a wide range of official resources related to Web pages and the Internet.

- WorldCat (www.worldcat.org): The world's largest aggregate library catalogue, offering access to the holdings of thousands of libraries around the world.
- Yahoo's Web directory (http://dir.yahoo.com): A well-organized catalogue of resources and discussion groups for a wide range of subject areas.

Software

There are many safe sources for software downloads, and by spending a little time searching these sites, you can find a wide range of useful utilities, many free or inexpensive. Here are a few of my favorites:

- Apple's listing of software for OS X (www.apple.com/downloads/macosx)
- Computer magazines: The Web site of your favorite computer magazine is another reliable sources of safe software downloads, most accompanied by review articles and ratings by the magazine's editors. Try Macworld (www.macworld.com), PC World (www.pcworld.com), and PC Magazine (www.pcmag.com) for starters.
- Tucows (www.tucows.com): A Web site that offers a wide range of safe downloads for Windows, Macintosh, and Linux, and each program has been rated by those who downloaded it.
- VersionTracker (www.versiontracker.com) and MacUpdate (www.macupdate.com): Two well-respected sites for finding and downloading Macintosh software and updates to that software.

Antivirus and security

- Ad-Aware 2007 Free edition (www.lavasoft.de): Well-respected free antispyware software for Windows. The company also sells a commercial version of this software with more features.
- AVG (www.grisoft.com): Antivirus software (free and paid versions) for Windows computers.
- ClamXav (www.markallan.co.uk/clamXav): Free antivirus software for Macintosh OS X.
- Comodo (http://www.comodo.com/): This firewall software has recently received better ratings than the previously popular ZoneAlarm firewall.
- F-Prot (www.f-prot.com): Antivirus software for Windows computers.

- Intego (www.intego.com): The NetBarrier firewall, Virus Barrier antivirus software, and Internet Security Barrier antispyware program for the Macintosh.
- PGP (www.pgp.com): Powerful encryption software.
- RSA Security Systems (www.rsasecurity.com): Powerful encryption software and other tools for safeguarding your data.
- Spybot Search and Destroy (www.safer-networking.org/en): Useful but very basic free antispyware software for Windows.
- Symantec's Norton Antivirus (www.symantec.com): Antivirus software available for both Macintosh and Windows. A steady, reliable choice for many years, but recently losing favor on both operating systems because it has become slow and bloated, and some users have had serious problems installing and uninstalling it.
- WebRoot Spy Sweeper (www.webroot.com): Currently the top-rated antispyware program for Windows users.
- Zonelabs (www.zonelabs.com): Excellent free ZoneAlarm firewall software for Windows computers (www.zonelabs.com/store/content/company/products/znalm/freeDownload.jsp). The company also sells a commercial version of this software with more features, plus various additional security programs.

Communication

Instant messaging (chat) software for Macintosh

- Adium (www.adiumx.com)
- AOL Instant Messenger (www.aim.com)
- Fire (www.fireim.org)
- Google Talk and Google Chat (www.google.com/talk)
- iChat (www.apple.com/support/downloads/ichatav.html): included with Apple's OS X operating system
- Ircle (www.ircle.com)
- Meebo (www.meebo.com): Web-based alternative
- Proteus for Mac (www.proteusx.org)
- Yahoo! Messenger (http://messenger.yahoo.com/download.php)

Instant messaging (chat) software for Windows

- AOL Instant Messenger (www.aim.com)
- Gaim (Pidgin) for Windows (http://sourceforge.net/projects/pidgin/)

- Google Talk and Google Chat (www.google.com/talk)
- Meebo (www.meebo.com): Web-based alternative
- Trillian (www.ceruleanstudios.com)
- Windows Messenger (http://tinyurl.com/52cjh): comes free with Windows, or direct from Microsoft
- Yahoo! Messenger (http://messenger.yahoo.com/download.php)

Internet telephone services

- Skype (www.skype.com): also offers a chat service

File transfers

- Apple's .Mac (www.mac.com): Offers file transfers for both Macintosh and Windows computers.
- Dropload (www.dropload.com): transfer of files up to 100 megabytes.
- Mediafire (www.mediafire.com) claims unlimited disk storage space plus up to 100 megabytes per file. Files remain until you delete them.
- MegaUpload (http://megaupload.com): file transfers of up to 250 megabytes.
- SendThisFile (http://sendthisfile.com): free uploads, with no stated maximum file size, but with minimal security and only 3 days to download the file.
- Yahoo's Briefcase (http://briefcase.yahoo.com): Yahoo offers 30 megabytes of free storage that you can use to transfer large files.
- YouSendIt (www.yousendit.com): file transfers of up to 2000 megabytes.

Utilities

If you don't see a specific type of software in this admittedly short list, see the more general list of download sites earlier in this section.

- Applescript and Automator: Apple's system-wide utility for creating scripts (macros) to automate certain processes. This Web page has moved sufficiently often that I've removed the link. Try the online help instead!
- Apple's Voiceover software (www.apple.com/accessibility/voiceover): Accessibility software for those who may need assistance from a screen reader.

- Backup software:
  - Retrospect (www.dantz.com) for Macintosh and Windows
  - Backup (www.mac.com) for users of Apple's Mac.com service
- IBM home page reader (http://www-03.ibm.com/able/solution_offerings/hpr3upgrade.html): Screen reader software for Windows.
- JAWS (www.freedomscientific.com/fs_products/software_jaws.asp): Screen reader software for Windows.
- Macro Express (www.macros.com): A utility for recording system-wide Windows macros.
- MegaReplacer (www.editorium.com/14843.htm): A friendlier, more powerful way to harness the power of Microsoft Word's search and replace functions. Available for both Windows and the Macintosh.
- Microsoft XMLDiff utility (http://msdn.microsoft.com/library/default.asp?url=/library/en-us/dnxmlnet/html/xmldiffgui.asp): A utility for comparing XML files and highlighting differences (e.g., as a result of editing).
- QuicKeys (www.quickeys.com): A utility for recording system-wide Macintosh or Windows macros.
- StuffIt (www.stuffit.com): An excellent file compression utility for both Windows and the Macintosh, with free decompression software available for your clients.
- Time tracking software recommended by various colleagues (Macintosh and Windows versions available unless otherwise noted):
  - Inertrak (Macintosh, Windows, Linux) and PicoTrak (Palm): http://inertron.com
  - Personal Timeclock: www.kmrconsulting.com/timeclock.html (Windows)
  - Timeless Time & Expense: www.magsoftwrx.com (Windows)
  - TimeSlice: www.timeslice.us (Macintosh and Windows)
  - Timeslips: www.timeslips.com (Windows)
  - TraxTime: www.spudcity.com (Windows)
- UCLA online statistical calculator (http://calculators.stat.ucla.edu/twosamp): A free, quick, and simple online tool for performing statistical comparisons of two sets of data (specifically, a two-sample *t*-test). If the link changes, use your favorite search engine to search for "two-sample test" and "online calculator"; you'll find plenty of options. The main site also offers a range of other useful calculators.

- Windows scripting host (http://msdn.microsoft.com/library/default.asp?url=/library/en-us/script56/html/a7362f02-ea57-451e-8033-5c0c42a4ed02.asp): A system-wide utility for creating scripts (macros) for current versions of Windows.

Writing and editing software

- BBEdit (www.barebones.com): A powerful text editor for the Macintosh with much of the power of the emacs editor for Unix. The company also produces the free TextWrangler software, which offers many of the features of BBEdit.
- emacs: A powerful text editor invented for Unix but now available for many operating systems—sometimes referred to, with only a little exaggeration, as a toolkit for building your own word processor. (To find a copy for your operating system, search the Web using the keywords *emacs* and *download*, followed by the name of your operating system.)
- FrameMaker (www.adobe.com): A powerful structured document authoring system. Although versions still exist for the Macintosh, the program is currently being developed only for Windows.
- OpenOffice suite (www.openoffice.org): A free suite of tools, including a word processor, that compares favorably with Microsoft Office. Though somewhat behind the current versions of Word and WordPerfect in terms of functions and polish, the OpenOffice word processor is an increasingly credible competitor.
- Proofreading in Adobe Acrobat: See John Clifford's 2004 article *Traditional proofreading in PDF* at the PlanetPDF Web site (www.planetpdf.com/creative/article.asp?contentid=6667&ra).
- ReferenceChecker (www.goodcitations.com): Software for checking references will never replace an editor until it can actually parse the references, but an automated version can at least spot and help you fix the more obvious errors.
- Templates: Providing authors with a template can solve a world of problems, since the template does much of the formatting for them and thus, leaves fewer opportunities for them to mess up that part of the work. For some insights into how this might be done, see my article on dynamic style guides (Hart 2000). Need a template to start you off? Try the ever-reliable Jack Lyon's free Author Tools Template at the Editorium Web site (http://editorium.com/).

- WebWorks ePublisher for Word and FrameMaker (www.quadralay.com): Powerful tools for producing both printed and online information from a single Word or FrameMaker file (i.e., single-sourcing). The company also develops tools for online (e.g., Web-based) team review of documents.
- Word (www.microsoft.com): The world's most popular word processor, available for both Macintosh and Windows.
- WordPerfect (www.corel.com): A powerful Windows word processor and the main competitor for Word.
- XMetal reviewer (www.xmetal.com/index.x): Powerful software for collaborative editing of XML files, particularly those produced using the company's XMetal authoring software.

About the author

Legend has it I've been writing and telling stories (both occasionally landing me in trouble) since I was 6, but it took me nearly 25 years to realize I could earn a living at this trade. Fortunately, IBM (Toronto) was sufficiently intrigued by the compelling lack of qualifications exhibited by my résumé to call me and demand why I was wasting their time. They hired me that afternoon, suggesting that either (a) I'm very persuasive or (b) they were very desperate. Not long after donning the blue sararyman uniform, I ducked a massive workforce re-engineering [sic] and found a home with the Canadian Forest Service (Sault Ste. Marie), for whom I toiled happily for the next 6 years. Keeping an ear to the ground led to dusty ears, but helped me duck yet another major right-sizing [sic] and return to my home town (Montréal), where I worked for the Forest Engineering Research Institute of Canada for the next 10 years. Since 2004, I've been freelancing in scientific editing for authors who speak English as a second or third language, but need to publish in English.

I've been working as a technical communicator since 1987, during which time I've been onscreen editing (mostly), writing technically and creating online help (frequently enough to know better), translating French manuscripts, audience analyzing, technology transferring, designing Webs, instructionally designing and video scripting, slide presenting and speech-writing, and information designing. I'm pondering adding a hat rack to keep all those hats off my desk, but I'm afraid someone might notice and add more hats.

At the tender age of 40-some, I still have time for weekend hockey with a group that seems to be growing younger every year, and the various and sundry sweaty exertions intended to help me survive the hockey. In what time remains, I keep busy publishing articles in various places, including *Intercom*, magazine of the Society for Technical Communication (STC), and publishing *the Exchange*, the newsletter of STC's Scientific Communication special interest group. In idle moments, of which there are surprisingly many given all the other activities going on, I spend an inordinate amount of time in the copyediting-L and techwr-L discussion groups, where I occupy an altogether unconscionable amount of the bandwidth mentoring colleagues. Lately, I've spent

an increasing amount of time traveling to various STC chapters at home and abroad to teach what I know.

Somewhere along the way, STC seems to have noticed all this activity and made me a Fellow. Which goes to show that *maybe I really am that persuasive*.

Index

C

D

G

H

I

J

K

L

M

N

O

P

(continued)

Q

R

(continued)

(continued)

X

Z